UNSHAKABLE FOUNDATIONS

A Selection of Books by Norman L. Geisler

The Big Book of Bible Difficulties
 (Baker, 2008)
Who Made God? (Zondervan, 2003)
Systematic Theology, Volume One
 (Bethany House, 2002)
Systematic Theology, Volume Two
 (Bethany House, 2003)
Systematic Theology, Volume Three
 (Bethany House, 2004)
Systematic Theology, Volume Four
 (Bethany House, 2005)
Unshakable Foundations (Bethany
 House, 2001)
*Baker Encyclopedia of Christian
 Apologetics* (Baker, 1999)
Chosen But Free (Bethany House,
 1999, 2001)
Love Is Always Right (Thomas Nelson,
 1996)
Roman Catholics and Evangelicals
 (Baker, 1995)
In Defense of the Resurrection
 (revised, Witness, Inc., 1993)
Answering Islam (Baker, 1993)
Matters of Life and Death
 (Baker, 1991)
*Thomas Aquinas: An Evangelical
 Appraisal* (Baker, 1991)
The Life and Death Debate
 (Greenwood, 1990)
When Skeptics Ask (Baker, 1990)
Come Let Us Reason (Baker, 1990)
Apologetics in the New Age
 (Baker, 1990)
The Battle for the Resurrection
 (Thomas Nelson, 1989)

Christian Ethics (Baker, 1989)
The Infiltration of the New Age
 (Tyndale, 1989)
Knowing the Truth About Creation
 (Servant, 1989)
Worlds Apart (Baker, 1989)
Christian Apologetics (Baker, 1988)
Signs and Wonders (Tyndale, 1988)
Philosophy of Religion (revised, Baker,
 1988)
Introduction to Philosophy
 (Baker, 1987)
Origin Science (Baker, 1987)
The Reincarnation Sensation
 (Tyndale, 1986)
A General Introduction to the Bible
 (revised, Moody Press, 1986)
False Gods of Our Time
 (Harvest House, 1985)
Is Man the Measure? (Baker, 1983)
Miracles and Modern Thought
 (Zondervan, 1982)
What Augustine Says (Baker, 1982)
*The Creator in the Courtroom—Scopes
 II* (Baker, 1982)
Decide for Yourself (Zondervan, 1982)
Biblical Errancy (Zondervan, 1981)
*Options in Contemporary Christian
 Ethics* (Baker, 1981)
Inerrancy (Zondervan, 1980)
To Understand the Bible, Look for Jesus
 (Baker, 1979)
The Roots of Evil (Zondervan, 1978)
A Popular Survey of the Old Testament
 (Baker, 1977)
From God to Us (Moody Press, 1974)

UNSHAKABLE FOUNDATIONS

NORMAN GEISLER
& PETER BOCCHINO

BETHANYHOUSE
Minneapolis, Minnesota

Unshakable Foundations
Copyright © 2001 by Norman Geisler and Peter Bocchino

Text illustrations by Jennifer Horton
Cover design by Eric Walljasper

Published by Bethany House Publishers
11400 Hampshire Avenue South
Bloomington, Minnesota 55438

Bethany House Publishers is a division of
Baker Publishing Group, Grand Rapids, Michigan.

Printed in the United States of America

ISBN   978-0-7642-2408-9

Library of Congress Cataloging-in-Publication Data

Geisler, Norman L.
    Unshakable foundations : contemporary answers to crucial questions about the Christian faith / by Norman Geisler & Peter Bocchino.
        p.   cm.
    Includes bibliographical references.
    ISBN 0-7642-2408-5 (pbk.)
    1. Apologetics—Miscellanea.   I. Bocchino, Peter.   II. Title.
BT1102 .G437   2000
239—dc21   00–009487

ACKNOWLEDGMENTS

This book is affectionately dedicated to our wives, Barbara and Therese, who have faithfully and lovingly supported us over the years. We are especially grateful for their encouragement during the writing of this book.

We want to give special recognition to Bill and Charlotte Poteet, who worked on the initial grammatical edits of the manuscript to help prepare it to be sent to the publisher. We are also grateful to Wayne House for taking the time to review the chapter on law and for his helpful suggestions. Furthermore, we would be remiss if we did not thank all the students of apologetics who, through their various suggestions over the years, helped to make this book both practical and meaningful.

Finally, we wish to express our appreciation to Steve Laube for believing in this work and to all of the talented people at Bethany House Publishers in seeing this project through to completion. In particular, we are thankful for the diligent efforts and commendable editing skills of Christopher Soderstrom.

Above all, we are indebted to our God, who has given us the grace to be able to reason about Him and His creation. He even invites us to come into His presence and "reason together" with Him (Isaiah 1:18), and it is our hope that the reader would take Him up on His gracious offer.

NORMAN L. GEISLER is author or coauthor of more than sixty books and hundreds of articles. He has taught at the university and graduate level for nearly forty years and has spoken, traveled, or debated in all fifty states and in twenty-five countries. He holds a Ph.D. in philosophy from Loyola University and now serves as President of Southern Evangelical Seminary in Charlotte, North Carolina.

PETER BOCCHINO is President of Legacy of Truth Ministries, located in Atlanta, Georgia. He served as Director of Leadership for Ravi Zacharias International Ministries for nine years and was responsible for writing and teaching a multicultural curriculum on Christian apologetics in Europe, the Middle and Far East, Africa, and the Americas. Peter has held open forums and training sessions on campuses around the world and has served on the academic standards committee for the Georgia Department of Education. Peter and his wife, Therese, have two children and reside in Atlanta.

CONTENTS

CONTENTS

INTRODUCTION

*By space the universe encompasses and
swallows me up like an atom; by thought
I comprehend the world.*

—BLAISE PASCAL

On January 28, 1986, the people of the United States watched the nationally televised launch of the space shuttle *Challenger*. Although shuttle launches were becoming a routine event, this one was unique because among the *Challenger*'s seven crew members was Christa McAuliffe, a high school teacher from New Hampshire. At seventy-three seconds after takeoff, enthusiasm turned into horror as the world witnessed the most tragic event in the history of space exploration. *Challenger* exploded and in its wake left a trail of smoke that tracked the spacecraft as it fell into the ocean and took the lives of all aboard. The ensuing investigation traced the cause of the explosion to something as simple as a faulty O-ring seal. Even though the seal was a simple component, it had a very particular and critical function. The seal was designed to isolate the solid-fuel rocket gases from the main fuel tank. However, its faulty design, coupled with extreme environmental conditions, affected the seal's functional integrity. This defective seal allowed the hot combustion gases to leak through the booster rocket joint. Once these hot gases made contact with the shuttle's external fuel tank, the fatal explosion was imminent.

Perhaps the most disconcerting aspect of this catastrophe is that NASA engineers had warned mission-control executives of the impending danger prior to the launch. Despite the concerns of engineers, the decision was made to continue with the launch—all systems go! Other matters and pressures took priority over the odds that there might be some fatal disaster. After all, the shuttle had many capable backup systems to ensure the safety of its crew. Unfortunately, the crew of the space shuttle put themselves into the hands of those who made a wrong decision, and they lost their physical lives as a result.

We have written this book in an effort to keep you from making a similar mistake regarding your spiritual life. As you continue to learn, whether formally or informally, you will find yourself in situations that may have serious consequences with respect to the decisions you make about what you believe to be true. Teachers, colleagues, peers, and others may challenge you in ways that will force you to reevaluate your beliefs in light of what is being taught or said to you. Therefore, we implore you: Do not place your faith in the hands of someone else! This book offers credible reasons as to why Christianity is intellectually sound.

To help us show you why this is true, we turn to Aristotle, who noted long ago that every field of knowledge begins with certain truths he referred to as *first principles*. First principles are *not* conclusions found at the end of a set of premises, but rather basic premises from which conclusions are drawn. They are axioms, givens—self-evident truths. They are so obviously reasonable that they neither demand nor admit direct proof. First principles are beyond direct proof because they are known to be true based upon their self-evident and inescapable nature. They also cannot be disproved; any attempt (within any given field of study) will only end up in self-defeating statements.

Aristotle also explained how these first principles form the *unshakable foundations* upon which all thought and knowledge rest. This book is intended to confirm Aristotle's observations, and then to show that first principles lead only to the God of the Bible.

In chapter 1 we will introduce you to *Logic* and the first principle of all knowledge: the law of noncontradiction. The universal and inescapable nature of this simple but profound law leads us to question its origin and ultimate rational justification. The answer to this question is that there must be some ultimate Mind that exists as the foundation for the laws of human thought. In chapter 2 we examine the popular views of agnosticism, pluralism, and relativism. As we analyze each of these in light of the law of noncontradiction, we show how they are ultimately self-defeating. We then explain why it is credible to believe that absolute truth exists, defining *Truth* as a statement, idea, symbol, or expression that matches (corresponds to) reality. Chapter 3 gives a brief description of *Worldviews* and explains how they affect the beliefs and behaviors of individuals. We have also included a test to measure the credibility of truth claims that worldviews make, and we offer a few suggestions about how to handle worldview questions.

In chapter 4 we embark on a journey into the discipline of *Science*. Our goal is to gain a basic understanding of the foundations upon which science is built, its limitations with respect to knowledge, and how to apply the scientific method to the question of origins. In chapter 5 the discipline of *Cosmology* is brought to bear on the nature and structure of the universe. The question of its origin—namely, whether or not it needs a cause—is answered in this chapter. It is argued that based upon the first principle of science and the supporting observational evidence, it is most reasonable to believe that the universe is finite. This being the case, it is necessary to conclude that an infinite and eternally powerful Cause brought it into existence. In chapter 6 we explain why it is credible to believe that this infinite and eternally powerful Cause must also be intelligent. Our reasoning is based on the science of information theory, as it relates to the *Origin of Life*.

Chapter 7 is dedicated to evaluating various models of origins and answering the questions surrounding *Macroevolution*. Arguments are made and evidence presented to show that macroevolution is not a viable model of origins. In chapter 8 we show why theistic macroevolution fails to provide the scientific reasoning and empirical evidence needed to support its claims. Hence, we turn to the only logical alternative—the *Intelligent Design* model—and argue for its credibility as the most plausible model of origins.

Chapter 9 discusses *Law* and the shift in American legal theory from the classical understanding of natural law to a theory that finds its origin in human reason—positive law. The examination of this change includes the identification of danger signals that ultimately threaten not only the stability of the criminal justice system but also our basic human rights. Chapter 10 uses an historical context (Nazi Germany) to disclose how the wrong view of human nature (macroevolution) and law (established upon human reason alone) violates human rights. Furthermore, we show how the prosecution argued for *Justice* at Nuremberg based upon an intuitive knowledge of "higher laws" that transcends governments. The foundation for this higher law is a higher Lawmaker—the Creator—who bestowed upon humanity intrinsic value that no government or people have a right to take away. At the end of this chapter, we conclude that it makes sense to believe that we live in a theistic universe. However, if an infinitely powerful and just God exists, what about evil? Where did evil originate? Did God create it? Chapter 11 examines the questions concerning the nature of *God* and the problem of *Evil.*

With the problem of evil identified, and since we believe the answer to the problem came to earth two thousand years ago in the person of Jesus Christ, we turn to *History*—chapter 12—to discover the answer. However, a proper interpretation of historical events depends upon the belief that history is really knowable and that miracles can happen. After showing that history is indeed knowable and that miracles are possible in a theistic universe, we present the evidence to support the authenticity of the New Testament documents and the reliability of its authors. Once the New Testament is shown to depict a factual representation of the life and teachings of *Jesus*, we move to chapter 13, where we examine His claims to see if they are trustworthy, specifically those concerning His *Deity*, and look at the evidence He offered to substantiate His claim to be God. The three lines of evidence offered are (1) His fulfillment of Old Testament prophecies, (2) His sinless life and miraculous deeds, and (3) His resurrection from the dead. If indeed Jesus is God, then what He says about the problem with humanity is true.

In chapter 14 we turn to Jesus for His analysis of the human condition, but we do so after we deal with the popular belief that *Ethics* and *Morals* are purely subjective and merely a matter of feelings or instinct. A summary of various arguments given by C. S. Lewis is presented to refute those popular beliefs. Following this, we look to Jesus and see what He has to say about ethics, the root cause of humanity's moral disease, and the permanent cure for that disease. The decision one makes on whether to accept or reject the teachings of Jesus carries with it temporal and eternal consequences: a destiny of eternal bliss or eternal misery. Each person must individually decide whether or not to believe in Jesus.

In chapter 15 we examine more closely the consequences mentioned above. Our discussion centers on what gives life ultimate meaning, and we show why *True Meaning* cannot be found apart from a loving relationship with God. God designed us to run on the fuel of Himself, and apart from Him there can be no "ultimate" meaning—just temporary states of superficial fulfillment. For those who accept the cure Jesus offers for humanity's moral disease, there awaits an eternal state of true happiness in *Heaven*. However, for those who reject God there awaits a place of *True Misery*, a misery that will last forever. The Bible refers to this eternal state of misery as *Hell*. Chapter 16 is intended to show briefly why hell makes sense and how it logically follows from God's holy, just, and loving nature.

In addition to these chapters, we have included an appendix titled *First Principle Responses to Ethical Questions*. The topics addressed in the appendix are abortion, euthanasia, biomedical issues, and human cloning.

It is our hope that your doubts and questions will be answered somewhere in the pages of this book and that as a result you will better understand why your faith rests upon *Unshakable Foundations*. We also pray that this work will help to foster in you a nondefensive boldness to be a confident witness as you share the gospel of Jesus Christ.

1
QUESTIONS ABOUT LOGIC

The fundamentals of logic should be as transcultural as the mathematics with which the principles of logic are associated. The principles of logic are neither Western nor Eastern, but universal.

—MORTIMER J. ADLER

WHAT ARE FIRST PRINCIPLES?

In a group of essays called the "Logic" or "Organon," Aristotle established the difference between valid and invalid forms of human reasoning. His aim was to make plain the steps by which a body of knowledge ought to be logically constructed. Aristotle showed how every science begins with certain obvious truths he referred to as *first principles,* explaining how these first principles form the foundations upon which all knowledge rests. First principles are the fundamental truths from which inferences are made and on which conclusions are based. They are self-evident, and they can be thought of as both the underlying and the governing principles of a worldview.

A *worldview* is like an intellectual lens through which we see the world. If someone looks through a red-colored lens, the world looks red to him. If another individual looks through a blue-colored lens, the world will look blue to her. So the question we must answer is "What color lens (worldview) is the right color to wear in order to have a correct view of the world?" Prior to finding out, a more fundamental question needs to be answered: "Is there only one intellectually justifiable lens through which the world can accurately be viewed?" In other words, "Is there only one true worldview?"

If our worldview is only as trustworthy as our first assumptions and the logical inferences we draw from them, then that must be the place to start. Since first principles cannot be avoided, due to their fundamental nature, we ought to be able to use them as common ground or starting points with any reasonable person before discussing his worldview. If we use a correct reasoning process, we should be able to discover which worldview is the most credible.

This "first principles" approach will form the basis for our methodology, which seems to have been overlooked or forgotten by many contemporary thinkers. Mortimer J. Adler notes an important distinction between modern thinkers and some of the great philosophical minds of the past, specifically Aristotle and Thomas Aquinas:

> In every case the correction of an error or the repair of a deficiency in the philosophy of Aristotle and Aquinas rests on the underlying and controlling principles of Aristotelian and Thomistic thought. In fact, the discovery of such errors or deficiencies almost always springs from close attention and leads to a deeper understanding of those principles.
>
> Here lies what for me is the remarkable difference between the faults I have found in modern philosophy and the faults I have found in the tradition of Aristotelian and Thomistic thought. The errors and deficiencies in this or that modern philosopher's thought arise either from his misunderstanding or, worse, his total ignorance of insights and distinctions indispensable to getting at the truth—insights and distinctions that were so fruitful in the work of Aristotle and Aquinas, but which modern philosophers have either ignored or, misunderstanding them, have dismissed. In addition, the errors or deficiencies in the thought of this or that modern philosopher cannot be corrected by appealing to his own most fundamental principles, as in the case with Aristotle or Aquinas. *On the contrary, it is usually his principles—his points of departure—that embody the little errors in the beginning which, as Aristotle and Aquinas so well knew, have such serious consequences in the end.*[1]

Most Christians are too quick to respond to an opposing worldview by critiquing it *at the conclusion* of an argument. Mortimer Adler rightly points

---

[1]Mortimer J. Adler, *A Second Look in the Rearview Mirror* (New York: Macmillan, 1992), 240 (emphasis added).

out that most of the time the errors exist *in the beginning*. This means we must focus on these "points of departure" used by philosophers, professors, authors, and skeptics to see if any errors exist in their foundations (most basic assumptions).

If Aristotle was right when he said that first principles form the foundations of all knowledge (academic disciplines), then it is essential that we learn how to identify and use them to support our faith in Christ. This is not the only method that can be employed to defend and communicate Christianity, but we consider it to be one of the best ways to build bridges of truth with those who reject our beliefs. If we can gain an understanding of first principles, we will be on our way to establishing common ground with those who oppose Christian theism. If these first principles of thought do actually reflect the nature of the God of the Bible, as will be argued, then the opposing questioners or listeners will be stranded if they reject them. That is, *they must either deny the validity of the first principles upon which the academic disciplines are based—thus undermining all knowledge—or they must grant the intellectual credibility of these first principles and with it the intellectual soundness of theism.*

WHY BEGIN WITH LOGIC?

The overall task before us is to construct a lens through which we can accurately view reality (defined as "that which is").[2] An intellectual lens contains many assumptions, but the real focal power can be found in the laws that guide human thought. *Everyone* uses logic to think about life. The reality of our existence, therefore, is the object of focus for this lens. All people have at one time or another given thought to the fact that they exist; existence and human reason are the two most fundamental assumptions that all people have in common. These two assumptions are unavoidable; in order to deny existence and reason, one would have to use reason to think about the denial. Further, one would

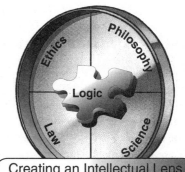

Creating an Intellectual Lens by Discovering First Principles

---

[2]We are using the term *reality* to signify that which exists independent of and external to our minds. This view is called *realism*. In chapter 2 we will show how agnosticism (the belief that one cannot know anything about reality) is self-defeating and how realism is unavoidable.

have to exist in order to be engaged in the reasoning process. Therefore, existence and reason must be the place to start an honest and impartial search for truth.

Our thoughts about our existence raise one of the most fundamental questions in philosophy: "Why is there something rather than nothing at all?"[3] The moment we begin to use our focal power of reason to ponder our existence, we begin the philosophical task of constructing an intellectual lens. With this in mind, the most sensible place for you to begin is to gain an understanding of the laws that guide correct thinking. If our thought processes are incorrect, they will almost always lead us to false conclusions. If human reason is the focal point of an intellectual lens, then it only makes sense to make sure that this lens is clean and polished. If it isn't, you run the risk of blurring your view of reality.

When we think about thinking, we automatically engage ourselves in the academic discipline known as *logic*. Logic is the branch of philosophy that involves an understanding of the laws that govern our thought processes. Logic is the order that reason discovers in thinking about thinking; therefore, it is the necessary precondition for all thought. Since people everywhere engage in the act of thinking, and since all thinking is based on logic, we can safely assume that logic is a universal practice. Once the focal power of reason has been set into place and is clear of any obstructions, we can apply it to the facts of reality and begin to bring a worldview into focus. Since all knowledge depends upon the act of thinking, logic must be the place to start constructing our intellectual lens.

WHAT IS THE FIRST PRINCIPLE OF LOGIC?

Can opposite truth claims both be true? Some people would say yes. Their position is entailed in the philosophy of *pluralism*. A pluralist would insist, for example, that Christians view reality one way, whereas Hindus view the same reality in a different manner, and conclude that both views are true. However, at this point we are not interested in why two groups of people espouse different views, but whether or not opposite conclusions about reality can both be accurate. Can the Christian affirmation (evil is real) and an opposing Hindu denial (evil is an illusion) both be right? If one view of evil is true, the other must necessarily be false; both claims about evil cannot be true and both cannot be false.

---

[3]See Martin Heidegger, *An Introduction to Metaphysics* (New York: Anchor, 1961), chapter 1.

Another way for us to grasp this is to analyze the word *tolerance*. The opposite of tolerance is intolerance. Imagine that we are taking a philosophy of religion class and we make it known that we believe Christianity is right and Hinduism is wrong. It won't take too long before we are labeled *intolerant*. Yet those who are opposed to us stamp themselves as tolerant because they believe that all religions are true, the *opposite* of what we believe. When one acknowledges that the intolerant position is the opposite of the tolerant one, she thereby establishes the credibility of the first principle of all knowledge, the *law of noncontradiction*.

When those who oppose Christians acknowledge the self-evident nature of the law of noncontradiction, it is analogous to setting the first piece of our intellectual lens into place. It establishes a primary and mutual point of contact for all people who believe something about anything. In other words, taking *any* opposing view on *any* issue, whether it is an unexpressed thought or a verbalized one, is equivalent to submitting to the power and validity of the law of noncontradiction. *One is forced to admit that this law of logic is true, because all other conclusions about reality necessarily depend upon it.*

A study of the formal discipline of logic is not for everyone, and it would go beyond the scope of this book to delineate the rules of logical inferences (called syllogisms) or to engage in an examination of how to avoid formal and informal fallacies.[4] However, you must at least acquire a working knowledge of the law of noncontradiction; it is the most powerful logical principle you can learn. *All thinking (whether about physics or about metaphysics) is alike to the extent that it is governed by this foundational first principle of logic—the law of noncontradiction.*

IS THE LAW OF NONCONTRADICTION UNAVOIDABLE?

The law of noncontradiction is both self-evident and unavoidable; again, *it must be used in any attempt to deny it.* It must be assumed to be true by anyone who wants to think or say anything meaningful; it is necessary for making any sort of distinction, affirmation, or denial. For example, if someone were to say, "I deny the law of noncontradiction," it would be the opposite of saying, "I affirm the law of noncontradiction." In the very act of denying the law of noncontradiction, that person must use it. The statement "You Christians are

---

[4]For further study of the laws of logic, including formal and informal fallacies, see N. L. Geisler and R. M. Brooks, *Come Let Us Reason: An Introduction to Logical Thinking* (Grand Rapids, Mich.: Baker, 1990).

intolerant because you don't accept all religions as true" is the opposite of being tolerant and accepting all religious truth claims as true! (From now on we will abbreviate the spelling of the law of noncontradiction with the initials LNC.)

The LNC is so powerful that we cannot get around it or behind it; its intuitive focal power has been securely fixed into the thought processes of all human beings. If someone were to say, "There is no such thing as truth, and the LNC is meaningless," he has done two things. First, he has assumed that his view is true as opposed to false, and thus he uses the LNC (which, of course, implies that the LNC has meaning, because his view is assumed to be meaningful). Second, he has violated the LNC by suggesting that *there is no such thing as truth* while at the same time and in the same sense insisting that *there is such a thing as truth*—the truth of his own view. By doing so, he automatically validates the LNC.

Thus far we have been exposed to three basic beliefs that must be assumed to be true for every worldview. The first is the belief in the fact of reality; it is actually undeniable. The second is that anyone who thinks about reality immediately assumes that reason applies to reality. The third is that both of these assumptions necessarily depend upon a more fundamental self-evident truth, the validity of the LNC.

Since the LNC is the focal point of the intellectual lens under construction, the trustworthiness of this lens is dependent upon the clarity and integrity of each component that is added to it hereafter. Consequently, before we continue we need to answer some questions as to the relationship between logic and reality, and as to the universal nature of logic. Everything we have concluded, and all that we will conclude from this point on, depends upon the answers to these questions.

WHAT IF ALL IS NOTHING BUT AN ILLUSION?

If all were an illusion, the search for truth would be a meaningless task. Let's begin answering this question, then, by clarifying the meaning of the terms *reality* and *illusion*. The words we use and accept from other people in dialogue must be understood if we are aiming to have good communication. When we assign words (symbols) to correspond to certain aspects of reality (referents), we are using another law of logic called the *law of identity* (LID). This law simply states that something is what we say it is: A is A. A correlative principle, the law of excluded middle (LEM), asserts that it is either A or non-A (but not both). All valid thinking rests on these principles: they are absolute, and without them thinking would not be possible. Mere symbols, terms, or words can be relative to a particular language or culture, but as long as they refer to the same reality, meaning can be, and is, universal. Universal statements translate into all languages as universal statements.

Therefore, the basic laws of logic are universally valid, and when properly used, the LNC, LEM, and LID act as the main logical gears that form the power train of the reasoning process that produces correct thinking. Later in this volume, we will see how these two seemingly simple laws can be used to help us defend our beliefs against some of the most ardent objections to Christianity. For now, notice how the LID can be used to determine if reality exists or if it is an illusion.

Throughout this chapter we have used the words *existence* and *reality* as equivalent terms because to be real is to exist and to exist is to be real. The term *reality* denotes that which exists and manifests certain attributes (whether we think about these attributes or not). Reality *is*, regardless of our knowledge of it. For example, gravity exists; it is part of reality. Even if Sir Isaac Newton had never defined gravity and we had no knowledge of its existence, it would not stop existing. When we forget about the reality of gravity, we can be abruptly reminded of it if we miss a step or slip on an icy sidewalk. Reality, like gravity, is something that exists no matter what we think: *reality is independent of our minds.*

We can also show that reality exists by analyzing the term *illusion.* An illusion is defined as *a misleading perception of reality.* When someone says that something is an illusion, she means that the illusion misrepresents what is real. However, if objective reality did not exist to provide a contrast, there would be no way of knowing about the illusion. In other words, in order to know that we are dreaming we must have some idea of what it means to be awake; only then can we contrast the two states. Similarly, we only know what an illusion is because we have some idea of what it means to be real. If everything were really an illusion, we would never come to know about it. *Absolute illusion is impossible!* Therefore, it is only logical to conclude that it is an illusion to believe that reality is an illusion.

WHAT IF LOGIC DOESN'T APPLY TO REALITY?

We have already defined logic as the order reason discovers in thinking about thinking, and we found logic to be a necessary precondition for all thought. When we apply our thoughts to the nature of reality and then make truth claims about what we discover, our truth claims will either be logical (sense) or illogical (nonsense). For that reason, the initial question to ask the person who thinks that logic does not apply to reality is, "What do you assume to be true about logic and reality?" The first assumption this individual must make, in order to answer this question, is that it is a logical question about reality and is therefore worthy of a logical answer.

In the same way, his counterquestion "What if logic does not apply to reality?" is assumed to be a logical question about that which exists (reality). Therefore, he assumes that logic does apply to reality. But in that case, the question contains an implied contradiction (it violates the LNC) and consequently is meaningless. On the other hand, if this question were not a logical question about reality, it wouldn't be necessary to answer it. If he truly does not believe that logic applies to reality—that all of reality doesn't make sense—then nothing should make sense, including his own question.

Since everyone uses logic to think about reality, everyone automatically assumes that logic applies to reality. When someone denies this truth, she also affirms the truth of the LNC in the process of the denial. Consequently, her denial becomes self-defeating and we are right back where we started: *logic is unavoidable.* C. S. Lewis explained the utter futility of trying to account for reality without the use of reason when he said,

> A theory which explained everything else in the whole universe but which made it impossible to believe that our thinking was valid, would be utterly out of court. For that theory would itself have been reached by thinking, and if thinking is not valid that theory would, of course, be itself demolished. It would have destroyed its own credentials. It would be an argument which proved that no argument was sound—a proof that there are no such things as proofs—which is nonsense.[5]

WHAT ABOUT THE USE OF EASTERN LOGIC?

Some say that there is another kind of logic, Eastern logic, which holds to the idea that reality, at its very core, embraces contradictions. However, trying to put limitations on any universal law is also self-defeating. Imagine someone

---

[5]C. S. Lewis, *Miracles* (New York: Macmillan, 1960), 14–15.

who believed in an Eastern view of gravity. For that person gravity must undergo an essential change because it is viewed in light of an Eastern culture. As preposterous as this idea sounds, the same is true of anyone who would believe that logic could undergo an essential change based upon its geographic location.

To say logic changes with respect to the observer's position is to undermine the word *logic*. As stated by Eastern logic, reality can be logical and illogical. But if something is both logical and illogical, it is a contradiction and has no meaning. So according to Eastern logic, everything is ultimately meaningless. Yet if everything were ultimately meaningless, so would be the distinction between Western and Eastern logic. If there were no basis for judging between correct and incorrect thinking, there would be no way to say that Eastern logic is more accurate than Western logic. Furthermore, there would be no way to conclude that the Eastern view of reality is more accurate than the Western view of reality. The only way anyone could make such an assertion would be to assume that reality does not essentially embrace contradictions and that it exists independently of our opinions. However, if this is true, then *the laws of logic, in particular the LNC, must be universal.*

Therefore, there is no such thing as Eastern logic or Western logic. It doesn't matter where thinking is happening or what culture is involved—logic is the same. Mortimer J. Adler underscores this universality:

> The fundamentals of logic should be as transcultural as the mathematics with which the principles of logic are associated. The principles of logic are neither Western nor Eastern, but universal.[6]

Anyone who visits the Far East will note that computers operate in the same manner as they do in the West. The logic used in places like India is identical to the logic used in North America, because logic is universal in nature, and the laws of logic are universal. When we think about the nature of reality, we engage in what is called *metaphysics* (that which is beyond the physical). Metaphysics deals with the existence or nonexistence of nonphysical realities. As applied to metaphysics, logic asserts that contradictories cannot coexist in reality. For example, *either* God exists *or* God does not exist; both cannot be true and both cannot be false (LEM). The Eastern view of reality, which is generally the pantheist's view,[7] accepts the metaphysical form of the

---

[6]Mortimer J. Adler, *Truth in Religion: The Plurality of Religions and the Unity of Truth* (New York: Macmillan, 1990), 36.

[7]Pantheism is explained in chapter 3. Basically, a pantheist believes that God pervades all things and is found within all things. God is the world, and the world is God.

LNC. If this weren't true, pantheists could be atheists; however, pantheists are not atheists because they believe that *either* God (Brahman) exists *or* no ultimate Being exists, but not both. They believe that *either* atheists *or* pantheists are correct, but not both. *Either* the universe is all that there is, a material reality and nothing else (atheism), *or* there is an ultimate Being (Brahman) who is the universe. Matter is *either* an illusion (in the case of pantheism) *or* it is real (in the case of atheism), but not both.[8] People in the Far East use the same kind of logic as people in the West: human logic.

Earlier we noted that the laws of logic are necessary for making any sort of distinction, affirmation, or denial. The very act of making a distinction between Eastern and Western thinking depends upon this universal law. To say that there is an Eastern view *as opposed to* a Western view depends upon the validity and universal nature of this law of logic. It is unmistakable: we must conclude that the LNC is as universal as the act of thinking itself.

CAN THE LAWS OF LOGIC BE USED AS A TEST FOR TRUTH?

Alexander Pope correctly observed that a little knowledge is a dangerous thing! This cliché could be true in our case if we fail to point out the principal limitation of logic. When we use logic as the focal point of our intellectual lens, we must be very careful to recognize that its effectiveness is limited to finding error alone. Logic's (i.e., the LNC's) function is to correct faulty thinking, or groundless reasoning, and is therefore a negative test for truth. This is a very important characteristic: *logic by itself will not help us find truth but will only help us detect error. What is true must be logical, but what is logical is not necessarily true.*

The statement "two plus two equals four" is logical. Similarly, the statement "two leprechauns plus two leprechauns equals four leprechauns" is also logical. Both statements are logical; however, the second statement does not mean that leprechauns actually exist. You would have to test and see if there is any evidence to support the claim that leprechauns are real. Consequently, what is real or true must be logical, but what is logical is not necessarily real or true.

If logic, by itself, only detects error, then how can we discover truth? We have designed this book in such a way that it will answer this question through the cumulative understanding and application of the foundational first princi-

---

[8]As pointed out earlier, this technically is called the *law of excluded middle* (LEM), which is a companion of the LNC.

ples of several fields of knowledge (academic disciplines) as they are applied to reality. In other words, we will see that once these first principles are properly put together, like the pieces of a puzzle, they will show us which worldview is most reasonable or true. Then it will be a matter of finding answers to questions that make sense within the parameters of that worldview and that seem to fit most consistently with what we know from our experiences in life as well. However, the cumulative application of first principles to reality must not violate previously established first principles. For example, when we identify the first principle of science and draw conclusions from it, it must not violate the first principles of logic or philosophy. We will expand on this test for truth in the chapters that follow.

2

QUESTIONS ABOUT TRUTH

What is truth?

—PILATE

WHAT IS TRUTH?

According to Aristotle, philosophy begins with the natural desire we all have to know the truth. However, a desire to know the truth is one thing, while finding the truth is quite another. Appearances can be deceiving; many things appear to be true, but in reality they are not. At first glance a straight steel rod immersed in a glass of water may look as though it's bent, but it isn't. If it's so easy to misperceive the true nature of physical things, what about the truth concerning metaphysical things?

Metaphysics is concerned with issues such as the existence and nature of God. Yet how can we ever hope to find true answers to questions regarding the truth about the existence and nature of reality when physical, tangible things can be so deceiving? Before we begin to answer this question, we must answer the more fundamental questions concerning the ability to know reality and the nature of truth.

If we are seriously in pursuit of truth, we must learn how to apply philosophy correctly to life. We may not feel comfortable with the term "philosophy," but we use philosophy all the time. When we think about life we use logic, and logic is a branch of philosophy. It's not a matter of whether one uses it, but whether one uses it correctly or incorrectly. Some people think that philosophy is reserved for the highly educated, but this idea is not true. Even those who have a very limited education are capable of following an argument. C. S. Lewis reminds us:

> Uneducated people are not irrational people. I have found that they will endure, and can follow quite a lot of sustained argument if you go slowly. Often, indeed, the novelty of it (for they have seldom met it before) delights them.[1]

Lewis shared the belief of the ancient Greeks that philosophy, by definition, had to be practical and meaningful. They believed philosophy was as useful for the uneducated craftsman of their day as it was for the educated metaphysician. So we need not veer away; regardless of a person's educational background, philosophy can become a meaningful tool.

The word *philosophy* comes from two Greek words: *phileo*, "love," and *sophia*, "wisdom." It is interesting to note that *phileo* signifies the kind of love that one has for a friend; the true philosopher loves wisdom as if it were a close friend. The Greeks combined these two words in an attempt to describe a distinctive type of mental exercise, the exercise of reason in search for truth. Philosophy can also be thought of as an inquiry into, and an analysis of, the fundamental realities of our existence—including the very words and concepts that constitute everyday language.

Moreover, philosophy is an effort to engage in a rational and consistent examination of the truth claims of any system of belief. Yet if truth does not exist, why bother with philosophy? Think of all the philosophers and philosophy books in the world today. If the academic discipline of philosophy is devoid of truth, then philosophers are in a vain pursuit. Something must be seriously wrong with philosophers who write and speak about the love of a close friend who does not exist!

The first major assumption that needs to be made by everyone searching for answers is that true answers can be found. Some people do deny that true answers exist. The problem with their view, though, is that they assume this view to be true; if it is, it is self-defeating. If they believe that all views of reality are false, then their view must also be false, for if it were true, then all views would not be false. *To deny the existence of truth is to affirm its existence—truth*

---

[1]C. S. Lewis, *God in the Dock* (Grand Rapids, Mich.: Eerdmanns, 1970), 99.

is inescapable! Therefore, the affirmation that true statements can be made about reality is a rationally justifiable one.

If truth and reality are inescapable, then how are they related? What is the connection between the nature of truth and the nature of reality? In chapter 1, we used the law of gravity to illustrate a truth. We said that even if Sir Isaac Newton hadn't defined gravity, the reality of its existence wouldn't be changed; that is, the existence of gravity does not depend upon our knowledge of it. If reality exists independently of our knowledge, then truth must be linked to the process of investigating and discovering an attribute of reality. When we investigate and discover some aspect of reality and make accurate statements about it, we speak the truth. Conversely, when we make statements that are supposed to match reality but do not, we do not speak the truth.

What is truth? By definition, *truth is an expression, symbol, or statement that matches or corresponds to its object or referent* (i.e., that to which it refers, whether it is an abstract idea or a concrete thing). When the statement or expression is about reality, it must correspond to reality in order to be true. Yet there are so many statements and views of reality; why should Christians believe that they have the only correct view? Shouldn't people interpret reality for themselves and personally decide what is true on an individual basis? When it comes to religion, isn't truth a matter of preference and therefore relative?

IS TRUTH RELATIVE?

A relative view of truth has been deeply ingrained into the minds and hearts of contemporary people, especially in academic circles. Relativistic thinking has influenced us so much that it is now considered anti-intellectual to believe in absolute truth. The majority of educators and students regard truth to be obsolete, not absolute. Allan Bloom, author of one of the most compelling books depicting the deterioration of higher education, has said:

> There is one thing a professor can be absolutely certain of: Almost every student entering the university believes, or says he believes, that truth is relative. If this belief is put to the test, one can count on the students' reaction: they will be uncomprehending. That anyone should regard the proposition as not self-evident astonishes them, as though he were calling into question 2+2=4. These are things you don't talk about.
>
> The students' backgrounds are as various as America can provide. Some are religious, some atheists; some are to the Left, some to the Right; some intend to be scientists, some humanists or professionals or businessmen; some are poor, some rich. They are unified only in their relativism and in

their allegiance to equality. And the two are related in a moral intention. The relativity of truth is not a theoretical insight but a moral postulate, the condition of a free society, or so they see it. They have all been equipped with this framework early on, and it is the modern replacement for the inalienable natural rights that used to be the traditional American grounds for a free society. That it is a moral issue for students is revealed by the character of their response when challenged—a combination of disbelief and indignation: "Are you an absolutist?" the only alternative they know, uttered in the same tone as "Are you a monarchist?" or "Do you really believe in witches?" . . .

Relativism is necessary to openness; and this is the virtue, the only virtue, which all primary education for more than fifty years has dedicated itself to inculcating. . . .

The true believer is the real danger. The study of history and of culture teaches that all the world was mad in the past; men always thought they were right, and that led to wars, persecutions, slavery, xenophobia, racism, and chauvinism. The point is not to correct the mistakes and really be right; rather it is not to think you are right at all.

The students, of course, cannot defend their opinion. It is something with which they have been indoctrinated. The best they can do is point out all the opinions and cultures there are and have been. What right, they ask, do I or anyone else have to say one is better than the others? . . . The purpose of their education is not to make them scholars but to provide them with a moral virtue—openness.[2]

If this analysis is accurate, and we believe that it is, how can we defend the Christian view of the credibility of absolute truth? To make matters worse, some professors are determined to undermine a student's religious beliefs. One professor told his class,

Our ethics are based on the ancient belief that there are supernatural forces at work in the world, that these supernatural forces provide the basis for ethics, that we have moral responsibility based on free will. This is all false. And even people who think it is true must recognize that there is no longer consensus on these beliefs. . . . I tell my religious students to look at the person sitting on each side of them. . . . Chances are, at least one of those persons doesn't share their belief in God that provides the ultimate foundation for ethics. There is no going back to a world in which our ethics can be based on a revelation of what God demands of us.[3]

---

[2] Allan Bloom, *The Closing of the American Mind* (New York: Simon and Schuster, 1987), 25–26.
[3] G. Liles, quoting Cornell biologist William Provine in "The Faith of an Atheist," *MD*, March 1994, 61.

The Christian's belief in absolute truth and the God of the Bible is not usually tolerated in secular intellectual settings. There is generally tremendous pressure exerted by peers, colleagues, educators, and unbelieving friends to get Christians to abandon their beliefs and to accept the idea that their narrow-minded thinking is the same mindset that ultimately causes travesties like the medieval Crusades and all kinds of persecution. They are then classified as intolerant bigots who can only see things their own way and refuse to accept the views of others. To help us better understand what this kind of environment could be like, consider the following scenario.

IS ABSOLUTE TRUTH INTOLERANT?

Imagine that you are a student in college or university and it's your first week on campus. In general, it has been a time of new experiences and making new friends. Today is your second day of classes, and you are waiting for the professor to show up. Calculus was tough, but you know that you will do well with some hard study on your part. Literature sounds like fun, since your professor said most of it will be dedicated to the review and critique of the books of your choice. But the class you're in right now is being met with great anticipation on your part because you don't know what to expect. You're not quite sure about introduction to philosophy. You don't know what will be said and how you will respond. So you comfort yourself with the idea that a philosophy class at an institution of higher learning like this one would surely offer you some sound guidance with respect to finding answers to ultimate questions. Well, you'll know soon enough, because here comes your professor.

"Hello, I'm Professor Leslie Stone, and I want to welcome you to philosophy class. I would like to use our time today to get to know one another. So please think about your views of truth and get ready to share them with the rest of the class. You are free to tell us whatever you believe about God, the universe, good and evil, or anything else that you feel would help us to get to know your personal religious convictions."

Okay, now what? You were afraid something like this might happen! Listen to your classmates—nobody has said a word about the Bible or Jesus, and it's almost your turn. Well, Professor Stone said to feel free to share whatever you believe. Hey, get ready, you're on!

"Yes, my name is John Tate, and I'm from Texas. I grew up in a religious home, with loving parents who taught me to believe in the Bible as the Word of God. I believe God created the universe as stated in the book of Genesis and that He also created Adam and Eve. I believe that Adam and Eve disobeyed

God and everyone born from that time on inherited a sinful nature. So all of us are born evil and have a natural bent to sin, which is the bad news. It's bad because, according to the Bible, everyone is destined for hell. However, the good news is that God sent His only Son, Jesus, to save us from eternal punishment. Jesus died for our sins and made it possible for us to go to heaven. Jesus made it very clear that He is the only way to God."

Hey, that wasn't so bad; Professor Stone actually thanked you and went right on to the next student. This won't be as unpleasant as you thought. There are only a few students left, and maybe you'll be able to ask Professor Stone if you can share your personal testimony. . . .

Well, that was the last student, and Professor Stone still has some class time left; this could be your chance. Wait, Professor Stone is getting ready to say something herself.

"Okay, class, now that we've heard what each of you believes, I would like a show of hands in response to my next question. Since what is true for one person may not be true for someone else, how many think that we ought to be tolerant of one another's religious beliefs? In other words, how many believe that all religious truth is personal and therefore relative?"

Oh no! Now what? Every hand in the room is being raised, and you're the only one who hasn't agreed. Professor Stone is looking right at you. What will you say?

"Mr. Tate."

"Yes, Professor Stone."

"Mr. Tate, I don't see your hand raised. How is it that everyone in this class recognizes the truth of what I have just said except you?"

"I don't know, Professor Stone. The only thing I know is that all of us can't be right. I believe that we should respect one another, but how can all of our answers be true?"

"Well, Mr. Tate, welcome to higher education and to my class. Let me take a few minutes to explain why all religious truth is relative.

"There is an old parable about six blind Hindus touching an elephant that may help you to see my point. One blind man touched the side of the elephant and said it was a wall.

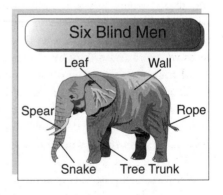

Another blind man touched the ear and said it was a large leaf of a tree. Yet another blind man was holding a leg and thought it was a tree trunk. Still another blind man took hold of the elephant's trunk and said it was a snake. Someone else was touching the elephant's tusk and believed it to be a spear. Another blind man had the elephant's tail in his hand and was calling it a rope. All of the blind men were touching the same reality but were understanding it differently. They all had the right to interpret what they were touching in their own personal way, yet it was the same elephant.

"You see, Mr. Tate, since we are all blind to the reality that may exist beyond this physical world, we must interpret that reality in our own way. Just as the parable illustrates, different religions have different interpretations of reality, but the reality is the same. It appears to be one thing for the Buddhist and another for the Muslim. A Christian sees it one way, and a Hindu another way, and so on. Reality is one, but views of it are many.

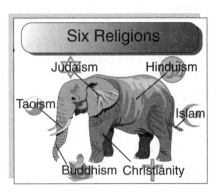

There are many paths that can lead you to the top of a mountain.

"Similarly, you have just heard your classmates share their personal views about ultimate reality, each right in his or her own eyes. Hence, we must accept each view and be tolerant of one another. Did not Jesus say, 'Love your neighbor as yourself'? Look around, Mr. Tate. These are your fellow students. Do you want to love them, or do you want to condemn them to hell with your belief in absolute truth? You must learn that there is enough hate in the world and that the only way to live in peace is to love, tolerate, and respect the religious convictions of others. You must understand that their views are as true for them as your view is for you. They see the truth in what I am saying, and that's why they raised their hands.

"I hope that you are now ready to agree with the rest of your fellow students, Mr. Tate, because we do not want to be religious bigots. Do we? This school advocates *pluralism* and *tolerance* as valuable tools in order to create a liberal environment where students can learn from their different personal preferences. Does that help you see what I am saying with respect to the relative nature of religious truth claims?"

"Yes, Professor Stone, I can see the truth in what you have said."

"Good for you, Mr. Tate! Our time is up, so class dismissed."

We need to look at some of the obstacles that keep people from believing in absolute truth. Pluralism is the first barrier, so we'll start by gaining an understanding of what it is and how it affects academics.

WHAT IS PLURALISM?

An institution of higher learning is a place where you would expect to find the right answers to some of the most important questions in life. Yet a secular college or university is usually one of the last places to find such answers with respect to the pursuit of absolute truth. Christian students who arrive on these campuses normally find themselves in an environment that offers many different answers to the same ultimate questions in life. This philosophical position is known as pluralism.

Contemporary pluralism manifests itself primarily as the diversity that is encountered in a multicultural society. There is certainly much to be gained by learning from the various ways the world is viewed, but how does that relate to truth? In philosophical terms, pluralism teaches that all views are true, even opposing ones. A pluralistic view of reality will undermine Christianity, which teaches that all views cannot be true. Ultimately, only one view is true, and everything opposed to it is false.

Religious pluralism consists of a belief system that holds in tension a diversity of thoughts, values, and convictions that are considered primarily to be a product of a person's family, culture, and society. As in the scenario above, a professor who teaches this philosophy will tell you that you must learn to accept alternative views of reality as true and to take delight in the fact that others can enrich your view of life by offering you a new perspective on reality. Therefore, according to religious pluralism, it only makes sense that the same ultimate questions can have different answers depending upon the way a person views the world. You may see the world as blue. Another may believe it is yellow. Still another perceives the world as red. Consequently, the answers to the ultimate questions in life will be colored or biased by the way the world is viewed.

We do have many of the same ultimate questions in life, such as: Does God exist? What is truth? Why are we here? What is evil and why does it exist if there is a loving God? What gives us meaning in life? According to pluralism, the answers to these questions depend upon how a person views the world. Since this kind of truth is a relative and personal matter, no one should believe that there is only one way to look at the world. *Pluralism is the logical conclusion of a relative view of truth.* It is also a denial of the laws of logic, for it insists that both A and non-A can be true.

The battle for absolute truth commences the moment we begin to answer ultimate questions with absolute answers based on the historical Christian view of the world. For students, this is an extremely difficult battle considering their environment. Many professors and classmates will be quick to point out that there is a problem with giving answers from a narrow-minded Christian perspective. It doesn't take long to be told—directly or indirectly—that Christians are not the sole possessors of truth and that to hold such a worldview is just a religious form of discrimination. That kind of intolerance will not be tolerated, and students are advised to liberate their minds by ridding themselves of a biased and constricted view of reality. They are exhorted to jettison their belief in an archaic Bible and to step into the realm of higher education where the intelligent people live. The only view that will be tolerated in such academic circles is a view that agrees with pluralism.

SHOULD PLURALISM BE EMBRACED IN ACADEMICS?

The word *university* is based on the concept of the unity of truth, the "one in the many." It was once believed that there was an overall *unity* in di*versity* (i.e., uni-versity) that formed the basis of the academic disciplines. This foundation for truth was also based on absolutes. Now, however, this kind of thinking is no longer tolerated, and the university has become a *pluraversity*. There is now a plurality in the diversity that does not consider truth as a harmonious whole to be pursued and discovered among the many diverse views of the world—and to think that it is, is equivalent to academic heresy. There are three words we must include in our vocabulary of truth terms in order to be academically, socially, and politically correct. These words are *pluralism, tolerance,* and *liberalism.*

However, it is vitally important that we understand when it makes sense to use and appreciate these terms and when it does not. Mortimer J. Adler explains:

> Pluralism, tolerance, and liberalism (the kind of liberalism that is doctrinaire) are twentieth-century terms that have few antecedents in modern thought, especially in that of the nineteenth century, but they have none in antiquity and the Middle Ages.
> The doctrinaire liberals of the twentieth century espouse pluralism and tolerance as if they were desirable values on which no restrictions or qualifications should be placed when they are applied to the life of society and of thought. . . . Pluralism is a desirable policy in all realms of action and

thought *except* those in which unity is required. When unity is required, pluralism must be restricted. . . .

In the sphere of all matters subject to individual thought and decision, pluralism is desirable and tolerable only in those areas that are matters of taste rather than matters of truth. Preferences with regard to cuisine, dress, patterns of dance, social manners, artistic style, do not raise any questions of truth. Where that is the case, pluralism has always existed on earth. . . . When, within a single society or culture, the attempt is made to regiment the conduct of individuals with respect to matters of taste, that regiment aims at a monolithic control of individual preferences and decisions.

The reaction against such monolithic or totalitarian regimentation is the motivating force of liberalism's spirited defense of toleration of diversity in all matters where individuals have a right to be free in expressing and acting on personal preference. Such matters belong in the sphere of the voluntary. But with regard to matters that belong in the sphere of intellect, matters involving truth not taste, a persistent pluralism is intolerable. . . . But such intolerance is entirely a private matter. It does not call for the suppression of the false opinions that others may still hold. . . . It calls only for the continued discussion between individuals. . . .

To view pluralism in regard to values as desirable and tolerable is tantamount to dismissing all value judgments as matters of taste rather than matters of truth. If, however, the prescriptive judgments we make about how to conduct our lives and our communities—judgments that contain the word "ought"—can be true or false, then they are subject to the unity of truth, as much as our judgments in mathematics and empirical science.[4]

We want to be clear on two critical points Adler stressed. Basically, *there is a place for pluralism in society with respect to matters of taste*, and Adler gave solid reasons why this makes sense in a free society. On the other hand, *there is no place for pluralism when it comes to deciding matters of truth*, involving a unity of thought. Therefore, we want to address the question "Are philosophical and religious ideas matters of *taste* or matters of *truth?*"

The simplest way to answer this question is to let those who believe that truth is a matter of taste decide for themselves. Let's say that we are having a discussion with some people who believe that all philosophical and religious statements are merely a matter of taste. If this is the case, they should not defend themselves when we disagree. If they begin to defend their view that these statements are matters of taste (or even think their statements are true),

---

[4]Mortimer J. Adler, *Truth in Religion: The Plurality of Religions and the Unity of Truth* (New York: Macmillan, 1990), 1–4.

the truth is revealed. Why should they get upset if we prefer one view to another as a matter of *taste*?

For example, if they were to say, "There is no such thing as truth with respect to philosophy," we can simply ask, "Is your statement true?" An intellectually honest individual should see the self-defeating nature of his assertion. Hence, *philosophical statements are matters of truth*. But what about religion? Do religious claims belong in the realm of taste and personal preferences? Imagine once again that you are John Tate, and let's take a closer look at what was communicated in your class.

Your professor strongly held that religious beliefs were matters of taste, of personal preferences. She believed that, with respect to religion, what was true for one individual was not necessarily true for another. The easiest way to check the validity of her belief is to simply apply her claim to itself and see if it passes its own test. You can accomplish this task by asking your professor the right question,[5] such as, "Is your idea—that what is true for one individual is not necessarily true for another—is that true for you or is it true for me and everyone else in the class also?"

If Professor Stone's view were only true for her, because she prefers to believe it as a matter of taste, why was she trying to convince you that it must be true for the entire class? If religious beliefs are just a matter of personal taste, then it makes no sense for Professor Stone to argue that her position is true for everyone. *Her perspective only makes sense if she really holds to the conviction that religious beliefs are matters of truth.* Both positions cannot be true at the same time and in the same sense; that violates the LNC. Professor Stone contradicted herself by preaching a personal view of tolerance while being intolerant of John's belief in "religious" absolute truth. It is clear that philosophical *and* religious ideas are matters of truth and not matters of taste.

Consequently, it makes sense to give reasons for the truth of one view of reality as opposed to another, and thus institutes of higher learning should not embrace pluralism with regard to philosophical and religious ideas. Students and professors ought to have the liberty to share and debate such issues, but ultimately they belong in the sphere of the intellect because they are matters of truth, not taste.

We said that truth is an expression, symbol, or statement that matches or corresponds to its referent (i.e., that to which it refers, whether it is a conceptual [abstract] idea or an actual [concrete] thing). When the statement or expression is about reality, then to be true it must match or correspond to reality.

---

[5]To learn how to ask the right questions, see chapter 3.

However, this definition of truth assumes we can know something about reality. So before we continue we must contend for the truth of that assumption and show that those who believe that reality cannot be known are in error.

AGNOSTICISM: WHAT IS THAT?

Think about what it means to know that something exists. Existence is the most basic fact about something. Take away its existence and nothing is left. However, many people believe that something exists while also believing that it is impossible to know anything else about it. This view is called *agnosticism.* The word *agnosticism* literally means "no knowledge." Thomas Henry Huxley invented the term in 1869 to denote the philosophical and religious attitude of those who claim that metaphysical ideas can neither be proved nor disproved. The two basic forms of agnosticism are represented by those who believe that reality is *not known* ("soft" agnosticism or skepticism) and those who claim that reality is *unknowable* ("hard" agnosticism). Later, we will show the soft agnostic why some of the fundamental aspects of reality are knowable. The hard agnostic view, though, must first be answered before we can continue our search for truth.

The eighteenth-century philosopher Immanuel Kant (1724–1804) established the view known as hard agnosticism. The central tenet of hard agnosticism is that although we know *that* reality exists, *what* reality is in itself (its essence) cannot be known by human reason. Even though Kant wrote centuries ago, his writings have formed the basis for much of modern philosophy. It was his pen that put an abrupt end to metaphysical reasoning (offering reasons for the existence of God). Kant drew the line that set the boundary for human reason, a line that fixed an impassible gulf between what reality is in itself and our ability to know it as such.

To help visualize the result of Kant's philosophy, think of ultimate reality as what actually exists beyond the physical world. According to Kant, we can never reason across the chasm from *what we see* to *what really is* and answer the question, "What is that?" "Kantsequently," *that* reality exists can be known, but *what* reality actually is in itself cannot be known. If we were to agree with Kant, we would believe that the categories of the mind form or structure reality for us, but that we could never truly know what it is. We only see reality *as it appears to us* after we have molded the "stuff" of reality via the categories and forms of the mind and the senses.

The majority of philosophers who followed Kant adopted his *metaphysical agnosticism.* Later, some reasoned that if we cannot know whether or not our ideas correspond to reality, then all truth must be relative to the individual way our minds interpret reality. Hence, the modern view of truth called *relativism* (all truth is relative) in due time gave rise to *pluralism* (all views are true).

DO PLURALISM AND RELATIVISM MAKE SENSE?

Relativism is subtler than hard agnosticism, for relativists believe that all views of reality are true within the context of an individual's culture or environment. If ideas do not correspond to objective reality, then we can never establish the truth of any one system of thought over another. A view can be logically coherent within its own set of ideas, but that does not mean it corresponds to reality. If we cannot know reality, then it makes sense to believe that truth claims at best reflect a different aspect of the same reality. Relativists do not believe there is only one true map, or worldview, that actually corresponds to reality. A *worldview* is a set of beliefs, a model that attempts to explain all of reality and not just some aspect of it.

According to relativism, all views depict the same reality from different perspectives, because different perspectives of the same object can yield different results. For example, an observer viewing an object from one angle may see it, as it is, a cylinder. However, if another person looked at the same cylinder from another view, it may appear to be a circle. Still another may see it as a rectangle from a third viewpoint. The cylinder doesn't change its shape; the difference is in the mind of the observer. Hence, relativists believe that there are many equally valid ways to view the same reality.

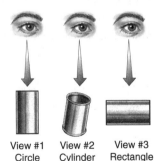

View #1 Circle   View #2 Cylinder   View #3 Rectangle

In the earlier scenario, a Christian student was exposed to pluralism in a philosophy class. His professor said,

Since we are all blind to the reality that may exist beyond this physical world, we must interpret that reality in our own way. . . . Different religions have different interpretations of reality, but the reality is the same. It appears to be one thing for the Buddhist and another for the Muslim. A Christian sees it one way, and a Hindu another way, and so on. Reality is one, but views of it are many. There are many paths that can lead you to the top of a mountain.

Yet if every view points to truth in everything it claims about reality, how can we ever find what is actually true?

For example, relativists and religious pluralists are asking us to believe that atheism points to the truth when atheists claim that God does not exist, and that theism points to the truth when theists claim God does exist. Relativists want us to accept both the pantheistic belief that God is the world and the theistic claim that God is not the world. Yet how can something exist as the world and not as the world—at the same time and in the same sense? For that matter, how can it exist and not exist? If everyone believed that all the tenets of every worldview were true, what would the word *truth* mean? If all views of reality are true, all views of reality must also be false, and ultimately there would be nothing to say about anything. If every statement points to truth, then nothing points to truth—*to point in every direction is the same as not to point at all!* This is called nonsense because it makes no sense and violates logic (the LNC), and logic is necessary for making sense.

With this in mind, we want to find out which claims about reality correspond to it in a more accurate way than the others do. In order to accomplish this task, we must first refute Immanuel Kant's hard-agnostic claim that reality is essentially unknowable. Since pluralism is linked to relativism and since relativism is an offshoot of agnosticism, all three views stand or fall together. Before we critique these three views it is important to make a distinction with respect to pluralism. Once we understand this distinction, we will be better equipped to advance our argument in favor of absolute truth.

ARE AGNOSTICISM, RELATIVISM, AND PLURALISM TRUE?

The fundamental flaw in Kant's hard-agnostic position is his claim to have knowledge of what he declares to be unknowable. In other words, if it were true that reality cannot be known, no one, including Kant, would know it. Kant's hard agnosticism boils down to the claim "I know that reality is unknowable." Therefore, we need to ask some basic questions about Kant's agnosticism: Is Kant's view only true for him, or does his view actually correspond to reality? If Kant's view doesn't correspond to reality, is it false? If Kant's agnosticism does correspond to reality, then how is it that we can know the most essential thing about reality—*that something exists*—but we cannot know anything about *what reality* is? If knowledge about reality is impossible for everyone, then it must also be impossible for Kant.

If reality were actually unknowable, how would Kant know this was true? We have already demonstrated that existence is the most essential thing that can be stated of something. Take away its existence and nothing is left. Think about it: the truth that follows Kant's sequences of thought tells us that he had to apply reason to reality to conclude other truths about *what* reality is in addition to his determination *that* reality existed.

TRUTH OR KANT'S SEQUENCES:

1. Kant *knows* that something real, in itself, exists on the other side of the fixed gulf.
2. Kant *knows* that this reality is the cause of all appearances (effects) in the human mind.
3. Kant *knows* that this reality is powerful enough to cause a universal effect.

This is certainly some critical *knowledge* about reality, which runs contrary to the claim of agnosticism.

It is not possible to know merely *that* reality exists without knowing something about *what* it is. All knowledge requires knowing some attribute of the object being known. It is impossible to affirm *that* something exists without simultaneously declaring something about what it is. For example, if someone brought an unknown electronic *gadget* into the room (see illustration), we would immediately know several things about it—even if we did not know its function. We would know that it exists, that it is physical, that it is a certain color and shape, that it has illuminated dials, that it has power, etc. We cannot know *that* it is without knowing something about *what* it is (even if we don't know *why* it is). Therefore, *hard agnosticism is self-defeating and false.* The truth about reality is that it exists and we can know something about it. Therefore, we may be able to discover some other attributes of reality and see which worldview most accurately corresponds to it.

We think it is fair to say that relativists and pluralists really do believe in absolute truth. They may deny it, but they cannot escape the reality of this assumption: that dialogues concerning the true nature of reality (metaphysics) only make sense if different views can be compared to that actual reality. In other words, anyone who attempts to defend one view ("all truth is relative" or "pluralism is true") over another ("absolute truth exists" or "pluralism is false") automatically assumes that ultimately only one view is true because it most accurately corresponds to reality. C. S. Lewis illustrated this point with the use of a map.[6] He explained that if two people drew a map of New York, the only way to say that one map is better than the other is to compare both of them with the real place that exists, New York itself. The actual reality of New York is the standard by which the maps must be measured. If New York did not exist or if it was impossible to know anything about it, how could we ever conclude that one map is better, or more accurate, than the other?

One way to illustrate the absurdity of "absolute relativity" is to imagine that we are sitting in a train that is ready to leave the train station. Our destination is a city to the north of our present location. Parked next to us is another train also ready to depart. A second glance reveals that motion is occurring, but we are not sure who is moving. Is our train moving or is the other train moving? The only way to answer this question is to look at a fixed point, a tree or a building, outside the window. But what if the tree or building begins to move as well? It would then be impossible to tell who or what was actually moving and in which direction. The only thing we could conclude about this situation is that there is motion occurring. If everything were moving, how would we ever know if we were moving in the direction of our destination (truth)? We would not be able to say that we were making progress (developing a better view of reality). We could only conclude that motion (thinking) was occurring. Lewis applied this kind of logic to ethics when he said,

> If things can improve, this means that there must be some absolute standard of good above and outside the cosmic process to which that process can approximate. There is no sense in talking of "becoming better" if better means simply "what we are becoming"—it is like congratulating yourself on reaching your destination and defining your destination as "the place you have reached."[7]

---

[6]C. S. Lewis, *Mere Christianity* (New York: Macmillan, 1952), 25.
[7]C. S. Lewis, *God in the Dock* (Grand Rapids, Mich.: Eerdmanns, 1970), 99.

In the same manner, it makes no sense to say that relativism or pluralism represents a better way to view reality than a view that believes in absolutes, unless these views are being compared with some absolute fixed point or standard. Without a fixed point, it only makes sense to say that these views are different from each other and that no one view is any better than another view. Hence, relativists and pluralists cannot logically label a view incompatible with their view as wrong; they can only logically say that the other view is different. Yet *the minute they decide they are right and that those who believe in absolutes are wrong, they must logically conclude that some absolute standard exists, even if they do not verbally admit it.* Consequently, relativism and pluralism cannot be true.

IS IT CREDIBLE TO HOLD TO ABSOLUTE TRUTH?

Now apply the train illustration to what we are trying to accomplish in this book. We are on a journey in search of truth; truth is our destination. But if all truth is relative, how will we know if we are heading in the right direction? It doesn't make sense to say that we are progressing in our search unless there is a fixed point (unchanging reality) that exists by which to measure our progress. Everyone has a fixed point (or an *absolute*), even relativists. Otherwise, they cannot claim to have a true view of reality. Advocates of relativism can, and often do, state their beliefs in subtle and covert ways. However, when stated in forthright English, their absolutes become rather obvious.

Think about it: why do relativists argue for the truth of their view? In other words, if there are no better views of reality and all views are just different views, why bother arguing for the truth of relativism—unless, of course, relativists really believe that they have a better view of reality! Consider the writings of one famous relativist, Joseph Fletcher (one of the signatories of "Humanist Manifesto II"). In his book *Situation Ethics*, Fletcher said, "The situationist avoids words like 'never' and 'perfect' and 'always' and 'complete' as he avoids the plague, as he avoids 'absolutely.' "[8]

What Fletcher is in effect saying is (1) "one should *never* use the word 'never,' " (2) "one should always avoid using the word 'always,' " and (3) "one should *absolutely* deny all 'absolutes.' "[9] Denying the validity of absolutes violates logic (the LNC) and is self-defeating.

Since it is self-defeating to believe that all views of reality are false or relative, and it is contradictory to believe that all views of reality are true, then the

---

[8]Joseph Fletcher, *Situation Ethics: The New Morality* (Philadelphia: Westminster, 1966), 43–44.
[9]Norman L. Geisler, *Is Man the Measure?* (Grand Rapids, Mich.: Baker, 1983), 180.

only logical option is to believe that some views represent reality in a better, or more accurate, way than others. Therefore, *in order for philosophical inquiry to make sense, one is forced to believe in absolute truth.* It makes sense to believe that there is a knowable, transcendent, and unchanging reality (a fixed point or referent). In this respect, we have demonstrated that the truth about reality can be known or discovered. How we go about understanding other character- istics of reality, or formulating a test for judging other truth claims about it, constitutes the next step in our journey.

HOW CAN WE KNOW THE TRUTH ABOUT REALITY?

Since reality is knowable, we need to learn how to utilize first principles in order to know which claims about reality are true. The academic discipline associated with how to know which view of reality is true is called *epistemology.* Epistemology is the systematic study of the nature, sources, and validity of the theory of knowledge (Greek *episte,* "knowledge," and *logos,* "word" or "dis- course"). As mentioned earlier, logic, by itself, can tell us what is false, but it cannot establish what is true. Logic is concerned with the specific and formal problem of valid reasoning; epistemology addresses the nature of both correct reasoning in relation to truth *and* the process of knowing what is true. It is the branch of philosophy that concerns itself with the methods of how to know truth, utilizing logic as a negative test. Epistemology deals with the ways in which beliefs are justified, that is, the ways in which we can test our beliefs to see if they constitute knowledge.

Mortimer J. Adler, distinguished author and philosopher, has written extensively on some of the greatest philosophical ideas debated down through the centuries. He is probably best known for his editing of the *Great Books of the Western World.* In connection with this project, Adler produced *Syntopicon,* two volumes containing 102 essays about "the 102 objects of thought that have collec- tively defined Western thought for more than 2,500 years. . . . These es- says . . . remain the centerpiece of En-

The Sphere of Truth

First Principles

cyclopedia Britannica's *Great Books of the Western World.*[10] With respect to the search for truth, Adler defends the position that truth is a harmonious whole, or sphere, which is constructed of many parts. However, each part of this coherent sphere of truth differs with respect to the method by which it is discovered. He calls this idea *the principle of the unity of truth.* Adler said, "All the diverse parts of the whole of truth must be compatible with one another regardless of the diversity of the ways in which these parts of truth are attained or received."[11]

Adler is referring to what is known as the coherence of all truth. We will employ this theory and establish a test method that will allow us to discover the truth about reality in a manner that upholds the principle of the unity of truth (*coherence*). The procedure we are proposing will involve identifying the first principles of the academic disciplines that make up the various parts of the sphere of truth. As we do so, we must also make every effort to see that their coherence (unity) is protected. For example, *what we discover to be true according to the first principles of science must be united with, and not violate, the previous truths established by the first principles of logic and philosophy.* (As we have shown, the LNC is preeminent.) As we continue to discover, identify, and unite the first principles of the other academic disciplines and form an intellectual lens, we will begin to see how the diverse parts of the sphere of truth can be united to form a coherent whole. Once this comprehensive lens is put together, we will be able to look through it and make certain inferences that will *correspond* to the overall reality that exists. These two elements of epistemology (coherence and correspondence) will constitute our method of testing the truth claims of a particular worldview.

As we envision this

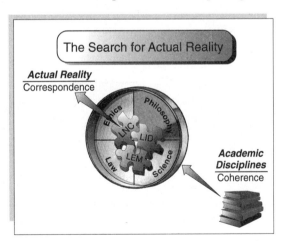

The Search for Actual Reality

Actual Reality
Correspondence

Ethics · Philosophy · LNC · LID · Law · LEM · Science

Academic Disciplines
Coherence

---

[10]Mortimer J. Adler, *The Great Ideas: A Lexicon of Western Thought* (New York: Macmillan, 1992), front dust cover.

[11]Mortimer J. Adler, *Truth in Religion: The Plurality of Religions and the Unity of Truth* (New York: Macmillan, 1990), 105.

test methodology, we can think of it as placing each part (first principle) of the intellectual lens together in a coherent manner. Little by little, the most essential characteristics of reality will come into focus as correct inferences are made through the use of this lens. This view of reality (worldview) will then become for us the interpretive structure through which the facts of this world can be explained.

We now have three parts of the lens in place, the first principles of logic (the LNC, LEM, and LID) and philosophy (the fixed point of unchanging reality). The LNC, in the strict sense, is absolutely first in the order of knowing because all human knowledge depends upon it; therefore, it deserves to be the centerpiece of the lens, as it will be utilized by every academic discipline. Each field of knowledge is dependent upon the proper use of the LNC in order to be classified as valid. The fixed point in philosophy is what gives us the academic credibility to continue our search for truth. The other branches of human knowledge also have first principles associated with them in the sense that each principle is first as the source of, and basis for, that particular branch of human knowledge. The first principles we are searching for are the fundamental starting points, or self-evident truths, of the academic disciplines: science, law, history, and ethics. If we can show that each piece of the intellectual lens represents some essential attribute of the nature of reality, then the intellectual lens will become the standard by which we must test all truth claims about the world.

In conclusion, it may help us to think of the cylinder illustration we used in discussing relativism and pluralism. We agree that some views of an object are a matter of perspective because they are relative to the viewer, as depicted in this illustration. However, we insist that it is not meaningful to claim that all views are simply a matter of perspective. For instance, it is not a matter of perspective that a cylinder exists to be perceived—the actual reality of the cylinder is what gives each perspective its validity. View #2 gives a clearer or better view

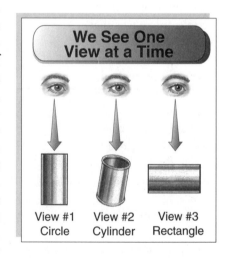

of the characteristics of the cylinder than view #1 or view #3. But to say that view #2 is the same reality as view #1 or view #3—that the cylinder is the circle or the rectangle—just doesn't make sense. Rather, it does makes sense to say that each view holds some truth, and that view #2 gives us a more accurate picture of what is being perceived. If we were looking for the view that gives us a clear understanding of what the object really is, then view #2 would be better than view #1 or view #3. Of course, we are finite and can only see the whole cylinder one view at a time, unlike God who sees the cylinder as a whole—from every possible perspective.

Let's return also to the elephant illustration. Your professor said the parable illustrated that different religions have different interpretations of reality, but the reality is the same. (It appears to be one thing for the Buddhist and another for the Muslim. A Christian sees it one way, and a Hindu another way, and so on.) Before we address this parable, we need to explain that religions and philosophies can be examined in light of the worldview into which they fit. In other

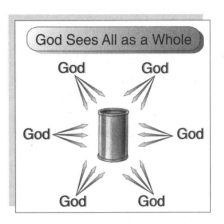

words, the worldview provides the infrastructure or basic foundation for the various religions and philosophies of life as shown in the adjacent table. Therefore, rather than analyzing each religion and philosophy of life, we can examine the worldview upon which a particular religion or philosophy is built. Since each worldview holds to central beliefs that are opposed by the others, then logically only one worldview can be true; the others must be false. The chief tenets of atheism, pantheism, and theism (the worldviews under consideration in this book) will be explained in chapter 3.

With respect to the elephant parable, relativists must assume knowledge of the whole elephant in order to know that each person has touched a part of it. We cannot know the *whole elephant* from one view, but we can see its various parts *one view at a time*. However, just as in the cylinder example, God sees the elephant *as a whole*. For us, each view of the ele-

WORLDVIEWS & RELIGIONS

ATHEISM	PANTHEISM	THEISM
Taoism	Hinduism	Judaism
Jainism	New Age	Islam
Secular Humanism	Zen Buddhism	Christianity

phant depicts a different part of it. If so, one would think that when an atheist, pantheist, and theist touch the same part of the elephant, they ought to be able to agree on what that part is. Moreover, since first principles form the foundations upon which all knowledge is built, including the tenets of these three worldviews, then we ought to be able to show which worldview makes correct inferences and reaches true conclusions. In order to accomplish this task, we have suggested a test methodology that utilizes first principles, explained in chapter 3. For now, we are merely showing how the same part of the elephant (reality) cannot be one thing for a theist and also be something completely opposite for an atheist or pantheist.

Since we are finite beings and cannot see all of reality at once, our view of reality is necessarily limited by our finitude. Even so, we believe that we can have sufficient knowledge of reality to find the answers to some of the most important questions in life without having an exhaustive knowledge of reality. Using logic and philosophy we have established the existence of a reality that is fixed and knowable. In keeping with the elephant analogy, let's say that we have just touched the ear and the side of the elephant (two aspects of reality), and since we used first principles to touch those parts, there was no particular worldview or religious bias involved. Therefore, using first principles from other disciplines as our sensing mechanism, we can continue to make inferences and draw conclusions about reality in the same way. Our first conclusion about reality, namely that it exists and is knowable, is known as *realism*.

Reaching this first checkpoint known as realism means that we have made significant progress in our journey toward truth. We arrived here by way of applying the first principles of logic and philosophy to the reality we undeniably know exists. If we are to make further headway in our pilgrimage, we cannot turn back. In other words, now that we have established the truth of these principles and the conclusions reached by using them, we cannot logically deny them at some future moment in an effort to escape the reality we discover. This is our point of no return, and it is at this point that we can define the nature of truth.

TRUTH BY ITS VERY NATURE IS:

- Noncontradictory—it does not violate the basic laws of logic.
- Absolute—it does not depend upon any time, places, or conditions.
- Discovered—it exists independently of our minds; we do not create it.
- Descriptive—it is the agreement of the mind with reality (correspondence).
- Inescapable—to deny its existence is to affirm it (we are bound by it).
- Unchanging—it is the firm standard by which truth claims are measured.

We will continue to apply the test mentioned above to the various beliefs that each worldview holds to be true. This is how we will discover which worldview has the correct explanation of reality. The first column of the adjacent table lists the subject matter with respect to each of the academic disciplines that will be utilized in this work. The columns to the right of the subject matter list the truth claims of each worldview: atheism, pantheism, and theism respectively. Thus far, we have shown that it would be self-defeating to believe truth is relative. As the highlighted

	Atheism	Pantheism	Theism
Truth	Relative, No Absolutes	Relative to This World	Absolute Truth Exists
Cosmos	Always Existed	Not Real– Illusion	Created Reality
God	Does Not Exist	Exists, Unknowable	Exists, Knowable
Law	Relative, Determined by Humanity	Relative to This World	Absolute, Objective, Discovered
Evil	Human Ignorance	Not Real– Illusion	Selfish Heart
Ethics	Created by Humanity, Situational	Relative, Transcends Good/Evil	Absolute, Objective, Prescriptive

box in the table on the right indicates, only *theism agrees with the conclusions drawn from the first principles of logic and philosophy.* Hence, we can eliminate hard agnosticism and soft agnosticism/skepticism,[12] since they are self-defeating in claiming that they know they cannot know anything and that they do not doubt that they should doubt everything.

Soon we will apply our test for truth to each worldview concerning its claims about the cosmos: the origin of the universe, the origin of life, and the origin of new life forms. However, before we employ the academic discipline of science to decide which worldview of the cosmos is true, we must first gain a proper understanding of what a worldview is and how it affects an individual's beliefs and actions. Therefore, let's take a closer look at the meaning of the term *worldview* and the claims of the worldviews of atheism, pantheism, and theism.

---

[12] *Agnostics* claim to know that they cannot know. *Skeptics* do not doubt their doubt, nor do they suspend judgment on their claim that we should suspend judgment.

3

QUESTIONS ABOUT WORLDVIEWS

Ideas have consequences.

—Richard M. Weaver

WHAT IS A WORLDVIEW?

We have already said that a *worldview* is analogous to an intellectual lens through which people view reality and that the color of the lens is a strong determining factor that contributes to what they believe about the world. Moreover, a *worldview* is a philosophical system that attempts to explain how the facts of reality relate and fit together. Once the pieces of the lens are put together, it will bring into focus the big picture of reality that provides the framework into which the smaller pieces of life then fit. In other words, a worldview shapes or colors the way we think and furnishes the interpretive condition for understanding and explaining the facts of our experience.

As important as it is to understand what a worldview is, it is even more critical to comprehend the logical consequences associated with living out the convictions of what a particular worldview holds to be true. This thought leads us to our next question.

WHY ARE WORLDVIEWS IMPORTANT?

Since our thoughts influence our emotions, reactions, and behaviors, it is particularly important for us to know what we believe and why we believe it.

Think about the kind of historical consequences that are the direct and logical results of a worldview—of beliefs or convictions. One man, Adolf Hitler, appealed to the people of his country to have the backbone to advance the logical outworking of their worldview. He said,

> The stronger must dominate and not mate with the weaker, which would signify the sacrifice of its own higher nature. Only the born weakling can look upon this principle as cruel, and if he does so it is merely because he is of a feebler nature and narrower mind; for if such a law did not direct the process of evolution then the higher development of organic life would not be conceivable at all. . . . If Nature does not wish that weaker individuals should mate with the stronger, she wishes even less that a superior race should intermingle with an inferior one; because in such a case all her efforts, throughout hundreds of thousands of years, to establish an evolutionary higher stage of being, may thus be rendered futile.[1]

Hitler referred to this dispensation of nature as "quite logical." In fact, it was so logical to the Nazis that they built concentration camps to carry out their convictions about the human race as being "nothing but the product of heredity and environment" or, as the Nazis liked to say, "of blood and soil."[2] Auschwitz was one such camp where theoretical precepts were applied to the real world. If we were to visit Auschwitz today, we could walk down the hallways of some of the buildings where we would see the unimaginable impact a worldview can and did have on people in the world. Most visitors are unprepared and shocked to see the photos of pregnant women and little children who were eventually tortured to death by Nazi officials. In preparing a cover story in remembrance of the fiftieth anniversary of the liberation of Auschwitz, *Newsweek* interviewed Lieutenant General Vasily Petrenko, the only surviving commander among the four Red Army divisions that encircled and liberated Auschwitz:

> Petrenko was a hardened veteran of some of the worst fighting of the war. "I had seen many people killed," Petrenko says. "I had seen many people hanged and burned people. But still I was unprepared for Auschwitz." What astonished him especially were the children, some mere infants, who had been left behind in the hasty evacuation. They were the survivors of the medical experiments perpetrated by the Auschwitz camp doctor, Josef Mengele, or the children of Polish political prisoners rounded up after the ill-fated revolt in Warsaw.[3]

[1]Adolf Hitler, *Mein Kampf,* trans./annot. James Murphy (New York: Hurst and Blackett, 1942), 161–62.
[2]Viktor Frankl, *The Doctor and the Soul: Introduction to Logotherapy* (New York: Knopf, 1982), *xxi.*
[3]Jerry Adler, "The Last Days of Auschwitz," *Newsweek,* January 16, 1995, 47.

The earlier quote from *Mein Kampf*, along with this brief excerpt from *Newsweek*, ought to be a sober reminder of the fact that worldviews lead to conclusions and consequences. The strong convictions of men like Adolf Hitler and Josef Mengele show that a worldview can change the face of the world. Understanding what different worldviews teach, and the logical outworking of each, is very crucial. Therefore, we plan to summarize some of the main tenets of the worldviews under examination in this book so that we can check their beliefs to see which ones are credible. However, there are many ways to view reality; perhaps it seems as if there can be as many worldviews as there are people in the world. So before we look at the main tenets of the worldviews we will be discussing, let's identify which ones we plan to examine.

HOW MANY WORLDVIEWS ARE THERE?

There are seven worldviews: theism, atheism, pantheism, panentheism, deism, polytheism, and finite godism. We know that all of these views have permeated our culture and exist, in one form or another, on virtually every secular college or university campus in North America and much of the rest of the world. In this book we will investigate only the three predominant worldviews that exist in our culture—atheism, pantheism, and theism.[4]

First, let us consider the worldview under which orthodox Christianity belongs, the worldview called *theism*. Theism teaches that there is only one infinite and personal Being who is beyond this finite physical universe. Theists believe that the attributes of the God of the Bible can be partially known through nature, just as the attributes of an artist can be recognized through the artist's painting. The Bible informs us that God has put a deep-seated knowledge in the hearts and minds of all the people of the world about some of His attributes and that this knowledge can be clearly seen through the observation of nature:

> What may be known about God is plain to them [all people], because God has made it plain to them. For since the creation of the world God's invisible qualities—his eternal power and divine nature—have been clearly seen, being understood from what has been made, so that men [all people] are without excuse.[5]

The battle for truth will focus on what God has revealed to all people about

---

[4]Finite godism is briefly examined in chapter 11 with respect to Rabbi Harold Kushner's book *Why Do Bad Things Happen to Good People?* Also, for more information about worldviews, see N. L. Geisler and R. M. Brooks, *When Skeptics Ask* (Grand Rapids, Mich.: Baker, 1990), chapter 3.
[5]Romans 1:19–20.

Himself. According to biblical theism, this verse makes it clear that God will hold everyone, regardless of his or her culture or society, accountable for what He has revealed about Himself through nature. The first two chapters of the book of Romans help us understand exactly what has been made clear by God—that He is the infinite and eternal power source that caused and sustains the existence of the physical universe, and that His divine nature is the basis for ethics. However, God also says that this truth has been suppressed by the evil moral condition of individuals and not because of their intellectual ignorance.

HOW DO WORLDVIEWS DIFFER?

The most fundamental dissension between worldviews is based on the existence and nature of God. In a book documenting a debate between an atheist and a theist, Peter Kreeft makes the following observation about the existence of God:

> The idea of God has guided or deluded more lives, changed more history, inspired more music and poetry and philosophy than anything else, real or imagined. It has made more of a difference to human life on this planet, both individually and collectively, than anything else ever has.[6]

To get an understanding of the primary differences that exist among atheism, pantheism, and theism, we only need to define each worldview and list its major tenets. The reason for this comparison is to demonstrate the logically incompatible nature of the essential truth claims each worldview makes concerning God, reality, humanity, evil, and ethics. Further study of each worldview is recommended, but these tenets will serve our purpose. Ultimately, we want to see which set of worldview tenets most accurately matches the fundamental truths used as the basis for each academic field of knowledge under consideration in this book.

WHAT DO ATHEISTS BELIEVE?

Atheism believes that no God exists, either beyond the universe or in it. The universe or cosmos is all there is or ever will be; it is self-sustaining. Some of the more famous atheists were Karl Marx, Friedrich Nietzsche, Sigmund Freud, and Jean-Paul Sartre. Their writings have had a tremendous influence

---

[6]J. P. Moreland and Kai Nielsen, *Does God Exist?* (Nashville: Thomas Nelson, 1990), 11.

upon the world. These men expressed their views in different ways, but all of them held to the basic belief that God does not exist. Some of the main tenets of atheism, in general, are as follows:

- GOD—He does not exist; only the universe exists.
- UNIVERSE—It is eternal; or it randomly came to be.
- HUMANITY (origin)—We have evolved, are made of molecules, and are not immortal.
- HUMANITY (destiny)—We have no eternal destiny and will be annihilated.
- EVIL (origin)—It is real, caused by human ignorance.
- EVIL (destiny)—It can be defeated by man through education.
- ETHICS (basis)—They are created by, and grounded in, humanity.
- ETHICS (nature)—They are relative, determined by the situation.

WHAT DO PANTHEISTS BELIEVE?

Another major worldview is the belief that God *is* the universe. This view is called *pantheism*, manifest in popular form as *the New Age movement.* For a pantheist there is no creator beyond the universe; creator and creation are two different ways of viewing the same reality, and ultimately only one reality exists, not many different ones. God pervades all things and is found within all things. Nothing exists apart from God: God is the world and the world is God; God is the universe and the universe is God. People hold to different kinds of pantheism, which are represented by certain forms of Hinduism, Zen Buddhism, and the New Age. Their views differ as to how God and the world are identified, but they all believe that God and the world are one. Some of the main tenets of pantheism are as follows:

- GOD—He is one, infinite, usually impersonal; he is the universe.
- UNIVERSE—It is an illusion, a manifestation of God, who alone is real.
- HUMANITY (origin)—The human's true self (atman) is God (Brahman).
- HUMANITY (destiny)—Our destiny is determined by karma/cycles of life.
- EVIL (origin)—It is an illusion, caused by errors of the mind.
- EVIL (destiny)—It will be reabsorbed by God.
- ETHICS (basis)—They are grounded in lower manifestations of God.
- ETHICS (nature)—They are relative, transcending the illusion of good and evil.

WHAT DO THEISTS BELIEVE?

Conversely, *theism* is the worldview that holds to the belief that the world is more than just the physical universe (atheism). At the same time, theists do not accept the idea that God is the world (pantheism). They believe in the existence of God and see His existence as the essential component of the theistic worldview. Theists are convinced that the universe had a supernatural First Cause who is infinitely powerful and intelligent. An infinite God is both beyond and manifests Himself in the universe. This God is a personal God, separate from the world, who created the universe and sustains it. Theists believe that God can act within the universe in a supernatural way. The traditional religions of Judaism, Islam, and Christianity represent theism. Some of the main tenets of theism are as follows:

- GOD—He is one, personal, moral, infinite in all His attributes.
- UNIVERSE—It is finite, created by an infinite God.
- HUMANITY (origin)—We are immortal, created and sustained by God.
- HUMANITY (destiny)—By choice we'll be either eternally with or separated from God.
- EVIL (origin)—It is privation or imperfection caused by choice.
- EVIL (destiny)—It will be ultimately defeated by God.
- ETHICS (basis)—They are grounded in the nature of God.
- ETHICS (nature)—They are absolute, objective, and prescriptive.

WHAT IS WORLDVIEW CONFUSION?

Our judgments concerning certain issues in life depend upon how we view the world. Our worldview will bias our conclusions because of the assumptions we make when we formulate it. For example, atheists who have decided that macroevolution accounts for the life we observe in the universe base their theory on purely naturalistic assumptions made within the atheistic worldview. Consequently, atheists have concluded that there is no God. At the same time, theists can look at the identical evidence and show that the only way to account for intelligent life in the observable universe is by positing an intelligent First Cause (God). The same facts of the universe are available to the atheist and the theist, yet their conclusions are irreconcilable. These incompatible answers result from what is referred to as *worldview confusion*. Since our judgments about life are biased by our worldview, and since different worldviews arrive at essentially different answers to the same questions, where do we go from here?

We suggest taking a closer look at the structure of the intellectual lens (worldview) being used to interpret the data under investigation and gaining an understanding of how that lens is put together. Understanding the assumptions that constitute the main structure of worldviews will be an essential aspect of learning how to communicate our beliefs across various worldviews without having them misinterpreted through other-colored lenses. Therefore, this lens is the place to begin to look for common ground—principles that are used in formulating any and every worldview. At first glance, the worldviews represented above do not seem to have many shared attributes. Yet as lenses they both are made of curved glass surfaces, and each has a focal point. For that reason, we may be able to find some mutual assumptions upon which to build a logical discussion before we argue about which interpretation of the evidence is the correct one. We are suggesting that one good way to communicate across worldviews is to ask the right questions.

WHY ARE QUESTIONS SO IMPORTANT?

There are many good reasons for asking honest questions during a dialogue. One important reason is that a sincere question lets the other person know that we are genuinely interested in her opinion. Remember that the ultimate goal in apologetics (giving reasons for our faith) is to gently confirm and defend our beliefs, in the hope that God will draw individuals into a relationship with Himself through Jesus Christ. Just spouting off answers or obnoxiously stumping for the Christian faith will not help to build relationships with people who need to know God. Therefore, it is essential to recognize that a properly focused question, *asked in an attitude of love and concern*, can be much more effective than just trying to prove a point and win an argument.

It has been rightly said that one can win an argument but lose the person in the process. Asking the right kinds of questions can help to disarm a potentially explosive dialogue and turn it into an effective discussion. When someone gets emotionally involved with an issue, it becomes increasingly difficult for him to follow a logical argument. The distraction can become so great that the result usually ends up with the discussion "producing more heat than light." Our primary task is to get away from the emotional aspect of the dialogue and try to establish some common ground for helpful communication to take place. The classroom is just the kind of place where emotions might get out of hand, so let's use that arena to take a look at what can happen when a professor or classmate questions Christianity.

Imagine that you are a college student and your biology professor knows that you believe God created the universe. One day he decides to ask you to justify your position in class and asks, "How can you believe in the Bible when it contradicts everything we know from science? For example, science has demonstrated that miracles are impossible. Yet you choose to believe in the miracles recorded in the Bible instead of science—why?" How should you respond to your professor? Most of us have been taught to respond to questions with answers. However, this is not always the wisest approach. It could be the case that your biology professor's question needs to be better understood. Christian philosopher Peter Kreeft says,

> There is nothing more pointless than an answer to a question that is not fully understood, fully posed. We are far too impatient with questions, and therefore far too shallow in appreciating answers.[7]

Rather than give an immediate response to your professor's question, it may be wiser to clarify his position first by asking *him* a question. However, your question had better be a good one, or else you may end up getting yourself into an emotionally charged conversation. For that reason, we want to discuss a method that will help you to ask the right kinds of questions in difficult surroundings; questions designed to neutralize a potentially emotional discussion.

HOW CAN WE HANDLE WORLDVIEW QUESTIONS?

First of all, we should keep in mind that not every question is asked in a sincere manner. Yet we should try to respond to what seems to be an insincere question in the most gracious and truthful way. We may not win over the questioner, but we may influence others who could be in the background waiting to hear our response. For example, it is highly unlikely that a professor who is standing in front of a class will be convinced of the truth of Christianity on the spot. However, God may use that situation to influence the minds of other students. The essential principle we want to teach about asking the right kind of questions concerns itself with shifting the discussion from a particular issue to the general truth principle behind the issue. We consider this to be the master key to unlocking a dialogue. Once we apprehend this key, we should be able to open the minds of our listeners with the turn of a simple question! We would like to suggest using this method in as many situations as possible. However, its success depends upon asking not just *any* questions, but on asking the *right* questions.

[7] Peter Kreeft, *Making Sense Out of Suffering* (Ann Arbor, Mich.: Servant, 1986), 27.

Imagine once again that you are the student taking the biology class mentioned above. Now, rather than responding to your professor with an answer, let's see what happens if you answer him by asking him the right question. Your professor asked you, "How can you believe in the Bible when it contradicts everything we know from science? For example, science has demonstrated that miracles are impossible. Yet you choose to believe in the miracles recorded in the Bible instead of science—why?" Let's

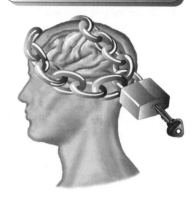

Questions: The Master Key to Unlocking the Mind

say that at this point in the semester you know your professor is a naturalist who believes that nothing exists outside of nature. How could you ever expect him to believe in the Word of God if there is no God? In the same manner, how could a naturalist believe in miracles, or acts of God, if there is no God who can act? Telling him your reasons as to why you believe the Bible is true—because it is the Word of God—may only serve to isolate you from him and the rest of the class. Where do you go from here?

At this point there is no common ground between this professor and you. For that reason, it is time to ask the right question in order to shift the discussion from this particular issue (the credibility of the Bible and miracles) to the general truth principle behind it. This will expose the hidden assumption in your professor's question. In order to do that, you must think about what your professor believes as a naturalist and find a way to ask him a question that puts both of you in shared territory.

Since logic is a fundamental area where common ground exists, we suggest using one of the first principles of logic, such as the law of noncontradiction (LNC), to formulate the right question. Your professor made a very confident and crucial statement when he said, "Miracles are impossible." You might notice, though, that he never offered you a definition of a miracle. Therefore, one place to begin would be to make sure that you and your professor agree on the definition of the significant terms you are using. Ask him to define what he means by *miracle*. He is most likely to respond by saying something like, "A miracle is an event in nature caused by something outside of nature." But since he does not believe that anything outside of nature exists, he is *forced* to conclude that miracles are impossible.[8]

Now you have located his assumption: he believes that nothing exists outside of nature and that science has demonstrated this to be the case. Moreover, as a naturalist he believes that science only concerns itself with nature and is thereby restricted to natural causes of events within nature. Consequently, your professor has defined miracles out of existence but *not by using the scientific method—rather by a philosophical assumption.* How can science prove that something does not exist outside of nature when, according to your professor, science cannot go beyond nature? There is something wrong here! Your professor is applying the wrong academic discipline to the question of miracles. C. S. Lewis explained how science cannot disprove the miraculous:

> [The] scientific method merely shows (what no one to my knowledge ever denied) that if miracles did occur, science, as science, could not prove, or disprove, their occurrence. What cannot be trusted to recur is not material for science: that is why history is not one of the sciences. You cannot find out what Napoleon did at the battle of Austerlitz by asking him to come and fight it again in a laboratory with the same combatants, the same terrain, the same weather, and in the same age. You have to go to the records. We have not, in fact, proved that science excludes miracles: we have only proved that the question of miracles, like the innumerable other questions, excludes laboratory treatment.[9]

Your professor was not only being unscientific when he claimed that miracles are impossible, he also committed a logical fallacy called *begging the question.* This fallacy is committed when someone argues in a circle. Lewis has also pointed out that if someone claims miracles are impossible, he must know that all reports of miracles are false. Yet the only way to know that all reports of miracles are false is to already know that miracles have never occurred—because they are impossible![10] The only alternative to this circular reasoning is to be open to the possibility that miracles have occurred. If you think about it, you may also want to consider asking your professor to define the term *natural,* even though he did not use this word in his question to you. Let's use Lewis's definition and see where it leads us.

---

[8]For a thorough philosophical analysis of this topic, see Norman L. Geisler, *Miracles and Modern Thought* (Grand Rapids, Mich.: Zondervan, 1982); and C. S. Lewis, *Miracles* (New York: Macmillan, 1978).

[9]C. S. Lewis, *God in the Dock* (Grand Rapids, Mich.: Eerdmans, 1970), 134.

[10]C. S. Lewis, *Miracles* (New York: Macmillan, 1978), 102.

If the "natural" means that which can be fitted into a class, that which obeys a norm, that which can be paralleled, that which can be explained by reference to other events, then Nature herself as a whole is *not* natural. If a miracle means that which must simply be accepted, the unanswerable actuality which gives no account of itself but simply *is*, then the universe is one great miracle.[11]

The only thing that your professor believes exists is the universe, and now, by definition, it turns out to be the biggest miracle of all. We are not suggesting that he will agree with you; we are demonstrating how to handle these kinds of questions. Asking for clarification will push your professor's original question back to a common principle where you may be able to build bridges of truth to the Christian worldview. You can share with your professor that if he agrees with the stated definitions of *miracle* and *natural*, both of you share a common belief. In fact, you can further justify how the Bible is harmonious with the scientific method because it is consistent with the principle of causality. In Genesis 1:1, the Bible declares God to be the uncaused Cause of the finite universe.[12]

We hope that the aforementioned scenario helped to show how asking the right kind of questions could be useful in guiding the direction of a discussion. Our goal is to shift the burden of proof from us to our questioners. By requesting clarification and using the LNC, we can ask our inquirers to define their terms, which in turn may compel them to think about their assumptions. As pointed out above, seeking the definition of the terms *miracle* and *natural* and probing until the assumptions were exposed showed how this professor either reasoned in a circle or accepted the greatest miracle of all—the universe. This method and reasoning process may or may not sway a college professor, but it can make a difference in the way other listeners perceive what we believe. It can be a very powerful tool, but don't expect to be able to master it in a short amount of time; it will require practice and insight to effectively use it in real-life situations. Once again, its success depends not merely upon asking any questions but rather upon asking the right questions.

HOW CAN WE ASK THE RIGHT KINDS OF QUESTIONS?

Asking the right kinds of questions depends upon our ability to know and properly use general precepts (first principles) that are related to the particular

---

[11]C. S. Lewis, *God in the Dock* (Grand Rapids, Mich.: Eerdmans, 1970), 36.
[12]The principle of causality, with respect to the origin of the universe, is thoroughly examined in chapter 4.

issue being discussed. Remember that when beliefs become convictions, a personal dimension enters the dialogue where emotions can run very deep! The right question can move a conversation back to common ground, a first principle, where it is more probable that a healthy discussion will take place. With this in mind, we are calling the right kinds of questions the *principle questions*. A principle question can catapult a conversation out of an emotional, subjec-

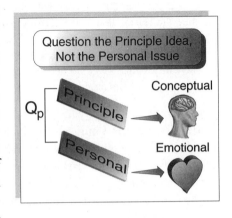

Question the Principle Idea, Not the Personal Issue

Q_p

Principle → Conceptual

Personal → Emotional

tive level and put it on a rational, objective level. Questioning principles rather than personal beliefs in order to engage people at the level of concepts rather than the level of convictions makes a difference! Remember: our first objective is to work from shared assumptions. We must endeavor to find the first principle related to the issue or question. Allow us to illustrate what we mean by using this technique on a popular question concerning God's ability to create a rock bigger than He can lift.

Imagine once again that you are at school and a certain student named Tom has been emotionally boiling over with your seemingly nonsensical belief in God. He can't wait for the opportunity to embarrass you in front of some of the other students who are interested in hearing more about your faith. One day, while you are having lunch with some of those responsive students, Tom decides to sit at your table and says, "Do you mind if I ask you a few questions?"

You respond by telling him that you would welcome his inquiries.

Tom then asks you, "Didn't Jesus say in Matthew 19:26, 'With God all things are possible'?"

You answer, "Yes."

Tom continues, "Do you believe that God is all-powerful and can do all things?"

Again, you answer, "Yes."

Now Tom thinks his moment is about to unfold, so with a sarcastic grin he asks, "Okay, can God create a rock so big that He cannot lift it?"

You ponder the question for a moment, thinking to yourself, *If I say yes, I'll be admitting that God is powerful enough to create the rock but not powerful enough to move it! However, if I say no, I'll be admitting that God is not all-*

powerful, because He cannot create a rock of that magnitude. It seems that either answer will force you to violate the LNC and contradict your view of God, defined as an all-powerful Being. It also seems as if Tom is using first principles to discredit you and your view of God. It is true that Tom is speaking correctly about God's power, but is he using first principles correctly?

Before we examine Tom's questions, remember that *now is not the time to appeal to ignorance* and tell Tom that he is trying to use human reason and that there are some things we just cannot understand about God. Nor should you say that somehow God is exempt from such a question. This will only give Tom more emotional fuel to think of other pointed issues to raise with you and accomplish his goal of discrediting your faith in front of your peers. Instead, you must focus in on this question and think of a principle question to ask him that moves the conversation from unstable *emotional* ground to firm *conceptual* territory.

Let's think about Tom's question and apply to it what we have learned from the proper use of the LNC. Tom wants God to create a rock so big that He cannot lift it. What is Tom really asking God to do? In order to find out, we need to define and clarify the use of Tom's words. The first question that comes to mind is, "How big of a rock does Tom want God to create?" Well, Tom wants God to create a rock so big that it would be impossible for Him to move it. Now, how big would a rock have to be in order for God not to be able to move it? What is the biggest physical entity that exists? Of course, the biggest physical entity is the universe, and no matter how much the universe expands it will remain a limited, finite physical reality—a reality that God can "lift." Even if God created a rock the size of an ever-expanding universe, God could still lift it or control it. The only logical option is for God to create something that exceeds His power to lift or control. But since God's power is infinite, He would have to create a rock of infinite proportions! This is the key: Tom wants God to create a rock, and a rock is a physical, finite thing. How can God create an *object* that is *finite* by *nature*—and give it an infinite size? There is something terribly wrong with Tom's question. So let's apply the correct use of the LNC to analyze it.

It is logically and actually impossible to create a physically finite thing and have it be *infinitely* big! By definition, an infinite, uncreated thing has no limits, and a finite, created thing does. Consequently, Tom has just asked if God can create an infinitely finite rock, that is, a rock that has limits and, at the same time and in the same sense, does not have limits. This question, then, violates the LNC and turns out to be utter nonsense. Tom thought he was asking an important question, one that would put the Christian on the horns of a dilemma. Instead, he only managed to show his own inability to think clearly.

Now that we have a clear understanding of Tom's question, it's simply a matter of formulating a principle question to ask him in order to reveal his error. How about this one: "Tom, how big do you want God to create that rock? If you tell me how big, I'll tell you if He can do it." Well, we can keep asking Tom that question until his answers approach the size of the universe and eventually introduce the idea of infinity. Once Tom reaches the point where he begins to see what he is really asking God to do, to create an infinite rock, he needs to be shown that he is asking God to do something that is logically irrelevant and impossible. God could no more create an infinitely finite rock than He could create a square circle: both are examples of *intrinsic impossibilities*. Commenting on intrinsic impossibility and an all-powerful God, C. S. Lewis said,

> It [the intrinsically impossible] is impossible under all conditions and in all worlds and for all agents. "All agents" here includes God Himself. His Omnipotence means power to do all that is intrinsically possible, not to do the intrinsically impossible. You may attribute miracles to him, but not nonsense.[13]

Not every question being asked is automatically meaningful just because it is a question. The question may sound meaningful, but we must be sure to test it with first principles to see whether it is valid. Be careful, then, not to be too quick to respond to questions; you may wind up trying to find a cogent answer to a question that has no logical relevance. Remember what Peter Kreeft said: "There is nothing more pointless than an answer to a question that is not fully understood." We would do well to heed his warning and utilize our understanding of first principles before we reply.

We have presented logical principles, such as the LNC, that can be called upon over and over again in situations such as the ones presented above. To be effective, one must practice this methodology and combine it with a solid understanding of the LNC until it becomes second nature. Questioning assumptions and using the LNC to detect error is essential to keeping a conversation moving toward the direction of truth.

At the end of the chapter on logic we pointed out that logic's primary function is to correct faulty thinking, or groundless reasoning, and is therefore a negative test for truth. We also said that we have designed this book in such

---

[13]C. S. Lewis, *The Problem of Pain* (New York: Macmillan, 1962), 28.

a way that its cumulative understanding and application of the foundational first principles of several fields of knowledge would help us to discover which worldview is most reasonable or true. As we have already shown, and as the worldview chart illustrates, they cannot all be true. Subsequently, it will be a matter of finding answers to questions that make sense within the parameters of that worldview and that seem to fit most consistently with what we know from our experiences in life as well. Since many people believe that only what is scientifically verifiable is true, let's begin with the discipline of science— the topic of our next chapter.

	Atheism	Pantheism	Theism
Truth	Relative, No Absolutes	Relative to This World	Absolute Truth Exists
Cosmos	Always Existed	Not Real– Illusion	Created Reality
God	Does Not Exist	Exists, Unknowable	Exists, Knowable
Law	Relative, Determined by Humanity	Relative to This World	Absolute, Objective, Discovered
Evil	Human Ignorance	Not Real– Illusion	Selfish Heart
Ethics	Created by Humanity, Situational	Relative, Transcends Good/Evil	Absolute, Objective, Prescriptive

—4—
QUESTIONS ABOUT SCIENCE

*The things best to know are first principles
and causes. For through them and from them
all other things may be known.*

—ARISTOTLE

IS SCIENCE A MATTER OF FAITH?[1]

Many people believe that only what is scientifically verifiable is true. Unfortunately, no scientific experiment can verify that assertion, for the claim is *philosophical* in nature, not scientific. Furthermore, science is based on logic, and no scientific experiment can verify logic. Logic, rather, is assumed to be a valid component of the scientific method. So before we use the scientific method, we need to understand the foundation upon which the discipline of science is built.

The word *science* literally means "knowledge"; it has its origin in the Latin term *scire* ("to know"). However, science assumes a certain interdependent order of knowledge, and ignoring or abusing this order can lead to highly questionable inferences and conclusions concerning reality. We must realize that *the*

[1]The response to this question was originally written in an article by Peter Bocchino titled "Keep the Faith." This article appeared in the 1996 spring communiqué called *Just Thinking*, distributed by Ravi Zacharias International Ministries.

discipline of science is based on certain first principles and assumptions established in philosophy. These assumptions are metaphysical[2] in nature and have priority over all scientific investigations. One philosopher of science summarizes:

> Philosophy undergirds science by providing its presuppositions. Science (at least as most scientists and philosophers understand it) assumes that the universe is intelligible and not capricious, that the mind and senses inform us about reality, that mathematics and language can be applied to the world, that knowledge is possible, that there is a uniformity in nature that justifies inductive inferences from the past to the future and from examined cases of, say, electrons, to unexamined cases, and so forth. . . . All of them are philosophical in nature.[3]

What is the logical justification for these metaphysical assumptions of science? Are our thoughts merely a product of the chemical reactions in our brains? If reason and logic *are* ultimately reducible to pure chemical reactions, how do we decide between good logic and bad logic? Which assumptions are reasonable and which are not? G. K. Chesterton noted that without some basis for reason, the reasoning process would be a pure act of faith:

> It is an act of faith to assert that our thoughts have any relation to reality at all. If you are merely a skeptic, you must sooner or later ask yourself the question, "Why should *anything* go right; even observation and deduction? Why should not good logic be as misleading as bad logic? They are both movements in the brain of a bewildered ape."[4]

We have already confirmed that first principles are self-evidently true; they are beyond all direct proof. First principles need no further justification; if they did, the justification process would need to go on without end. Consequently, we must get back to some starting point as the basis for reason itself. If not, we will end up trying to justify every justification or explain every explanation. C. S. Lewis provides us with a clear illustration of the absurdity of such a task:

> You cannot go on "explaining away" forever: you will find that you have explained explanation itself away. You cannot go on "seeing through" things forever. The whole point of seeing through something is to see something through it. It is good that the window should be transparent, because the street or garden beyond it is opaque. How if you saw through

---

[2]The term *metaphysical* comes from a Greek term meaning "beyond the physical." Metaphysics deals with what is real, what exists.
[3]J. P. Moreland, *Christianity and the Nature of Science* (Grand Rapids, Mich.: Baker, 1989), 45.
[4]G. K. Chesterton, *Orthodoxy* (New York: Doubleday, 1959), 33.

the garden too? It is no use trying to "see through" first principles. If you see through everything, then everything is transparent. But a transparent world is an invisible world. To "see through" all things is the same as not to see.[5]

Ultimately, the first principles of thought are rationally justifiable only if there is a Mind that provides the basis for their existence. As Lewis so aptly states,

> One man's reason has been led to see things by the aid of another man's reason, and is none the worse for that. It is thus still an open question whether each man's reason exists absolutely on its own or whether it is the result of some (rational) cause—in fact, of some other Reason. That other Reason might conceivably be found to depend on a third, and so on; it would not matter how far this process was carried provided you found Reason coming from Reason at each stage. It is only when you are asked to believe in Reason coming from non-reason that you must cry Halt, for, if you don't, all thought is discredited. It is therefore obvious that sooner or later you must admit a Reason which exists absolutely on its own.[6]

The very fact that logic can be valid or invalid presupposes a standard of logic that goes beyond human thought. Consequently, *in order for science to be sound, it must keep the faith it has in reason, and correct reasoning logically depends upon the existence of a thinking entity (God).* Therefore, this entity must necessarily be the *primary cause* or rational basis for all first principles, including scientific assumptions. Since scientific investigations are not isolated from philosophical assumptions, we need to examine assumptions to see if they are valid or invalid. The first principle of science is a philosophical assumption upon which the discipline of science rests: it is known as the *principle of causality.*

WHAT IS THE PRINCIPLE OF CAUSALITY?

The principle of causality states that *every event has an adequate cause.* This principle is firmly coupled to searching for explanations, and even the simple things we observe, like colors in a rainbow, must have a cause. So when asking for the explanation for a rainbow, we are actually looking for the cause of that rainbow.

---

[5]C. S. Lewis, *The Abolition of Man* (New York: Macmillan, 1947), 91.
[6]C. S. Lewis, *Miracles* (New York: Macmillan, 1947), 27–28.

In addition, when we are looking for the cause of an event, there are several kinds of causes that can be isolated. In this illustration we have noted two types of causes: a secondary (or instrumental) cause and a primary (efficient) cause. Sir Isaac Newton was the first person to use a prism to reveal that sunlight could be split up to yield a spectrum of colors. The spectrum of colors emanating from the prism is the effect we observe of light passing through it. The effect—the spectrum of colors—has a secondary (instrumental) cause, the prism. However, it also has a primary (first) cause, the sunlight. The color is inherent in the sunlight (primary cause), and the prism is the instrument (secondary cause) by which light is dispersed. Technically, however, the sun is caused and therefore

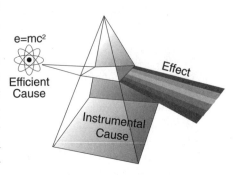

preceded by energy, so the ultimate question to be answered is, "Is the energy supply in the universe infinite and thus has it always existed, or is it finite and thus did it have a beginning?" In other words, "Is energy the first cause of the entire universe, or is there a cause prior to it?"

Before we use the principle of causality to answer this question, we need to verify its credibility, since it is the first principle of science. We must also remember that *the causality principle is philosophical in nature,* and as such it affirms that *a necessary and sufficient condition must exist for every effect.* Effects do not occur without causes; this is true of everything that is finite and comes into existence, including the universe. The father of modern science, Francis Bacon (1561–1626), said, "True knowledge is knowledge by causes."[7] If the universe is finite and had a beginning, then it would need to have a cause—*if* causality is a valid principle. A flaw in the causality principle would be equivalent to having a fatal crack in the foundation of science.

IS THE CAUSALITY PRINCIPLE RELIABLE?

David Hume (1711–1776) was a skeptic who believed that all knowledge comes through our five senses. Causal connection, according to Hume, is not one thing *caused* by another; it is one thing *followed* by another. He asserted that our belief about causality is based on experience, which is based on cus-

---

[7]Francis Bacon, *Novum Organum* (New York: Bobbs-Merrill, 1960 ed.), 121.

tom, which depends upon repeated conjunctions—not observed causal connections.[8]

We must note, however, that Hume did not actually deny the principle of causality itself. Rather, he challenged the basis some had for affirming this principle. He also stated the uncertainty of knowing which preceding causes are the causes of which effects. For example, we can experience that B follows A (A, B), but we can't experience A causing B (A→B). Hume believed that we can only know customary *conjunctions*, or relationships, rather than the actual causal *connections*.

Hume was not saying that there is no cause of an effect; he was saying that we cannot be certain as to which cause is causing which effect. We see routine relational events happen over and over again, but we do not observe what actually causes them. For example, the sun rises regularly *after* the rooster crows, but certainly not *because* the rooster crows. Consequently, Hume argued for the suspension of all judgments about real causal connections. Again, Hume did believe that there is a causal connection. He even went so far as to say it is "absurd" to deny the principle of causality: "I never asserted so absurd a proposition as that anything might arise without a cause."[9]

Our response to Hume and to others who hold this view is focused on the certainty of this kind of skepticism. Simply stated, are we being asked to be uncertain about all of reality? If so, then are we not being asked to suspend judgment about every view of reality, *except this view?* Maybe instead we should be skeptical about skepticism. Furthermore, isn't it a judgment about reality to say that all judgments about reality ought to be suspended? How did Hume reach his conclusions if he knew of no necessary causal connections and if all judgments were suspended? The truth is that *Hume assumed causality throughout his argument.* In fact, his very denial of causality implies a necessary causal connection in his thought process. Otherwise, how could he have known for sure that his conclusions were correct? Without assuming a necessary basis (cause), his denial is meaningless. He also implicitly postulated that his argument (the cause) can be used to convince those who believe in causal connections to become a skeptic like himself (effect), or why bother writing books? For these reasons, we can say that Hume's claims are self-defeating.

---

[8]David Hume, *An Enquiry Concerning Human Understanding*, Great Books in Philosophy (Buffalo, N.Y.: Prometheus, 1988), 43.
[9]David Hume, *The Letters of David Hume*, ed. J. Y. T. Grieg (Oxford: Clarendon, 1932), 1:187.

DOES QUANTUM PHYSICS DISPROVE CAUSALITY?

Some scientists argue that the principle of causality is not valid in light of modern quantum physics. They say that the principle of causality breaks down at the subatomic level of reality, and Heisenberg's *uncertainty principle* is referenced as the basis for their opinion.[10] Therefore, according to these scientists, if causality does not exist at the most fundamental level of reality (the subatomic level), it must be invalid at all other levels as well. In other words, if causality does not exist at the smallest level of reality, why should it exist at the largest level—the cause of the universe?

During a debate with a theist, Bertrand Russell (1872–1970) commented on the relationship between the uncertainty principle and applying causality to the origin of the universe. He said,

> I see no reason whatsoever to suppose that the total [universe] has any cause whatsoever. . . . The concept of cause is not applicable to the total [universe]. . . . I should say that the universe is just there, and that's all. . . . I don't want to seem arrogant, but it does seem to me that I can conceive things that you say the human mind can't conceive. As for things not having a cause, the physicists assure us that individual quantum transitions in atoms have no cause.[11]

In light of this, one would think at first glance that the principle of causality must be suspended. However, *the uncertainty principle does not dethrone the principle of causality;* if it did, it would be self-defeating. If the principle of causality was not valid, *all* scientific conclusions would be questionable, since causality is foundational to the discipline of science. As quantum physics is a part of science, it would also fall into that category, for how could it be that the only time science can be certain about its conclusions is during the experiments that confirm uncertainty? It seems to us that these scientists have misinterpreted and misapplied the uncertainty principle, which basically states that the position and momentum of a subatomic particle cannot be established simultaneously.[12]

In his book *Truth in Religion,* Mortimer J. Adler has a chapter titled

---

[10]The uncertainty principle, or indeterminacy principle, refers to a restriction on the accuracy of measuring subatomic particles. One cannot measure simultaneously and exactly both the position (location) and the momentum (speed) of an electron.

[11]John Hick, *The Existence of God* (New York: Macmillan, 1964), 175–76.

[12]The uncertainty principle is not to be understood as or confused with the *uncausality principle,* with respect to effects occurring without causes.

"Reality in Relation to Quantum Theory." The following paragraphs are relevant to our learning.

> It is logically necessary to bear in mind one point that the quantum physicists appear to forget or overlook. At the same time that the Heisenberg uncertainty principles were established, quantum physicists acknowledged that the intrusive experimental measurements that provided the data used in the mathematical formulations of quantum theory *conferred on subatomic objects and events their indeterminate character.* . . .
>
> God knows the answer, as Einstein at the beginning of his controversy with Bohr declared when he said that God does not throw dice, which implied that the *unexamined* subatomic reality is a determinate reality. . . . Whether or not God knows the answer, experimental science *does not know it.* Nor does philosophy know it with certitude. But philosophy can give a good reason for thinking that subatomic reality is intrinsically determinate. The reason is that quantum theorists repeatedly acknowledge that their intrusive and disturbing measurements are the *cause of the indeterminacy* they attribute to subatomic objects and events. It follows, therefore, that the indeterminacy cannot be intrinsic to subatomic reality. . . .
>
> Einstein was right that quantum theory is an incomplete account of subatomic reality. But he was wrong in thinking that the incompleteness could be remedied by means at the disposal of science. Why? Because the question that quantum theory and subatomic research cannot answer is a question for philosophy, not for science.[13]

Scientists would do well to remember that the uncertainty principle is based on the validity of the causality principle. It is self-defeating to believe that the causality principle is unreliable based on the uncertainty principle, because causality, as we have shown, is a necessary precondition for discovering the uncertainty principle. Consequently, *the principle of causality is philosophically sound and stands firm as the first principle of science.*

We can say with confidence, then, that causality is a valid principle to use both when we look at inner space (e.g., the operation of an atom) and when we look at outer space (e.g., the operation of the universe). Having proven its reliability, now we want to know if the causality principle is applicable to the probable existence of a First Cause that lies beyond the space-time universe. In other words, can causality answer the question concerning the reality of the existence of God?

---

[13]Mortimer J. Adler, *Truth in Religion: The Plurality of Religions and the Unity of Truth* (New York: Macmillan, 1990), 93–100, last emphasis added.

DOES CAUSALITY APPLY TO GOD?

In his argument concerning a First Cause, Bertrand Russell also posited that if Christians want to be so adamant about pressing the causality question in seeking a cause for everything, then the First Cause (God) must have also had a cause. He said his father taught him that the question "Who made me?" cannot be answered, since it is immediately followed by another question: "Who made God?" If everything must have a cause, then God must have a cause. If something can exist without a cause, it may just as well be the world as God.[14]

Russell's objection can be answered by noting that he incorrectly defined the causality principle and committed a logical fallacy called a *category mistake*. The causality principle does not say that *everything* needs a cause. Rather, that which is *finite and limited* needs a cause; that is, anything that had a beginning must have had a cause. Russell confused two distinct and separate categories.

For example, seeing and tasting represent two different categories. Color is sensed by sight and is irrelevant to the sense of taste; therefore, the question "How does the color green taste?" is meaningless. The same is true with the question "Who made God?" This confuses the finite category with the infinite category. Only finite things, or entities, need a cause; they have had a beginning and come into existence. An infinite being, such as God, does not have a beginning. An infinite being must have always existed and is, therefore, uncaused. If it turns out that the universe has always existed, then it would not need to have had a cause. However, if it can be shown that the universe is finite and had a beginning (the topic of the next chapter), then we can conclude that it must have had a cause.

IS GOD A SELF-CAUSED BEING?

Jean-Paul Sartre (1905–1980) argued that the principle of causality affirms that everything must have a cause either inside itself or outside itself. Therefore, we must assume that if we arrive at a cause beyond this world (viz., God), this cause must have a cause for its existence within itself. That is, God must be a self-caused being. But a self-caused being is impossible since to cause oneself to exist, one would have to exist prior to one's own existence.

Sartre makes the same error as Russell by incorrectly defining the principle of causality. As noted above, the principle of causality does not affirm that

---

[14]Bertrand Russell, *"Why I Am Not a Christian" and Other Essays on Religion and Related Subjects*, ed. Paul Edwards (New York: Simon and Schuster, 1957), 3–4.

everything needs a cause but rather that finite things do. Yet Sartre is right in stating that a self-caused being is impossible. What, then, is God? If God is not caused and He is not self-caused, what is He? The only logical alternative is the one to which most theists adhere: God is an *uncaused* Being. An uncaused Being has always existed and does not need a cause. God is the First Cause of every finite thing that comes into existence, and there is nothing prior to God as the Cause of all finite things because God has always existed. Consequently, Sartre's conclusion, that causality must lead to an impossible self-caused Being, does not follow.

Understood properly, the principle of causality leads us back to something that must be the First Cause, the uncaused Cause of every finite thing that exists. We are claiming that God has always existed as the First Cause of the universe, while, on the other hand, atheists and naturalists insist that the universe has always existed. Before we can decide which worldview is correct, we must determine whether or not the scientific method can be utilized to discover the cause of past events, such as the origin of the universe. All scientists may not agree on every aspect of how to employ the scientific method with respect to past events, but they must agree on the first principles that are necessary for proper inferences to be made about past events. Thus far, we have seen that the principle of causality is a fundamental statute that must be accepted by anyone who engages in the discipline of science. With this in mind, let's take a closer look at the scientific method.

CAN SCIENCE DETERMINE PAST CAUSES?

Science provides us with knowledge in the sense that it deals with the present observation and operation of the physical world and repeatable events. If an event can be repeated and observations made, then the principles of philosophy and the laws of science can be used to discover what causes effects. This search for the causes of observable effects is *operation science*. It is the kind of science that concerns itself with the causes (actions) and effects (reactions) of the present workings of the physical world. For that reason, operation science is limited to discovering secondary or natural causes for a regular pattern of events. When it comes to dealing with past events that are no longer happening in the present, another kind of science must be applied. This kind of scientific method can be referred to as *origin science*.

Origin science is comparable to *forensic science*, which superintends the kinds of investigations of events that were not observed and are not repeatable. This kind of event is called a *singularity*. All that is needed for one to posit an intelligent cause for some past singularity is to show that similar events in the present can be constantly connected to an intelligent cause. Homicide detectives use this method to investigate murders and answer questions such as: What was the cause of death? Was it an accident, or was it a planned event? Did it happen by chance, or was it the result of an intelligent agent? As long as the basis for a forensic reconstruction of the past event is some regularly observed causal connection—observed in the present—the object of this speculation can be an unrepeated singularity. In the chapters that follow, we will apply this scientific practice to such singularities as the origin of the universe and the origin of life.

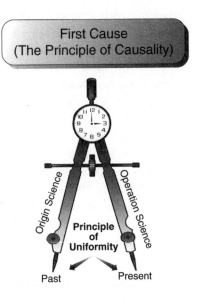

For now, it is essential to understand that operation and origin science are connected by a philosophical principle called *uniformity* (or *analogy*). This is another philosophical assumption by which science links the present to the past and makes predictions about the future. With respect to origin science, *the uniformity principle states that the present is the key to understanding the past.* If present observations indicate that it always takes a certain kind of cause to produce a certain kind of effect, the principle of uniformity tells us that a similar kind of event in the past must have had a similar kind of cause as observed in the present. If scientists are not clear on differentiating between operation and origin science and do not employ the principle of uniformity, their results will most assuredly be misleading. Therefore, we are obligated not to violate the principles of causality and uniformity as we use the scientific method to answer origin questions. Yet how far back can science go? Can it be used legitimately to determine whether or not God created the space-time universe?

CAN ORIGIN SCIENCE AFFIRM THE EXISTENCE OF GOD?

The ultimate origin question that challenges both philosophy and science is what Peter Kreeft refers to as that "haunting question," penned by the philosopher Martin Heidegger: "Why is there anything rather than nothing at all?"[15] In other words, why do we exist? Did God create this universe, or has it always existed? We believe that the first principles of philosophy and science, applied properly to these questions, can provide us with trustworthy answers. However, many modern scientists believe that science can neither affirm nor deny the existence of God. For example, Stephen Jay Gould, Harvard professor and paleontologist, has said,

> Science simply cannot (by its legitimate methods) adjudicate the issue of God's possible superintendence of nature. *We neither affirm it nor deny it; we simply cannot comment on it as scientists.* . . . Science can work only with naturalistic explanations; it can neither affirm nor deny other types of actors (like God).[16]

Yet if Gould speaks the truth, why does he (along with so many of his scientific colleagues) continue to write and speak so prolifically on this topic? If silence rules, why do we continue to hear so much opposition from them on this issue? With all due respect to Professor Gould, he is guilty of breaking his own rules because he has made many comments about "the issue of God's possible superintendence of nature." After critiquing William Paley's design argument for the existence of God, Gould said,

> Good design exists, and implies production for its current purpose; but adaptations are built naturally, by slow evolution towards desired ends, *not by immediate, divine fiat.*[17]

How can Gould as a scientist know this to be true if science cannot make such pronouncements? Many scientists, including Gould, not only "adjudicate the issue of God's possible superintendence of nature" but also write as if they have a passion to use science to come to terms with this question about God's existence. In the introduction to Stephen Hawking's book *A Brief History of Time,* Carl Sagan said,

> This is also a book about God . . . or perhaps the absence of God. The word God fills these pages. Hawking embarks on a quest to answer Einstein's famous question about whether God had any choice in creating the

---

[15]Peter Kreeft, *Three Philosophies of Life* (San Francisco: Ignatius, 1989), 9.
[16]Stephen Jay Gould, "Impeaching a Self-Appointed Judge," *Scientific American,* July, 1992, 120 (emphasis added).
[17]Stephen Jay Gould, *Eight Little Piggies: Reflections in Natural History* (New York: W. W. Norton & Co., 1993), 144.

universe. Hawking is attempting, as he explicitly states, to understand the mind of God.[18]

Another great scientist, Albert Einstein, also spoke of God's creation of nature. He said,

> I want to know how God created this world. I am not interested in this or that phenomenon, in the spectrum of this or that element. I want to know his thoughts, the rest are details. . . . God does not play dice with the world.[19]

Our only point in mentioning these two eminent scientific minds of the twentieth century is to refute Gould's dogmatic statement that science can neither affirm nor deny the existence of God; we are not saying that Hawking and Einstein are referring to the God of the Bible. Yet there is a long history of great scientists who founded various scientific fields of knowledge while invoking a First Cause as the Designer of the universe and Author of the laws of nature. These scientists are listed below along with the scientific field they instituted:[20]

- Johannes Kepler (1571–1630)—Celestial mechanics, physical astronomy
- Blaise Pascal (1623–1662)—Hydrostatics
- Robert Boyle (1627–1691)—Chemistry, gas dynamics
- Nicolaus Steno (1638–1687)—Stratigraphy
- Isaac Newton (1642–1727)—Calculus, dynamics
- Michael Faraday (1791–1867)—Magnetic theory
- Charles Babbage (1792–1871)—Computer science
- Louis Agassiz (1807–1873)—Glacial geology, ichthyology
- James Young Simpson (1811–1870)—Gynecology
- Gregor Mendel (1822–1884)—Genetics
- Louis Pasteur (1822–1895)—Bacteriology
- William Thomson (Lord Kelvin) (1824–1907)—Energetics, thermodynamics
- Joseph Lister (1827–1912)—Antiseptic surgery
- James Clerk Maxwell (1831–1879)—Electrodynamics, statistical thermodynamics
- William Ramsay (1852–1916)—Isotopic chemistry

[18]Stephen W. Hawking, *A Brief History of Time* (New York: Bantam, 1988), x.
[19]Ronald W. Clark, *Einstein: The Life and Times* (New York: Avon, 1972), 37–38.
[20]Norman Geisler and J. Kerby Anderson, *Origin Science* (Grand Rapids, Mich.: Baker, 1987), 39–40.

Stephen Jay Gould claims that science is metaphysically neutral, yet one cannot separate science from metaphysics. We have already explained how science is based on metaphysical first principles that are not ultimately and rationally justifiable without granting the existence of God. In fact, naturalists must admit that some kind of reason is prior to nature in the sense that *we use reason to shape our concept of nature.* C. S. Lewis explains:

> Reason is given before Nature and on reason our concept of nature depends. Our acts of inference are prior to our picture of Nature almost as the telephone is prior to the friend's voice we hear by it. When we try to fit these acts into the picture of Nature we fail. The item we put into that picture and label "Reason" always turns out to be somehow different from the reason we ourselves are enjoying and exercising while we put it in. The description we have to give of thought as an evolutionary phenomenon always makes a tacit exception in favor of the thinking which we ourselves perform at that moment.[21]

Lewis put his finger on something that naturalists are hard pressed to explain—human rationality. It seems to be independent of nature in the sense that the picture of nature depends upon it. In other words, we reason about nature in a way that is independent of nature. It is akin to putting together the pieces of a puzzle called "nature"—and the one piece that cannot be put into the puzzle is human rationality, because it is being used to put the puzzle together!

Therefore, naturalists are forced to define human thoughts as products (or by-products) of mere secretions of the brain and accordingly, then, reduce thoughts to pure *nonrational* chemical reactions. Yet how can *rational* thoughts, inferences, insights, and knowledge be the pure result of chemistry? Could it be that the act of reasoning depends upon something more than mere brain chemistry? Could it be that mental occurrences, such as rational thoughts, are not purely the result of a physical phenomenon? Could it be that human reason, in particular the laws of logic, is anchored outside of nature in divine reason, and that what we observe in nature is the result of a greater rationality than human rationality? We agree with C. S. Lewis when he said,

> Acts of reasoning are not interlocked with the total interlocking system of Nature as all its other items are interlocked with one another. They are connected with it in a different way; as the understanding of a machine is certainly connected with the machine but not in the way the parts of the

---

[21]C. S. Lewis, *Miracles* (New York: Macmillan, 1947), 23.

machine are connected with each other. The knowledge of a thing is not one of the thing's parts. In this sense something beyond Nature operates whenever we reason. I am not maintaining that consciousness as a whole must necessarily be put in the same position. Pleasures, pains, fears, hopes, affections and mental images need not. No absurdity would follow from regarding them as parts of Nature. The distinction we have to make is . . . between Reason and Nature: the frontier coming not where the "outer-world" ends and what I should ordinarily call "myself" begins, but between reason and the whole mass of non-rational events whether physical or psychological. . . .

Rational thought is not part of the system of Nature. Within each [person] there must be an area (however small) of activity which is outside or independent of her. In relation to nature, rational thought goes on "of its own accord" or exists "on its own." It does not follow that rational thought exists *absolutely* on its own. It might be independent of Nature by being dependent on something else. For it is not dependence simply but dependence on the non-rational which undermines the credentials of thought.[22]

We conclude that it only makes sense to say that the justification of human reason must be based on a rational Being outside of nature. We plan to show how science, in particular the fields of cosmology and molecular biology, point directly to an infinitely powerful and intelligent First Cause of nature (the universe as a whole). Now, some would argue that once God is invoked into the scientific method, the result is devastating and undermines all scientific investigations. This is not the case, as we will explain.

DOES APPEALING TO A CREATOR NULLIFY THE SCIENTIFIC METHOD?

The principles and laws we utilize in the scientific method are the *secondary* causes that explain much of what we observe in the daily operation of the universe. The idea that invoking a Creator into the scientific method will nullify it has been shown to be false both in practice and in history. We have already listed the founding fathers of the various disciplines of science whose belief in a Creator actually motivated them to probe more deeply and pursue the study of the natural world as the logical outworking of its Designer. For example, Francis Bacon was inspired by the theistic doctrine of creation. He concentrated on the secondary scientific causes (natural laws) used by God to

[22]C. S. Lewis, *Miracles* (New York: Macmillan, 1947), 25, 27.

operate the universe. Bacon replaced the deductive method of Aristotle with a more inductive and experimental method that established a fresh new direction for modern science. Belief in a Creator who works through secondary causes did not harm science. In point of fact, this belief helped to inspire great thinkers and to advance science significantly.

The question we are seeking to answer is related to finding the primary cause of natural laws. For example, the cause of falling rocks can be explained simply as the result of the universal law of gravity, a natural cause, pulling them toward the center of the earth. Gravity is a part of physical reality and is one of the fundamental laws of physics. However, gravity is the result of the force of attraction between any two objects in the universe that have mass or substance. Moreover, mass can be thought of as the measure of the amount of matter in a body. Yet matter is a material substance, which has extension in space and time, and may also be considered a specialized form of energy ($E=mc^2$). Think about these causal connections:

1. The cause of falling rocks is gravity.
2. Gravity is a force of attraction caused by mass.
3. Mass is a measure of matter and mathematically equivalent to energy, which is caused by. . . ?

Well, what is the cause of the energy in the cosmos? Does it need a cause? If energy is matter, and the universe is made up of matter, is it infinite? Is there a limit to the universe? Is Carl Sagan's view—that "the Cosmos is all that is or ever was or ever will be"[23]—true? Is the cosmos the cause of all other things, including human life and rationality? Can the cosmos, as a whole, be explained by purely natural causes? We will address these questions in chapter 5.

---

[23]Carl Sagan, *Cosmos* (New York: Random, 1980), 4.

5
QUESTIONS ABOUT THE COSMOS

IF the existence of the cosmos as a whole needs to be explained, and IF it cannot be explained by natural causes, THEN we must look to the existence and action of a supernatural cause for its explanation.

—MORTIMER J. ADLER

DOES THE COSMOS NEED A CAUSE?

Two men were walking through the forest and happened across a glass sphere lying on the carpet of green moss. There were hardly any sounds other than the pair's own footsteps and certainly no signs of other people. But both of them saw that the very obvious inference from the evidence of the sphere was that someone had put it there. Now, one of these men was a skeptical scientist, trained in the modern view of origins, and the other a layman.

The layman said, "What if the sphere were larger, maybe ten feet around—would you still say that someone put it there?" Naturally, the scientist agreed that a larger sphere would not affect his judgment.

"Well, what if the sphere were huge—a mile in diameter?" probed the layman. His friend responded that not only would someone have put it there, but there also should be an investigation to find out what caused that someone to do it.

The layman then ventured one more question: "What if the sphere were as big as the whole universe? Would it still need a cause?"

"Of course not," snapped the skeptic. "The universe is just there."[1]

Is it credible to believe, as Bertrand Russell said, that "the universe is just there" and does not need a cause? If little spheres need causes and bigger spheres need causes, doesn't the biggest sphere need a cause too? This is the question we are seeking to answer. For now, take a look at how a very observant and logical detective goes about an investigation.

Through the pen of Arthur Conan Doyle, Sherlock Holmes has fascinated minds around the world with his use of seemingly simple logic as he is able to examine the evidence, unravel the mystery, and solve the case. Probing a little deeper into Holmes's methodology will reveal how he is able to connect clues with first principles and causes. In one episode involving a murder, the police had looked everywhere for clues, but there were no fingerprints to be found and no other evidence to indicate the presence of a murderer. Yet Holmes believed from experience that a natural phenomenon could not be the cause of death and was determined to scour that room until some piece of evidence had been found.

Following a diligent search, Holmes happened upon what he was looking for. It was so obvious that the officers had overlooked it: a small yet significant bloodstain on the wall. To everyone else who had searched the room, it was just another bloodstain, but not to Holmes. Holmes found a vital clue in the bloodstain: a fingerprint belonging to the murderer.

What caused the universe? Was it caused by some natural phenomenon? Is it self-caused? Has it always existed (uncaused)? Or did something or someone else cause the universe? *If the universe had a beginning, then it needs a first cause.* To appeal to natural causes—the laws of nature, as the justification for the origin of the cosmos—seems just as absurd as someone concluding that the glass sphere discovered in the forest was a result of some natural phenomenon. We can likewise rule out a self-caused universe as impossible; to be self-caused it would have had to have existed (in order to be the cause) and have not existed (in order to be caused) at the same time.

The next question is "Has the universe always existed?" Either the cosmos had a beginning, or Carl Sagan was right ("The Cosmos is all that is or ever was or ever will be"). Naturalistic cosmologists tell us that either the cosmos

---

[1]Adapted from N. L. Geisler and R. M. Brooks, *When Skeptics Ask: A Handbook on Christian Evidences* (Grand Rapids, Mich.: Baker, 1990), 211.

came *from* nothing *by* nothing, or it has always existed. But it is impossible for nothing to produce something. Therefore, the only plausible naturalistic alternative for these cosmologists to pursue is the belief that the universe must have always existed.

We believe that the scientific evidence substantiates the claim that the universe had a beginning. And again, if it did have a beginning, then it must have had a cause. We plan to argue for a proper understanding and application of origin science that will show that a Cause of the cosmos lies outside the realm of natural phenomena. As C. S. Lewis so aptly stated,

> On any view, the first beginning must have been outside the ordinary processes of nature. An egg which came from no bird is no more natural than a bird which had existed from all eternity. And since the egg-bird-egg sequence leads us to no plausible beginning, is it not reasonable to look for the real origin somewhere outside the sequence altogether? You have to go outside the sequence of engines, into the world of men, to find the real originator of the Rocket. Is it not equally reasonable to look outside Nature for the real Originator of the natural order?[2]

Was there a beginning to the universe? Are the laws we discover in nature, which give order and structure to the universe, grounded in the mind of a Designer, or do they exist on their own? There are only two alternatives to investigate: Either the universe had no beginning and is therefore uncaused, or the universe had a beginning and consequently needs a cause. The principle of causality states that everything that has a beginning must have a cause. If we can confirm that the universe had a beginning, then we must look outside of nature for the kind of cause it would take to bring it into existence. Where do we begin? A good place to start would be to differentiate between two fields of science. One field deals with what the cosmos is like, and the other field focuses on its origin.

WHAT'S THE DIFFERENCE BETWEEN COSMOLOGY AND COSMOGONY?

Cosmology (the theory of the cosmos) is the branch of astronomy that deals with the nature and structure of the universe as a whole. It is the *operation science* component of astronomy. As such, it concerns itself with the causes and effects of the present workings of the physical universe. Conversely, when we

---

[2]C. S. Lewis, *God in the Dock* (Grand Rapids, Mich.: Eerdmans, 1970), 211.

try to explain the origin of the universe, we enter another scientific discipline known as *cosmogony.* Cosmogony (the origin of the cosmos), the *origin science* component of astronomy, is concerned with formulating theories that give an account of the origin of the universe as a whole. It is vitally important for us to keep in mind that any valid model of the origin of the universe is to be based on the principle of uniformity: the present is the key to the past.

For example, imagine that we are standing on the branch of a tree, holding a saw, and we decide to use the saw to cut off the branch on which we are standing. It would be foolish: the branch and saw, along with us, would go crashing to the ground. Well, if the tree represented the field of astronomy, the branch represented the field of cosmology, and the saw represented the field of cosmogony, the same results would take place. That is, if we were to develop a theory about the origin of the cosmos (cosmogony) that did not conform to the laws and principles of science and the supporting observational evidence of the universe (cosmology), our theory would eventually self-destruct. The principle of uniformity (discussed in chapter 4) stipulates that the laws and principles of operation science are not to be violated as we investigate origins. Therefore, sound conclusions, based upon the laws and principles of science and observational evidences, must serve as the foundation for any valid theory of origins.[3]

After we establish a reliable cosmological framework and link the present to the past with the principle of uniformity, we should be able to test various origin models to see which one is philosophically sound and scientifically reliable. This test should utilize what we know from the principles and laws of science and the observational evidence from cosmology. We have already identified the principle of causality as the philosophical first principle of science; the task before us is to name its empirical (observable) counterpart. In other words, we need to identify the foremost empirical law of science and combine it with the principle of causality and other evidences from cosmology.

WHAT IS THE FOREMOST LAW OF SCIENCE?

Everyone—and everything—is growing older and becoming more and more deteriorated; we see this to be a universal truth. Consequently, people die, cars corrode, buildings fall, landscapes erode, and our natural resources gradually deplete. No matter how hard we try, we will never be able to reverse this process and get things back to their original highly ordered and uncor-

---

[3]This is true of the origin of the universe, the origin of the first life form, and the origin of new life forms.

rupted state. Things and systems are constantly breaking down and moving in the direction of higher states of disorder. We can keep fixing the car, painting the house, and repaving the driveway, and yet some counterforce seems to be at work—persistently undoing what we do. This bent toward deterioration is the result of the universal law of physics known as *the second law of thermodynamics.*[4]

Thermodynamics is the scientific discipline that studies heat (*thermo*) and its ability to do mechanical work (*dynamics*). The effects of the second law of thermodynamics are directly observable from an overwhelming body of scientific evidence. This law's greatest power is its universal predictive quality that, on the whole, the rise of disorder (along with the decrease in useable energy) will eventually prevail. This means that as time ticks away, the universe will eventually run out of usable energy and reach a state of ultimate disorder. When we look at the nature and structure of the universe with respect to cosmology, this one scientific law stands above the rest. Therefore, we must use this law as our empirical counterpart to the first principle of causality and understand its implications with respect to cosmology and the origin of the cosmos (cosmogony).

Imagine finding a sealed container with rows of marbles compiled in an orderly manner. If we take the container and shake it over a period of time, it will resemble the container portrayed on the right. If it represents a closed, isolated system (a system that has no interference from the outside), no matter how long we shake the container, according to the second law of thermodynamics, the marbles will never be able to return to their original highly ordered state. Their final state will be one of disarray.

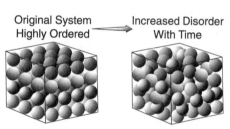

Original System Highly Ordered ⟶ Increased Disorder With Time

The simple reason we know this final state of disorder will occur is because of the universal power and predictive quality of this law. By definition, the second law only occurs in systems that are closed and isolated, and all closed and isolated systems will eventually end up in a state of disorder. The technical term that scientists use to measure the level of disorder of a system is called *entropy.* The original container on the left is in a low state of entropy (disorder)

---

[4] The first law of thermodynamics (the law of the conservation of energy) states that the *actual* amount of energy in the physical universe remains constant, while the second law states that the *usable* amount of that fixed energy is constantly decreasing.

because it is a highly ordered system. Conversely, after some period of time has elapsed, the condition of the container on the right reaches a state of high entropy because its level of disorder has significantly increased. The discovery of the second law as the foremost law at work in the universe meant that scientists had to treat the universe as a closed, isolated system. That the second law of thermodynamics will eventually permeate and dominate the entire cosmos raises the following question.

IS THE COSMOS RUNNING OUT OF USABLE ENERGY?[5]

Before we jump into a system as big as the universe, let's examine how the second law affects a familiar mechanical system, like a car. If we build an engine, we'll design it in such a way as to keep the level of disorder (in the form of wasted energy) to a minimum. As the car engine burns gasoline, the heat generated by that

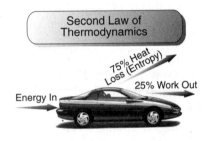

combustion process is converted into mechanical energy—which turns the wheels of the car. Ideally all of the fuel we put into the engine would be directly converted into mechanical energy to move the car. If 100% of the energy *could* be directly converted to power the car, we would have built a highly ordered system with no amount of disorder (entropy) in the form of wasted fuel.

To keep the accounting straight, we must bear in mind that the total amount of energy that goes into this car must equal the total amount of energy that comes out of it—into whatever form it happens to be converted. This law is known as the *first law of thermodynamics* and assures the conservation of energy. Unfortunately, the second law of thermodynamics will not allow us to build a car that is 100% efficient (no wasted energy). In reality, a heat engine is only 25% efficient; eventually, only 25% of the gasoline we put into the tank of a car gets converted into mechanical energy that propels the car. Where does the other 75% of the energy go? It obeys the second law and is radiated from the car in the form of wasted heat energy—unburned gasoline particles that exit through the exhaust pipe, friction of mechanical parts and the tires on the

[5]The response to this question was originally written in an article by Peter Bocchino titled "In the Beginning?" This article appeared in the 1996 fall communiqué called *Just Thinking*, distributed by Ravi Zacharias International Ministries.

road, and other heat losses. Therefore, the typical car engine operates at a fairly high level of disorder or wasted energy (entropy), and as time goes by the car will eventually run out of fuel.

Cars run out of gas all the time—we expect them to do so. This fact is not a devastating one because the car is an open system, and we can refuel it at a filling station. However, the same is not true of the universe as a whole. As the universe runs out of usable energy, there is no evidence to support the idea that a cosmic filling station exists. Cosmologists treat the universe as a gigantic heat engine with no external source of energy input. This means that the total amount of usable energy in the universe is fixed and is decreasing as time passes (nuclear fusion is occurring throughout the universe).

We can think of the universe as a large hourglass that is running out of usable energy. As depicted in this illustration, the bottom portion of the hourglass contains *unusable* energy. This means that at some very early point in time, the universe must have been in a highly ordered state, which fits nicely with what we know about the universe and the second law of thermodynamics. According to the second law, the universe is expected to run out of usable energy, resembling the marbles (from an earlier illustration) that eventually get vibrated into a high state of disorder. Consequently, as the "grains" of usable energy are used up and fall into an unusable state, disorder is on the rise and the usable energy is decreasing.

Second Law—A Closed System

Unusable Energy

When we consider the consequences of a universe that obeys the second law, there is only one logical conclusion: the universe will eventually run out of usable energy. Since there is no place for the universe to obtain more fuel, *we live in a finite universe.* Cosmologists recognize that someday there will be no more usable energy available for the universe to operate. Left to itself, the temperature of the entire universe will eventually plunge to a freezing –460°F (–273°C), a temperature referred to as *absolute zero.* In other words, the universe is running out of time, and at some point in the future our cosmic heat engine will come to a grinding and frigid halt.

CAN SCIENTISTS EVADE THE SECOND LAW OF THERMODYNAMICS?

We have established that cosmology is the operation science component of astronomy, and the second law of thermodynamics is the foremost law that cosmologists use to describe the nature of the cosmos. The implication is that theorists may choose to overlook some scientific law or principle when developing a theory of origins, but a *valid* origin model cannot escape the death grip of the second law. If scientists disregard the second law, in order to be logically consistent they must ignore the other laws of operation science as well. No matter how complex or exotic an origin model may be, if it violates the second law it must be ruled out as a credible "scientific" origin model.

Paul Davies, professor of mathematical physics at the University of Adelaide in Australia, says that whereas some scientists try to escape the second law, most scientists have only confirmed the absolutely fundamental nature of it. In essence Davies says that every honest and serious cosmologist must deal with the second law and factor it into their theory of origins. He quotes Sir Arthur Eddington, contemporary of Einstein and one-time professor of astronomy at the University of Cambridge, on the hopelessness of avoiding the relentless rise of disorder:

> The law that entropy always increases—the Second Law of Thermodynamics—holds, I think, the supreme position among the laws of Nature. If someone points out to you that your pet theory of the universe is in disagreement with Maxwell's equations—then so much for Maxwell's equations. If it is found to be contradicted by observation—well, these experiments do bungle things sometimes. But if your theory is found to be against the Second Law of Thermodynamics I can give you no hope; there is nothing for it but to collapse in deepest humiliation.[6]

Roy Peacock, visiting professor of aerospace sciences at the University of Pisa and an authority on thermodynamics, has penned a response to Stephen Hawking's book *A Brief History of Time*. Professor Peacock's book, *A Brief History of Eternity*, was written with the intent of demonstrating how astronomical discoveries, coupled with the laws of thermodynamics, logically lead to the conclusion that the universe is finite. He explains:

> The Second Law of thermodynamics is probably the most powerful piece of legislation in the physical world. It ultimately describes every proc-

---

[6]Paul Davies, *The Cosmic Blueprint* (New York: Simon and Schuster, 1988), 20.

ess we have ever discovered: it is the final Court of Appeal in any dispute relating to actions and procedures, whether they are naturally generated or man inspired. It draws the conclusion that in our universe there is an over-all reduction in order, a loss of available energy that is measured as an increase in entropy. So the available stock of order is being exhausted. Akin to the dying battery of a flashlight, useful energy is being dissipated into entropy after which none remains for use. . . . For us to live in a universe in which the Second Law of thermodynamics holds, then, it must be a universe that has a starting point, a creation.[7]

The second law of thermodynamics is the "final Court of Appeal." If astro-nomical discoveries can also be introduced into the courtroom as supplemen-tary evidence of a created cosmos, then it is only logical to conclude beyond a reasonable doubt that the universe is finite and needs a cause. In addition to the second law of thermodynamics, there are many empirical evidences to sup-port the finite nature of the cosmos. The two most staggering pieces of data are presented below (Exhibits A and B).

WHAT EVIDENCE SUPPORTS BELIEF IN A FINITE UNIVERSE?

EXHIBIT A—THE RADIATION ECHO

Arno Penzias and Robert Wilson, two physicists at the Bell Telephone Lab-oratories, discovered that the earth is bathed in a faint glow of radiation. For this they were awarded the Nobel Prize in 1978.[8] The measurements taken by Penzias and Wilson demonstrated that the earth could not possibly be the source of this radiation glow. Their data indicated that they had found radia-tion left over from the initial explosion of the beginning of the universe, com-monly referred to as the *Big Bang*.

To help us visualize the radiation glow of a past event, think of what we see when we turn off a television set in a dark room. The television continues to glow (radiate) even after the source of power (electrons) has been cut off. The glow on the television tube is the *radiation echo* that was caused by elec-tron beams bombarding the screen while the power was on.

Although Penzias and Wilson won the Nobel Prize, there were skeptics who resisted the idea of a beginning and wanted to discredit what they found, call-ing into question the accuracy of the data. However, within a few years cynics

---

[7]Roy Peacock, *A Brief History of Eternity* (Wheaton, Ill.: Crossway, 1990), 106.
[8]Stephen W. Hawking, *A Brief History of Time* (New York: Bantam, 1988), 42.

were silenced by another discovery that was celebrated as one of the most, if not the most, significant in the history of cosmology.

On November 18, 1989, a satellite named COBE ("cosmic background explorer") was successfully launched into space with instruments aboard capable of measuring the radiation echo left behind from the Big Bang—if indeed it had actually happened. COBE was designed to measure the intensity of the radiation and its overall shape in order to determine what produced it. Soon after the launch mission control, located at NASA's Goddard Institute for Space Studies, began receiving data from COBE that would be analyzed over the next few years. In April of 1992, the final summation of COBE's data was made public and hailed as unprecedented—even referred to as the Holy Grail of cosmology. George Smoot, University of California astrophysicist, said, "If you're religious, it's like looking at God."[9] The COBE mission successfully mapped out a picture of the cosmic background radiation caused by the initial explosion of the universe. Stephen Hawking called this discovery "the most important discovery of the century, if not all time."[10] *The most convincing aspect of this background radiation is the fact that it had the exact pattern and wavelength for the light and heat of an explosion calculated to be of the magnitude of the Big Bang.* Hence, we submit this observational evidence as Exhibit A in support of a theory of origin that affirms that the universe had a beginning.

EXHIBIT B—THE EXPANDING UNIVERSE

If we were standing in an elevator moving upward, we would experience a sense of getting heavier. The increase of speed (acceleration) would produce an effect that would push us toward the floor, indicating that there is a force being exerted upon us analogous to that of gravity. Now imagine that the elevator was somewhere out in space accelerating at the same rate as that of the force of gravity on earth. If the elevator had no transparent panels and an oxygen supply, we would not be able to tell if we were standing in an elevator on earth or in one somewhere out in space. Furthermore, if the elevator were a spaceship traveling at an acceleration that exerted the same magnitude of force as the force of gravity on earth, there would be no way for us to tell the difference between being in space and being on earth.

This idea, that acceleration and gravity are somehow equivalent at a deeper level, is the principal assertion of Albert Einstein's *general theory of relativity.*

---

[9]Michael D. Lemonick, "Echoes of the Big Bang," *Time*, May 4, 1992, 62.
[10]Quoted by George Smoot and Keay Davidson, *Wrinkles in Time* (New York: Avon, 1993), 283. The original quote can be found in the *London Times*, April 25, 1992, 1.

Interesting, yes—but what do gravity and acceleration have to do with cosmology and the origin of the universe?

In probing the origin and nature of gravity and linking it to an accelerating universe, the general theory of relativity predicted that the universe had a beginning and is expanding in all directions. Hence, if Einstein's theory proved to be valid, then the universe was (and is) actually expanding. Reversing that expansion and going back in time means that the universe would get smaller and denser until it vanished into nothing. This is what disturbed Einstein; his own theory demanded a beginning (or initial starting point) for the universe.

In 1917, Einstein published his theory in a paper called "Cosmological Considerations on the General Theory of Relativity." However, in realizing the solution for his equations Einstein decided to introduce a simple mathematical device called *the cosmological constant* into his theory. He did so because the solution required a finite, expanding universe, which was offensive to him. This constant represented a counterforce that kept the universe from blowing up— keeping it stable and unchangeable in time. Unfortunately, the introduction of the cosmological constant into his equations turned out to be one of Einstein's biggest blunders, documented in a book by one of America's top astronomers, Robert Jastrow.

Robert Jastrow founded NASA's Goddard Institute for Space Studies and served for twenty years as its director; he is also a recipient of NASA's Medal for Excellence in Scientific Achievement. In *God and the Astronomers*, Jastrow summarized the reactions of scientists concerning a finite, expanding universe. He relayed the findings of a Russian mathematician, Alexander Friedman, who discovered that the renowned Albert Einstein had made a grave error in his calculations: at one point, Einstein had actually divided by zero! Jastrow also mentions the response of a Dutch astronomer, Willem de Sitter, who quickly recognized that the solution to Einstein's equations predicted an expanding universe. Jastrow continues by noting Einstein's reaction:

> Around this time, signs of irritation began to appear among the scientists. Einstein was the first to complain. He was disturbed by the idea of a Universe that blows up, because it implied that the world had a beginning. In a letter to de Sitter—discovered in a box of old records in Leiden some years ago—Einstein wrote, "This circumstance [of an expanding Universe] irritates me," and in another letter about the expanding Universe, he said: "To admit such possibilities seems senseless." This is curiously emotional language for a discussion of some mathematical formulas. I suppose that

the idea of a beginning in time annoyed Einstein because of its theological implications.[11]

According to Einstein's theory of general relativity, the universe is finite and expanding in all directions. Beginning in 1919 and through the rest of this century, general relativity has been empirically verified by numerous experiments in operation science. The first observational proof of general relativity concerned itself with the prediction that a beam of light would bend under the influence of a large mass similar to that of the sun.

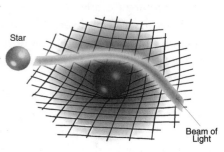

According to general relativity, a beam of light has weight and is attracted toward a large mass in the same way that an object is pulled toward the earth. In 1919, during a total eclipse of the sun, the effect of the sun's mass on a group of bright stars was measured before and after the sun was in the vicinity of the stars. When the true and apparent positions of the stars were compared, the results were found to be exactly what the theory predicted. This verification gave Einstein international recognition.

Another observation, which turned out to be the most convincing proof of general relativity, involved the measurements of the precise shape of planetary orbits. General relativity predicted that a massive object (a planet or the sun) would literally warp the space around it. Consequently, the warped fabric of space would create a depression or gravity well, which in turn would have an affect on

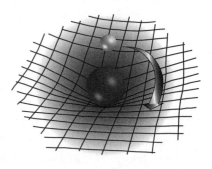

the orbital paths of planets. For example, if we dropped a heavy object, such as a cannon ball, onto a piece of stretched elastic as depicted in this illustration, it would create a very deep cavity. The maximum curvature, or warping of the elastic, takes place nearest to the surface of the cannon ball. If we rolled a marble (a lighter object) in the direction of the cannon ball, the warped elastic fabric would pull the marble closer to the surface of the cannon ball. Although this drawing is depicted in two dimensions, it is analogous to the warping of

[11]Robert Jastrow, *God and the Astronomers* (New York: W. W. Norton & Co., 1992), 20–21.

the fabric of space by the mass of objects the size of planets. This description was formulated by Einstein's theory and solved an essential mystery associated with the orbit of the planet Mercury.

Mercury is the innermost planet in our solar system because it is the nearest planet to the sun. When the validity of general relativity was being considered, the orbit of Mercury was a mystery to astronomers. Mercury's orbit did not align itself with what Newton's laws predicted: that Mercury's orbit would shift *slightly* every year due to the gravitational influence of other planets. The actual shift measured was more than the value Newton's theory predicted. This observation led astronomers to consider the idea of the existence of another planet closer to the sun that would account for Mercury's behavior.

However, according to Einstein's new theory this speculative planet need not exist. General relativity predicted the extreme curvature of space near the sun, which would account for the discrepancy. Measurements of Mercury's orbit proved that Einstein was right. As Mercury approached the gravity well near the sun's surface (as in the marble/cannon ball/elastic analogy), it would follow that depression, causing a marked shift in its orbit. Scientists have also made extremely accurate measurements of the orbital positions of the Earth, Mars, and Venus and have found them to be precisely what general relativity predicted. It is important to note that Einstein's equations represent a *refinement* of Newton's calculations and not a *contradiction*. This difference or refinement is insignificant for a small object but crucial for an object of planetary size.

Perhaps the most stunning prediction of general relativity is the idea that if a large enough mass was concentrated into a small enough volume, the space around that object would be severely distorted. This high degree of distortion in space would produce a phenomenon that has come to be known as a *black hole* (black is the name we attribute to a material that absorbs all the colors of the spectrum of light). A black hole's tremendous warping of space (analogous to a hole) results in a correspondingly high gravitational field. This field is so powerful that nothing, not even light, can generate enough energy to escape its gravitational grip.

When a star, such as the sun, begins to go through its final stages of death, it reaches a point where it enters total gravitational collapse. In other words, the only energy left in the star is its gravitational force, which eventually causes the star to collapse on itself. A black hole is eventually formed as the imploding star's gravitational momentum increases and the volume of the star decreases. The gravitational field of the black hole becomes so intense that nothing can evade it. A black hole is like a gigantic cosmic vacuum cleaner, absorbing anything that gets within its grasp.

Since by its very nature a black hole literally leaves no visible evidence to observe, astronomers must infer that black holes exist from the gravitational effects they have on other celestial bodies. Astronomers can also detect the emission of X-rays and gamma rays left behind by matter falling into black holes. In June of 1994, the Hubble Space Telescope was used to infer the reality of a massive black hole at the core of galaxy M87.[12] More recently, a team of astrophysicists at the Harvard-Smithsonian Center for Astrophysics in Cambridge, Massachusetts, has concluded that a supermassive black hole exists deep within the spiral galaxy NGC 4258. According to *Science News,*

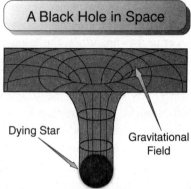

A Black Hole in Space

Dying Star

Gravitational Field

> Astronomers have repeatedly reported evidence that black holes lurk at the centers of galaxies. However, the latest finding all but settles the case, many scientists assert. Using a continent-wide array of radio telescopes, a U.S.-Japanese team last week reported "compelling evidence" that the center of a relatively nearby galaxy harbors a black hole as massive as 40 million suns.[13]

Direct proof of the existence of black holes has now surfaced through the observation of energy vanishing from volumes of space without a trace. Astronomers have been able to observe matter falling into black holes and "disappearing forever" by observing the "radiation that is emitted from the vicinity" that helps "astronomers to demonstrate that the strangest objects in the cosmos [black holes] are a reality."[14]

Therefore, black holes offer strong observational evidence to support the theory of general relativity. Add this evidence to the predictions of the deflection of light rays and the orbital paths of planets, and we can reasonably conclude that general relativity is a valid theory. In fact, through very sophisticated experimentation, general relativity has been confirmed up to at least five deci-

---

[12]R. Cowen, "Repaired Hubble Finds Giant Black Hole," *Science News,* vol. 145, no. 23, June 4, 1994, 356.

[13]R. Cowen, "New Evidence of Galactic Black Hole," *Science News,* vol. 147, no. 3, January 21, 1995, 36.

[14]Jean-Pierre Lasota, "Unmasking Black Holes," *Scientific American,* May, 1999, 42.

mal places.[15] Based upon the soundness of general relativity, we can correctly surmise that the universe had a beginning and is expanding in all directions.

We believe, then, that Carl Sagan was philosophically and scientifically incorrect to conclude that the universe has always existed. We established that operation science must set the stage for a valid origin science model. For this reason, in order to believe Sagan's model one must be willing to call into question the causality principle and the second law of thermodynamics. Furthermore, one must also ignore the conclusive observational evidence of the radiation echo and the general theory of relativity secured from the field of cosmology. Therefore, with the confirmation of the data presented above and its consistency with the principles of causality and uniformity, the second law of thermodynamics, and the principles of operation science, we conclude that *the universe had a beginning and, thus, is finite.*

WHICH ORIGIN MODEL BEST FITS THE COSMOLOGICAL EVIDENCE?

As mentioned above, any valid origin model must never violate the well-established principles and laws of science and must be consistent with the observational evidence secured from cosmology. The cosmological framework has now been established and leads to the direct and logical conclusion that the universe is finite and must have had a beginning. The most compelling reason for this conclusion is the second law of thermodynamics. Furthermore, the data altogether implies that the expanding universe is a direct result of its initial explosion into existence at some point in the past. Therefore, the view that we propose as being the most valid origin model, and the one that is most widely accepted among cosmologists, is the *Big Bang*. However, we reject the naturalistic assumptions that are often associated with the Big Bang model.

The Big Bang model is often misunderstood as a theory that states that at some point in the past, and at a certain location in space, a preexisting, superdense particle of matter suddenly exploded. However, we must remember that *space and time were also part of this superdense particle*—the whole universe, including the space between stars and planets, was condensed into it. Since space, time, and matter are interdependent, they must have been created together. It is this initial act of creation that we are referring to when we say "Big Bang model." Included in this model of origins is a cause that is consistent with, and is the logical conclusion of, the cosmological evidence and laws of

---

[15]For a listing of the observational verifications of general relativity, see Hugh Ross, *The Fingerprint of God* (Orange, Calif.: Promise, 1991), 46–47.

science. That is, *an infinite uncaused Cause that must also be eternal* (outside of time) caused the initial creation event that brought the space-*time* universe into existence. Moreover, the Big Bang was not just any old explosion; strong evidence suggests that it was an orchestrated cosmic detonation. This event had to have precisely the right balance of forces in order to produce the universe that we live in. Theoretical physicist John Polkinghorne, a colleague of Stephen Hawking, notes:

> In the early expansion of the universe there has to be a close balance between the expansive energy (driving things apart) and the force of gravity (pulling things together). If expansion dominated then matter would fly apart too rapidly for condensation into galaxies and stars to take place. . . . [The possiblity of our existence] requires a balance between the effects of expansion and contraction which at a very early epoch in the universe's history (the Planck time) has to differ from equality by not more than 1 in 10^{60}. The numerate [mathematician] will marvel at such a degree of accuracy. For the non-numerate I will borrow an illustration from Paul Davies of what that accuracy means.[16] He points out that it is the same as aiming at a target an inch wide on the other side of the observable universe, twenty thousand million light years away, and hitting the mark![17]

This kind of accuracy seems to indicate strongly that this infinite and eternal power must also be knowledgeable, given the magnitude of precision observed in bringing the universe into existence. What could have caused this kind of explosion? As Mortimer J. Adler has said, "IF the existence of the cosmos as a whole needs to be explained, and IF it cannot be explained by natural causes, THEN we must look to the existence and action of a supernatural cause for its explanation."[18] Adler's statement calls for a First Cause that acted from a completely unconstrained dimension of reality, independent of, and preexistent to, the dimensions of our space-time universe. Since it is impossible for nothing to produce something, something must have always existed as the First Cause of the universe. Furthermore, this First Cause must be eternal (outside of time, since time is part of the finite universe) and powerful enough to account for the origin and existence of the universe. It also is highly probable that this Cause must also be knowledgeable[19] (and since it is infinite, it must be infinitely knowledgeable). Hence, we conclude that *the Superforce*

---

[16]Paul Davies, *God and the New Physics* (New York: Simon & Schuster, 1983), 179.

[17]John Polkinghorne, *One World* (London: SPCK, 1986), 57.

[18]Mortimer J. Adler, *How to Think about God* (New York: Macmillan, 1980), 131.

[19]We will present a more substantial case for the highly probable conclusion that this Cause is intelligent in chapter 6.

that brought the universe into existence is a supernatural entity that is infinitely powerful, eternal, and knowledgeable.

WHY DID THE SUPERFORCE BRING THE COSMOS INTO EXISTENCE?

It is credible to believe that the cosmos had a beginning and therefore a First Cause. So the basic question "Why is there something rather than nothing at all?" is answered: something exists now because a Superforce with the attributes noted above created it. Is our presence an accident, or did the Supermind behind the universe have a purpose for creating us? Paul Davies posits that "science may explain the world, but we still have to explain science." He continues:

> The laws which enable the universe to come into being spontaneously seem themselves to be the product of exceedingly ingenious design. If physics is the product of design, the universe must have a purpose, and the evidence of modern physics suggests strongly to me that the purpose includes us.[20]

When we consider the question of purpose, we are considering the question of a *final cause.* However, when we raise the question of a purposeful cause, we are really raising the question of an *intelligent, efficient cause.* Is Paul Davies correct? Are we the product of an intelligent cause? Richard Dawkins believes that we are "survival machines—robot vehicles blindly programmed to preserve the selfish molecules known as genes."[21] Are we merely the accidental by-product of some infinite superforce that has no intelligence? If we were caused by some ultimate and aimless superforce, then the question of purpose is meaningless. In fact, one wonders why the question of why we exist is raised at all. If Dawkins is right, why do mere molecular robots ponder such questions? Is there a Supermind that designed into our being the desire and intelligence to ask these kinds of questions? We believe that there is, and we have dedicated the next chapter to the justification of an infinite, eternal, all-powerful, and super-intelligent First Cause.

(Note: If you agree with our conclusion as stated above, then you may want to go directly to chapter 6. However, you may be familiar with various origin models that attempt to evade the conclusion that the universe had a beginning.

---

[20]Paul Davies, *Superforce* (New York: Simon & Schuster, 1984), 243.
[21]Richard Dawkins, *The Selfish Gene* (Oxford University Press, 1976), preface.

If so, continue reading to see how the first principles of philosophy and laws of science can be employed to refute some of these speculative and complex alternative origin models.)

WHY COULDN'T THE COSMOS BE OSCILLATING (OR PULSATING)?

One theory that seeks to avoid a beginning of the space-time universe is often referred to as the *oscillating*, or *pulsating*, model of the universe. This origin model is founded on the conjecture that the universe is expanding as the result of one of many big bangs. Theorists speculate as to how the universe will stop expanding at some point and will start contracting under the universal attracting force of gravity. The phrase used to describe the collapse of the universe is the *Big Crunch*, theoretically similar to the implosion of a star and its resulting black hole. According to the oscillating model, the ensuing implosion is supposed to trigger another explosion, or big bang, starting the whole process over again. Hence, this model states that the universe cycles through an infinite number of explosions and implosions that have no beginning and no end.

To hypothesize that the Big Bang is only the latest of a series of explosions still forces us to ask, "What caused the first explosion?" To believe that there was no first explosion and that these bangs and crunches go back infinitely in time, violates both science and philosophy. It is a violation of the foremost law of science because

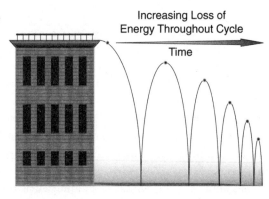

the oscillation process must conform itself to the second law of thermodynamics. According to the second law, the available amount of usable energy in the universe must progressively be reduced until there can be no more cycles. It is analogous to dropping a Superball off of a skyscraper. If left unobstructed, it may bounce for a very long time, but eventually the second law will dominate the process and ensure that it stops bouncing. Gravity pulls the ball to the ground, but the second law impedes it from having the same amount of energy that would cause it to rise back to its original height. In a similar manner, even if this is a bouncing universe, the second law states that usable energy would continue to decrease throughout the entire process. Hence, the universe must have had a beginning.

Moreover, is it possible that the universe could produce even a single bounce? Astronomer Hugh Ross explains why this idea is not feasible:

> The universe, with a specific entropy of about a billion, ranks as the most entropic phenomenon known. Thus even if the universe contained sufficient mass to force an eventual collapse, that collapse would *not* produce a bounce. Far too much of the energy of the universe is dissipated in unreclaimable form to fuel a bounce. Like a lump of wet clay falling on a carpet, the universe, if it did collapse, would go "splat."[22]

For these reasons, we reject the oscillating (or pulsating) universe model. Furthermore, any origin model that violates the second law of thermodynamics and is compelled to adopt an infinite view of time, will also be forced to commit an error in philosophy, namely, that there cannot be an infinite number of actual moments of time. We will identify and explain this error later when we analyze Stephen Hawking's proposal.

WHY COULDN'T THE COSMOS BE IN AN ETERNAL STEADY STATE?

Some cosmologists claim that the expanding universe takes on an eternal and unchanging quality as the voids resulting from the expansion are filled by the spontaneous generation of new matter. Consequently, they assert that the second law of thermodynamics does not apply to the universe as a whole. Others maintain that the second law applies to the universe as a whole but was not in effect at 10^{-43} seconds (beginning of the space-time universe). All of these cosmologists conclude that Carl Sagan was right ("The Cosmos is all that is or ever was or ever will be"). They may hold varying opinions on how the universe evades the second law, but they all agree that the universe is somehow ultimately exempt from the final death grip of the second law of thermodynamics.

As far as the evidence is concerned, *the laws of thermodynamics hold throughout the entire knowable universe.* When spacecraft are designed to meet the very demanding standards necessary for long journeys, the aerospace engineers assume that all the known laws of physics apply throughout the universe. In August of 1989, *Voyager 2* discovered six additional Neptunian moons before

---

[22]Hugh Ross, *The Fingerprint of God* (Orange, Calif.: Promise, 1991), 105.

it departed from our solar system. Up to that point the laws of physics were still valid, and there is no scientific reason to believe that these laws do not hold throughout the entire universe. Furthermore, the knowable universe has been calculated to have a radius of 20 billion light-years. So when we observe quasars, the most distant objects, we assume that the laws governing electromagnetic radiation (particle and wave physics) hold at these ranges. If this is true, would not the most prominent laws of physics, the laws of thermodynamics, be expected to be in effect as well? Of course they would, and there is no philosophical or scientific reason to think otherwise. Hence, all of the scientific evidence supports the universal application of the laws of thermodynamics and leads us to the only logical conclusion—the universe had a beginning.

The other aspect of this model, the idea that the second law does not apply at 10^{-43} seconds in time, must be carefully weighed. We already concluded that some Superforce transcends the laws of physics. If this is the case, then there are only two options: (1) If any law or principle of science is in effect at 10^{-43} seconds, then the second law (which has priority over all the laws) must be in effect as well, or (2) Origin models cannot utilize any of the laws or principles of operation science at 10^{-43} seconds.

The first option leads us back to the conclusion of this chapter—the spacetime universe had a beginning. The second option rules out all origin models that attempt to give an explanation of what happened before the Big Bang, including Stephen Hawking's proposal (discussed below). However, the latest ideas about what happened at 10^{-43} seconds seem to have captured the attention of researchers and amateur cosmologists. As *Astronomy* magazine explains:

> In the leading physics laboratories around the world, the universe before the big bang has become one of the hottest areas of research. There is a tangible air of excitement as we witness the birth of a new science called quantum cosmology. *Although there is no experimental proof for quantum cosmology,* the theory is so compelling and beautiful that it has become the center of intense research.[23]

The problem with this "new science called quantum cosmology" is that it is beyond scientific investigation and is essentially philosophical in nature. As a philosophy, quantum cosmology is riddled with problems that will be identified and discussed in the next origin model, Stephen Hawking's proposal.

---

[23]Michio, Kaku "What Happened Before the Big Bang?" *Astronomy*, vol. 24, no. 5, May, 1996, 36 emphasis added.

WHAT ABOUT QUANTUM COSMOLOGY AND STEPHEN HAWKING'S MODEL?

Stephen Hawking has assembled one of the most imaginative origin models that seeks to avoid a universe that has a beginning. Hawking proposes a universe that is finite, yet without limits, similar to a sphere which has no edge (the edge represents the beginning of time).

For instance, if we were able to continually walk around the earth, we would never fall off because it has no edge. In this way, we can think of the earth as a finite sphere, yet without limits, that can be circled infinitely with respect to time. Hawking argues that if the universe were to have no edge, it would be "completely self-contained and not affected by anything outside itself. It would neither be created nor destroyed. It would just BE."[24] However, Hawking adds the following caution:

> I'd like to emphasize that this idea, that time and space should be finite without boundary, is just a *proposal:* it cannot be deduced from some other principle. Like any other scientific theory, it may initially be put forward for aesthetic or metaphysical reasons, but the real test is whether it makes predictions that agree with observation.[25]

Hawking's proposal seeks to avoid what has been called a *singularity*—a point at which all the known laws of physics no longer apply. The Big Bang singularity clearly indicates the beginning of the space-time universe. However, Hawking averts it by assuming that there was no beginning. He has endeavored to develop a model of the universe that is finite and measurable, but without limits in time. He incorporates into his proposal the often-misinterpreted uncertainty principle of quantum theory[26]; he also employs a concept he calls *imaginary time.* Simply stated, imaginary time, in mathematical terms, is equivalent to imaginary numbers (the square root of a negative number). Consequently, the integrity of Hawking's model rests on two assumptions: (1) It is credible to utilize the concept of imaginary time in a model that must describe

---

[24]Stephen W. Hawking, *A Brief History of Time* (New York: Bantam, 1988), 136.
[25]Ibid., 136–37.
[26]For an explanation and analysis of the uncertainty principle, see chapter 4, "Does quantum physics disprove causality?"

a universe that functions in real time, and (2) It is valid to employ the uncertainty principle at 10^{-43} seconds in order to avoid the beginning of the space-time universe.

Hawking describes the use of imaginary time as a "mathematical device (or trick) to calculate answers about real space-time."[27] But does his proposal answer the ultimate origin question when it is applied to real space-time? Hawking admits:

> When one goes back to the real time in which we live, however, there will still appear to be singularities. The poor astronaut who falls into a black hole will still come to a sticky end; only if he lived in imaginary time would he encounter no singularities.[28]

When Hawking converts his work back into real time, the singularity (the beginning of time) reappears. In an effort to avoid a beginning, he suggests that "the so-called imaginary time is really the real time, and that what we call real time is just a figment of our imaginations."[29] If this were true, then every scientific law and principle must also be a figment of our imaginations because they were developed in real time. According to Hawking's proposal we would have to recalculate these laws and principles by converting their real associated time scales into imaginary-time coordinates.

Therefore, we propose that the real time is real and that Hawking's proposal is a "figment of the imagination." As soon as the numbers in his theory are converted back into real time (the dimension of time in which science operates), the singularities and boundary conditions show up again. The only *scientific* conclusion that can be deduced from this proposal is that it is a clever mathematical trick—not a meaningful description of reality. It may be an exotic and highly imaginative way of thinking about the origin of the universe, but that is all we can say for it.

Hawking's suggestion is similar in nature to Einstein's cosmological constant. Einstein needed, and created, a mathematical constant to stop the universe from expanding because of its implications with respect to the beginning of time. However, as we have shown, a universe that exists in real time and space must have had a beginning—a conclusion that is consistent with the laws of science. Roy Peacock noted the true scientific beauty of Hawking's proposal when he said,

> The elegance of Hawking's model is not that it leads us to a universe

[27]Hawking, op. cit., 134.
[28]Ibid., 139.
[29]Ibid., 139.

that was without beginning and will be without end; it is that it brings us back in real time and space, to one which includes singularities—and that is a conclusion lining up nicely with the Second Law of thermodynamics.[30]

As we have seen, one major philosophical problem associated with Hawking's view is its contradictory assumption: if all the laws of physics no longer apply at 10^{-43} seconds, then none of the laws of physics can be utilized to create a model, including the principle of uncertainty. Hawking is very careful not to violate the uncertainty principle,[31] but he does not seem to take equal precaution with keeping the second law of thermodynamics intact. Either all the laws do apply or they do not; to say that they do not and then to use the principle of uncertainty is a violation of the foremost precept of logic, the law of noncontradiction. Also, arbitrarily picking the principle of uncertainty over the second law not only *begs the question* in philosophy but is out of order in science. If the uncertainty principle can be employed for a model developed at 10^{43} seconds, then the second law of thermodynamics must take priority over it, since it is more firmly established by observation.

Since Hawking admits that the underlying assumptions in his proposal are metaphysical in nature,[32] we can critique it as such. In order to believe that time is infinite, one must be willing to commit an error in logic. It is an error known as a *category mistake* (introduced earlier), which in this case confuses the mathematically possible with the actual.

For example, mathematical concepts are *logically* possible but not always *actually* possible in a material universe. Consider the ancient dilemma known as Zeno's paradox, which was an attempt to prove that all motion is an illusion. Zeno based his argument on the mathematical concept of a line containing an infinite number of points. We have adapted his argument, for illustrative purposes, and show a line that is connecting point A to point B.

In mathematics, the number of points on line A, B is infinite. Conceptually speaking, in order to get from point A to point B, we would have to

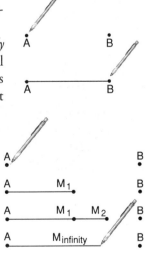

[30]Roy E. Peacock, *A Brief History of Eternity* (Wheaton, Ill.: Crossway, 1990), 95.
[31]Op. cit., 148–49.
[32]Ibid., 136.

pass the midpoint—M_1. However, after passing midpoint M_1, we must pass the midpoint between M_1 and point B, which is M_2. This is an endless process because there are an infinite number of mathematical midpoints between point A and point B. Therefore, it seems logically impossible to move from point A to point B; doing so would require crossing an infinite number of midpoints—$M_{infinity}$, as indicated in the second illustration.

Zeno applied these mathematical concepts to a runner attempting to run a race starting at point A and crossing the finish line at point B. He argued that it would be logically impossible for the runner to move in any direction because in order to do so the runner would have to cross an infinite number of midpoints. Therefore, Zeno concluded that motion is an illusion, a "figment of the imagination." Sound familiar? It should, because Zeno and Hawking essentially commit the same philosophical mistake.

The problem is that they both have confused the abstract and the concrete. An abstract infinite number of points (or moments) is possible, but a concrete (actual) infinite number is not.

In a very similar manner, we must reject the idea that an actual infinite universe exists; as a concept it fails to meet the material (observational) test for truth. As Hawking says, "When one goes back to the real time in which we live, however, there will still appear to be singularities."[33] Referring to the validity of his proposal, Hawking states that "the real test is whether it makes predictions that agree with observation."[34] According to his own criteria, the no boundary proposal fails the real test of a credible theory both scientifically and philosophically. There is more than enough evidence to conclude that general relativity is a valid theory, and by doing so we are once again confronted with a singularity—the beginning of the universe. Even Hawking concludes,

> According to the theory of relativity, there must have been a state of infinite density in the past, the big bang, which would have been an effective beginning of time. . . . At the big bang and other singularities [e.g. black holes], all the laws would have broken down, so God would still have had complete freedom to choose what happened and how the universe began.[35]

---

[33]Ibid., 139.
[34]Ibid., 137.
[35]Ibid., 173.

6
QUESTIONS ABOUT THE ORIGIN OF LIFE

Is it really credible that random processes could have constructed a reality . . . which excels in every sense anything produced by the intelligence of man?

—MICHAEL DENTON

WHICH CAME FIRST, MIND OR MATTER?

"And so," said the lecturer, "I end where I began. Evolution, development, the slow struggle upwards and onwards from crude and inchoate beginnings towards ever-increasing perfection and elaboration—that appears to be the very formula of the whole universe.

"We see it exemplified in everything we study. The oak comes from the acorn. The giant express engine of today comes from the Rocket. The highest achievements of contemporary art are in a continuous line of descent from the rude scratchings with which prehistoric man adorned the wall of his cave.

"What are the ethics and philosophy of civilized man but a miraculous elaboration of the most primitive instincts of savage taboos? Each one of us has grown through slow prenatal stages in which we were at first more like fish than mammals, from a particle of matter too small to be seen. Man himself springs from beasts; the organic from the inorganic. Development is the key word. The march of all things is from lower to higher."

None of this, of course, was new to me or to anyone else in the audience. But it was put very well (much better than it appears in my reproduction) and the whole voice and figure of the lecturer were impressive. At least they must have impressed me, for otherwise I cannot account for the curious dream I had that night.

I dreamed that I was still at the lecture, and the voice from the platform was still going on. But it was saying all the wrong things. At least it may have been saying the right things up to the very moment at which I began attending; but it certainly began going wrong after that. What I remembered on waking went like this: ". . . appears to be the very formula of the whole universe. We see it exemplified in everything we study. The acorn comes from a full-grown oak. The first crude engine, the Rocket, comes not from a still cruder engine, but from something much more perfect than itself and much more complex, the mind of a man, and a man of genius. The first prehistoric drawings come, not from earlier scratchings, but from the hand and brain of human beings whose hand and brain cannot be shown to have been in any way inferior to our own; and indeed it is obvious that the man who first conceived the idea of making a picture must have been a greater genius than any of the artists who have succeeded him. The embryo with which the life of each of us began did not originate from something even more embryonic; it originated from two fully-developed human beings, our parents. Descent, downward movement, is the key word. The march of all things is from higher to lower. The rude and imperfect thing always springs from something perfect and developed."

I did not think much of this while I was shaving, but it so happened that I had no 10 o'clock pupil that morning, and when I had finished answering my letters I sat down and reflected on my dream.

It appeared to me that the Dream Lecturer had a good deal to be said for him. It is true that we do see all around us things growing up to perfection from small and rude beginnings; but then it is equally true that the small and rude beginnings themselves always come from some full-grown and developed thing. All adults were once babies, true; but then all babies were begotten and borne by adults. Corn does come from seed: but then seed comes from corn. I could even give the Dream Lecturer an example he had missed. All civilizations grow from small beginnings; but when you look into it you always find that those small beginnings themselves have been "dropped" (as an oak drops an acorn) by some other and mature civilization. The weapons and even the cookery of old German barbarism are, so to speak, driftwood from the wrecked ship of Roman civilization. The starting point of Greek culture is the remains of older Minoan cultures, supplemented by oddments from civilized Egypt and Phoenicia.

For the first time in my life I began to look at the question with both eyes open. In the world I know, the perfect produces the imperfect, which again becomes perfect—egg leads to bird and bird to egg—in endless succession. If there ever was a life which sprang of its own accord out of a purely inorganic universe, or a civilization which raised itself by its own shoulder-straps out of pure savagery, then this event was totally unlike the beginnings of every subsequent life and every subsequent civilization. The thing may have happened; but all its plausibility is gone. On any view, the first beginning must have been outside the ordinary processes of nature. An egg which came from no bird is no more natural than a bird which had existed from all eternity. And since the egg-bird-egg sequence leads us to no plausible beginning, is it not reasonable to look for the real origin somewhere outside the sequence altogether? You have to go outside the sequence of engines, into the world of men, to find the real originator of the Rocket. Is it not equally reasonable to look outside Nature for the real Originator of the natural order?[1]

The above scenario, written by C. S. Lewis, accurately portrays the task at hand. We want to know if it is reasonable to affirm the existence of an intelligent mind as the "real Originator of the natural order." We are trying to discover which came first: Did mind create matter, or did matter create mind? Did God create man, or did man create God? Does intelligence arise from nonintelligence, or does it always take intelligence to produce intelligence?

WHAT ARE THE TWO COMPETING ORIGIN-OF-LIFE MODELS?

In order to be consistent with the previous investigation, we again need to make a differentiation between operation science and origin science. In doing so, we should be able to rule out theories of the origin-of-life that are based on unjustified assumptions and not supported by scientific laws and observations. It is vitally important to keep in mind that any valid model of the origin of life should never violate the scientific-laws evidence procured from observation. This methodological rule is known as the *principle of uniformity*[2] (or *analogy*).

---

[1]C. S. Lewis, *God in the Dock* (Grand Rapids, Mich.: Eerdmanns, 1970), 208–11.
[2]The *principle of uniformity* should not be confused with the naturalistic view known as *uniformitarianism*. Uniformitarianism assumes that only natural causes can be applied to past events. However, this assumption is not scientifically justifiable; it is a philosophical presupposition of naturalism. The basis of uniformitarianism is the principle of continuity, that there is a *continuos*, an unbroken series of natural physical causes. However, the conclusion presented in chapter 5, that the universe is finite and had a beginning, undermines the credibility of uniformitarianism. That conclusion clearly demonstrated a need for a supernatural force or cause beyond the natural space-time universe in order to account for its origin.

Although we discussed this principle in chapter 4, it may be wise to quickly review it before we proceed.

The principle of uniformity tells us that unobserved causes of events in the past are assumed to be similar to causes of like events observed in the present. For example, we are looking for the kind of cause in the present that is necessary to produce a single cell (the first life form), and by proper use of the principle of uniformity we must assume that the same kind of cause produced it in the past. Ultimately, by correctly applying the laws and observational evidences from operation science and the principles of causality and uniformity, we should be able to determine which origin model most accurately describes the origin of life. There are two competing origin-of-life models under consideration in this chapter: the macroevolutionary model and the design model.

The macroevolutionary model states that life was self-generated from nonliving (inorganic) matter. Once the gap from nonlife to life was bridged, the first living cell began to evolve by random changes (mutations) in its genetic information system, creating new characteristics that were not in the original organism. This model will be expanded with respect to new life forms in the next chapter; for now, we are interested in how it explains the origin of life. According to this model, the first living organism evolved from lifeless matter by the accidental assembly of matter, without the intervention of a super-intelligent mind.

The design model states that nonlife never produces life and that the first life forms were the direct result of a super-intelligence. This model will be extended in chapter 8. For now, we plan to show how it offers a more accurate description of life's beginnings in that it is more philosophically sound and scientifically accurate than the macroevolutionary explanation of the origin of life.

In order to keep within the scope of this overall work, it will be necessary to stay focused on testing these two models with respect to how they account for the origin of life. We will use operation science as our guide in establishing the first principle of molecular biology as the foundational building block for any origin-of-life model. Once that first principle has been identified and shown to be true, it will be combined with other scientific laws and observational evidence in order to construct a framework for a trustworthy origin-of-life model. The model that most accurately accounts for the tremendous gap between nonliving matter and life, without violating the first principle of molecular biology, philosophical principles, scientific laws, and observational evidence, will be considered to be the authoritative model. The best place to start this investigation is at the beginning with an understanding of what must be explained: the nature of a single cell—the first living organism.

DID DARWIN UNDERSTAND THE COMPLEX NATURE OF THE CELL?

Biology is the science of life and of living organisms, including their structure, function, growth, origin, and microevolution.[3] The smallest component of life and living organisms is called a *cell.* Molecular biology consists of the study of the components of a cell on the molecular level. It was not too long ago that the cell was considered to be a *black box,* a term used to describe an apparatus whose inner components are mysterious in that they are not observable or are incomprehensible. This is how one author, Michael J. Behe, characterizes the history of biology—as a chain of black boxes. Behe explains,

> Computers are a good example of a black box. Most of us use these marvelous machines without the vaguest idea of how they work, processing words or plotting graphs or playing games in contented ignorance of what is going on underneath the outer case.[4]

Behe continues by depicting the history of biology as the opening of one black box after another, and in the mid–1800s, the time of Charles Darwin, the cell was still a black box to the mind of Darwin and every other scientist. Behe says that although Darwin was able to make sense of much of biology above the cell level, he was not knowledgeable of the inner workings of a living cell. He notes that it was not until after World War II, with the help of electron microscopy, that new subcellular structures were discovered. The same cell that looked so simple to scientists of the past was now seen as an overwhelmingly complex molecular entity, equipped with its own power plant and information center. Behe records,

> This level of discovery [of subcelluar structures] began to allow biologists to approach the greatest black box of all. The question of *how life works* was not one Darwin or his contemporaries could answer. They knew that eyes were for seeing—but how, exactly, do they see? How does the blood clot? How does the body fight disease? The complex structures revealed by the electron microscope were themselves made of smaller components. What were those components? What did they look like? How did they work?[5]

---

[3]We are making a differentiation between the term *microevolution*, which accounts for changes that occur within a type's own natural biological limits as it adapts to changes in its environment (varying climate and other environmental factors), and *macroevolution*, which extrapolates those changes by assuming that specific types of life have no natural biological limits.
[4]Michael J. Behe, *Darwin's Black Box: The Biochemical Challenge to Evolution* (New York: Free, 1996), 6.
[5]Ibid., 10.

"How does life work?" was not the only question Darwin or his contemporaries were powerless to address; they were also incapable of answering the question "How did life begin?" How did the first living cell become alive from nonliving matter? To gain a better understanding of the magnitude of such a question, Michael Denton illustrates the kind of complexity that must be accounted for with respect to a living cell. He says,

> To grasp the reality of life as it has been revealed by molecular biology, we must magnify a cell a thousand million times until it is twenty kilometers in diameter and resembles a giant airship. . . . What we would then see would be an object of unparalleled complexity and adaptive design. On the surface of the cell we would see millions of openings, like the portholes of a vast space ship, opening and closing to allow a continual stream of materials to flow in and out. If we were to enter one of these openings we would find ourselves in a world of supreme technology and bewildering complexity. We would see endless highly organized corridors and conduits branching in every direction away from the perimeter of the cell, some leading to the central memory bank in the nucleus and others to assembly plants and processing units. The nucleus itself would be a vast spherical chamber more than a kilometer in diameter, resembling a geodesic dome inside of which we would see, all neatly stacked together in ordered arrays, the miles of coiled chains of DNA molecules. A huge range of products and raw materials would shuttle along all the manifold conduits in a highly ordered fashion to and from the various assembly plants in the outer regions of the cell. . . . Is it really credible that random processes could have constructed a reality, the smallest element of which—a functional protein or gene—is complex beyond our own creative capacities, a reality which is the very antithesis of chance, which excels in every sense anything produced by the intelligence of man?[6]

What caused the first single cell, a highly specified and complex entity, to exist? Did it take intelligence to produce the first life form? Or did life arise through purely natural forces and processes over a long period of time? What criteria ought we to use to determine whether or not macroevolution is a feasible model to account for the origin of life? How about Darwin's own?

> If it could be demonstrated that any complex organ existed, which could not possibly have been formed by numerous, successive, slight modifications, my theory would absolutely break down.[7]

---

[6]Michael Denton, *Evolution: A Theory in Crisis* (Bethesda: Adler & Adler, 1986) 328, 342.
[7]Charles Darwin, *On the Origin of Species* (New York: NAL Penguin Inc., 1958), 171.

We plan to demonstrate that the theory of macroevolution is scientifically implausible with respect to offering an account for the origin of life, according to Darwin's criteria. The bulk of our critique with respect to Darwin will appear in the next chapter. Before we examine in depth the macroevolutionary model of origins, we need to establish whether there exists any basis for that theory at the molecular level. Relying on the current scientific understanding of the nature and function of the cell, we concur with Behe, who concludes that macroevolution is a "fact-free" science. To begin, let's open "Darwin's black box" and take a closer look at the basic structure and function of a living cell.

HOW COMPLEX IS A SINGLE CELL, AND HOW DOES IT WORK?

Today, the cell is usually understood as the smallest unit of matter considered to be alive—a tiny construct that can be less than a thousandth of an inch in diameter. First we'll identify the various fundamental parts of the cell, and later we'll discuss their respective functions.

Inside the cell wall are *proteins* (see following graphic), which are the fundamental components of all living cells and include many substances, such as enzymes, hormones, and antibodies. These components are necessary for the proper functioning of an organism. Next, notice that the cell nucleus contains the nucleolus and an essential molecule called *deoxyribonucleic acid (DNA)*. The *nucleolus* is a small, typically round, granular body

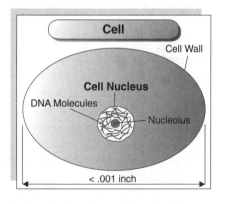

composed of protein and ribonucleic acid (RNA). DNA, combined with protein, is organized into structural units called *chromosomes*, which usually occur in identical pairs. The DNA molecule forms the infrastructure in each chromosome and is a single, very long, highly coiled molecule subdivided into functional subunits called *genes*. A gene occupies a certain place on the chromosome and embodies the coded instructions that determine the inheritance of a particular characteristic or group of characteristics that are passed on from one generation to the next. Together the chromosomes contain all the information needed to build an identical functioning copy of the cell.

Cells have two primary functions: to provide a framework to sustain life and to produce exact copies of themselves so that the organism can continue to live even after those original cells die. One way to understand the structure and operation of a cell is to think of it as a chemical factory in a large city (organism). This factory operates in such a way that it takes raw materials from the environment, processes them, and yields a product that can be used in its own environment (inside the cell) as well as be sent out to be used somewhere else in that city (the organism). This chemical plant is fully equipped with a biological library located in the computer center (cell nucleus), where the blueprints for the entire city are stored. These blueprints also come with a complete set of instruction manuals that explain the necessary steps for the construction and replication of life. The blueprints and instruction manuals are stored in code form on compact discs (DNA) in the computer center (cell nucleus).

To help us visualize how the various components of a cell work together, imagine that the wall (cell wall) enclosing the chemical factory gets damaged. A messenger (mRNA) is dispatched to the computer center (genetic library), located in the cell nucleus, where it locates the blueprints and the instructions (DNA) needed to repair the injury to the wall. Next, the mRNA makes an exact copy of the information it requires from the computer and stores it on a CD. When the copying process is complete, the mRNA heads off to the site where the damage occurred and begins to manufacture little robots (specific protein molecules), based on the information it copied, in order to accomplish the work of repairing the wall. This explanation is very basic, but it will help us gain a fundamental understanding of the structure and operation of a cell.

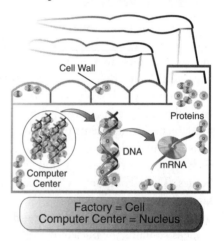

The next step is to probe a bit deeper into the operation of a cell in order to discover more about the information content that is stored in the computer center (located in the cell nucleus). One way to think about the information content inside a cell is to compare it to an instruction manual of the type that comes with the purchase of an item requiring assembly.

Most likely, we have all had the experience of being frustrated after purchasing some such item. Sometimes the instructions that accompany these objects can be vague, only elevating the level of aggravation. Perseverance is usually the key factor in overcoming the irritation and getting the project finished. Now, what would you do if you purchased something as complex as a computer system and then found out that its full assembly was required? Imagine opening the box containing the parts of a computer system and seeing that they all needed to be assembled. Furthermore, think about the headache that would be associated with all of the instruction manuals necessary for the construction of such a technical object. But—what if all the parts arrived *without* the blueprints or instruction manuals? How would you even begin to assemble it? Without the specific information that communicates the know-how or skills associated with the construction of a computer, the components alone are useless.

This analogy is one very rudimentary way of showing how raw materials alone will not produce a specified and complex system. In a similar manner, all the components for life would be useless without the blueprints and instruction manuals necessary for the assembly and correct operation of a living cell. Energy, matter, and time are not the only ingredients needed to assemble living things; *information* must also be present to get the job done. With this in mind, let's take a closer look at the kind of coded information that exists in the cell's computer center.

WHAT KIND OF CODED INFORMATION DOES A CELL UTILIZE?

The DNA molecule is the fundamental building block of all living things. It determines the form and function of the cell and passes on genetic information from one generation to the next by making exact copies of itself. The complex systems of every known organism are reproduced and assembled on the basis of the information stored on the DNA molecular system. Since the entire chemical metabolism is preprogrammed by the genetic code, it is essential to know the level of complexity associated with this genetic information. This means the DNA molecular system must be uncoiled in order for us to find out what kind of information base exists in the cell.

Once we look inside the cell

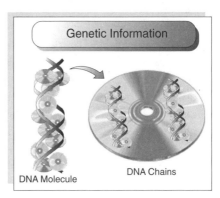

Genetic Information

DNA Molecule

DNA Chains

nucleus, we see that all of the genetic information is stored on the DNA molecule. Probing deeper into the DNA molecule, notice how the DNA chains are stored on compact discs (like CDs). These DNA information chains contain specific information about the organism. This information has been compressed and saved in a coded form (as depicted below). The genetic code consists of a sequence of letters (A, T, C, and G) similar to a child's toy blocks with each side of a block stamped with one of the four letters of the alphabet. If these letters are linked together in a certain coded sequence, they can be used to construct a message (set of instructions) in order to communicate an action. Looking at the blocks, we can read what appears to be a message in coded form. Reading the letters from left to right and linking them together from the top set of blocks down to the bottom set, the message reads: *TAG-CAT-ACT*. This message could be decoded to mean that it is time to get a license *TAG* for the *CAT*, so *ACT* now! Admittedly, this is obviously a very limited and vague way to communicate instructions. However, picture the code as consisting of the four letters—A, T, C, and G—and using certain specific and complex sequences to convey a number of ideas or commands. It

could become rather involved, but if a set of rules determined that a certain arrangement of letters signified a specific concept or action, that code could be utilized to transmit an enormous amount and unparalleled variety of messages.

Morse Code is an example of a coded system of communication that uses only two units in varying sequences to communicate messages. Morse Code consists of combinations of dots and dashes representing the letters of the alphabet and numerals. Similarly, the genetic alphabet only has four letters—A, T, C, and G (explained later)—which are used to store and communicate specific instructions in a coded form. In the previously stated example, we explained what happens in a cell with respect to its coded information. First, the information is read and copied and then is transported to the place where a certain task needs to be performed. Then the coded information must be translated into a specific sequence in order to accomplish the exact activity that is required by the cell. The next step we want to take is to examine the information content of the cell and discover the nature of that coded information.

Molecular biology is essentially dependent upon a sub-discipline known as *information theory*. This discipline is a relatively new science, not around during the days of Darwin, and was never considered when Darwin developed the theory of macroevolution. Information theory is indispensable to understanding what biology is all about—information storage and retrieval systems. These systems are analogous to the blueprints and instruction manuals that provide the know-how concerning the construction and operation of the mechanisms of life. They specify what to do and how to do it, just as software does for a computer.

The Morse Code

A	.-		S	...
B	-...		T	-
C	-.-.		U	..-
D	-..		V	...-
E	.		W	.--
F	..-.		X	-..-
G	--.		Y	-.--
H	....		Z	--..
I	..		1	.----
J	.---		2	..---
K	-.-		3	...--
L	.-..		4	....-
M	--		5	.....
N	-.		6	-....
O	---		7	--...
P	.--.		8	---..
Q	--.-		9	----.
R	.-.		0	-----

Every software program makes use of a programming language that employs a code consisting of two units, ones and zeros. When these numbers are put into a certain specific arrangement, the computer is designed to respond to that sequence in a particular manner. For example, the sequence 111001100111 would communicate a certain lingual message that the computer has been designed to act upon. However, the code must be set up with very specific rules in order for the system to function properly. The programmer must create a language, along with a set of regulations that govern it, that will guarantee the precise operation of the computer system.

Now, imagine that we have been assigned the task of breaking the code utilized by a certain computer. If we were able to break the code and understand how the language worked, we would also be able to gain some insight into the mind of the original programmer. The complexity of the language used by a computer is directly proportional to the kind of mind that created the coded information system. The same is true for the information content of the genetic code and the language of a living cell. Once the code is broken and its complexity determined, we should be able to discern whether or not the information content of the genetic code had an original, intelligent programmer, or if it came into being by random processes.

HOW DOES THE DNA MOLECULAR-INFORMATION SYSTEM WORK?

The DNA molecule is a single, very long, highly coiled molecule that can be subdivided into functional subunits called *genes*. Genes that contain the coded information we have been discussing consist of tinier units referred to as *nucleotides*. A nucleotide is the technical name for the smallest unit (letter) in the genetic code. By itself, a nucleotide conveys no information. However, if several nucleotides are strung together into a precise sequence or chain similar to the computer language example of 111001100111, the letters begin to construct specific messages in code form. In 1952 two geneticists, James D. Watson and Francis H. Crick, discovered that the DNA molecule's parts fit together in a *specified* manner. This precise configuration of the DNA molecule became known as the *genetic code*. Ten years after this discovery the genetic code was deciphered and proven biologically correct. In other words, it was empirically verified that the parts of the genetic code, represented by the letters

A, T, C, and G, only fit together in certain sequences that specify the blueprints and instruction manuals for all living things.

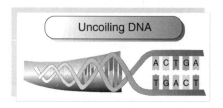

Watson and Crick discovered that the structure of a DNA molecule is in the shape of a double helix, resembling a long spiraling rope ladder. If we were able to uncoil it we would see the sides and steps of this ladder. The strands (or sides) of the rope ladder are composed of alternating sections of sugar and phosphate molecules. The steps of the ladder carry the genetic information (genetic code) and are made of four nitrogen-containing bases: adenine (A), thymine (T), cytosine (C), and guanine

(G). The rungs of the ladder are made up of a nucleotide that links itself with a complementary base on the opposite side of the strand.

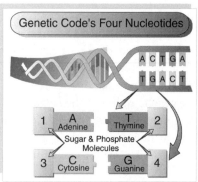

For example, adenine (A) always binds to thymine (T), and cytosine (C) always attaches to guanine (G). Hence, each step of the rope ladder consists of two bases and only two possible combinations for each step: A/T and C/G, which equates to two nucleotides per step. Each nucleotide is a subunit of the DNA molecule and contains a phosphate, a sugar, and any one of the four nitrogen bases. *The specific order of nucleotides determines the genetic code for each of us.* This code may seem rather insignificant, but it is the means by which all living things operate at the molecular level. To better our understanding, let's take a look at what happens during the copying process.

The DNA of a specific life form has the responsibility of designating that life form and its functions. It also designates genetic information that will be passed from one generation to the next by making exact copies of itself. The technical term for this procedure is *replication*. One way to imagine the DNA replication process is to untwist the rope ladder we have been referring to and separate the pairs of letters (nucleotides). It is this sequence of letters that determines the unique genetic code for each individual. Once the DNA molecule has been uncompressed and uncoiled, we can see each pair of letters (base pairs) and their particular arrangement. These arrangements, or chains of information, are extremely important because they determine the characteristics of a particular organism. Consequently, the copying process must be a precise operation.

This diagram illustrates the replication process. In stage 1 the base pairs

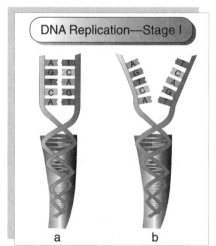

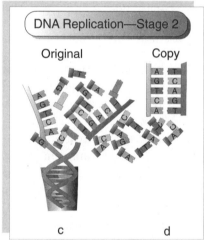

pull at one end of the DNA ladder (a), separating the bases (b). Next, in stage 2, the disconnected base pairs of the original DNA ladder recombine with free floating nucleotides (c) and form an exact copy of the original (d). Adenine fuses with thymine (A/T) and cytosine with guanine (C/G) until two identical DNA strands result. This completes the copying process and cell division is ready to begin. The next area of investigation has to do with the complexity level of the information that exists within the DNA molecular system.

WHAT KIND OF INFORMATION IS STORED IN THE DNA MOLECULE?

We already know that the genetic code consists of the four letters, A, T, C, and G. Now we need to understand just how complex the genetic code is in order to determine whether or not the code is a random by-product of purely natural forces. Can energy, matter, and time alone produce the type of order that is found in the genetic code? Let's see what molecular biologists found when they deciphered the genetic code.

As previously mentioned, information theory, the sub-discipline of molecular biology, seeks to describe the data storage and retrieval systems in biological entities. With respect to the kind of information that was discovered to make up the genetic code, molecular biologists classify it as equivalent to that of a written language! Information scientist Hubert P. Yockey explains:

> The statistical structure of any printed language ranges through letter frequencies, digrams, trigrams, word frequencies, etc., spelling rules, grammar and so forth and therefore can be represented by a Markov process given the states of the system. . . . It is important to understand that we are not reasoning by analogy. The sequence hypothesis applies directly to the protein and the genetic text as well as to written language and therefore the treatment is mathematically identical.[8]

Yockey is saying that speaking about the genetic code as being the language of life is not merely an analogy. The indescribable significance of this discovery is that the cell has a language of its own, fully equipped with rules—equivalent to a written language—that governs how it communicates. In a more recent work, Yockey explains that information theory has demonstrated that there is a one-to-one correspondence, an *isomorphism*,[9] between the logic system of the genetic text on the one hand, and communication systems, computers, and mathematical logic systems on the other. Yockey says,

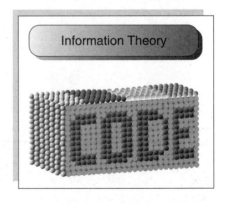

Information Theory

[8]Hubert P. Yockey, "Self Organization, Origin-of-life Scenarios and Information Theory," *Journal of Theoretical Biology*, vol. 91 (1981): 16. A *Markov process* is a phrase used in the discipline of statistics. It concerns itself with analyzing a succession of events within certain parameters, each of which is determined by the event immediately preceding it. This process was named after the Russian mathematician Andrei Markov (1856–1922).

[9]Yockey uses the term *isomorphism* in the mathematical sense, as the one-to-one correspondence between the elements of two sets such that the result of an operation on elements of one set directly corresponds to the result of the operation on their images in the other set. This is indicative of a direct cause-and-effect relationship.

The basic principle on which computers operate is that of the Turing machine (Turing 1937). [Alan Mathison] Turing conceived this abstract model of a computing machine to solve problems in the foundations of mathematics. . . . Turing imagined an abstract machine in which a message or sequence is recorded on an output tape that could be weightless and of infinite length. In computer terminology these messages or sequences are called bit strings because they are expressed in a string of the alphabet (0, 1). . . . There is a reading head that may move in either direction along the tape to read the input, which interacts with a finite number of internal states. These states are called a program in modern computer technology. The program carries out its instructions on the message read from the input tape and the machine stops when the program is executed.

The logic of Turing machines [computers] has an isomorphism [one-to-one relationship] with the logic of the genetic information system. The input tape is DNA and the bit string recorded is the genetic message. The internal states are the tRNA, mRNA, . . . and other factors that implement the genetic code and constitute the genetic logic system. The output tape is the family of proteins specified by the genetic message recorded in DNA. There is also an isomorphism between the information in the instructions on the Turing machine tape and the information in the list of axioms from which theorems are proved. Without noticing these isomorphisms, corresponding properties would appear to be unrelated. But in each of these four cases one has an information source, a transmission of information, a set of instructions or tasks to be completed and an output.[10]

Yockey's work utilizes the concepts and principles developed in communication systems and computers to demonstrate their direct applicability to the problems encountered in molecular biology. For that reason, according to information theory, the genetic logic information system directly corresponds to the logic systems used in computer technology.

To help us visualize the one-to-one correspondence between a written language and the language of the DNA information system, we have referenced two researchers, Lane P. Lester and Raymond G. Bohlin, who offer the following explanation:

The DNA in living cells contains coded information. It is not surprising that so many of the terms used in describing DNA and its functions are language terms. We speak of the genetic *code*. DNA is *transcribed* into RNA. RNA is *translated* into protein. Protein, in a sense, is coded in a foreign *language* from DNA. RNA could be said to be a *dialect* of DNA.

---

[10]Hubert P. Yockey, *Information Theory and Molecular Biology* (Cambridge University Press, 1992), 87–88.

Such designations are not simply convenient or just anthropomorphisms. They accurately describe the situation. . . . The genetic code is composed of four *letters* (nucleotides), which are arranged into sixty-four *words* of three letters each (triplets or codons). These words are organized in sequence to produce *sentences* (genes). Several related sentences are strung together and perform

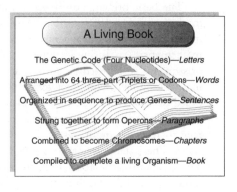

A Living Book

The Genetic Code (Four Nucleotides)—*Letters*

Arranged into 64 three-part Triplets or Codons—*Words*

Organized in sequence to produce Genes—*Sentences*

Strung together to form Operons—*Paragraphs*

Combined to become Chromosomes—*Chapters*

Compiled to complete a living Organism—*Book*

as *paragraphs* (operons). Tens or hundreds of paragraphs comprise *chapters* (chromosomes), and a full set of chapters contains all the necessary information for a readable *book* (organism).[11]

What kind of cause can account for the kind of specialized order and complex information found in the genetic logic system? One way to answer this question is to know what we mean when we say that something is alive.

WHEN DOES NONLIVING MATTER BECOME A LIVING ORGANISM?

We have already learned that the second law of thermodynamics results in an overall high level of disorder in the universe with the increase of time. Naturally, the inverse function of that law (1 divided by the second law or 1/entropy) produces higher overall levels of order as time increases. This reciprocal function of the second law of thermodynamics is called the *law of specificity*. With respect to information (not energy), this law is analogous to turning back the hand of time and getting a system back into its original highlyordered state. In his book *The Philosophical Scientists*, David Foster explains this relationship:

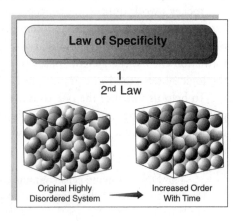

Law of Specificity

$$\frac{1}{2^{nd}\ Law}$$

Original Highly Disordered System → Increased Order With Time

---

[11]Lane P. Lester and Raymond G. Bohlin, *The Natural Limits to Biological Change* (Grand Rapids, Mich.: Zondervan, 1984), 86 (emphasis added).

The running-down of the universe and its winding-up depends upon the same general mathematics with an inverse or NOT relationship. We must agree with Eddington that the Second Law of Thermodynamics is a major law of nature. But we find that it is only half the likely truth and that it has a complement in a sort of *Law of Specificity* which is its obverse using the same general mathematics.[12]

When we study biology, it doesn't take long to encounter the word *species*. The choice of this term, as opposed to some other, is based on the law of *spec*ificity. In fact, it is this law that gives biologists a clear differentiation between nonliving matter and life. This essential distinction was summarized by the famous biologist Leslie Orgel when he said,

> Living organisms are distinguished by their *specified complexity*. Crystals ... fail to qualify as living because they lack *complexity*; random mixtures of polymers fail to qualify because they lack *specificity*.[13]

In other words, when we observe the kind of order found in the crystals of a piece of quartz, it has redundant characteristics—like the message, "CAT, CAT, CAT, CAT"—but it *lacks complexity*. A chain of random polymers (small molecules linked together to form a macromolecule, such as a protein or nucleic acid) has a complex nature, but it *lacks specificity* in that it has no function or carries no message and would appear in a form such as "AG TCTT ACTGG TTCC." However, *specified complexity* has the kind of order that communicates a clear message or function, such as, "THIS SENTENCE IS CARRYING A MESSAGE BY INDICATING THE SPECIFIED COMPLEXITY OF A LIVING ORGANISM." So crystals in a piece of quartz are specified but not complex; random mixtures of polymers are complex but not specified. Life is distinct from nonliving matter in an essential way: it is both *specified* and *complex*.

Can natural forces alone, then, cause this kind of specified complexity? What is the difference between random processes producing order, and intelligence producing highly specified and complex order?

WHAT KIND OF CAUSE PRODUCES HIGHLY SPECIFIED COMPLEXITY?

The following illustration is my (Norman Geisler) updated version of William Paley's famous "watchmaker argument" in light of modern molecular

---

[12]David Foster, *The Philosophical Scientists* (New York: Dorset, 1985), 41.
[13]Leslie Orgel, *The Origins of Life* (New York: Wiley, 1973), 189 (emphasis added).

biology and information theory. It deliberately borrows the format and language of Paley to make the point.

> In crossing a valley, suppose I come upon a round stratified stone and were asked how it came to be such. I might plausibly answer that it was once laid down by water in layers which later solidified by chemical action. One day it broke from a larger section of rock and was subsequently rounded by the natural erosional processes of tumbling in water. Suppose then, upon walking further, I come upon Mount Rushmore where the forms of four human faces appear on a granite cliff. Even if I knew nothing about the origin of the faces, would I not come immediately to believe it was an intelligent production and not the result of natural processes of erosion?
>
> Yet why should a natural cause serve for the stone but not for the faces? For this reason, namely, that when we come to inspect the faces on the mountain we perceive—what we could not discover in the stone—that they manifest intelligent contrivance, that they convey specifically complex information. The stone has redundant patterns or strata easily explainable by the observed natural process of sedimentation. The faces, however, have specially formed features, not merely repeated lines. The stone has rounded features like those we observe to result from natural erosion. The faces, on the other hand, have sharply defined features contrary to those made by erosion. In fact, the faces resemble things known to be made by intelligent artisans. These differences being observed, we would rightly conclude there must have existed at some time and at some place some intelligence that formed them.
>
> Nor would it, I apprehend, weaken the conclusion if we had never seen such a face being chiseled in granite, if we had never known an artisan capable of making one, or if we were wholly incapable of executing such a piece of workmanship ourselves. All this is no more than what is true of some lost art or of some of the more curious productions of modern technology.
>
> Neither, secondly, would it invalidate our conclusion that upon closer examination of the faces they turn out to be imperfectly formed. It is not necessary that a representation be perfect in order to show it was designed.
>
> Nor, thirdly, would it bring any uncertainty in the argument if we were not able to recognize the identity of the faces. Even if we had never known of any such person portrayed, we would still conclude it took intelligence to produce them.
>
> Nor, fourthly, would any man in his senses think the existence of the faces on the rock was accounted for by being told that they were one out of many possible combinations or forms rocks may take, and that this con-

figuration might be exhibited as well as a different structure.

Nor, fifthly, would it yield our inquiry more satisfaction to be answered that there exists in granite a law or principle of order which had disposed it toward forming facial features. We never knew a sculpture made by such a principle of order, nor can we even form an idea of what is meant by such a principle of order distinct from intelligence.

Sixthly, we would be surprised to hear that configurations like this on a mountainside were not proof of intelligent creation but were only to induce the mind to think so.

Seventhly, we would be not less surprised to be informed that the faces resulted simply from the natural processes of wind and water erosion.

Nor, eighthly, would it change our conclusion were we to discover that certain natural objects or powers were utilized in producing the faces. Still the managing of these forces, the pointing and directing them to form such specific faces, demands intelligence.

Neither, ninthly, would it make the slightest difference in our conclusion were we to discover that these natural laws were set up by some intelligent Being. For nothing is added to the power of natural laws by positing an original Designer for them. Designed or not, the natural powers of wind and rain erosion never produce human faces like this in granite.

Nor, tenthly, would it change the matter were we to discover that behind the forehead of a stone face was a computer capable of reproducing other faces on nearby cliffs by laser beams. This would only enhance our respect for the intelligence that designed such a computer.

And, furthermore, were we to find that this computer was designed by another computer we would still not give up our belief in an intelligent cause. In fact, we would have an even greater admiration for the intelligence it takes to create computers that can also create.

In addition, would we not consider it strange if anyone suggested there was no need for an intelligent cause because there might be an infinite regress of computers designing computers? We know that increasing the number of computers in the series does not diminish the need for intelligence to program the whole series. Neither would we allow any limitation on our conclusion (that it takes intelligence to create such specific and complex information) by the claim that this principle applies only to events of the near past but not the most remote past. For what is remote to us was near to those remote from us.

And would we not consider it arbitrary for anyone to insist that the word *science* applies to our reasoning *only* if we assume the face had a natural cause, such as erosion, but not if we conclude it had an intelligent source? For who would insist that an archaeologist is scientific *only* if he posits a non-intelligent natural cause of ancient pottery and tools?

Neither, lastly, would we be driven from our conclusion or from our confidence in it by being told we know nothing at all about how the faces were produced. We know enough to conclude it took intelligence to produce them. The consciousness of knowing little need not beget a distrust of that which we do know. And we do know that natural forces never produce those kinds of effects. We know that the faces on the rock manifest a form such as is produced by intelligence. For as William Paley remarked, "Wherever we see marks of contrivance, we are led for its cause to an intelligent author. And this transition of the understanding is found upon uniform experience."

Suppose also that in studying the genetic structure of a living organism, we discover that its DNA has a highly complicated and unique information code, distinguished by its specified complexity. Also, suppose we observe that living organisms are distinguished by their *specified complexity.* . . . Suppose we discover that the information in living cells follows the same patterns as do combinations of letters used by intelligent beings to convey such information. . . . Noting all this, would we not conclude that it most probably took intelligence to produce a living organism? And would we not arrive at this position with the same degree of confidence with which we conclude that it took to inform the rock to take the specifically complex shape of the face?

What is the basis of the confidence that it takes intelligence to originate such information? Is it not our uniform experience? Is it not true, to quote David Hume, that a "uniform experience amounts to a proof, [so that] here a direct and full proof from the nature of the fact."[14]

In short, is not our belief in the high probability that intelligence produced the various complex information codes of living things based on the scientific principle of uniformity—that "the present is the key to the past"? And since we did not observe the origin of living things, does it not follow that our speculations about these past events are entirely dependent on the trustworthiness of the principle of uniformity (analogy)? But in view of the fact that our experience uniformly indicates the need for intelligence to create such information, is not the hypothesis of a non-intelligent natural cause of living things contrary to the principle of uniformity on which scientific understanding of the past depends?[15]

Yes, science affirms over and over again that it *always* takes intelligence to produce the specified complexity found in *any* living entity. There is no scien-

[14]See David Hume, *An Enquiry Concerning Human Understanding*, ed. Charles W. Hendel (New York: Bobbs-Merrill, 1955; orig. ed. 1748), 123.

[15]Norman L. Geisler and J. Kerby Anderson, *Origin Science: A Proposal for the Creation-Evolution Controversy* (Grand Rapids, Mich.: Baker, 1987), 159–64.

tific law or observational evidence to support the idea that the highly specified and complex information found in a cell can be produced by natural laws.

WHY CAN'T THE FORCES OF NATURE ACCOUNT FOR THE ORIGIN OF LIFE?

The table below provides us with a few illustrations of the distinction between things caused by natural laws and things caused by intelligent design. The left-hand column lists examples exhibiting characteristics produced by non-intelligent natural forces, and the right-hand column displays examples of highly specified and complex order that is always shown to be the result of an intelligent cause.

Non-Intelligent Forces of Nature Random, Redundant, and Complex	Intelligent Design of a Mind Highly Specified and Complex
Redundant patterns in sand drifts	A sand castle
Random/redundant cloud patterns	A message written in the sky
Complex patterns in raw marble	Marble statue of Abraham Lincoln
Random/redundant noise patterns	Highly specified, complex message
Self-generating computer programs	Mind of the computer programmer

The question we must answer for ourselves is "Can the results of an enormous natural explosion the magnitude of the Big Bang, left to itself over a long period of time, produce the kind of highly specified and complex order found in a living organism without the guidance of intelligence?" The evidence from repeated observation strongly confirms that it always takes intelligence to produce the highly specified and complex order that exists in living organisms. Nonliving matter and living organisms may utilize the same basic molecular building, but their essential difference is found in the message on those blocks when they are linked together in a highly specified and complex manner (genetic code).

Recalling the marbles illustration from chapter 5, we ask, "How probable is it that time, energy, and natural (random) forces alone could organize these marbles in such a manner as to spell out the word *code* against a background of so many other possibilities?" This same question applies to the highly specified and complex order we find in living organisms. In fact, it would be interesting to consider the level of improbability associated with the theory that life could emerge merely as the result of time, energy, and natural forces.

Scientists use the second law of thermodynamics to measure the level of disorder (entropy) in a system. The reciprocal function, the law of specificity (1/entropy), is also used to measure the degree of order (specificity) produced in a system. What is the level of improbability of generating the kind of order found in living organisms without the intervention of intelligence, against a backdrop of other possibilities? Let's consider two factors that affect the answer to this ques-

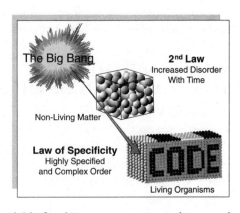

tion. The first is the time that was available for this process to occur; the second is the probability associated with the idea that life might have emerged as a result of random natural forces alone. David Foster helps us with the question of time:

> Specificity is the measure of the improbability of a pattern *which actually occurs* against a background of alternatives. . . . Let us imagine that there is a pack of 52 cards well shuffled and lying face-downwards on a table. What are the chances of picking all the cards up in the correct suit sequence starting with (say) the Ace of Spades and working downwards and then through the other suits and finishing (say) with Two of Clubs? Well, the chance of picking up the first card correctly is 1 in 52, the second card 1 in 51, the third card 1 in 50, the fourth card 1 in 49 and so forth. So the chance of picking up the whole pack correctly is Factorial 52 (i.e., 52!) as one chance in . . . (about) 10^{68}. This number is approaching that of all the atoms in the universe. . . .

- Number of seconds back from now to the estimated date of the Big Bang is 4×10^{17} (say 10^{18}).
- Number of atoms in the universe: 10^{80}.
- Number of photons in the universe: 10^{88}.
- Number of stars in the universe: 10^{22}.
- Number of wavelengths of light to traverse the universe: 2×10^{33}.[16]

If someone believed that the universe was approximately 10^{18} seconds old, how probable is it that natural forces would produce life? Using the law of specificity, the probability of life arising by natural forces alone has been seriously considered by both mathematicians and astronomers.

---

[16]David Foster, *The Philosophical Scientists* (New York: Dorset, 1985), 39–40, 81.

Mathematicians, drawn in by the statistical nature of the problem, have denied the feasibility of random minor mutations producing biological novelty and complexity. Using computers, mathematician Marcel Schutzenberger, found the odds against improving meaningful information by random changes were $10^{-1,000}$. The astronomers Fred Hoyle and Chandra Wickramasinghe placed the probability that life would originate from non-life as $10^{-40,000}$ and the probability of added complexity arising by mutations and natural selection very near this figure.[17]

Scientific conclusions must be based on probability. At best, scientific conclusions depend on a level of probability that a certain cause produced a certain effect. If we were to consider the possibility that life arose without an intelligent cause, we would be forced to move completely out of the realm of science. The number of $10^{40,000}$ is unimaginably larger than the number of atoms in the known universe (10^{80}); therefore, the probability of life arising by chance is much less than the probability of finding one particular atom in the entire universe. Now if scientific models ought to be built upon the highest degree of probability, and $1/10^{1,000-40,000}$ power is in the range of impossibility, then to believe that it is true is to go beyond the scope of science! The *rule of thumb* in physics is that once the probability of an event decreases below $1/10^{50}$, it has entered the realm of the *impossible.*

The amount of numbers involved with the odds mentioned above is hard to imagine. Michael Denton may help us grasp their order of magnitude.

> Numbers in the order of 10^{15} are of course completely beyond comprehension. Imagine an area about half the size of the USA (one million square miles) covered in a forest of trees containing ten thousand trees per square mile. If each tree contained ten thousand leaves, the total number of leaves in the forest would be 10^{15}, equivalent to the number of connections in the human brain![18]

For us to believe that purely natural forces could have produced the kind of highly specified and complex order mentioned above, we would have to make an utterly blind leap of faith! Moreover, in light of the science of information theory, we would be forced to reject the conclusions discovered in that field, which confirm the need for life to have an intelligent cause. For these reasons, we reject the idea that life could have risen out of non-living matter by natural forces alone.

[17]Lane P. Lester and Raymond G. Bohlin, *The Natural Limits to Biological Change* (Grand Rapids, Mich.: Zondervan, 1984), 86.
[18]Michael Denton, *Evolution: A Theory in Crisis* (Bethesda: Adler & Adler, 1986), 330.

HOW DOES INFORMATION THEORY CONFIRM AN INTELLIGENT CAUSE?

Actually, it is misleading to cast the argument for an intelligent cause of life in terms of probability, for the sciences of information theory and molecular biology have verified that the genetic code in a living cell (A, T, C, and G) is *mathematically identical* to a written language. Therefore, we can think of it as being characteristic of having intelligently imposed boundaries, or conditions, on it in the same manner as an author who uses specific letters to write a book.

There are all kinds of books that utilize the same letters of the alphabet, but they communicate radically different ideas. For example, the same author may write one book on ethics and another book on science. Now consider the fact that both books consist of the same material (paper and ink), but the messages are distinctly different. The essential discrepancy between the two books is the way the author specifies which letters of the alphabet to use to signify certain words and their order (specified boundaries).

Next, the words are linked together by the mind of the author to formulate sentences. Sentences are constructed in such a way that they form paragraphs. When enough paragraphs are written, a chapter emerges. Finally, the chapters are compiled to produce a book on ethics. Each step along the way requires the author to intelligently manipulate the letters and organize the words, sentences, paragraphs, and chapters by imposing specified boundary conditions upon the written materials. However, when the same author writes a book on science, the process, spelling rules, and principles of grammar are the same, but the author must use *intelligence* to specify different boundary conditions.

A *boundary condition* is a restriction on the working of nature. It is a term that has a long history of use in physics. In information theory, the equivalent of a boundary condition is the term *specified complexity*. What is of critical importance in communication is not the agency or material being used to communicate, but the boundary conditions associated with the material.

Consider the effects of a skywriter who imposes a boundary on smoke by intelligently controlling its release from an airplane. No physical boundary has been imposed. The only boundary imposed upon the smoke is a boundary of thought. In other words, the material itself does not form its own boundaries—an intelligent agent imposes them on the material. A boundary of thought was also imposed on the stone of Mount Rushmore in order to form the faces of the presidents there. Likewise, a boundary condition of thought would need to be imposed on the sand of the beach if we were to write a message such as "It took no intelligence to write this message." In each case the boundary condition had its origin in intelligent thought and was *then* imposed on inert material, whether it was smoke, stone, or sand.

Two points arise out of the discussion about boundary conditions and specified complexity. First, in a communication system like a book, the boundary condition itself is what is of interest. In other words, the communication is the boundary condition, and the communication is independent of the medium by which it is conveyed. The communication is the same whether it is written on paper, stone, sand, or with smoke released from a plane. The medium, however, does affect the degree of permanency. The second point arising from the discussion is that specified complexity and communication-type boundary conditions are known experientially to arise by the intelligent shaping of matter, that is, by a primary efficient cause.[19]

Operation science confirms that the specified complexity associated with things such as books are accounted for by intelligent causes. It has never been demonstrated that books result from explosions in printing factories! Herein lies an essential problem for anyone who believes that matter, time, and natural forces represent the only reality in the universe. One scientist described the purely naturalistic macroevolutionary model of the origin of life as

> an attempt to explain the formation of the genetic code from the chemical components of DNA without the aid of a genetic concept (information) originating outside the molecules of the chromosomes. This is comparable to the assumption that the text of a book originates from the paper molecules on which the sentences appear, and not from any external source of information (external, that is, to the paper molecules). . . . Hence the genetic "Book of Life," genetic information, stems allegedly from the "paper" on which it is written—the nucleotides, bases, and amino acids which comprise DNA. Chance is believed to have synthesized this genetic information onto matter.[20]

It is time to draw this discussion to a close and decide whether or not the origin of life happened as the result of natural forces alone or by intelligent design. We believe that the macroevolutionary explanation for the origin of the genetic text violates the laws and observational evidence of science. As previously mentioned, in studying the information content of the DNA molecular

---

[19]Norman L. Geisler and J. Kerby Anderson, *Origin Science: A Proposal for the Creation-Evolution Controversy* (Grand Rapids, Mich.: Baker, 1987), 141–42.
[20]A. E. Wilder-Smith, *The Natural Sciences Know Nothing of Evolution* (Costa Mesa, Calif.: Word for Today, 1981), 4–5.

system, one discovers that there are very specific terms used to describe the DNA molecule and its function. When molecular biologists use words such as *information, code translation,* and *program,* are they not using words that everyone associates with the concept of intelligence? *Intelligence* is a term used to signify the capacity for reasoning and understanding and for similar forms of mental activity.[21] If so, what kind of intelligence can have the know-how needed to produce the specified complexity of life?

WHAT KIND OF INTELLIGENT CAUSE DESIGNED THE GENETIC TEXT?

NASA's Search for Extra Terrestrial Intelligence (SETI) has prompted the use of large radio telescopes aimed into deep space. The purpose of SETI is to receive some type of transmission (communication). Carl Sagan said,

> The receipt of a *single message* from space would show that it is possible to live through such technological adolescence; the transmitting *civilization,* after all, has survived. Such knowledge, it seems to me, might be worth a great price.[22]

A single message from outer space, even one sentence, would be enough proof for scientists of the caliber of the late Carl Sagan to conclude that intelligent life had caused it. Using the same kind of reasoning, one can also conclude that the origin of the genetic code discovered in the first living cell had an intelligent cause. In fact, the conclusion would be even more probable if the information content in the first form of life was greater than a single message from space. This thought prompts us to ask, "How much information existed in the first life form of a single cell?"

The science of information theory tells us that DNA and its functions are mathematically identical to a written language. But how much information is there in a single cell, the kind of primitive cell that we have been investigating? Atheist Richard Dawkins, professor of zoology at Oxford University, acknowledged that

> each [cell] nucleus . . . contains a digitally coded database larger in information content than all 30 volumes of the *Encyclopedia Britannica* put together. And this figure is for *each* cell, not all the cells of a body put together. . . . Some species of the unjustly called "primitive" amoebas have

---

[21] *Webster's Encyclopedic Unabridged Dictionary of the English Language* (Avenel: Gramercy, 1989), 739.
[22] Carl Sagan, *Bocca's Brain* (New York: Ballantine, 1988), 322 (emphasis added).

as much information in their DNA as 1,000 [volumes of the] *Encyclopedia Britannica.*[23]

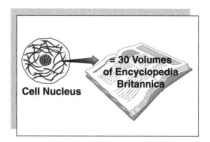

Accounting for the amount of information stored in a single cell apart from an intelligent cause is only one aspect of the problem. Just consider the kind of mind needed to design the mechanisms necessary to compress and encode *1,000 volumes of data* to fit into a highly compressed area (less than one-thousandth of an inch) as that of a single cell!

So if a single cell can contain up to 1,000 volumes of highly specified and complex information, how much information is the human brain capable of storing? Carl Sagan said,

The information content of the brain expressed in bits is probably comparable to the total number of connections among the neurons— about a hundred trillion, 10^{14}, bits. If written out in English, say, that information would fill some twenty million volumes, as many as in the world's largest libraries. The equivalent of twenty million books is inside the heads of everyone of us. The brain is a very big place in a very small space.[24]

The human brain is capable of storing twenty million volumes of genetic information—an inconceivable amount! In fact, it is roughly equivalent to the Library of Congress. Is this kind of information and retrieval system the cumulative result of random processes?

We mentioned that according to Carl Sagan, a single message would be enough to convince us that an intelligent cause was behind that message. *If a single message from space can bring about the conviction that it had an intelligent cause, what about 1,000 volumes of information found in a single cell?* The appearance of life on earth was a clear message, 1,000 volumes long! What if NASA's radio telescopes captured from space a few dozen CDs containing the information equivalent of 1,000 volumes of the *Encyclopedia Britannica?*

---

[23]Richard Dawkins, *The Blind Watchmaker* (New York: W. W. Norton & Co., 1987), 17–18, 116.
[24]Carl Sagan, *Cosmos* (New York: Ballantine, 1980), 230.

Would they not immediately recognize that the cause of such information had to be intelligent? Of course they would, and so do we!

Therefore, we conclude that the law of specified complexity, coupled with the first principles of uniformity and causality, justifies the belief that the origin of life had a super-intelligent cause. Since this super-intelligent cause also brought the space-time universe into existence, it must be more than natural. Consequently, the supernatural power that brought the universe into existence also designed and created the first life forms and must be a supernaturally intelligent Being.

WHAT ELSE CAN WE KNOW ABOUT THIS SUPER-INTELLIGENT BEING?

Take a moment to consider once again the computer analogy. Computers are composed of two major elements: *hardware* and *software*. The hardware is the material part of a computer, while the software corresponds to the intelligence that gives the computer its know-how or instructions. With regard to our inquiry of this super-intelligent Being who designed and created the genetic logic system, David Foster notes,

> In searching for "what is behind the DNA" it would seem that we have entered the realm of *software*. Molecular biology can find no trace of further hardware which is upstream from the DNA, and since the DNA is known to be coded, then *we are not looking for more physical facts but for mental functions*. Until the invention of electronic computers such an approach might have been considered as pure metaphysics, but the opening up of the computer art tells us that software is both "real" and as important as hardware. . . . If we now transfer our thoughts from man-made computers to "what is behind DNA," we have little choice but to imagine that there is a correspondence. Now "what is behind man-made computers" is not a thing; it is pure logic. In the DNA we have seen the "thing" or hardware of natural computing, but we need to invent a term for the logic of the system and there seems no more appropriate word than *LOGOS*. This Greek word means word or reason, the mind-stuff itself.[25]

The "what" behind the DNA is really anchored in the mind of the "who," *Logos*, behind the design of the DNA information system. This Supermind programmed the genetic logic system and all physical reality. However, science is limited to what it can discover about this *Logos*. Science cannot get behind

[25]David Foster, *The Philosophical Scientists* (New York: Dorset, 1985), 88–89 (emphasis added).

the hardware in order to detect anything else about what the software or its programmer is like. It is up to other disciplines to provide correspondence to the programmer—*Logos*. Science was used to discover three major attributes that correspond to this *Logos*—it is infinitely powerful, eternal (outside of time), and super-intelligent. Since this *Logos* is outside of time, we can also logically conclude that it is not subject to temporal change because change requires time. Therefore, this *Logos* must be an infinitely powerful, intelligent, and unchanging Being.

WHICH WORDVIEW IS TRUE (BEST CORRESPONDS TO REALITY)?

It may be a good idea to review the cumulative conclusions that have been drawn thus far. The test method[26] being used to discover the truth about reality utilizes the principle of the unity of truth (the coherence principle) and identifies and prioritizes the first principles of the academic disciplines that make up the various parts of the intellectual lens. As the first three parts (first principles) of this intellectual lens[27] were set into place in a coherent manner, we ob-

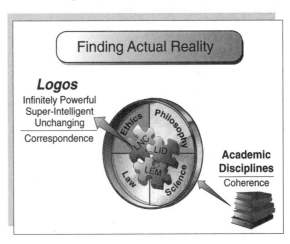

served a *correspondence* between the conclusions reached and the most essential characteristics of reality. This view of reality (worldview) has now become our interpretive framework by which the facts of this world can be explained. In other words, the conclusions drawn from the first disciplines of logic, philosophy, cosmology, molecular biology, and information theory have ruled out atheism and pantheism as viable worldviews. As we continue to learn more about reality from the first principles in the forthcoming chapters, we must also make every effort to see that their *priority* and *coherence* are protected.

---

[26]See chapter 2 in order to review the method of testing the truth claims of worldviews.

[27]The law of noncontradiction in logic, the unchanging reality in philosophy, and the principle of causality in science.

Only theistic conclusions agree with the first principles related to the nature of truth, the nature of the cosmos, and the existence and knowability of an infinitely powerful, intelligent, and unchanging Being (*Logos*). In a few of the forthcoming chapters we will be dealing with topics such as law, human rights, evil, and ethics. We plan to show that only

	Atheism	Pantheism	Theism
Truth	Relative, No Absolutes	Relative to This World	Absolute Truth Exists
Cosmos	Always Existed	Not Real– Illusion	Created Reality
God (Logos)	Does Not Exist	Exists, Unknowable	Exists, Knowable

theism in general (and Christian theism in particular) offers a rational justification for, and coherent explanation of, the questions arising from a study of these issues. Furthermore, we will offer reasons as to why atheism and pantheism violate the first principles associated with these subjects and fail to offer valid answers to the questions raised by discussing them.

7
QUESTIONS ABOUT MACROEVOLUTION

If it could be demonstrated that any complex organ existed, which could not possibly have been formed by numerous, successive, slight modifications, my theory would absolutely break down.

—CHARLES DARWIN

WHAT IS MACROEVOLUTION?

Macroevolution is a theory or model of origins that holds to the idea that all varieties of life forms emanated from a single cell or "common ancestor." Macroevolutionists believe that once the first living cells came into existence, it was just a matter of time, natural selection,[1] and random molecular biological changes in their genetic information systems (mutations) that caused new characteristics (*microevolutionary* changes) to occur. According to Darwinism, these small, successive microevolutionary changes came about via random genetic variations initiated by a changing environment, which exerted various pressures

---

[1]Natural selection, according to Darwinism, is the process by which plants and animals adapt to a changing environment over a long period of time; eventually this process is supposed to give rise to organisms so different from the original population that new species are formed. See *Oxford Dictionary of Biology* (New York: Oxford University Press, 1996), 338.

on the organisms. This prompted them to mutate in order to survive, and eventually the most adaptable organisms did (survival of the fittest). Survival was accomplished in certain organisms by surpassing the natural biological limits with respect to their species and giving rise to a new species[2] (*macroevolution*).

Based upon this Darwinian model of the "origin of species," macroevolutionists believe that *every* species has a common ancestor, including the human race. Hence, according to macroevolution, human life ultimately is the result of a series of microevolutionary changes over a long period of time, starting with the first living cells and eventually giving rise to humanity.

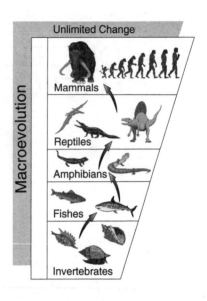

ARE THERE VARIATIONS OF MACROEVOLUTION?

The most commonly held view of macroevolution is known as *gradualism*. Following Darwin, two famous scientists who hold this view, which is the classical understanding of Darwinism, are Stephen Hawking and Richard Dawkins. Gradualism asserts that very long periods of time are needed to accomplish what is known as *transitional* or *intermediate* forms of life. An intermediate form of life is macroevolution "in process." In other words it is a life form in transition that possesses some of the characteristics of the species it once belonged to and some of the attributes that will eventually make it a completely new species. Consequently, this model of origins states that new life forms appeared gradually as a product of natural selection and genetic mutations over very long periods of time (usually millions of years).

The most recent variation of the macroevolutionary model is called *punctuated equilibria.* One prominent name associated with this theory is one of its designers, Stephen Jay Gould (paleontologist and professor of biology at Har-

---

[2]We are using the term *species* as understood in biology to mean "a category used in the classification of organisms that consist of a group of similar individuals that can usually breed among themselves and produce fertile offspring." See *Oxford Dictionary of Biology* (New York: Oxford University Press, 1996), 477.

vard University). Gould's colleague, Niles Eldredge (paleontologist at the American Museum of Natural History in New York City), assisted in conceptualizing this variation. Both men have acknowledged that the observational evidence (fossil remains of a life form in transition) predicted by the theory of macroevolution and needed to support gradualism is severely lacking. They have thus proposed a variant explanation of macroevolution, which states that new life forms were created by "rapid bursts of speciation" (this view is explained and analyzed below). Gould and Eldredge have suggested that these rapid bursts of macroevolution happened over relatively short periods of time (usually hundreds to thousands of years) as opposed to the millions of years required by gradualism.[3] This theory still maintains that new life forms appear as a product of unlimited random genetic mutations, but *at a highly accelerated rate*, leaving little or no trace of intermediate forms of life in the fossil record.

WHAT IS THE DESIGN MODEL?

The design model is a theory of origins asserting that all life forms were designed to experience only limited genetic variations (microevolution) in order to adapt to and survive the stresses caused by environmental changes. Some forms of life were not able to adapt to their surroundings because they had reached their design limitations and consequently died out (extinction). Theists who hold to this form of the design model believe that observation confirms microevolutionary variations in degree within a certain *kind*.[4] This model predicted that the fossil record would not bear witness to transitional forms but would manifest evidence of life forms appearing on earth abruptly and fully formed, confirming their cause: sudden bursts of creation. Moreover, this model predicted that the basic life forms would experience limited change and exhibit no directional modifications during their tenure on earth.

The design model maintains that life forms experience only limited microevolutionary changes over long periods of time and also asserts that the similarities among the life forms are the result of common design specifications—not a common ancestor. According to the design model, this interdependent design criterion is linked to the fact that all life forms share a com-

---

[3]Stephen Jay Gould, *The Panda's Thumb* (New York: W. W. Norton & Co., 1982), 181–84.
[4]It is important to note that the term *kind*, in the design model, refers to a created kind. This model suggests that information theory, as it is applied to molecular biology, demonstrates that there exists a definite limit to biological change. Although variation occurs to allow for adaptation, we plan to show that the evidence clearly confirms that all alternative expressions are still essentially of the same basic created kind. This allows for extensive variability *within the created kind* with respect to the limitations imposed on the organism by the laws governing the information content of the genetic text.

mon environment and must be able to function properly within their ecosystem. Therefore, based upon that design, this model also predicted that some severe environmental changes could cause a mass extinction of certain life forms.

ARE THERE VARIATIONS OF THE DESIGN MODEL?

Basically, there are three variant forms of the design model. Two vary with respect to time and the third with respect to mechanism. The first variation of the design model is held by theists who believe that the space-time universe and all life forms were constructed in six successive twenty-four-hour days. Their view is known as the *young earth view.* Other theists maintain that the material universe and all life forms were assembled in a progressive series of stages, each stage separated by a long period of time. Theists holding this view believe each time interval allowed the newly created entity in the environment to be properly *phased in*—which gradually allowed the ecosystem to reach its natural equilibrium, or balancing point. This variation of the design model is referred to as the *progressive creation view.* These views differ with respect to time but essentially agree that operation science and the observational evidence of the existing fossil record do not support any kind of macroevolutionary model of origins.

The third variation of the design model is known as *theistic evolution.* Theistic evolutionists affirm the need for an intelligent first cause of all life forms. However, they believe that this intelligent cause used the process of macro-evolution to bring about new life forms. Theistic evolutionists borrow ideas from both the design and macroevolutionary models. Although theistic macro-evolution can be placed under the design variation category, we will critique it as a variant form of macroevolution. Our reason for doing so is that if we can show that macroevolution is not a viable scientific model, then any form of macroevolution will automatically be disqualified as well. If our argument holds—that is, if the observational evidence and laws of science do not support macroevolution—then we need not concern ourselves with any prefix or label (such as "theistic") that is attached to a macroevolutionary model.

In considering the basic variations of all the origin models under consideration in this chapter, we have put together the following flowchart.

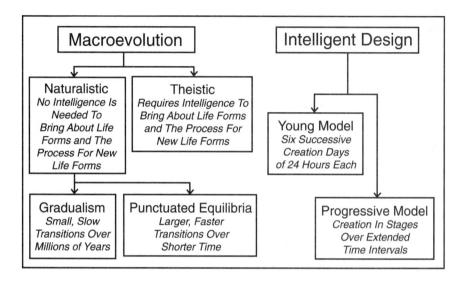

As we examine the variations of both design and macroevolution, it is critically important to be constantly aware of the differentiation that must be made between *operation* science and *origin* science. We cannot allow any unsupported ideas about the origin of new life forms to be injected into the flow of this analysis prior to operation science conclusions. If we do so, we will be *begging the question*, which occurs when an unjustifiable assumption is slipped into an argument to support a conclusion that has not yet been established.

For example, Stephen Jay Gould has said that the mechanism for macroevolution is indeed unknown, yet he also stated in the same breath that it is insignificant with respect to the *fact* of macroevolution. He said, "Our continuing struggle to understand how evolution happens (the theory of evolution) does not cast our documentation of its occurrence—the 'fact of evolution'—into doubt."[5] Gould has openly acknowledged that the mechanism (*how* macroevolution happened) is not really known, but the "fact of evolution" (*that* it happened) is certain. This is a simple case of *question begging*—the conclusion (macroevolution is a fact) is used as an assumption (macroevolution happened). Stated more forthrightly, Gould should have said, "I know that macroevolution is true because it has happened, and I know it has happened because it is true."

Taking for granted that somehow macroevolution came to pass and that there are no natural limitations to biological change is an extremely substantial

---

[5]Stephen Jay Gould, "The Verdict on Creationism," *New York Times Magazine*, July 19, 1987, 34.

and highly questionable assumption that must be justified. With respect to the "documentation" of macroevolution, we will attempt to show that the fossil record reveals no such evidence. We will keep all assumptions, hidden or open, from influencing origin models until they can be shown to be both philosophically and scientifically justified.

HOW SHOULD ORIGIN MODELS BE EVALUATED?

We are suggesting that in order to determine if any origin model is credible, it should adhere to philosophical first principles and must not violate the laws of science. Our goal is to ascertain which model, design (limited biological adaptation—microevolution) or macroevolution (unlimited biological adaptation), best conforms to these criteria. Stephen Hawking also adds two more test elements:

> A theory is a good theory if it satisfies two requirements: It must accurately describe a large class of observations on the basis of a model that contains only a few arbitrary elements, and it must make definite predictions about the results of future observations.[6]

Besides conforming to first principles and scientific laws, the credibility of each model depends upon the accuracy of explaining a "large class" of observational evidence and testing the exactness of the "definite" predictions each model makes with respect to future observations. For example, the macroevolutionary model asserts that there are no biological limits to microevolutionary change and predicts that the fossil record will support this claim with the discovery of transitional fossils. In contrast, the design model states that there are boundaries to biological adaptation (microevolution) and predicts that the fossil record will show the abrupt appearance of fully developed new life forms. *The goal of each model should be to offer an explanation for the appearance of new life forms, with special attention given to the emergence of human life.* Once the laws of science and the empirical evidence have been set forth, we should be able to judge for ourselves which model of origins conforms most nearly to the established criteria.

We plan to argue that the theory of macroevolution is untenable by showing that it is not substantiated by operation science. First, we will analyze the alleged mechanism by which the process of macroevolution is supposed to have taken place (natural selection and genetic mutations). Next, we will examine

[6]Stephen W. Hawking, *A Brief History of Time* (New York: Bantam, 1992), 9.

the fossil record to see if there is enough observational evidence to satisfy the predictions made by the gradualist view of the macroevolutionary model.

After showing the deficiencies associated with the gradualist view, we will turn to the relatively new variant form of macroevolution, an hypothesis called *punctuated equilibria.* We intend to argue for its implausibility as well. Furthermore, it will be shown that the only logical alternative is the design model. We will then test this model in order to determine if it is a viable scientific option, that is, if it meets the criteria of a good theory. If it is and does, we need only present all the data concerning origins in a systematic way to see which variation of the design model—the young earth view or the progressive creation view—most accurately corresponds to all of the evidence.

DOESN'T NATURAL SELECTION SUPPORT MACROEVOLUTION?

Every origin model must answer the question "What produced this effect?" A model of origins needs a cause that accomplishes the work involved. In the case of natural causes, there must be a natural process or mechanism that can produce the effect. Microevolution accounts for variation *within* a given kind, but macroevolution must provide a mechanism that explains how one form of life is eventually transformed into another. For that reason, one of the first questions that needs to be answered is "Are there any genetic or biological boundaries (design limitations) that exist within the structure of genetic kinds?"

If, as evolutionary theory asserts, there are no limits to biological change, one must also ask, "How does the organism know what kind of genetic mutation is needed in order to become the kind of entity that will be able to survive in the new environment?" Let us not forget that a selection implies the concept of choosing between alternatives and that to do so requires intelligence. *DNA, in and of itself, has no mind for choosing anything, let alone selecting a new code for survival.* How can there be a goal or selection without intelligence involved in the process? In other words, how does an organism know that it must adapt to its environment in order to keep existing? Why doesn't it just die out? These questions bring us back to the only logical answer—cells must have been pre-programmed by an intelligent mind that designed them to experience limited adaptation to a changing environment. With these design parameters in place, certain environmental changes would trigger specific adjustments within the biological system and allow it to adapt itself to the changing ecosystem as far as its limits will allow.

For instance, think of a computer that monitors and operates an airplane when the pilot switches to autopilot. The computer was designed to sense the changes in pressure, altitude, wind velocity, and other dynamics in order to make the appropriate changes to the essential systems that will keep the plane on its course. However, if the environment is altered beyond the parameters programmed into the computer, either the pilot takes over or the results are disastrous.

Macroevolutionists insist, though, that there are no limitations to changing biological systems. Of course, macroevolution "in process" cannot be observed; the great evolutionary transitions are considered to be a singularity (they are alleged to have happened only once). Therefore, macroevolutionists appeal to an *analogy* called *artificial selection* to support their claim. They maintain that since artificial selection can produce significant changes over short periods of time, then natural selection would produce even greater changes over long periods of time. In order to decide if their analogy is valid, we need only test it.

First of all, we must recognize that analogies do not prove; they merely clarify or illustrate. An analogy is credible only if its elements have more similarities than differences. If the opposite is true, then it is not a valid analogy. Our task is to demonstrate the implausibility of this particular one, which has already been carefully examined and is cited in the following table[7]:

	The Crucial Differences	
	Artificial selection	**Natural selection**
Goal	• Aim (end) in view	• No aim (end) in view
Process	• Intelligently guided process	• Blind process
Choices	• Intelligent choice of breeds	• No intelligent choice of breeds
Protection	• Breeds guarded from destructive forces	• Breeds not guarded from destructive forces
Freaks	• Preserves desired freaks	• Eliminates most freaks
Interruptions	• Continued interruption to reach desired goal	• No continued interruptions to reach any goal
Survival	• Preferential survival	• Nonpreferential survival

The comparison clearly shows that rather than being similar, artificial selection and natural selection are in the most critical respects exactly the opposite.

---

[7]Norman L. Geisler and J. Kerby Anderson, *Origin Science* (Grand Rapids, Mich.: Baker, 1987), 149.

For this reason, the analogy is not a good one and does not provide any observational evidence to support the credibility of natural selection as a valid mechanism for macroevolution. Even so, some macroevolutionists still maintain that artificial selection demonstrates the validity of natural selection, and they appeal to operation science by citing research projects such as the fruit fly experiments.

WHAT ABOUT THE FRUIT FLY EXPERIMENTS?

Macroevolutionists maintain that blind processes produced the specified complexity of life by mutations mainly occurring during DNA replication, through the deletion, addition, or change of a single nucleotide. But the truth is that *mutations are mistakes, errors that violate the rules of spelling and grammar in the language of DNA*. These mistakes are analogous to errors made while retyping a manuscript. Macroevolutionists claim that this is the means by which the genetic structure of an organism changes and brings about biological breakthroughs capable of producing new life forms. Yet how can mistakes be the basis for adaptation? Adaptations to environmental change require knowledge of what is needed to change in order to survive as one of the fittest. What we can see is that for adaptations to be meaningful they must be the result of intelligent design, not the product of blind forces and time.

In an attempt to provide observational evidence to sustain their view, macroevolutionists put their hypothesis to the test with what has come to be known as the "genetic workhorse" of macroevolution: a fruit fly named *Drosophila*. Macroevolutionary scientists have tried to change Drosophila through a variety of means over the past seventy-five years or so in an effort to force it to mutate into some new life form. However, *even with intelligent intervention*, and under laboratory-controlled conditions, all of the efforts of macroevolutionists have been in vain. Drosophila remains what it has always been—a fruit fly. Instead of demonstrating that genetic boundaries do not exist, Drosophila has proved just the opposite.[8]

Why can't macroevolutionary geneticists get Drosophila to become a new life form? The simple answer is that the genetic code of the fruit fly was constructed with certain limits, and the information needed to transform that code into a new life form does not exist within the molecular structure or design parameters of Drosophila. Furthermore, a new genetic type requires more than just gene modification—it needs new genetic information/material, including

---

[8]Lane P. Lester and Raymond G. Bohlin, *The Natural Limits to Biological Change* (Grand Rapids, Mich.: Zondervan, 1984), 88–89. (To be fair, we should point out that turning Drosophila into some type of novel entity was not a stated goal of original researchers.)

the intelligence to construct it. Consequently, if intelligent macroevolutionists cannot accomplish this task by their own ingenuity, why should we consider the idea that it could happen by acci-dental genetic variations? We there-fore conclude that if scientific theories are to remain scientific, they must re-side strictly within the parameters of operation science. The fruit fly exper-iments provide solid observational ev-idence confirming the implausibility of both artificial and natural selection as viable mechanisms in support of macroevolution. In fact, their research serves as strong observational evidence to authenticate the design model's

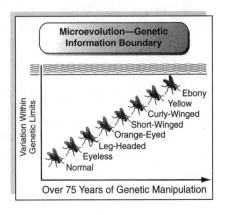

claim that microevolutionary variation occurs within the range of genetic limits.

WHAT ABOUT THE USE OF COMPUTER MODELS AND ANALOGIES?

Some scientists call upon mathematical models and other analogies to show that chance genetic mutations, over long periods of time, can produce the spec-ified complexity required for life and for new life forms to arise. For example, Stephen Hawking refers to "the well-known horde of monkeys hammering away at the typewriters—most of what they write will be garbage, but very occasionally by pure chance they will type out one of Shakespeare's sonnets."[9] In a similar manner, could not random mutations produce this kind of order that would eventually give rise to the first form of life (a single cell) and new life forms?

The test we used to determine the credibility of the analogy between arti-ficial and natural selection could also be used to test the monkey analogy as well. Before we do so, it is important to note that macroevolutionists use many other analogies based on circumstantial evidence, including comparative anat-omy, embryology, comparative biochemistry, and comparative chromosome structure. Yet *all fail to prove anything with respect to observational evidence and operation science.* On that account, this will be the last analogy we analyze be-

---

[9]Stephen W. Hawking, *A Brief History of Time* (New York: Bantam, 1988), 123.

cause our purpose is to test the validity of the foundational aspects of origin models, not to give a survey of the circumstantial evidence.

We need only go back to operation science and the first principle of molecular biology with respect to information theory—the law of specified complexity. This law has confirmed that the information content of the genetic text cannot arise without an intelligent cause. Intelligence is a necessary precondition for the origin of any informational code, including the genetic code, no matter how much time is given. Therefore, any analogy that attempts to account for the genetic code without the use of intelligent intervention automatically disqualifies itself as a scientific explanation.

Furthermore, to propose that monkeys sitting at typewriters, given enough time, will eventually type out one of Shakespeare's sonnets goes far beyond the scope of science with respect to statistics. One statistician decided to tackle the probability of such an endeavor:

> On a computer, William Bennett set one trillion monkeys to typewriters, typing ten keys a second at random. We would have to wait a trillion times the estimated age of the universe before we would even see the sentence, "To be, or not to be: that is the question." It may not be theoretically impossible for a pot of water to freeze when placed on a lighted stove burner, but the *real* probability is so absurd that it is hardly worth talking about.[10]

As hard as it is to imagine monkeys sitting quietly at their work stations typing away, it is harder still to imagine that there are no monkeys tearing up papers and throwing typewriters off of desks—not all monkeys are constructive. And neither are mutations. In fact, almost all, if not all, mutations are destructive mistakes that are harmful to the survival of the organism.

Richard Dawkins gives a more creative and modified version of the same analogy, but in such a way as to make it appear more feasible. He says,

> I don't know who first pointed out that, given enough time, a monkey bashing away at random on a typewriter could produce all the works of Shakespeare. The operative phrase is, of course, given enough time. Let us limit the task facing our monkey somewhat. Suppose that he has to produce, not the complete works of Shakespeare but just the short sentence "Methinks it is like a weasel," and we shall make it relatively easy by giving him a typewriter with a restricted keyboard, one with just 26 (capital)

---

[10]William R. Bennett, Jr., *Scientific and Engineering Problem Solving With the Computer* (Englewood Cliffs: Prentice Hall, 1976), referenced in Lane P. Lester and Raymond G. Bohlin, *The Natural Limits to Biological Change* (Grand Rapids, Mich.: Zondervan, 1984), 157–58.

letters, and a space bar. How long will he take to write this one little sentence? . . . The chance of it getting the entire phrase right is . . . about 1 in 10,000 million million million million million million. To put it mildly, the phrase we seek would be a long time coming, to say nothing of the complete works of Shakespeare. So much for single-step selection of random variation. What about cumulative selection; how much more effective should this be? Very very much more effective. . . . We again use our computer monkey, but with a crucial difference in its program. It again begins by choosing random sequence of 28 letters [characters], just as before:

WDLMNLT DTJBKWIRZREZLMQCO P

It now "breeds from" this random phrase. It duplicates it repeatedly, but with a certain chance of random error—"mutation"—in the copying. The computer examines the mutant nonsense phrases, the "progeny" of the original phrase, and chooses the one which, *however slightly*, most resembles the target phrase, METHINKS IT IS LIKE A WEASEL.[11]

Note how Dawkins' analogy is moving further and further away from nonintelligent, chance mutations. He agrees that "single-step" selection will not work. (By "single-step," he is referring to a mutation that gets "erased" after it mutates and must begin again from where it was before it mutated.) He then suggests that the mutation that is heading in the "right" direction is stored in order to be acted upon at a later time. This cumulative effect (the storage of favorable mutant forms of the organism) allegedly will help the organism reach its intended goal, which he calls the "target." Yet how this organism "knows" what that target is or even how it can "know" is not explained.

That doesn't stop Dawkins. He continues his illustration by pointing out how much faster the computer monkey was able to reach its "target phrase" by using the cumulative selection method as opposed to the single-step selection.

There is a big difference, then, between the cumulative selection (in which each improvement, however slight, is used as a basis for future building), and single-step selection (in which each new "try" is a fresh one). If evolution had to rely on single-step selection, it would never have got anywhere. If, however, there was any way in which the necessary conditions for *cumulative* selection could have been set up by the *blind forces of nature*, strange and wonderful might have been the consequences. As a matter of fact that is exactly what happened on this planet.[12]

We must stop right here and look at those last two sentences again. "If . . .

[11]Richard Dawkins, *The Blind Watchmaker* (New York: W. W. Norton & Co., 1987), 46–48.
[12]Ibid., 49 (emphasis added).

the *necessary conditions . . .* could have been set up by *blind forces . . .* As a *matter of fact* that is exactly what happened." Wait a minute—what happened and how did it happen? Are we to accept the scientifically unjustified assumption "If the necessary conditions could have been set up by blind forces" as a true major premise by a pure leap of "blind" faith? Are we supposed to believe it is "a matter of fact" and not just some desperate effort to help Dawkins explain how macroevolution is a viable model? How did the "blind forces of nature" set up the *necessary conditions* and write a software program (information) similar to Dawkins' computer program when only hardware (matter) existed? Who wrote the original program? The validity of Dawkins' entire proposition rests upon the credibility of his major premise. And this major premise contains an incredibly unjustifiable assumption that again reveals circular reasoning.

How the *necessary conditions* for highly specified and complex information were established is the most significant aspect of the theory of macroevolution. Dawkins neglects and, in doing so, fails to speak directly to the fundamentals of science by giving an account for how that information came to be (the principle of causality). He circuitously shows, by his computer analogy, that there must be a direct relationship between information (mind/software) and molecular structure (matter/hardware). Yet he never offers an explanation for how mindless matter is able to set up the necessary conditions for anything, let alone the specified complexity needed for life and new life forms.

The following citation is extensive and may be difficult to follow. However, if you take your time and read it carefully, it will help you to see why the mutation of matter, single-step or cumulative, is insufficient to produce new life forms.

The ink molecules mediating the contents of this book possess their own chemical architecture, rendering the written sentences black, legible, and perceptible. This architecture of the molecules exists as a closed system and makes the ink—or the printer's ink—black. Simultaneously, it also provides a basis for the superimposed

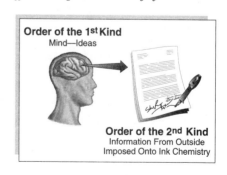

Order of the 1st Kind
Mind—Ideas

Order of the 2nd Kind
Information From Outside
Imposed Onto Ink Chemistry

code-form of a language. This written form of language is based on the architecture of the printer's ink, without originating from it. The information contained within the molecules of printer's ink does not in the least provide the basis for the contents, the coded contents of the completed book, although the architecture of the ink and the architecture of a sentence or of writing are certainly interdependent. However, the chemical constitution of ink is *totally independent* of the coded contents of the text of the book. *Information from without has been imposed onto ink chemistry; this information belongs to order of the second kind.*

If water is poured onto a text written in ink, this text will thus be modified or partly smudged; but never is fundamentally new information added to the text in this manner. The chemistry of *mutations* in the genetic code information has an effect similar to that of water on our text. Mutations modify or destroy already existing genetic information, but *they never create new information.* They never create, for example, an entirely new biological organ, such as an eye or ear. Herein lies an error . . . that fundamentally *new* information is created by mutations. . . .

The chemical properties of carbon atoms which affect the nature of the DNA molecule have little to do with the coded contents of the nucleic acids, although both are interdependent—just like the printer's ink and the contents of the text. These two stages may be distinguished from each other in the following manner: The first type of order includes no "projects" or teleonomy,[13] whereas the second type of order (writing) includes coded teleonomy and coded projects. Just as ink and printer's ink do not intrinsically contain any code indicating grass, the first order contains neither a simulated code nor stored information. But the coded writing set down with the aid of printer's ink contains both the first and second type of order. In the second type, additional information exceeding and transcending that of pure chemistry is included.

Naturally the phenomena of two superimposed orders is widespread. A piece of cast iron contains the order harbored by iron. But this order does not suffice to build the order of the cylinder block of a car. The information necessary to build a car's cylinder block is not inherent to iron. However, additional "foreign" information for cylinder blocks may be imprinted onto the information harbored by the iron. By taking a car blueprint and the iron and combining the two in a workshop, a car cylinder block is formed. The iron itself, however, does not possess the coded information on the blueprint, but can receive and carry the same, so that a car cylinder block results. Thus the car cylinder block possesses at the same time the properties of the blueprint and also those of the iron molecules. Thus the car cylinder block is a sort of *hybrid* between the two types of order.

Similarly, the chemical components of nucleic acids or the proteins of life do not possess sufficient information to build an amoeba or a man. But by taking a concept of life (a blueprint, so to say) and combining this coded information with the properties of the components of nucleic acids

---

[13] *Teleonomy* is used here as having a design or purpose in mind. That is, phenomena are guided by a force other than mechanical, in that they are intentionally moved toward certain goals.

(or of proteins), a man or an amoeba can be formed. However, matter alone—not even the matter from which nucleic acids or proteins are built—does not possess the information of a coded blueprint needed to build a man. A living organism is a *hybrid* between the two types of order.[14]

The relationship between software and hardware is the relationship between mind and matter. This realization is all that is necessary to see the impossibility of the monkey/computer macroevolutionary metaphor. The same impossibility applies to all the other comparisons made by macroevolutionists based on circumstantial evidence, including comparative anatomy, embryology, comparative biochemistry, and comparative chromosome structure.

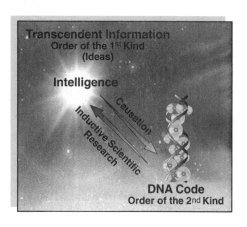

We therefore conclude that intelligence is the real "missing link" in the chain of macroevolutionary theory. Without the original programmer to write the software, the computer cannot operate at all. Not only so, the hardware alone would never be able to spontaneously generate a self-replicating software program that cumulatively modifies itself to produce a more wonderfully specified and complex version of its original. This is what has to be demonstrated if macroevolution is to be based on scientific laws and observational evidence. However, *operation science knows of no mechanism to support biological novelty by way of cumulative mutations.* The fossil record is the only observational evidence available to help support the claim that accumulation of small mutations over long periods of time was responsible for new life forms. We thus turn to the discipline of *paleontology* to examine that evidence.

WHAT ABOUT THE FOSSIL RECORD (PALEONTOLOGICAL EVIDENCE)?

If macroevolutionists such as Richard Dawkins are correct about gradualism—if the accumulation of small changes over long periods of time *has* oc-

---

[14]A. E. Wilder-Smith, *The Natural Sciences Know Nothing of Evolution* (Costa Mesa, Calif.: Word for Today, 1981), 46–48 (emphasis added).

curred—then this fact of history should be verifiable in the fossil record. If macroevolution did occur in a gradual manner through unbounded and cumulative microevolutionary changes, then transitions between life forms should appear in paleontological evidence as part of what the organism was in its original state and part of what it was becoming as a new form of life.

The gradualist view predicts that a large class of intermediate or transitional fossils should be discovered in the fossil record. This prediction can be verified by producing fossil evidence of gradual transitions of relatively simple forms of life into more and more complex forms of life. For example, the fossil record should be filled with some type of combination

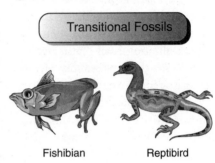

Transitional Fossils

Fishibian   Reptibird

of a fish in a transition stage as it is becoming an amphibian (say, *fishibian*), or a mixture of a reptile in transition as it is becoming a bird (say, *reptibird*).

Paleontology is the study of life forms existing in prehistoric times as represented by the fossil remains of plants, animals, and other organisms. A fossil is a remnant of an organism from a past geological age, such as an animal skeleton or leaf imprint that is embedded and preserved in the earth's crust. With this in mind, let's start at the beginning, a point in history known as the *Precambrian* period, and see what the record has to say.

In geology, the Precambrian time period is the earliest and largest division of time for which rock strata are recognized. This era is taken to include the entire time interval that began with the formation of the solid crust of the earth and ended when life in the seas had begun to flourish. It is the span of time preceding the *Cambrian* period and is characterized by the appearance of primitive forms of life. The major macroevolutionary processes are supposed to have taken place during the Precambrian and Cambrian time frames, making this the largest and widest gap in the fossil record to fill. Therefore, the geological strata bridging these two eras ought to be overflowing with fossilized evidence to support the claims of gradualists.

However, *there is absolutely no evidence indicating how the five thousand genetic types of marine and animal life allegedly evolved during these two eras.* This is a curious reality that does not fit the gradualistic macroevolutionary model. In fact, the first evidence of invertebrate[15] animal life appears with startling and

---

[15]An invertebrate is an animal, such as an insect or a mollusk, that lacks a backbone or spinal column. A vertebrate, in contrast, has a backbone or spinal column; examples include fish, amphibians, reptiles, birds, and mammals.

remarkable suddenness in the Cambrian period. The general public became aware of this primarily through a *Time* magazine cover story, which said,

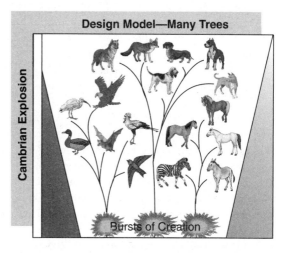

543 million years ago, in the early Cambrian [period], within the span of no more than a million years, creatures with teeth and tentacles and claws and jaws materialized with the suddenness of apparitions. *In a burst of creativity like nothing before or since,* nature appears to have sketched out the blueprints for virtually the whole of the animal kingdom. This explosion of biological diversity is described by scientists as biology's *Big Bang.*

Over the decades, evolutionary theorists beginning with Charles Darwin have tried to argue that the appearance of multi-celled animals during the Cambrian [period] merely seemed sudden, and in fact had been preceded by a lengthy period of evolution for which the geological record was missing. *But this explanation, while it patched over a hole in an otherwise masterly theory, now seems increasingly unsatisfactory.* Since 1987, discoveries of major fossil beds in Greenland, in China, in Siberia, and now in Namibia have shown that the period of biological innovation occurred at virtually *the same instant in geological time all around the world. . . .*

It was during the Cambrian (and perhaps only during the Cambrian) that nature invented the animal body plans that define the broad biological groupings known as phyla, which encompass everything from classes and orders to families, genera and species. For example, the chordate phylum includes mammals, birds and fish. The class Mammalia, in turn, covers the primate order, the hominid family, the genus *Homo* and our own species, *Homo sapiens.*

Scientists used to think that the evolution of phyla took place over a period of 75 million years, and even that seemed impossibly short. Then two years ago a group of researchers led by John Grotzinger, Samuel Bowring from MIT, and Andrew Knoll [paleontologist at Harvard University] took this long-standing problem and escalated it into a crisis. First they recalibrated the geological clock, chopping the Cambrian period to about half its former length. Then they announced that the interval of major evolutionary innovation did not span the entire 30 million years, but rather was concentrated in the first third. "Fast," Harvard's [Stephen Jay] Gould observes, "is now a lot faster than we thought." . . . Of course understanding what made the Cambrian explosion possible doesn't address the larger question of what made it happen so fast. *Here scientists delicately slide across data-thin ice, suggesting scenarios that are based on intuition rather than solid evidence.* . . .

The Cambrian explosion has caused experts to wonder if the twin Darwinian imperatives of genetic variation and natural selection provide an adequate framework for understanding evolution. "What Darwin described in the *On the Origin of Species*," observes Queen's University paleontologist Narbonne, "was the steady background kind of evolution. But there also seems to be a non-Darwinian kind of evolution that functions over extremely short time periods—and that's where all the action is."[16]

Researchers are now saying that this Cambrian explosion took even less time than previously thought and have revised it downward to ten million years. But no matter how they set up the model, this rapid burst of the creation of life is diametrically opposed to gradualism. Michael Behe, associate professor of biochemistry at Lehigh University, says,

Careful searches show only a smattering of fossils of multicellular creatures in rocks older than about 600 million years. Yet in rocks just a little bit younger is seen a profusion of fossilized animals, with a host of widely differing body plans. Recently the estimated time over which the explosion took place has been revised downward from 50 million years to 10 million years—a blink of the eye in geological terms. The shorter time estimate has forced headline writers to grope for new superlatives, a favorite being the "biological Big Bang." Gould has argued that *the rapid rate of appearance of new life forms demands a new mechanism other than natural selection for its explanation.*"[17]

The prediction of macroevolution's slow change over long time periods—gradualism—has been found to be false with respect to the very beginning of the appearance of life and new life forms. Right from the start, the discipline of paleontology offers no observational evidence in its support. If this is true of the largest and widest gap to fill, on what basis should any intelligent person

---

[16]J. Madeleine Nash, "When Life Exploded," *Time*, December 4, 1995, 49–56 (emphasis added).
[17]Michael J. Behe, *Darwin's Black Box: The Biological Challenge to Evolution* (New York: Free, 1996), 27–28.

accept the claim that transitional fossils exist throughout the rest of the record, with the exception of a few so-called missing links? Let's examine this claim as well.

ISN'T THE FOSSIL RECORD COMPLETE EXCEPT FOR A FEW MISSING LINKS?

Again, Charles Darwin admitted, "If it could be demonstrated that any complex organ existed, which could not possibly have been formed by numerous, successive, slight modifications, my theory would absolutely break down."[18] We have already shown that Darwin's theory has broken down at the molecular biological level. In fact, Michael Behe has dedicated his entire book, *Darwin's Black Box*, to that end. His central thesis focuses on the fact that there are many organs that have not been and cannot be "formed by numerous, successive, slight modifications."

Behe explains how some biological systems are *irreducibly complex;* that is, they could not have evolved as independent parts to form an integrated whole—they come in one entire package. A mouse trap, for instance, is irreducibly complex—if any one part of the trap is removed, it cannot function. Behe cites elements from the human body that could not have evolved because they are likewise irreducibly complex: the DNA molecule, vision, blood-clotting, cellular transport, and many more fall into this classification.

In DNA replication, for example, proteins are necessary to process the information on the double helix structure. Yet the information to build those proteins is already stored as encoded data on the double helix![19] This is what we mean when we say that at the molecular level, according to his own criterion for falsification, Darwin's theory has "absolutely" broken down. Next, let's apply Darwin's test to the fossil record and transitional forms.

The macroevolutionary view of origins based on gradualism predicts a large class of transitional fossils; these should exist as evi-

One Fossilized Skull Fragment
Two Conflicting Models

Macroevolutionary Artist

Design Model Artist

---

[18]Charles Darwin, *On the Origin of Species* (New York: NAL Penguin Inc., 1958), 171.
[19]Michael J. Behe, *Darwin's Black Box: The Biological Challenge to Evolution* (New York: Free, 1996), 39–46.

dence of gradual transitions of relatively simple forms of life evolving into more and more complex forms of life over very long periods of time. For approximately 140 years (over 500 million geological years' worth of fossil evidence) macroevolutionists predicted that it would only be a matter of time before paleontological evidence would be discovered in support of this theory. Rather than debate how artists should visualize what type of flesh and muscle belongs on what kind of bone or skull fragments,[20] we need only quote the intellectually honest macroevolutionists who have now admitted to the lack of evidence with respect to the "missing links."

The truth of the matter is that *the fossil record shows no evidence of transitional fossils and consequently does not accurately describe a large class of observations.* Yet for many decades science textbooks kept the truth about these major gaps a secret and actually depicted macroevolution as a life chain with a few missing links. For example, according to macroevolution, humans and apes are supposed to have shared a common ancestor; they are also thought to have shared a common ancestor with the horse. Similar relationships are imagined to be linked throughout the entire animal and plant kingdoms. These interrelationships are referred to as *phylogeny* and are portrayed in flowchart types of associations in a so-called *phylogenetic tree.*[21] As shown here, the concept of this tree was developed by macroevolutionists to show how their model accounts for the divergence of all living things from a "common ancestor." The branches represent the transitions leading back to a common ancestor, and the new life forms appear as the leaves on the phylogenetic tree.

The majority of science textbooks depict macroevolution as a tree with branches revealing various speciations; however, the phylogenic tree analogy is a gross misrepresentation of the facts. Only in relatively recent times have macroevolutionists faced the truth and made public confessions like the following from Stephen Jay Gould:

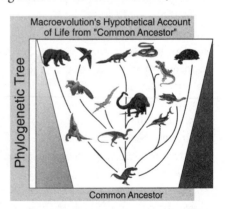

Macroevolution's Hypothetical Account of Life from "Common Ancestor"

Phylogenetic Tree

Common Ancestor

---

[20]See Duane Gish, *Evolution: The Challenge of the Fossil Record* (Green Forest, Ariz.: Master, 1986), 149. An example of two macroevolutionary artists is given showing two contrasting drawings of the same fossilized remains of *Zinjanthropus bosei*, or "East-Africa Man." One sketch depicts the fossil with a human-like appearance, while the other shows it to have ape-like features.

[21]The illustrations we have inserted with respect to the phylogenetic tree are offered as visual aids only. They are not a technically accurate representation of the phylogenetic tree or a formal blueprint of the supposed macroevolutionary relationships between species.

> *The extreme rarity of transitional forms in the fossil record persists as the trade secret of paleontology.* The evolutionary trees that adorn our textbooks have data *only at the tips and nodes* of their branches; the rest is inference, however reasonable, *not the evidence of fossils.*[22]

In short, we don't have a tree at all; only the twigs and leaves with no branches or trunk! The lack of paleontological evidence to support gradualism has been hidden over the years in an effort to suppress the truth and to build a case in favor of macroevolution based on a level of appealing to the public. This particular tactic was used to gain the support of the nonscientific populace in order to make macroevolution a widely accepted model of origins. Lest you think this is our own opinion, think again in light of the following quotation written over forty years ago in the introduction to the 1956 reprint of Charles Darwin's *On the Origin of Species:*

> As we know, there is a great divergence of opinion among biologists, not only about the causes of evolution but even about the actual process. This divergence exists because the evidence is unsatisfactory and does not permit any certain conclusion. It is therefore right and proper to draw the attention of the non-scientific public to the disagreements about evolution. But some recent remarks of evolutionists show that they think this unreasonable. *This situation, where scientific men rally to the defense of a doctrine they are unable to define scientifically, much less demonstrate with scientific rigor, attempting to maintain its credit with the public by the suppression of criticism and the elimination of difficulties, is abnormal and undesirable in science.*[23]

The majority of macroevolutionists ignored this admonition and instead tried to establish their position by misleading the public and appealing to popular sentiments or to opinions instead of operation science and the observational evidence. However, the truth is that the evidential data and laws of science do not support a credible mechanism for gradualistic macroevolution.

There is no phylogenetic tree, but gradualists excuse themselves from this empirical pretense by blaming it on the fossil record. Gould cites Darwin on this matter and points out that Darwin called the geological record "extremely imperfect." He also describes how Darwin claimed that this fact explains why intermediate fossils do not exist.[24] Gould says, *"Darwin's argument still persists*

[22]Stephen Jay Gould, *The Panda's Thumb* (New York: W. W. Norton & Co., 1982), 181 (emphasis added).
[23]W. R. Thompson, quoted from the introduction to *On the Origin of Species* (New York: E. P. Dutton & Co., 1956), referenced in the *Journal of the American Scientific Affiliation* March 1960, 135 (emphasis added).
[24]Charles Darwin, *On the Origin of Species* (New York: NAL Penguin Inc., 1958), 159.

*as the favored escape of most pale-
ontologists from the embarrassment
of a record that seems to show so little of evolution directly."*[25] Richard
Dawkins adds, "Some very important gaps really are due to imperfections in the fossil record.
Very big gaps, too."[26]

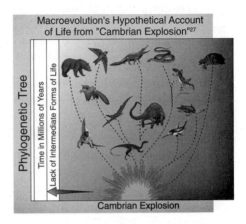

Are Darwin and Dawkins
correct? Could the fact that the
fossil record does not support the
predictions of gradualism be attributed to the idea that the rec-
ord is imperfect? Gould thinks that this excuse is hard to imagine:

> All paleontologists know that the fossil record contains precious little
> in the way of intermediate forms; transitions between major groups are
> *characteristically* abrupt. Gradualists usually extract themselves from this di-
> lemma by invoking the extreme imperfection of the fossil record. . . . Al-
> though I reject this argument, let us grant the traditional escape and ask a
> different question. Even though we have no direct evidence for smooth
> transitions, can we invent a reasonable sequence of intermediate forms—
> that is, viable, functioning organisms—between ancestors and descendants
> in major structural transitions? Of what possible use are the imperfect in-
> cipient stages of useful structures? What good is half a jaw or half a wing?
> The concept of *preadaptation* provides the conventional answer by permit-
> ting us to argue that incipient stages performed different functions. The
> half jaw worked perfectly well as a series of gill-supporting bones; the half
> wing may have trapped prey or controlled body temperature. I regard pre-
> adaptation as important, even an indispensable concept. *But a plausible
> story is not necessarily true. I do not doubt that preadaptation can save gradu-
> alism in some cases, but does it permit us to invent a tale of continuity in most
> or all cases? I submit, although it may only reflect my lack of imagination, that
> the answer is no.*[28]

---

[25]Stephen Jay Gould, *The Panda's Thumb* (New York: W. W. Norton & Co., 1982), 181 (emphasis added).
[26]Richard Dawkins, *The Blind Watchmaker* (New York: W. W. Norton & Co., 1987), 229.
[27]See Footnote 21.
[28]Op. cit., 189 (emphasis added).

It is untrue that the fossil record is complete except for a few missing links. The phylogenetic tree is nothing but twigs (microevolution) and leaves. The truth is that there are no missing links, but rather a *missing chain*, representative of enormous gaps in the record. For example, if you had one link in New York City, one in London, and another in Berlin, would it be correct for you to say that you had missing links in your chain? No, it would be more correct to say that you just had some links and were imagining that a chain existed. Consequently, we conclude that *gradualism is not supported by any known mechanism in operation science, nor is there any credible observational evidence available to sustain it based on paleontology.*

This remarkable absence of intermediate forms required for the verification of the macroevolutionary model is a solemn charge that cannot be ignored. Charles Darwin himself wrote, "Why then is not every geological formation and every stratum full of such intermediate links? Geology assuredly does not reveal any such finely graduated organic chain. *This is perhaps the most obvious and gravest objection which can be urged against my theory."* [29] We agree.

Where does that leave macroevolutionists? Will they admit that their theory has been falsified and give it up? No, instead they continue to do what they have always done; they "delicately slide across data-thin ice, suggesting scenarios that are based on intuition rather than solid evidence."[30] One such scenario is called *punctuated equilibria* and we analyze its validity below.

WHAT IS THE "PUNCTUATED EQUILIBRIA" MODEL, AND IS IT VALID?

In what certainly appears to be a desperate effort to save a dying theory, macroevolutionists have resorted to inventing a remarkably "data-thin" view of their model. The main advocates of this new hypothesis are Stephen Jay Gould, Niles Eldredge, and Steven Stanley (paleontologist at John Hopkins University). These men have referred to their new hypothesis as *punctuated equilibria.* Punctuated equilibria is not a newly discovered scientific mechanism; it is merely an attempt to keep the macroevolutionary model alive by restating the facts. According to Stephen Jay Gould,

> Paleontologists have paid an exorbitant price for Darwin's argument. We fancy ourselves as the only true students of life's history; yet to preserve our favored account of evolution by natural selection we view our data as

---

[29]Charles Darwin, *On the Origin of Species* (New York: NAL Penguin Inc., 1958), 287 (emphasis added).
[30]J. Madeleine Nash, "When Life Exploded," *Time*, December 4, 1995, 55 (emphasis added).

so bad that we almost never see the very process we profess to study. . . . The history of most fossil species includes two features particularly inconsistent with gradualism:

1. *Stasis.* Most species exhibit no directional change during their tenure on earth. They appear in the fossil record looking much the same as when they disappear; morphological change is usually limited and directionless.

2. *Sudden appearance.* In any local area, a species does not gradually appear by the steady transformation of its ancestors; it appears all at once and "fully formed." . . .

Eldredge and I refer to this scheme as the model of *punctuated equilibria.* Lineages change little during most of their history, but events of rapid speciation occasionally punctuate this tranquillity. Evolution is the differential survival and deployment of these punctuations. (In describing the speciation of peripheral isolates as very rapid, I speak as a geologist. The process may take hundreds, even thousands of years; you might see nothing if you stared at speciating bees on a tree for your entire lifetime. But a thousand years is a tiny fraction of one percent of the average duration for most fossil invertebrate species—5 to 10 million years. Geologists can rarely resolve so short an interval at all; we tend to treat it as a moment.)[31]

Within the macroevolutionary framework, punctuated equilibria and gradualism stand diametrically opposed to each other in regard to transitional time frames. Gradualism calls for an organism to change at a very slow pace by the process of natural selection and random microevolutionary mutations at the genetic level, which would gradually lead to the emergence of a

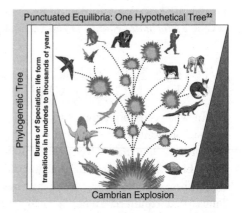

Punctuated Equilibria: One Hypothetical Tree[32]

Phylogenetic Tree

Bursts of Speciation: life form transitions in hundreds to thousands of years

Cambrian Explosion

new life form. The newer punctuated view, however, demands that life forms remain within their own genetic limits for very long periods of time (stasis), until environmental pressures force them to "burst forth" (sudden punctuations) into new life forms. As noted in the illustration above, in an effort to patch up the holes in the macroevolutionary phylogenetic tree, the large gaps

[31]Stephen Jay Gould, *The Panda's Thumb* (New York: W. W. Norton & Co., 1982), 181–84.
[32]See footnote 21.

in the fossil record have been covered by explosion symbols, indicative of "punctuated bursts" of new genetic types.

These "rapid speciations" are macroevolutionary "quantum leaps," occurring in a geological moment, with the living entity instantly becoming a new life form. We believe that this view is punctuated, not with scientific reasoning or observational evidence, but instead with implausible attempts to explain away, and not account for, the very large gaps that so obviously exist in the fossil record. Again, it is merely a rearranging of the facts to save a theory built on unjustified philosophical and scientific assumptions of the naturalistic view of the universe. Before we look at the punctuated view of macroevolution from a purely scientific perspective, let's make it clear that *gradualism and punctuated equilibria are philosophical views and are not based on scientific laws or observational evidence.* In fact, Gould admits this to be true:

> If gradualism is more a product of Western thought than a fact of nature, then we should consider *alternate philosophies of change* to enlarge our realm of constraining prejudices. In the Soviet Union, for example, scientists are trained with a very different philosophy of change—the so-called dialectical laws, reformulated by [Friedrich] Engels from [G. W. F.] Hegel's philosophy. The dialectical laws are explicitly punctuational. They speak, for example, of the "transformation of quantity into quality." This may sound like mumbo jumbo, but it suggests that change occurs in large leaps following a slow accumulation of stresses that a system resists until it reaches the breaking point. . . . *I emphatically do not assert the general "truth" of this philosophy of punctuational change. . . . I make a simple plea for pluralism in guiding philosophies.*[33]

Scientific pluralism? In other words, since there is no scientific evidence to support either gradualism or punctuated equilibria, Gould would like us to be open-minded about science and accept all the views of how macroevolution occurred. If we prefer to be gradualists, we need to be open to a punctuated view when gradualism cannot explain the facts. If we lean toward a punctuated account, we need to not be too hard on the gradualists. That is, don't let our philosophical prejudices undermine the macroevolutionary model of origins.

What is really being requested of us is that we be open-minded (pluralistic) *only* within the possibilities of naturalism. Consequently, we are being asked to believe that macroevolution is the only explanation available to account for the origin of life and new life forms. We are also being asked to be open-minded about the two severe scientific flaws of the macroevolutionary model in general: (1) It has no scientific mechanism to account for unlimited genetic change, and (2) It has no observational evidence (facts) to support its claims. We agree

---

[33]Ibid., 184–85 (emphasis added).

with Gould's earlier assessment of gradualism as "a plausible story [which] is not necessarily true."[34] We not only see his statement as applicable to gradualism but to the punctuated view as well.

Therefore, we reject the punctuated view, along with Gould's "scientific pluralism," on purely scientific grounds, and we agree with Michael Denton's scientific critique of punctuated equilibria. He says that even if one were to accept the punctuated view as a possible explanation of the gaps between life forms, one would also have to account for the larger systematic gaps. Denton summarizes what are perhaps the essential pitfalls of the punctuated view:

> The gaps which separate species: dog/fox, rat/mouse, etc. are utterly trivial compared with, say, that between a primitive terrestrial mammal and a whale or a primitive terrestrial reptile and an Ichthyosaur; and even these relatively major discontinuities are trivial alongside those which divide major phyla such as mollusks and anthropods. . . . Surely such transitions must have involved long lineages including many collateral lines of hundreds or probably thousands of transitional species. To suggest that the hundreds, thousands or possibly millions of transitional species which must have existed in the interval between vastly dissimilar types were all unsuccessful species occupying isolated areas and having very small population numbers is verging on the incredible! . . .
>
> Whatever view one wishes to take of the evidence of paleontology, it does not provide convincing grounds for believing that the phenomenon of life conforms to a continuous pattern. The gaps have not been explained away. It is possible to allude to a number of species and groups such as *Archeopteryx,* or the rhipidistian fish, which appear to be to some extent intermediate. But even if such were intermediate to some degree, there is no evidence that they are any more intermediate than groups such as the living lungfish or monotremes which are not only tremendously isolated from their nearest cousins, but which have individual organ systems that are not strictly transitional at all. *As evidence for the existence of natural links between the great divisions of nature, they are only convincing to someone already convinced of the reality of organic evolution.*[35]

Like gradualism, punctuated equilibria is nothing more than speculation. As mentioned, it is unsupported by operation science and it violates the law of uniformity, offering no scientific mechanism and no empirical data to support its claims. Furthermore, Gould notes that new life forms emerge in a geological

---

[34]Ibid., 189.

[35]Michael Denton, *Evolution: A Theory in Crisis* (Bethesda: Adler & Adler, 1986), 193–95 (emphasis added).

moment, which only multiplies the genetic obstacles associated with macro-evolution and the need for an even more efficient mechanism to produce bio-logical novelty. For these reasons we must reject punctuated equilibria as a valid explanation for the appearance of life and new life forms. The rejection of both variant forms of macroevolution—gradualism and punctuated equilibria—as valid models that account for the origin of new life forms automatically dis-qualifies theistic macroevolution as well. As with the punctuated view, theistic macroevolution is only convincing to someone already predisposed to believing it. However, we will address the problems associated with theistic evolution in the next chapter when we examine the design model of origins.

We conclude this analysis with comments from Dr. Colin Patterson, author of the book *Evolution* and a lifelong macroevolutionist. In 1981 he gave a series of lectures to some of the top macroevolutionists in the United States. At that time Dr. Patterson was the senior paleontologist at the British Museum of Nat-ural History in London and editor of its journal. The following citations are extracted from a transcript of his lecture given at the American Museum of Natural History in New York City on November 5, 1981.

> One of the reasons I started taking this anti-evolutionary view, or let's call it non-evolutionary view, was last year I had a sudden realization that for over twenty years I had thought I was working on evolution in some way. One morning I woke up and something had happened in the night and it struck me that I had been working on this stuff for twenty years and there was not one thing I knew about it. That's quite a shock to learn that one can be so misled so long. . . . For the last few weeks I've tried putting a simple question to various people and groups of people.
>
> *The question is: Can you tell me anything you know about evolution, any one thing, any one thing that is true?* I tried that question on the geology staff at the Field Museum of Natural History and the only answer I got was silence. I tried it on the members of the Evolutionary Morphology Seminar at the University of Chicago, a very prestigious body of evolution-ists, and all I got there was silence for a long time and eventually one person said, *"I do know one thing—it ought not to be taught in high school."* . . . The level of knowledge about evolution is remarkably shallow. We know it ought not to be taught in the high school and that's all we know about it. . . . So I think many people in this room would acknowl-edge that during the last few years if you had thought about it at all, you've experienced *a shift from evolution as knowledge to evolution as faith.* I know that's true of me and I think it's true of a good many of you in here.[36]

---

[36]Colin Petterson, "Evolutionism and Creationism," speech given at the American Museum of Natural History, New York, November 5, 1981 (transcribed by Wayne Frair), 1, 4 (emphasis added).

Patterson is not alone in his declaration of macroevolution as being impoverished with respect to scientific knowledge. When Michael Behe did his research for *Darwin's Black Box,* he decided to look into the number of published articles that appeared in a special publication entitled *Journal of Molecular Evolution* (*JME*). This journal was established in 1971 to accommodate the increasing number of research papers dedicated to molecular evolution. Behe noted that the JME is run by "prominent figures" in the field, including around a dozen or so who are members of the National Academy of Sciences. After Behe surveyed ten years' worth of articles, he drew the following conclusion:

> Molecular evolution is not based on scientific authority. There is no publication in the scientific literature—in prestigious journals, specialty journals, or books—that describes how molecular evolution of any real, complex, biochemical system either did occur or even might have occurred. There are assertions that such evolution occurred, but absolutely none are supported by pertinent experiments or calculations. . . . "Publish or perish" is a proverb that academicians take seriously. If you do not publish your work for the rest of the community to evaluate, then you have no business in academia (and if you don't already have tenure, you will be banished). But the saying can be applied to theories as well. If a theory claims to be able to explain some phenomenon but does not generate even an attempt at an explanation, then it should be banished. Despite comparing sequences and mathematical modeling, molecular evolution has never addressed the question of how complex structures came to be. In effect, the theory of Darwinian molecular evolution has not published, and so it should perish.[37]

The theoretical research that tries to account for a macroevolutionary view of life is, as one author notes, a "fact-free" science.[38] The more researchers learn, the more perplexed they become in trying to fit their findings into the macroevolutionary model. We therefore conclude that the macroevolutionary model of origins is not a valid model and turn our attention to the only logical alternative—the design model. We consider the design model to be the most reasonable model of origins because it is the most consistent model with respect to philosophy (causality and uniformity), operation science (observation and repetition), and paleontology (empirical data/facts).

---

[37]Michael J. Behe, *Darwin's Black Box: The Biological Challenge to Evolution* (New York: Free, 1996), 185–86.
[38]Ibid., 191 (cited from issue of *Scientific American,* June 1995,"From Complexity to Perplexity").

8

QUESTIONS ABOUT INTELLIGENT DESIGN

*In the beginning God created the heavens
and the earth.*

—GENESIS 1:1

WHAT ABOUT THE THEISTIC MACROEVOLUTIONARY MODEL OF ORIGINS?

The principles of causality and uniformity, the law of specified complexity, and the science of information theory show us that the first life form must have had an intelligent cause. Furthermore, operation science has demonstrated that mutations cannot produce the new information necessary to bring about biological novelty. Moreover, the observational evidence confirms that there are natural limitations to genetic change that supports *micro*evolution, but there is no evidence (scientific, paleontological, or otherwise) to support the claim that microevolution can be extrapolated to the *macro* level. Paleontology confirms that the abrupt appearance of the first life forms—the five thousand genetic types of marine and animal life—suddenly arose in an amazingly short and fast global explosion of life. From that point on, paleontology also confirms that all other new life forms appear just as abruptly in the fossil record. Macroevolutionist Stephen Jay Gould admits,

Most species exhibit no directional change during their tenure on earth. They appear in the fossil record looking much the same as when they disappear; morphological change is usually limited and direction-less. . . . In any local area, *a species does not gradually appear by the steady transformation of its ancestors; it appears all at once and "fully formed."*[1]

All of the evidence shows that there are no objective scientific reasons why we ought to accept *any* form of the macroevolutionary model. This leaves us with the intelligent design model alternative.

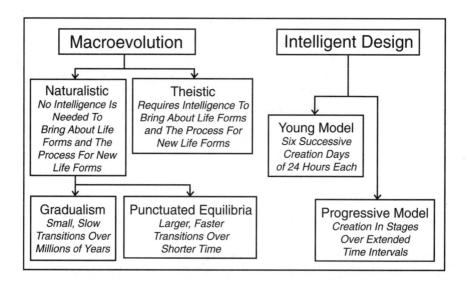

However, before considering which view of the design model most accurately corresponds to the facts, we'll analyze one other option, the theistic macroevolutionary view. We intend to show that from an evidentiary point of view, there is no difference between atheistic or naturalistic macroevolution and theistic macroevolution.

Theistic macroevolutionists believe that God is the cause behind life on earth, but that He used the process of macroevolution to bring about new life forms and eventually the human race. This theory includes God and was developed by theists who thought that macroevolution had some academic merit. Theistic macroevolutionists generally endeavor to address some of the more severe problems associated with macroevolution by interjecting God's handi-

[1]Stephen Jay Gould, *The Panda's Thumb* (New York: W. W. Norton & Co., 1982), 182 (emphasis added).

work where the evidence is severely lacking.

Many theistic macroevolutionists who believe in gradualism believe that bringing God into the model relieves them of the nagging problem of the need for an intelligent cause. Of course it solves the main difficulty with respect to the initial needed information, but it does not help with the fossil record. Theistic macroevolutionists are faced with the same difficulty that atheistic or naturalistic macroevolutionists are faced with, namely, the lack of paleontological evidence. Therefore, the same evidence that nullifies the atheistic macroevolutionary models also serves to refute theistic macroevolution—the evidence needed to support any macroevolutionary model of origins does not exist.

This leaves us with theistic macroevolutionists who believe in the punctuated view of the origin of life and new life forms. As defined earlier, the punctuated view demands that life forms remain within their own genetic limits for very long periods of time (stasis), until environmental pressures force them to "burst forth" (sudden punctuations) into new life forms. Theistic macroevolutionists would argue that God pre-timed these new species to burst forth, and thus the difference between someone such as Stephen Jay Gould and a theistic macroevolutionist is the belief in intelligent design. So our questions for theistic macroevolutionists who believe in the punctuated view is "What is left of the macroevolutionary model?" Is it not a "fact-free" view? Is it not wanting for empirical evidence to support it?

If theistic *gradualism* is not a plausible view, and the theistic *punctuated* view reduces to God as the Cause behind the bursting forth of new life forms, then on what scientific basis do theistic macroevolutionists build their case? We can see an atheist going to such extremes to save the macroevolutionary model, but why would a theist do so? We can understand someone in Gould's shoes trying to go far beyond the observable evidence because he believes that the statement "created in God's own image" is "fallacious."[2] According to his worldview, he has no other option! However, this is not the case for theists. Not only do they have at least two other options—the young and progressive design views—but if they still choose to embrace macroevolution, they must also honestly deal with the biblical questions this embrace raises. One author succinctly captured those difficulties in his writings. He said,

> There are devout Christians who hold that the process by which man was created was biological and genetic, in other words that man's physical being was produced by evolution. A form of this theory, I well remember, appealed to me in my undergraduate days in the university. I devoutly

---

[2]Stephen Jay Gould, *The Mismeasure of Man* (New York: W. W. Norton & Co., 1981), 324.

believed in the inerrancy of the Bible, but I thought the Bible record could be harmonized with the idea that Adam was produced by mutation, and that he was constituted as man in the image of God by a special supernatural act. . . . However, I became thoroughly convinced many years ago that this hypothesis is untenable. . . .

Evolution does not solve any difficulties. It is more complicated than the simple special creation view. . . . The statement of Genesis 2:7, to the effect that "The Lord God formed man of the dust of the ground," seems to indicate rather strongly that man's body was formed, not from some previously existing animal, but rather from inorganic material.

There is an observable gap which some anthropologists have called a bio-cultural gap between man and the other animals. This is to say, the alleged behavioral transition between non-man and man—between instinct-bound animal and . . . cultural man—is not documented by paleontological evidence and constitutes a more significant discontinuity than [those in] the fossil [record].

Finally, . . . the theory of the derivation of the human physical body from merely animal ancestry is extremely difficult to harmonize with the doctrine of man created in the image of God, man as a fallen creature, man as redeemable in Christ.[3]

We are compelled to conclude that human life, as observed, can only be explained as the direct result of a special act of creation such as recorded in the early chapters of the book of Genesis. There are many other reasons—both biblical and nonbiblical—as to why we reject theistic macroevolution, but it would be beyond the scope of this work to delineate them. Our next task is to consider the two remaining design models of origins—the young earth view and the progressive view.

WHICH DESIGN MODEL BEST MATCHES ALL THE SCIENTIFIC EVIDENCE?

Before we attempt to answer this question, it may help to get the overall picture of the origin of the universe, the origin of life, and new life forms. Consider the following summary that reflects previously drawn conclusions based upon philosophical first principles, the laws of science, and trustworthy observational evidence:

Big Bang of Cosmology—The Origin of the Universe: Based on the second

[3]James Buzwell, Jr., *A Systematic Theology of the Christian Religion*, vol. 1 (Grand Rapids, Mich.: Zondervan, 1962), 323–24.

law of thermodynamics and the principles of causality and uniformity (analogy), the space-time universe is considered to be finite and consequently was caused by an infinitely powerful, eternal, and uncaused entity.

Big Bang of Molecular Biology—The Origin of Life: Based on the principles of causality and uniformity, the law of specified complexity, and the science of information theory, we discovered that the first life form needed an intelligent Cause. This Cause designed all living things to be capable of limited microevolutionary changes that allowed them to adapt to varying environments. Therefore, we can add the attribute of intelligence to this infinitely powerful, eternal, and uncaused *Being*.[4]

Paleontology—The Origin of New Life Forms: As with the first form of life, new life forms appear suddenly in the historical record without signs of gradual transformation. In terms of the order of nature and appearance of new life forms, the fossil record indicates that they appear in the following order:

1. Age of Invertebrates
2. Age of Fishes
3. Age of Amphibians
4. Age of Reptiles
5. Age of Mammals
6. Age of Humans

Now, let's assume that the order of appearance is correct but that the corresponding dates, as proposed by gradualist macroevolutionary geologists, are in error. The punctuated model argues that a new species can fully evolve in merely hundreds to thousands of years (an overall short span of time). On the other hand, gradualism holds to transitions being in the neighborhood of millions of years (an overall long span of time). For the present, let's put ages and time frames aside (we'll come back to them later) in order to concentrate on the valid data and see what we can find out.

In presenting the design model, we are not interested in assigning exact dates and ages to all of these events; we leave that up to you to decide. We will offer a suggested time scenario later, but our purpose right now is to show that the Genesis account of the origin of all living things is essentially in accord with modern science. Consider the following order of creation as described in Genesis 1:

1. Universe/Earth (Genesis 1:1)
2. Sea (Genesis 1:6)
3. Land/Plants (Genesis 1:9, 11)
4. Sea Animals (Genesis 1:20)
5. Land Animals (Genesis 1:24)
6. Humanity (Genesis 1:27)

Of course, Genesis 1 was not written from a modern scientific perspective,

---

[4]Once we add the characteristic of intelligence to this infinitely powerful, eternal, and uncaused entity, we have one of the essential qualities of personhood.

but it does offer an extremely accurate account of the order of creation as compared to the discoveries of modern science. In other words, when we line up the order of nature with the creation account as recorded in Genesis 1—with respect to order of appearance—there is an amazing correlation. Let's consider the two variant forms of this design model and see which one best fits the scientific evidence. (We are not intending to give a point-by-point explanation of the design model and show how it relates to the technical details surrounding all of the events; we merely want to show why the design model is scientifically sound.)

The design model, especially at its most crucial points, is consistent and in agreement with the principles of causality and uniformity, the laws of operation science, and the known evidence. Considering the fact that the basis for this model comes from the book of Genesis, one has to wonder how its author, in view of the prevailing myths of origins in his day, could have had such an accurate picture of the essential elements that make up the universe and all life forms. The most plausible explanation is that the Designer/Creator gave the author of Genesis the information.

When it comes to deciding between the young earth view and the progressive view, we recognize that some people believe that the only correct way to interpret Genesis 1 is to understand it as referring to literal twenty-four-hour days. If this is true, then we are obliged to accept the belief that all of creation, including the space-time universe itself, occurred within a 144-hour time span (six solar days). Therefore, we want to be clear that it is not within the scope of this work to hammer out the technical details concerning the Hebrew language with respect to the correct interpretation of Genesis 1. Accordingly, if you hold to the belief that Genesis 1 can only be referring to six literal twenty-hour days of creation—the young earth view—we are not attempting to convince you otherwise. After all, the Creator could have created the universe in six hours, six minutes, or six seconds, and the young earth view is certainly a viable view of origins. We are merely offering an alternative view that is also viable and does not violate any principles of interpretation—it is kept within the proper context of Genesis 1. As stated by one recognized expert of the Hebrew language,

> A true and proper belief of the inerrancy of Scripture involves neither a literal nor figurative rule of interpretation. What it does require is a belief in whatever the biblical author (human and divine) actually meant by the words he used. . . . The message and purpose of Genesis 1 is the revelation of the one true God who created all things out of nothing and . . . brought forth His creation in an orderly and systematic manner. There were six

major stages in this work of formation, and these stages are represented by days of the week.[5]

With this in mind, if you are committed to the young earth view, there is nothing more to be said. We are not trying to challenge the scholarship or conclusions of other competent and dedicated scholars.[6] However, if you are open to considering the progressive view of origins, continue reading as we show why we think the progressive view of the design model fits all of the scientific evidence well.

WHY DOES THE PROGRESSIVE VIEW BEST FIT ALL THE EVIDENCE?

Earlier we stated that macroevolutionists use the analogy of the phylogenetic tree to illustrate their view. The macroevolutionary model predicted only one phylogenetic tree with many branches and leaves—one that represents no intelligent design and one common ancestor. However, the data does not support this prediction; it actually depicts no main branches, but many twigs and leaves (indicated by the appearance of new life forms). Again, this fact was clearly stated by Gould, who said that new

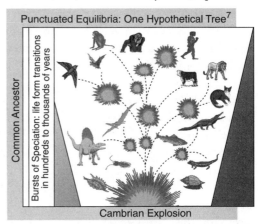

Punctuated Equilibria: One Hypothetical Tree[7]

Common Ancestor

Bursts of Speciation: life form transitions in hundreds to thousands of years

Cambrian Explosion

life forms "appear in the fossil record looking much the same as when they disappear; morphological change is usually limited and directionless. . . . In any local area, *a species does not gradually appear by the steady transformation of its ancestors; it appears all at once and "fully formed."*"[8]

---

[5]Gleason L. Archer, *Encyclopedia of Biblical Difficulties* (Grand Rapids, Mich.: Zondervan, 1982), 58, 60.
[6]Many sincerely honest and intellectually gifted scholars argue for either the young earth or old earth (progressive) view. Yet even macroevolutionists do not spend much time on intramural debates—they understand that there is power in having a united front. We need to do the same. It is our hope that some will reconsider the infighting over the question of age and concentrate on some of the more important aspects of the design model that we are presenting in the pages that follow. We trust that this form of argumentation will help resolve some of the internal conflict and foster unity as well.
[7]See Footnote 21 in chapter 7.
[8]Gould, *The Panda's Thumb*, 182 (emphasis added).

The model that predicted the data that has been discovered by paleontologists is the intelligent design model. It predicted what the fossil record has verified: many phylogenetic trees, with each tree having branches denoting microevolution, representing adaptation to the ecosystem within certain designated genetic parameters. We believe it is correct to say that one would expect similar kinds of creatures to share comparable biological systems and chromosome structures, since a common Designer created them to coexist within the same ecosystem. Therefore,

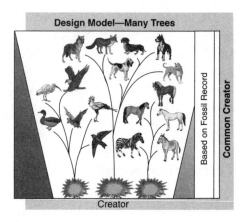

their similarities are directly related to their common designer and common ecosystem—not to a common ancestor. Since new life forms, then, appear with startling abruptness in the fossil record, there cannot be just one whole tree with a few missing branches (missing links). Rather, there must be many trees.

Stephen Jay Gould's punctuated model could be represented in graphical form as shown here. We believe that this graph is a fairly accurate and intellectually honest view of the data discovered in the fossil record.

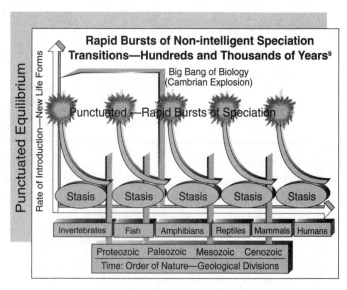

It pictures the paleontological evidence as it relates to the order of nature, the

---

[9]The data shows no evidence to support the idea that these life forms were "moving" (changing) in the "direction" of becoming new forms of life (new genetic types).

appearance of new life forms, and the geological divisions. Note that the first multicellular forms of life suddenly appear during what is now being called the *Cambrian explosion.* According to Gould, after life forms emerge they remain in stablity (stasis) until changing environmental conditions force nature into "rapid bursts of speciation" (Gould said that this "process may take hundreds or even thousands of years"[10]). Looking at this graph in the light of first principles and the laws of science, it becomes rather apparent that there is no mechanism to explain these bursts of speciation in purely natural terms. Moreover, we have already shown that biological change is limited and that new life forms require new information from an intelligent source.

Now consider once again the magnitude of the Cambrian explosion. Gould admits that "the Cambrian period is a period distinguished by the abrupt appearance of an astonishing array of multicelled animals.... *All around the world*... scientists have found the mineral remains of organisms that represent the emergence of nearly every major branch in the zoological tree."[11] The abrupt nature of this explosion of life, along with its global magnitude, can be better explained and accounted for by the progressive view of the design model. We believe this because the progressive view is consistent with the laws of science, as explicated in the various academic disciplines, and corresponds to the available observational evidence as discovered in the fossil record. We show this to be the case in response to the next question.

DOES THE PROGRESSIVE VIEW FIT ALL THE EVIDENCE?

The general answer to this question is provided in the table on the next page. Notice that it compares the order of creation described in Genesis 1 with the order of nature and appearance of new life forms as depicted by the paleontological record. Keep in mind, too, that a progressive view may interpret the Genesis days as overlapping stages of creation.[12] This time lag would be necessary to allow for the new life forms to be phased in and for the ecosystem to reach its equilibrium in accordance with the laws of nature. Moreover, there are different equilibrium time frames associated with each entity being created, directly related to the complexity and reaction time of the ecosystem to reach equilibrium. In light of this understanding of Genesis, let's take a closer look at what could have occurred during the six stages of creation.

[10]Op cit., 181–84.
[11]Ibid., 49 (emphasis added).
[12]There are, of course, different forms of the progressive creation view.

Instead of non-intelligent bursts of speciation, as with Gould's punctuated equilibria, this graph shows intelligent bursts of creation with new life forms being introduced into the ecosystem at precisely the right moments in time—when the ecosystem has reached its natural equi-

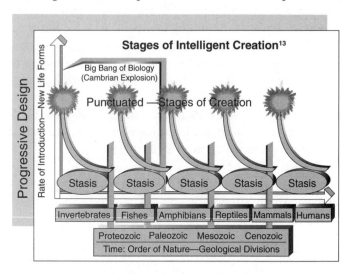

librium. As the graph indicates, the basic order of the stages of creation as described in Genesis 1 fits very nicely with the order of nature as depicted by the paleontological record and with the geological time divisions.

Since science is a progressive discipline and since there is variance in the interpretation of Genesis 1, it is not claimed that the following correlation is either definitive or final, but merely tentative and plausible in view of the present evidence.

Stages	Genesis Event	Verses	Science/Paleontology
1–2	Creation of the space-time universe	1–5	Big Bang of cosmology (light bursts forth from darkness)
2–3	Earth formed/water begins to condense/global sea emerges/atmosphere (expanse) created	6–8	Volcanic activity ends / Earth cools / atmosphere forms over the sea (troposphere—greenhouse effect)
3–4	Dry land created / Earth-moon system created / atmosphere becomes transparent (single-celled plant life created by now)	4, 9–10	Origin of double planet system (theory of the origin of the moon from the Earth would create a basin in the Earth for water to gather to one side)

---

[13] The data shows no evidence to support the idea that these life forms were "moving" (changing) in the "direction" of becoming new forms of life (new genetic types).

4–5	Creation of sea animals (multicellular to amphibians / reptiles / winged animals) creation of "great reptiles" (the largest reptiles are dinosaurs)	14–19	Cambrian explosion / age of fish (array of multicellular animals having the body plans of virtually all creatures that now swim, fly, or crawl throughout the world.)
5–6	Creation of land animals (domesticated livestock, non-domesticated—wild) Creation of mammals / human life	24–27	Age of amphibians / reptiles Age of mammals / humanity

The recorded events in Genesis 1 are not concerned with the details that a scientist would consider important. Yet we can safely assume that necessary life forms and atmospheric conditions were also being created to prepare the ecosystem of the earth for the creation of other anticipated life forms and eventually human life. In the outline that follows, we have substituted creation stages for creation days. We have also attempted to fill in some of the conditions that would most probably have needed to be present from the perspective of a model that allows for long periods of overlapping creation time frames.[14]

Stages 1–2: The "Big Bang" marked the creation of the space-time universe.[15] The Creator brought forth light from darkness in a single immensely concentrated burst of energy; electron orbits decayed and energy began to be converted to matter. During this stage solar and galactic systems would have taken shape, forming the Milky Way and igniting the sun, which began to burn as a main sequence star. The Creator formed the earth and our solar system from the shapeless nebula in dark space, which caused contrast between darkness and light (Genesis 1:1–5).

Stages 2–3: During this time span, the earth would have been steeped in volcanic activity, and the ensuing steam would have begun to condense. As the planet cooled down, water would have accumulated to form a sea that covered the surface of the earth. During these stages toxic gases from the volcanic activity probably dominated the atmosphere. The Creator thus formed an expanse

---

[14]Sources used for this summary and for further study include, Gerald Schroeder, *The Science of God* (New York: Free, 1997); Don Stoner, *A New Look at an Old Earth* (Eugene, Ore.: Harvest House, 1997); Hugh Ross, *The Fingerprint of God* (Orange, Calif.: Promise, 1991).

[15]It is fascinating to note that not until this century was it realized that space and time are correlative. Albert Einstein's discovery revealed time to be a fourth dimension. Hence, *time was created along with the universe.* Yet the Bible revealed this fact almost two thousand years before Einstein (see 1 Corinthians 2:7; 2 Timothy 1:9; and Titus 1:2).

(Genesis 1:6–8) or air space (troposphere[16, 17]), which created an oxygen-rich atmosphere, causing the sky to change from opaque (light-absorbing) to translucent (light-diffusing). This expanse would naturally have resulted in an atmosphere with temperature and pressure differentials producing violent electrical storms, resulting in the formation of an ozone layer.[18] The first forms of single-celled plant life could have been introduced to the ecosystem of the seas around this time: "Contrary to scientific opinion held until recently, fossil data have demonstrated that the first simple plant life appeared immediately after liquid water and not billions of years later."[19]

Stages 3–4: Genesis tells us that dry land was created by gathering the sea to one place (Genesis 1:9–10). One plausible explanation of "where" the water was placed is connected to the origin of the moon. Some scientists have speculated that the moon was once part of the earth. Isaac Asimov said, "This is an attractive thought, since the moon makes up only a little over one percent of the combined earth-moon mass and is small enough for its width to lie within the stretch of the Pacific. If the moon were made up of the outer layers of the earth, it would account for the moon's having no iron core and being much less dense than the earth, and for the Pacific floor being free of continental granite."[20]

After dry land was formed, the first terrestrial plants were created (Genesis 1:11–13). During this time various kinds (species) of vegetation, including plant life and trees, were phased in to the ecosystem. Plants are the earth's primary source of food and energy, deriving it through photosynthesis. For that reason, photosynthesis could have started to take place at this time as well, strengthening the already oxygen-rich atmosphere—which in turn enhanced the photosynthetic process. As photosynthesis continued, water would decompose, producing free oxygen and creating a greenhouse effect. Consequently, a thick cloud layer would have formed, covering the entire earth, and a stable water cycle (evaporation and condensation) would have been established as well.

Plant life requires the ecosystem to have the necessary microorganisms (bacteria and fungi) and insects (two million known species in the animal king-

---

[16]The troposphere is the lowest zone of the atmosphere. The composition of the atmosphere varies with altitude. About 75% of the total mass of the atmosphere and 90% of its water vapor are contained in its troposphere. Excluding water vapor, the air of the troposphere contains 78% nitrogen, 21% oxygen, and a balance of argon, carbon dioxide, and traces of other noble gases.

[17]Noble gases are rare (precious) gases such as helium, neon, and radon.

[18]Ozone is produced by subjecting oxygen to high-voltage electrical discharges.

[19]Gerald Schroeder, *The Science of God* (New York: Free, 1997), 68.

[20]Isaac Asimov, *Asimov's Guide to Science* (New York: Basic, 1972), 122.

dom) for proper equilibrium. Insects and other organisms are essential for such tasks as aeration, fertilization, pollination, and the like. Furthermore, the ecosystem would now have needed a food chain to sustain its balance.[21] The introduction of newly created entities would have shifted the ecosystem out of balance; therefore, fine-tuning was necessary, including the right amount of equilibrium time for the sequence of changes to lead to a new period of stabilization. When the ecosystem reached its equilibrium point, the next "burst of creation" would have taken place.

Stages 4–5: Once the volcanic activity had subsided and as the earth cooled, the carbon dioxide levels would have decreased along with the cloud coverage. Correspondingly, the stabilized atmosphere (with respect to pressure and temperature) and the consumption of carbon dioxide by the plants would have played a key role in clearing up the sky. As a result, the sun could be seen by day and the moon and stars by night (Genesis 1:14–19).

The Cambrian explosion most probably would have taken place during these latter stages of creation. The Creator brought forth an influx of aquatic life along with a host of small animal life, and probably toward the end of stage five, He introduced the "great creatures of the sea," including the reptiles, the greatest of which is the dinosaur.[22] After the ecosystem balanced that enormous explosion of aquatic life, the first true birds apparently were created as the atmosphere and ecosystem reached a somewhat stable temperature (Genesis 1:20–23). The stabilization of the atmospheric conditions would have been critically important, because birds are warm-blooded creatures and must generate and maintain heat within their own bodies to counteract temperature fluctuations of the environment.

Stages 5–6: These overlapping stages would prepare the ecosystem for the main purpose of fine-tuning the earth's environment: the creation of human life. Near the close of stage five, the Creator brought forth land animals and mammals known as livestock (domesticated), along with wild (non-domesticated) animals (Genesis 1:24–27). As the ecosystem adjusted to the introduction of animal life, and as the system reached a certain level of equilibrium, mammals were most probably created. We have endeavored to explain these stages below.

The following account is a bit involved and should be followed carefully. It is important to take the time to understand the terminology. Comprehending the terms and understanding their relationships will help bring to light the significance

---

[21]The number of links in an average food chain is between three and six.
[22]Gerald Schroeder, *The Science of God* (New York: Free, 1997), 193.

of applying the right terms to the right species, without a macroevolutionary bias.

There are two subclasses of mammals: the *prototheria* and the *theria.* The prototheria lay large yolky eggs and include only the duck-billed platypus and spiny anteater. Although warm-blooded, their body temperature is somewhat variable. The theria consists of the infra-classes called *metatheria* and *eutheria.* The metatheria are mammals that

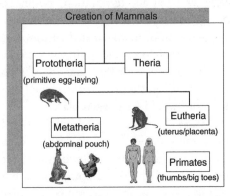

have an abdominal pouch into which the newly born young, in a very imma-ture state, move to complete their development. Modern examples of these mammals would be kangaroos, koalas, and bandicoots. Finally, the eutheria are mammals whose embryos are retained in a uterus in the mother's body and nourished by a placenta. With these, the young are fully protected during their embryonic development and kept at a constant temperature.

The increasing level of embryonic complexity with the mammals gives some insight into the order of creation leading up to humanity. Although hu-mans are classified as eutheria mammals, so are a large diversity of other mam-mals. Within the eutheria group, though, only primates are further distinguish-able by thumbs and big toes that are opposable (permitting manual dexterity) and opposing eyes (for binocular vision). Primates include monkeys, apes, and humans. The order of primates that includes humanity is known as *Homo,* and macroevolutionists place humans and all their supposed macroevolutionary an-cestors in a group called *hominids.* However, now that we have shown that macroevolution is not a plausible model of origins, we can dispense with this particular extension of terms and classify human life as a separate and distinct kind from monkeys and apes. On that account, the proper classification of humans is *Homo sapiens.*

Homo sapiens were created distinctly human, hence the use of the term *sapien. Sapien* is from a Latin word that conveys the idea of having intelligence, discernment, and wisdom. It has to do with having the intellectual wherewithal to make judgments and to deal with persons in a right manner, that is, to make correct ethical choices.[23]

---

[23]We will pick up this unique characteristic of Homo sapiens in the chapters on law, justice, and ethics when we define the concept of personhood and discuss the topics of morality and human rights.

Not even all macroevolutionists believe that Homo habilis and Homo erectus were common ancestors.[24] The following quotation is taken from Duane Gish's book *Evolution: Challenge of the Fossil Record;* we commend it to you if you are interested in knowing more about this issue.

> While certainly not entertaining any doubts about the fact of evolution, Stephen J. Gould, Harvard University paleontologist, has the following to say concerning this state of affairs:
>
> "What has become of our ladder if there are three coexisting lineages of hominids . . . none clearly derived from another? Moreover none display any evolutionary trends during their tenure on earth: none become brainier or more erect as they approach the present day."[25]

Gish continues by citing the discovery of another macroevolutionist, Louis Leaky, who found certain artifacts that led to only one conclusion: Homo habilis and Homo erectus existed contemporaneously with Homo sapiens.[26] Gish says,

> If *Australopithecus, Homo habilis,* and *Homo erectus* existed contemporaneously, how could one have been ancestral to another? And how could any of these creatures be ancestral to Man, when Man's artifacts are found at a lower stratigraphic level, directly underneath, and thus earlier in time to these supposed ancestors of Man? If the facts are correct as Leaky has reported them, then obviously none of these creatures could have been ancestral to Man, and that leaves Man's ancestral tree bare.[27]

Accordingly, toward the very end of stage six, once the ecosystem fully adjusted with the addition of mammals prior to Homo sapiens, the Creator

---

[24]*Homo* is Latin for "man." The terms *habilis* and *erectus* signify dexterity and walking upright, respectively. They are allegedly ancestral to Homo sapiens.

[25]Duane Gish, *Evolution: Challenge of the Fossil Record* (Green Forest, Ariz.: Master, 1985), 171.

[26]Ibid.

[27]Perhaps you are wondering why man is found at a lower stratigraphic level, since we have asserted that although these other creatures were not ancestral to man, other mammals were created first. There are two responses to this inquiry. First, if these fossil remains belonged to apes, and apes and humans existed together at some given point in time, there is no reason an ape couldn't have died in the same location that was inhabited by humans earlier in time. Second, the macroevolutionary conclusion that these fossil remains are ancestral to humans is by no means certain—they may be fossils of human beings. For example, Jack Cuozzo has documented with recent high-tech X-rays of Neanderthal skulls that they are not ape-like but human-like. In speaking of the famous Le Moustier fossil, he asserts that "it is not ape-like at all. . . ﹐ The lower jaw . . . is 30 mm (over an inch) out of the socket (TM fossa). This allowed the upper jaw to be pushed forward 30 mm, presenting a very ape-like appearance. This would be a dislocated lower jaw in any oral surgeon's office. How can a dislocated jaw be passed off as evidence for evolution?" (*Buried Alive: The Startling Truth About Neanderthal Man* [Green Forest, Ariz.: Master, 1998], 166.)

formed two humans and breathed life into them. They were made not only as living souls with bodies but were also highly endowed with spiritual, rational, moral, and volitional faculties. If the aforementioned explanation of the stages of creation are fairly accurate—and we believe there is no biblical or scientific reason to seriously call them into question—then it seems to us that the progressive view of the design model fits well with all of the available evidence from science.

This graph is an attempt to put all of the data together into one concise overview as represented by the progressive model. As we factor in the overlapping time periods, the data begins to align itself

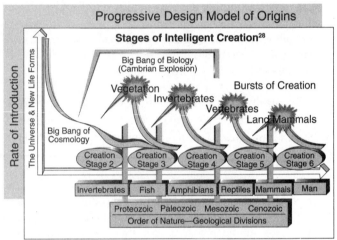

with the known facts (including the Big Bang of cosmology) in such a way as to depict all the sequences and correlate them with the known order of nature, appearances of new life forms, and geological ages. Note once again how the stages of creation allow for the newly created entities to be phased in to the environment, allowing for the ecosystem to reach its natural equilibrium.

After carefully considering all the evidence, the progressive view of the design model (or something like it) appears to be a viable model of origins. Three independent fields of study support its integrity: cosmology, molecular biology, and paleontology. The progressive view also proves to be consistent with first principles, the laws of science, and the observational evidence. Furthermore, it satisfies the criteria of a good theory in that (1) it adequately describes a large class of observations (i.e., the origin and nature of the universe, the origin and nature of life, new life forms, and the fossil record) and (2) it makes sound predictions about the genetic limitations of adaptation.

---

[28]The data shows no evidence to support the idea that these life forms were "moving" (changing) in the "direction" of becoming new forms of life (new genetic types).

DOES THE BIBLICAL AGE OF HUMANITY CONFLICT WITH MODERN SCIENCE?

The simple answer to this question is no; the biblical age of humanity and modern science are not at odds with respect to the age of the universe or the human race. Since macroevolutionists are wrong with respect to human ancestors, the time frames of any living thing prior to the human race is not relevant here for several reasons.

First of all, the Bible does not explicitly state the age of the human race; in fact, there are gaps in the genealogies recorded in the Bible. For example, Matthew 1:8 says that Jehoram was the father of Uzziah (another name for Azariah), while 1 Chronicles 3:11–14 lists three other generations between Jehoram and Azariah (Ahaziah, Joash, Amaziah). Likewise, Genesis 11:12 lists Shelah as the son of Arphaxad, while Luke 3:36 places another generation between them (Cainan). Since the Bible nowhere adds up the numbers listed in Genesis 5 and 11, and since there are intentional and significant gaps in the genealogies, we cannot determine from it exactly how old the human race is. Consequently, all attempts to calculate the age of humanity from biblical history are replete with potentially fallible human assumptions. The Bible's purpose in recording these genealogies was not to give a complete and exhaustive ancestral account but rather a proof of lineage and descent.[29]

Secondly, relatively recent discoveries by molecular biologists have challenged the long-standing and widely accepted macroevolutionary age of humanity. This issue has become a point of contention among molecular biologists, anthropologists, and paleontologists as they argue about the age of the human race. The following tabulation is a summary of the range of debated ages of humanity as noted in *Newsweek*,[30] *Discover*,[31] *Science*,[32] and *Nature*[33] magazines:

In the late 1950s: 5 to 15 million years old
In the mid–1970s: 5 to 7 million years old
In the late 1970s: 1 million years old

[29]See Norman L. Geisler, "Genealogies: Open or Closed" in *Baker Encyclopedia of Christian Apologetics*. (Grand Rapids, Mich.: Baker, 1999), 267–270.
[30]John Tierney, Linda Wright, and Karen Springen, "The Search for Adam and Eve," *Newsweek*, January 11, 1988, 46.
[31]James Shreeve, "Argument Over a Woman," *Discover*, August 1990, 54.
[32]Ann Gibbons, "Mitochondrial Eve: Wounded, but Not Dead Yet," *Science*, vol. 257, August 14, 1992, 873.
[33]L. Simon Whitfield, John E. Sulston, and Peter N. Goodfellow, "Sequence Variation of the Human Y Chromosome," *Nature*, vol. 378, no. 6558 (1995), 379, referenced in Hugh Ross, "Searching for Adam," *Facts & Faith*, vol. 10, no. 1 (1996), 4.

In the mid–1980s: 800,000 years old
In the late 1980s: 50,000 to 200,000 years old
In the mid–1990s: 43,000 years old

It's hard to ignore the obvious direction that the age of humanity seems to be heading—younger all the time! More recent Y-chromosome studies[34] fix an even younger age to Homo sapiens, suggesting that they appeared somewhere between 37,000 to 49,000 years ago.[35] It is possible that this date can be reduced even more to between 10,000 and 20,000 years ago or less.

Let's calculate the margin of error associated with the age of the human race, using the macroevolutionary average estimated age of ten million years[36] in the late 1950s and the macroevolutionary average estimated age of 43,000 years in 1995:

$$[10 \text{ million}–43,000]/10 \text{ million} \times 100 = 99.57\% \text{ difference.}$$

It is clear that this macroevolutionary "dating game" operates at an incredibly high margin of error—nearly 100% on the human level. Take a look at the following graph:

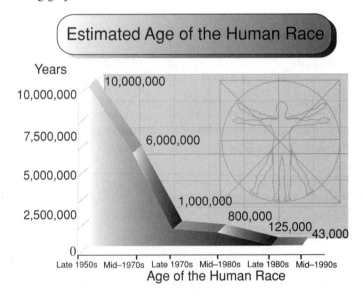

Estimated Age of the Human Race

Years — 10,000,000 — 7,500,000 — 5,000,000 — 2,500,000 — 0

10,000,000 — 6,000,000 — 1,000,000 — 800,000 — 125,000 — 43,000

Late 1950s Mid–1970s Late 1970s Mid–1980s Late 1980s Mid–1990s
Age of the Human Race

---

[34]Chromosomes are threadlike bodies composed of genes that carry genetic information responsible for the inherited characteristics of the organism. X and Y chromosomes are the chromosomes that will determine the sex of the offspring. A female has two X chromosomes (XX), while a male has one of each (XY).

[35]Op. cit.

[36]This number is found by averaging the estimates of five and fifteen million.

In view of what has been presented, there is no basis to the charge that the biblical age of humanity conflicts with modern science. Taking the upper-limit estimate of the Y-chromosome studies estimated age (49,000) and the upper limit of the Hebrew scholars' estimated age (35,000), the margin of error drops considerably:

$$[49,000-35,000]/49,000 \times 100 = 28.57\% \text{ difference.}$$

The Genesis account of the creation of the universe and all life forms is absolutely amazing! In thirty-one verses we read an account of the entire origin of the universe, all living things, and human beings. One physicist rightly states,

> These are events about which scientists have written literally millions of words. The entire development of animal life is summarized in eight biblical sentences. Considering the brevity of the biblical narrative, the match between the statements and timing in Genesis 1 and the discoveries of modern science is phenomenal, especially when we realize that all biblical interpretation used here was recorded centuries, even millennia, in the past and so was not in any way influenced by the discoveries of modern science. It is modern science that has come to match the biblical account of our Genesis.[37]

This has been a remarkable investigation ending with the beginning—Genesis. When Robert Jastrow pondered the scientific discoveries of this century and his colleagues' reactions to them, he was quite mystified. As a self-proclaimed agnostic astronomer, Jastrow basically could not understand why scientific men found scientific evidence hard to accept. He said that they were reacting with their feelings and not their minds. After citing evidence for the beginning of the universe and giving examples of the emotional reactions of some of his associates and other men of science, Jastrow said,

> Now we see how the astronomical evidence leads to a biblical view of the origin of the world. All the details differ, but the essential element in the astronomical and biblical accounts of Genesis is the same; the chain of events leading to man commenced suddenly and sharply, at a definite moment in time, in a flash of light and energy. . . . The scientist's pursuit of the past ends in the moment of creation. This is an exceedingly strange development, unexpected by all but the theologians. They have always accepted the word of the Bible: *In the beginning God created the heaven and*

---

[37]Gerald Schroeder, *The Science of God* (New York: Free, 1997), 70.

earth. . . . For the scientist who has lived by faith in the power of reason, the story ends like a bad dream. He has scaled the mountains of ignorance; he is about to conquer the highest peak; as he pulls himself over the final rock, he is greeted by a band of theologians who have been sitting there for centuries.[38]

We have arrived at the overall conclusion that an uncaused, infinitely powerful, eternal, and intelligent Being (God) exists. This was accomplished without being biased by unjustifiable philosophical assumptions. Through an examination of the known facts, and through an application of the first principles of the in-

	Atheism	Pantheism	Theism
Truth	Relative, No Absolutes	Relative to This World	Absolute Truth Exists
Cosmos	Always Existed	Not Real– Illusion	Created Reality
God (Logos)	Does Not Exist	Exists, Unknowable	Exists, Knowable

volved academic disciplines, we can say that atheism and pantheism hold false views of reality. Furthermore, it is most reasonable to say that we can know with a high degree of probability (in scientific terms) that God (*Logos*) does exist and is knowable.[39] If God does exist and is infinitely powerful and intelligent, He should know what is right and what is wrong. This conclusion leads us to our next topic: the credibility of believing in universal moral laws.

[38]Robert Jastrow, *God and the Astronomers* (New York: W. W. Norton & Co., 1992), 14, 106–7 (emphasis added).
[39]See chapter 2 to review the method of testing the truth claims of worldviews.

9
QUESTIONS ABOUT LAW

The philosophy in the schoolroom in one generation will be the philosophy of the government in the next.

—ABRAHAM LINCOLN

There is an often unrecognized but logical connection between creation and one's view of law and government. Our Founding Fathers recognized this truth and declared that because all "are created equal" they possess God-given "unalienable Rights" based on "the Laws of Nature," which come from "Nature's God." For that reason, in Congress on July 4, 1776, they unanimously declared,

> When in the Course of human events, it becomes necessary for one people to dissolve the political bands which have connected them with another, and to assume among the Powers of the earth, the separate and equal station to which the Laws of Nature and of Nature's God entitle them, a decent respect to the opinions of mankind requires that they should declare the causes which impel them to the separation.
>
> We hold these Truths to be self-evident, that all men are created equal, that they are endowed by their Creator with certain unalienable Rights, that among these are Life, Liberty and the Pursuit of Happiness. That to secure these rights, Governments are instituted among men.[1]

WHAT IS LAW?

American law was originally based on the classical understanding of *jurisprudence*. Jurisprudence is the science or knowledge of law and is sometimes called the *philosophy of law*. The most substantial body of thought in this discipline focuses on the meaning of the concept of law itself (legal theory) and the relationship between this concept and the concept of morality. Throughout the history of jurisprudence, the view of law most commonly defended is called *natural law*. Natural-law proponents believe that all human beings are aware of certain laws that exist for the purpose of governing human conduct and protecting the rights of individuals. It is believed that these laws are discoverable through "sensible" intelligence. Ancient Greek and Roman thought, particularly Stoicism, introduced certain ideas of eternal laws. Of course, the Jews and Christians understood law to be a reflection of the eternal nature and character of God as given to Moses in the moral principles of the Ten Commandments (Mosaic law). Mosaic law is anchored in the belief that God created human life in His image (*Imago Dei*), and part of that image emulates God's moral attributes.

The New Testament describes natural law as something inherent in all human beings. It is a knowledge that is God-given, and it serves as the basis for morals and ethics. Speaking about people who never heard of Moses and the Ten Commandments, the New Testament tells us that they know about God's law because "*the requirements of the law are written on their hearts*, their consciences also bearing witness, and their thoughts now accusing, now even defending them" (Romans 2:15, emphasis added).

During the Middle Ages the leading theologians, the most enduring and influential being Thomas Aquinas, understood and defended natural law as a derivative of eternal law. The classical understanding of natural law, then, is the human participation in eternal law by way of reason. "In brief, natural law is the 'natural light of reason,' by which we discern what is right and what is wrong."[2] All rational creatures discover natural law by way of first principles and immediate precepts. It also can be said that human reason is the basis for natural law only insofar as it participates in the Creator's eternal law. As shown in this illustration, the Creator illuminates human reason so that natural law may be known and moral laws constructed upon the foundation of eternal law. Therefore, natural-law legal theory is based upon absolute and objective moral laws, and it values all human life. *"For 'all laws derive from the eternal law to the extent that they share in right reason' and right reason is only right if it participates in 'Eternal Reason.' "*[3]

---

[2]Norman L. Geisler, *Thomas Aquinas: An Evangelical Appraisal* (Grand Rapids, Mich.: Baker, 1991), 165.
[3]Ibid. (emphasis added).

(There are other very good explanations and articulations of natural-law legal theory that ought to be studied in order to gain a better understanding of this topic. C. S. Lewis eloquently defended it in his valuable work *The Abolition of Man.*[4] A more recent work was done by J. Budziszewski, a philosophy professor at the University of Texas who has given a forceful update of this view of law in his book *Written on the Heart: The Case for Natural Law.*[5])

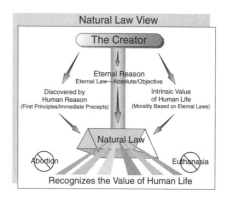

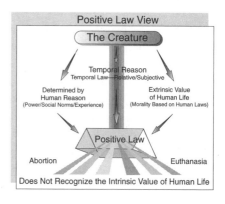

In contraposition to natural law is what has been referred to as *positive law* (which can refer to written law). Whether or not it is based in natural law, generally speaking, positive law is opposed to the classical understanding of natural law. Most advocates of positive law today believe that the only binding laws on humanity are laws imposed, not by the Creator, but by the creature—human government.

As depicted in this diagram, positivists believe that law is temporal because it has its basis in temporal reason, not eternal reason. Consequently, they believe that laws cannot be subject to any higher legal constraints.

The "legal prism" of positive law, then, is "characterized by two major tenets: (1) that there is no necessary connection between morality and law; and (2) that legal validity is determined ultimately by reference to certain basic social facts."[6] This makes positive law subjective because it is based upon relative social norms that differ with various cultures, experiences, and situations. Positive law advocates insist that *law* is determined by humanity, and that therefore human authorities are sovereign over it. This understanding of law leads to the idea that humanity is also sovereign over *life* and determines the

---

[4]C. S. Lewis, *The Abolition of Man* (New York: Macmillan, 1955).

[5]J. Budziszewski, *Written on the Heart: The Case for Natural Law* (Downers Grove, Ill.: InterVarsity, 1997), 196.

[6]*The Cambridge Dictionary of Philosophy* (Cambridge University Press, 1995), 425.

value of it. We strongly believe that this is why positive legal theory results in the devaluation of human life and thus undermines the basis for equality and human rights.

In this chapter, we want to examine the arguments for natural law and positive law views to see which one is preeminent. (Because of the law of non-contradiction, they cannot both be correct.) However, before we examine these two competing views of law, it may be helpful for you to understand the major trends of thought that led to the decline of the classical understanding of natural law and helped to establish and empower the positive law view.

WHAT CAUSED THE RISE OF POSITIVE LAW THEORY?

One of the best places to begin to understand the emergence of positive law is with the philosophy of the famous German atheist Friedrich Nietzsche (1844–1900), who said, "God is dead and we have killed him."[7] The phrase "God is dead" had different meanings for different thinkers; Nietzsche used it in the mythological sense. In other words, he asserted that the myth of God's existence, which was once widely believed, died, and that the myth of objective values died with Him. Therefore, for Nietzsche, reason was the only hope for humanity. He believed that with the exercise of reason, combined with the will to power to dominate the eternal recurrence of time, one could become the "self-sufficient man." Existence for Nietzsche was to "live dangerously!" To "send your ships into uncharted seas!"[8]

Nietzsche believed that there was no meaning in life (in and of itself) except the meaning man gives to it himself. He reduced everything in life to the will for self-assertion, and since God-given values were dead, it was up to humans to create their own values. He argued that we must go "beyond good and evil." Accordingly, "Since there is no God to will what is good, we must will our own good. And since there is no eternal value, we must will the eternal recurrence of the same state of affairs." Nietzsche said, in the last line of the *Genealogy of Morals*, that he would rather will nothingness than not to will at all. This willing of nothingness is what is called *nihilism* ("nothingness-ism").[9]

Utilitarianism also formed an essential part of the foundation that provided the philosophical support for positive law. Utilitarianism is "the moral theory

---

[7]Friedrich Nietzsche, *The Gay Science*, in *The Portable Nietzsche*, trans. Walter Kaufmann (New York: Viking, 1968), 95.
[8]Ibid., 97.
[9]Norman L. Geisler, *Christian Ethics: Options and Issues* (Grand Rapids, Mich.: Baker, 1989), 33.

that an action is morally right if and only if it produces at least as much good (utility) for all people affected by the action as any alternative action the person could do instead."[10] This view was advocated by Jeremy Bentham (1748–1832) and John Stuart Mill (1806–1873). Bentham held this view in the *quantitative* sense; he spoke of it as what brings the greatest amount of pleasure and the least amount of pain. This view is referred to as the "utilitarian calculus." Bentham believed that one ought to act in such a manner as to produce the greatest good for the greatest number of persons in the long run.

Mill used the same utilitarian calculus, only he argued that it should be understood in the *qualitative* sense: "Pleasures differed in kind, and higher pleasures are to be preferred over lower ones."[11] "Pleasures do not differ merely in their amount or intensity. One is higher and more valuable than another simply because most people who experience both decidedly prefer one over the other."[12] Mill held that "in any event, there are no absolute moral laws. It all depends upon what brings about the greatest pleasure. And this may differ from person to person and from place to place."[13]

Another thinker who influenced the rise of positive law was Charles Darwin (1809–1882). In 1859 Charles Darwin published his book on macroevolution, *On the Origin of Species*. His teaching eventually became widely accepted as the scholarly view to hold, and it effectively reduced humanity to the level of animals. For all practical purposes, the belief that humans are only different in degree from animals, and do not differ in kind, slowly influenced and eventually established macroevolution as an academic, political, legislative, judicial, and public mindset. Agreeing with Darwin, Karl Marx said, "In our evolutionary concept of the universe, there is absolutely no room for either a Creator or a Ruler."[14] In brief, if there is no Moral Lawgiver, there is no moral law on which to base civil laws. This belief strengthens positive law because it supports the view that there is no relationship between the concept of law and the concept of morality.

As educators integrated Darwinian thought into the various academic disciplines, students gradually learned that there is no transcendent basis for law and morality and that human behavior was a combination of instinct and genetics. As a result, the view that humans "ought" to be held responsible to treat other humans in a way prescribed by natural law was eventually expunged from

---

[10] *The Cambridge Dictionary of Philosophy* (Cambridge University Press, 1995), 824.
[11] John Stuart Mill, "Utilitarianism," in *The Utilitarians* (Garden City, N.Y.: Dolphin/Doubleday, 1961).
[12] Norman L. Geisler, *Christian Ethics: Options and Issues* (Grand Rapids, Mich.: Baker, 1989), 66.
[13] Ibid., 31.
[14] *Marx and Engels on Religion*, ed. Reinhold Niebuhr (New York: Schocken, 1964), 295.

classes on legal theory. It was replaced with a Darwinian understanding of human behavior, which is harmonious with macroevolution and supports the view of positive law. As a result, *positive law, reinforced by a Darwinian naturalistic worldview, eventually became the dominant theory that was taught in "higher education" and the view most widely accepted and practiced in courts of law.*

This raises a critically important question with respect to the relationship between morality and law: "If humans are not naturally moral and if they are genetically determined, how can they be held legally responsible for their behavior?" *Time* magazine once printed a ten-page article to defend and promote the idea that humans are genetically determined and morally impotent. The author of the article, Robert Wright, proposed that our sexual attitudes, fidelity being one among many, are determined by genetics—hence, the cover story: "Infidelity: It May Be in Our Genes." Wright said, "We are potentially moral animals—which is more than any other animal can say—*but we are not naturally moral animals.*"[15] Although the article focused on infidelity as one of the many varieties of sexual expression, the principle of genetically determined sexual behavior would logically apply to *all* sexual demeanors, including homosexuality, child molestation, pedophilia, rape, and others.

In his article, Wright explained how infidelity is a natural impulse, as natural as any sexual desire—even the desire to fall in love. He said,

> In the 1967 best seller *The Naked Ape*, zoologist Desmond Morris wrote with comforting authority that the evolutionary purpose of human sexuality is "to strengthen the pair-bond and maintain the family unit." . . . This picture has lately acquired some blemishes. . . . Of course you don't need a Ph.D. to see that till-death-do-we-part fidelity doesn't come as naturally to people as, say, eating. But an emerging field known as evolutionary psychology can now put a finer point on the matter. By studying how the process of natural selection shaped the mind, evolutionary psychologists are painting a new portrait of human nature. . . . The good news is that human beings are designed to fall in love. The bad news is that they aren't designed to stay there. According to evolutionary psychology, *it is only "natural"* for both men and women—at some times, under certain circumstances—*to commit adultery.* . . . It is similarly natural to find some attractive colleague superior on all counts to the sorry wreck of a spouse you're saddled with.[16]

If Wright is correct and if humans are essentially animals, then it makes

---

[15]Robert Wright, "Infidelity: It May Be in Our Genes," *Time*, August 15, 1994, 46 (emphasis added).
[16]Ibid. (emphasis added).

sense to say that it is only natural for humans to behave in the manner described above. If so, can adultery (or homosexuality, or child molestation, or pedophilia, or rape, or any sexual behavior) ever be wrong? Legally wrong, perhaps, if a government makes laws against such behavior. But could it ever be legally right and morally wrong? Not according to positive law, because there is no relationship between the concept of law (legal theory) and the concept of morality. Moreover, *if macroevolutionists are correct and sexual behavior is the direct result of genetics and environment, what about other types of behavior?* What about assault? What about murder? With this in mind, we ask, *"How does macroevolution and a positive view of law affect the judicial process?"*

DOES POSITIVE LAW JEOPARDIZE CRIMINAL JUSTICE?

Based upon Nietzsche's foundation of atheism, the utilitarianism of Bentham and Mill, and a Darwinian view of the development of human life, legal scholars started to formulate new theories of law. Eventually, positive law became known as *legal realism*. Legal realism is "a theory in philosophy of law or jurisprudence broadly characterized by the claim that the nature of law is better understood by observing what courts and citizens actually do than by analyzing stated legal rule and legal concepts."[17] Legal realism in the United States, in its contemporary form, is known as *critical legal studies.*

The critical legal studies movement has recently given rise to *postmodern legal theory.* Advocates of this theory believe that law is created and interpreted in such a way as to benefit the people in power and exclude the poor and minorities. As one postmodern professor said,

> If there is a single theme [in postmodern legal theory], it is that law is an instrument of social, economic, and political domination, both in the sense of furthering the concrete interests of the dominators and in that of legitimating the existing order. This approach emphasizes the ideological character of legal doctrine.[18]

If the positive or postmodern view of law is considered to be correct, then law ultimately depends upon the wills of human legislators. If those legislators believe that macroevolution is true, then they also believe that there is no essential difference between human nature and animal nature. If this is the case

---

[17] *The Cambridge Dictionary of Philosophy* (Cambridge University Press, 1995), 425.
[18] Mark Kelman, *A Guide to Critical Legal Studies* (Cambridge, Mass.: Harvard University Press, 1987), 1.

and human behavior is genetically determined, how does it affect the concept of justice?

Rather than give a speculative answer to this question, we cite two examples that actually happened. In 1991 Tony Mobley shot and killed a Domino's pizza manager execution-style and was sentenced to death. His attorneys contended that "Mr. Mobley's genes may have predisposed him to commit crimes. His actions may not have been a product of total free will."[19]

The article went on to describe how this case was seeking to break new legal ground by bringing into court a growing body of research linking genes and aggressive behavior. "Mr. Mobley's unusual defense has raised an additional concern among some legal experts, who worry that genetic research could tear at the fabric of the criminal-justice system by allowing people to argue that they were born without control over their actions."[20] Yet this view is not really new. The author of this article referred to an attorney who tried the same strategy many years ago. "The lawyer Clarence Darrow took an early stab at this approach in the notorious 1924 trial of Nathan Leopold and Richard Loeb, two wealthy Chicago boys who murdered a fourteen-year-old. Mr. Darrow suggested that one of the boys may have been corrupted by 'the seed' of 'remote ancestors.' "[21]

Mobley's attorneys and Darrow[22] used essentially the same tactic. They sought to excuse the behavior of their clients based upon the macroevolutionary theory of genetic determination. Their defensive strategy is harmonious with a positive view of law, and as a result, *this kind of defense strategy is an attempt to undermine the very essence of the criminal-justice system and thereby devalue human life itself.* Some criminal-law experts believe that the criminal-justice system will continue to meet this kind of defense, particularly as genetic research continues; they actually expect it to "mushroom." If this does happen, how will the Darwinian understanding of human nature and the belief in positive law influence legislature?

HOW CAN LAWMAKERS PASS GOOD LAWS?

Since referring to the various modifications of positive law by their different names can get confusing, and since the fundamental elements of each re-

---

[19]Edward Felsenthal, "Man's Genes Made Him Kill, His Lawyers Claim," *The Wall Street Journal*, November 15, 1994, B1.

[20]Ibid.

[21]Ibid.

[22]Clarence Darrow is widely remembered as the defense attorney in the well-known Scopes trial of 1925, which dealt with the prosecution of a high school biology teacher in Dayton, Tennessee, accused of teaching the theory of macroevolution.

main unchanged, we will hereafter refer to all views of man-made laws as positive law.[23] We take the term *positive law* to refer to that condition in which human legislatures have no objective and transcendent standard to measure human behavior, and in which laws are written by the governing powers of a society to protect their own interests. This understanding of law raises one of the most important questions of legal theory and the criminal-justice system, namely, "How can a society develop a set of laws that are considered to be good laws?" Since "the good" can refer to the good of the state or to the good of the individual, who decides which good is the "better" or "greater" good? In other words, how can a nation determine what constitutes "good laws"?

By "good laws," we are not referring to civil or legal rights, rights such as those enumerated in the first eight amendments to our constitution, or those rights explicitly defined in constitutions and in the positive laws enacted by legislatures. These rights can and have changed with time in our own country, and they significantly vary from culture to culture. *What we are referring to are human or natural rights, which are to be clearly distinguished from civil or legal rights.*

When President George H. Bush nominated Judge Clarence Thomas to fill a vacancy on the United States Supreme Court bench in 1991, liberal critics opposed him because they feared he would use his belief in natural law as a means of interpreting the Constitution. Democratic Senator Joseph Biden chaired the Judiciary Committee at that time. Biden said that he also believed in natural law; however, he was afraid that Thomas might believe in the "wrong kind" of natural law. Phillip Johnson (law professor at the University of California, Berkeley) has noted how Senator Biden differentiated between the "right kind" (good) and "wrong kind" (bad) of natural law. Citing an essay authored by Biden, Johnson says,

> According to Senator Biden's article, good natural law is subservient to the Constitution—i.e., to positive man-made law—and its use is therefore restricted "to the task of giving meaning to the Constitution's great, but sometimes ambiguous, phrases." Second, good natural law does not dictate a moral code to be imposed upon individuals. . . . Finally, good natural law is not a static set of "timeless truths" but rather an evolving body of ideals that changes to permit government to adjust to new social challenges and new economic circumstances. Bad natural law, by negative implication, would be an unchanging moral code that restricts either the freedom of individuals to do as they think best or the freedom of government to do whatever the public interest requires.[24]

---

[23]Other names used in this chapter for positive law include legal realism, legal relativism, critical legal studies, and postmodern legal theory.
[24]Phillip E. Johnson, *Reason in the Balance* (Downers Grove, Ill.: InterVarsity, 1995), 134.

Of course, Senator Biden is not using the term *natural law* in the classical sense, as the Founding Fathers did; rather, he puts positive law above objective natural law. In doing so, however, he raises the logical dilemma for moral and legal relativists. The "timeless truths" to which Senator Biden referred are how he describes the classical understanding of natural law, for natural law can be thought of as the "timeless truths" that constitute the objective standard of right and wrong against which all human behavior and legal standards are to be measured. In order to truly believe in natural law, one would have to submit to absolute moral laws that transcend governments. Phillip Johnson sheds a little more light on this contemporary dilemma.

> Anyone who says there is such a standard [that there are objective, transcendent, and absolute moral laws] seems to be denying that we are morally autonomous beings who have every right to set our own standards and depart from the traditions of our ancestors. If one attributes the enduring moral commandments to God, one invites the accusation that one means to force one's religious morality on persons with different views. On the other hand, anyone who denies that there is a higher law seems to embrace nihilism and therefore to leave the powerless unprotected from the whims of the powerful. Either alternative is unacceptable. The safest course . . . [is to] be impenetrably vague or platitudinous on the subject.[25]

If the classical understanding of natural law is not true, however, then there is no dilemma to worry about, and consequently leaders such as Senator Biden ought not to be concerned with embracing nihilism and leaving the powerless unprotected from the whims of the powerful. The late Arthur Allen Leff, Yale law professor, had a way of stating complex issues such as this one in profoundly simple terms. In a penetrating lecture delivered at Duke University a few years before his death, Leff precisely described not only the essence of the political battle between the supporters of natural law and positive law, but the essence of an internal struggle every person faces. He pointed directly to the dilemma of a society whose individuals yearn for both autonomy and enduring moral values at the same time. Leff said,

> I want to believe—and so do you—in a complete, transcendent, and immanent set of propositions about right and wrong, findable rules that authoritatively and unambiguously direct us how to live righteously. I also want to believe—and so do you—in no such thing, but rather that we are wholly free, not only to choose for ourselves what we ought to do, but to

---

[25]Ibid.

decide for ourselves, individually and as a species, what we ought to be. What we want, Heaven help us, is simultaneously to be perfectly ruled and perfectly free, that is at the same time to discover the right and the good and to create it.[26]

It is this kind of candor that brings us to the ultimate test of who is right in this debate concerning the nature of law and its relationship to morality. The twentieth century witnessed the loss of moral objectivity and the dangers associated with upholding the positive law view. As Peter Kreeft says,

> We have lost objective moral law for the first time in history. The philosophies of moral positivism (meaning that morality is *posited* or made by man) and of moral relativism and subjectivism have become for the first time not a heresy for rebels but the reigning orthodoxy of the intellectual establishment. University faculty and media personnel overwhelmingly reject belief in the notion of universal and objective values.[27]

Let's take this rejection of the classical view of natural law to its logical conclusion. Natural law is based upon the inherent, universal understanding that certain behaviors are immoral and, therefore, ought to be illegal. In the past, America embraced the truth that human life had God-given value that went beyond the scope of government. If this is true, it only makes sense that natural law is a necessary prerequisite for positive law. In this sense, natural law provides the basis for a standard of morality. This standard, or moral law, can be thought of as a *first principle* of jurisprudence upon which all law ought to be based and upon which true civilization depends.

Civilization is dependent upon natural law with respect to the conviction that human nature is distinct from animal nature because the Creator endowed all of humanity with certain characteristics (unalienable human rights). These qualities do not depend upon any government, and they must bear witness to the eternal nature and moral character of the Creator. Yet in order for law to be in effect, it must be proclaimed and upheld. The United States of America was founded upon belief in the classical understanding of natural law that served as the basis for the fundamental principles (self-evident truths) proclaimed in the Declaration of Independence. Furthermore, in an effort to uphold and secure the axiomatic truths proclaimed in that declaration, our Founding Fathers chartered the Constitution and established our system of government.

---

[26]Arthur Allen Leff, "Unspeakable Ethics, Unnatural Law," *Duke Law Journal*, December 1979, no. 6, 1229.
[27]Peter Kreeft, *Back to Virtue* (San Francisco: Ignatius, 1992), 25 (emphasis added).

Our Founding Fathers knew that in a country that would one day be filled with diversity, the founding principles must be based on truth, because *truth brings unity to diversity*. They considered the unifying first principles of the Declaration of Independence to be "self-evident" truths. They knew that if these truths were violated, it would eventually undermine and threaten the God-given human rights that they were meant to establish and for which governments were to be instituted to secure and uphold.

In contrast to many contemporary leaders, our Founding Fathers were judicious politicians because they were clear and penetrating thinkers. They understood the axiomatic truths of life and that their ultimate rational justification came from the Divine Lawgiver (Creator), who alone gave humanity life and value (human rights). To their way of thinking, the Creator is the basis for life, truth, law, freedom, and justice (true freedom implies justice). According to them, governments rest upon the shoulders of the Creator, not the creation.

Divine Lawgiver View

The Declaration of Independence

We hold these Truths to be self-evident, that all men are created equal, that they are endowed by their Creator with certain inalienable Rights, that among these are Life, Liberty and the Pursuit of Happiness. That to secure these rights, Governments are instituted among men.

Our Founding Fathers understood that the first principles that guarantee life, liberty, and justice must logically be anchored in a transcendent, absolute, and personal Being. The Declaration of Independence clearly states that governments are to be instituted in order to *secure* certain human rights—it was not believed, nor was it stated, that governments are to be instituted to *create* those rights. However, as a nation today we practice a vastly different declaration than the one our Founding Fathers authored. Rather than a declaration based upon a Creator, creation, and inalienable human rights, we practice a declaration based upon naturalism, macroevolution, and relative human rights.

Naturalistic Evolution View

A Declaration of Contingency

We hold these relative truths to be self-evident, that all Homo sapiens have evolved slowly; that they are endowed by nature with certain contingent and relative rights; that among these are the right to kill their babies, the right to full autonomy and the right to pursue what makes them happy. That to create and secure these rights, Governments are instituted among Homo sapiens.

Since we no longer practice law as founded upon the belief in a personal

Creator—and as articulated in the Declaration of Independence—our culture runs the risk of undermining the value of human life and the belief that all humanity is created equal and as such "ought" to be treated with God-given equal value. We plan to show that the prevailing understanding of positive law stands diametrically opposed to natural law and to the essential principles that provide the basis for the Constitution.

We believe that the classical understanding of natural law is justifiable and unbiased because it is objective and determinate. We will argue that, in contrast, positive law threatens the very moral fiber of the United States of America and the basic truths that secure human rights, which so many brave individuals have given their lives to defend. Moreover, positive law separates legal theory from any normative moral standards in rejecting all principles, distinctions, and categories that are thought to be binding for all times, persons, and places. Therefore, we also will demonstrate that positive law is a threat to life and basic human rights in our country and that it removes the rational justification to defend life and human rights on an international level.

HOW DOES POSITIVE LAW THEORY THREATEN BASIC HUMAN RIGHTS?

As we have already stated, once Darwin's macroevolutionary view of life entered the academic scene and merged Nietzsche's nihilistic atheism with the utilitarianism of Bentham and Mill, it was just a matter of time before law students graduated, entered into various leadership positions, and argued for the positive law model. Slowly but surely, the United States adopted a positive law framework. During this time, lawmakers developed laws and judges interpreted and applied laws from a legal positivist framework, undergirded by a purely naturalistic worldview. As this summary shows, beginning in 1962, every major federal and Supreme Court decision favored a macroevolutionary and naturalistic view of human life—and a relative view of values. The belief that humans are only different in degree from animals and not different in kind began to become, and is now established as, an academic, political, judicial, and public

Major Supreme Court Decisions From 1962 to 1987
1962: Removed class devotional prayer
1963: Removed class devotional Bible reading
1968: Protected teaching macroevolution
1973: Removed right to life for the unborn
1980: Removed Ten Commandments from schools
1987: Rejected the requirement of teaching creation alongside evolution

mindset. Combine that with the fact that the Creator has been removed from the public arena and is no longer considered to be the basis for moral laws, and you have the right political chemistry for legislating the devaluation of human life.

The shift from natural to positive law automatically leads to a shift in values—and in particular, the value of human life. It is now up to the courts to decide what constitutes "personhood" as well as if and when a "person" has the right to be protected by law. In the process, law and morality have become autonomous and situational. Consequently, the U.S. Supreme Court decision in 1973 (*Roe v. Wade*) marked the sanction of abortion on demand and the beginning of the widespread public devaluation of human life. After life in the womb was attacked, the next logical step in devaluing human life was taken: infanticide. The case of Infant Doe in Indiana in April of 1982 is an example of how genetically inferior newborns in the U.S. lost their God-given human right to life. Some babies are born with genetic deficiencies such as Turner's syndrome (forty-five instead of forty-six chromosomes) or Down's syndrome (forty-seven chromosomes). The Supreme Court of Indiana ruled that a newly born baby could literally be starved to death, even when other couples had the desire to adopt the child.

Abortion on demand and infanticide are on one end of the human-life spectrum. At the other end is euthanasia,[28] just one more example showing that positivists believe human judges ought to be sovereign over human life. *Euthanasia is not referring to allowing someone to die with dignity, and it does not mean removing a mechanical means of prolonging the experience of dying. Euthanasia is represented by the readiness of some people either to directly or indirectly kill someone who if treated properly could go on living.* Frankly speaking, it is the killing of a person on the grounds that he or she is better off dead. It usually hides behind misleading phrases like "the right to die."

On June 26, 1997, the Supreme Court decided that the average American has no constitutional right to a physician-assisted suicide. On the other hand, the Court left open the possibility that a state could permit it. Oregon has already passed a law permitting the same. So the battle must be fought on a state-by-state level. Since euthanasia is on the same trajectory as abortion on demand, it will probably only be a matter of time before it gains national acceptance.

As the view of positive law shaped the mindset of America's academic, political, and judicial leaders, the basic human rights of the defenseless were taken

[28]See the appendix for ethical analyses of abortion and euthanasia.

away. The question is "To what depth and breadth will positive law threaten human rights?" How far will we go with respect to redefining personhood? Nobelist Dr. James Watson won international recognition for his part in cracking the DNA code. He is considered to be an authority on human life. He also believes that no newborn infant should be declared to be a living person until it has passed certain tests regarding its genetic endowment. He says, "If a child were not declared alive until three days after birth, then all parents could be allowed the choice . . . [to] allow the baby to die . . . and save a lot of misery and suffering."[29]

Notice the dangerous direction that "defining a person" is taking—the direction is genetic purity! If genetic purity becomes one of the criteria for defining both personhood and the right to be protected by law, then where should the line be drawn, if it is drawn at all? Furthermore, who has the right to draw it? If the value of a human life is related to how physically, genetically, or mentally "perfect" a person is, or whether or not a baby is wanted by its mother or father, then as a nation we are in principle no better than Nazi Germany.

HOW DOES EDUCATION INFLUENCE LAW AND HUMAN RIGHTS?

As a nation we are teaching the next generation that we do not value human life either in the beginning (abortion and infanticide) or at the end (euthanasia). If we are teaching America's children that we do not value life at the beginning or end, what makes us think that somehow they will learn to value life anywhere in between? Surveys tell us that one of the greatest fears American children have is that they will be a victim of violence at school.[30]

What we do as a nation will be emulated by our children. We have showed them that statements like "one nation under God" are untrue not only in principle but also in practice. America's young people are being taught that God has no place in government, school, or courts of law. They are also learning that lawmakers and Supreme Court justices are the ones that decide who has value and ought to be protected by the Constitution.

The survival of our children's future depends upon all of us and our ability to think rationally about the ideas and philosophies that penetrate the various social systems in our country today. This is especially true of the educational institutions that lay the foundation for thoughts and ideas. History testifies to the fact that ideas and worldviews can have both good and bad consequences.

[29]Cited by Paul Kurtz in *Forbidden Fruit: The Ethics of Humanism* (Buffalo, N.Y.: Prometheus, 1988), 18.
[30]George H. Gallup, *Scared: Growing Up in America* (Harrisburg, Pa.: Morehouse, 1996), chapter 1.

If we do not learn from what history has taught us about law, human rights, and the value of even a single human life, then we run the risk of repeating the same mistakes—and possibly at an even higher price.

The late Oliver Wendell Holmes (1841–1935) was professor of law at Harvard Law School and is quoted abundantly in the judicial profession. In 1902 he was appointed to the U.S. Supreme Court by President Theodore Roosevelt and became nationally famous for his liberal interpretations of the U.S. Constitution.[31] Holmes once said, "When I want to understand what is happening today or try to decide what will happen tomorrow, I look back. A page of history is worth a volume of logic."[32]

Even a liberal-minded justice like Holmes recognized the value of history in understanding where a society is and where it is going. For that reason, it is incumbent upon everyone in the judicial profession to look back at history and learn from it. We have already done this in examining the impact that Bentham, Mill, Darwin, and Nietzsche had on education and the field of legal theory or law. Now let's look back again to see how education can have an effect on human rights.

We can learn how education influences human rights from Nazi Germany and the Holocaust. This page in history is a frightful reminder that bad ideas, even for the most highly educated people, can in fact have horrible consequences. Hitler's ideas eventually were incorporated into German legislation and became the laws that governed that nation. Once National Socialism took hold of Germany, lawmakers were faced with the task of creating and implementing laws that supported National Socialism. According to German legislators, good laws were laws that promoted and served the interests of the state. Therefore, laws were made that placed the state above individual human rights, for according to positive law, the German legislative body had a right to create those laws. So when it was decided who the genetically inferior races were, they made it legal to remove them from their society in order to strengthen their own race. This concept seems so radical that one has to wonder how Hitler was able to persuade an entire nation of its truth. But before we look at how Germany became convinced of Hitler's ideas, let's look at who convinced Hitler.

In 1948 Richard Weaver wrote a book called *Ideas Have Consequences*. In it he sent a warning:

That it does not matter what a man believes is a statement heard on

[31] *Microsoft® Encarta® 97 Encyclopedia*. S. V. "Holmes, Oliver Wendell."
[32] Laurence J. Peter, *Peter's Quotations* (New York: Bantam, 1977), 244.

every side today. The statement carries a fearful implication. If a man is a philosopher . . . what he believes tells him what the world is for. How can men who disagree about what the world is for agree about any of the minutiae of daily conduct? The statement really means that it does not matter what a man believes so long as he does not take his beliefs seriously. . . . But suppose he does take his ideas seriously?[33]

Not only did Hitler take his own ideas seriously, he also took Charles Darwin and *On the Origin of Species* seriously. In particular, he embraced the subtitle of Darwin's work: *The Preservation of Favoured Races in the Struggle for Life.* Hitler accepted Darwin's law of nature—"the survival of the fittest *race*"—and applied it to Germany and the rest of the world. He believed that in order for Germany to survive and thrive, it had to teach a generation of young leaders to value the Aryan race and the State over inferior races at the expense of individual human rights. Hitler knew that education was the master key to convincing Germany that as a nation they had a right to achieve genetic and racial purity.

Darwin's racial bigotry is not emphasized today, but it is clearly a crucial principle that is concomitant with the macroevolutionary view of life. In fact, the Scopes trial is often cited as the landmark case that was aimed at stopping educational bigotry in America. Macroevolutionists wanted their view of the origin of life to be taught as an alternative model alongside the creation model. However, what is often overlooked is the fact that macroevolution supported racial prejudice. The following is a quote from a biology text being used in Tennessee before the time of the Scopes trial. This text clearly sets forth the hierarchy of the five races on earth and the superiority of the white race. It reads,

> At the present time there exist upon the earth five races or varieties of man, each very different from the other in instincts, social customs, and, to an extent, in structure. These are the Ethiopian or Negro type, originating in Africa; the Malay or brown race, from the islands of the Pacific; the American Indian; the Mongolian or yellow race, including the natives of China, Japan, and the Eskimos; and finally, *the highest type of all, the Caucasians, represented by the civilized white inhabitants of Europe and America.*[34]

Hitler took that macroevolutionary racial bigotry and coupled it with his own twist on Nietzsche's idea of the "overman" (*superman*). Nietzsche's "overman" is

---

[33]Richard M. Weaver, *Ideas Have Consequences* (University of Chicago Press, 1948), 23.
[34]George W. Hunter, *A Civic Biology: Presented in Problems* (New York: American Book Co., 1914), 196 (emphasis added).

the one who can have victory over life's miseries, demonstrating worthiness through self-assertion and the will to power, which Hitler extended to a super race. Add Darwin's law of natural selection, with respect to racial survival, to a distortion of Nietzsche's "overman," and Hitler, along with National Socialism, drew the following conclusion:

Survival of the Fittest

"By means of natural selection or the preservation of favoured races in the struggle for life."
Charles Darwin, *On the Origin of Species*

"The superior race must not mate with the inferior races."
Adolf Hitler, *Mein Kampf*

> The stronger must dominate and not mate with the weaker, which would signify the sacrifice of its own higher nature. Only the born weakling can look upon this principle as cruel, and if he does so it is merely because he is of a feebler nature and narrower mind; for if such a law did not direct the process of evolution then the higher development of organic life would not be conceivable at all. . . . If Nature does not wish that weaker individuals should mate with the stronger, she wishes even less that a superior race should intermingle with an inferior one; because in such a case all her efforts, throughout hundreds of thousands of years, *to establish an evolutionary higher stage of being*, may thus be rendered futile.[35]

Hitler proposed a course of action that would give Germans victory over life's miseries in an effort to give their country back its dignity (specifically, from humiliation in previous wars). He wrote with extreme confidence and persuasive ability and set forth social and political goals for an economically ruined and morally devastated postwar Germany. With the condition of Germany being so debilitated, and considering the intellectual basis for Hitler's plan, Germans became convinced that his strategy would succeed. Hitler never gave a single hint of doubt that his plans would not work. He saw himself as Nietzsche's *superman* with the will to power and to cultivate an army of *supermen* (Nazis) who would set out to dominate the inferior races of the world and transform the Aryan race into the *super race*. Hitler saw this plan as perfectly consistent with the laws of nature and as the "final solution" to rid the world of "inferior" strains of the human species that he considered to be parasites and an impediment to achieving "an evolutionary higher stage of being."

How did Hitler propagate these ideas? Where did this all start? The answer

---

[35]Adolf Hitler, *Mein Kampf* (London: Hurst and Blackett, 1939), 161–62 (emphasis added).

to both questions is education! One survivor of Auschwitz was very aware of the impact education had on Nazi Germany. He said,

> The gas chambers of Auschwitz were the ultimate consequence of the theory that *man is nothing but the product of heredity and environment*—or, as the Nazis liked to say, "of blood and soil." I am absolutely convinced that the *gas chambers* of Auschwitz, Treblinka, and Maidanek *were ultimately prepared not in some ministry or other in Berlin, but rather at the desks and in the lecture halls of nihilistic scientists and philosophers.*[36]

The goal of National Socialism, with respect to education, was to train the next generation of German leaders in such a way that they would be capable of finishing what Hitler and the Nazis had started. Hitler knew that he needed to educate Germany's youth concerning the plan he presented in *Mein Kampf;* he realized education was the primary agency to propagate his ideas, and once Germany embraced the principles set forth in his writings the rest became a matter of history.

> By educating the young generation along the right lines, the People's State will have to see to it that a generation of mankind is formed which will be adequate to this supreme combat that will decide the destinies of the world. The nation will conquer which will be the first to take this road. The whole organization of education and training which the People's State is to build up must take as its crowning task the work of instilling into the hearts and brains of the youth entrusted to it the racial instinct and understanding of the racial idea. No boy or girl must leave school without having attained a clear insight into the meaning of racial purity and the importance of maintaining the racial blood unadulterated. Thus the first indispensable condition for *the preservation of our race* will have been established and thus future cultural progress of our people will be assured.[37]

America also is embracing such self-destructive principles. In light of Lincoln's dictum—"The philosophy in the schoolroom in one generation will be the philosophy of the government in the next"[38]—we feel morally obliged to point out the deep-seated dangers associated with governments who advocate legal positivism. We believe that legal positivism and macroevolution are bad ideas, and once bad ideas become convictions of educators and governments, the results can be devastating. For that reason, the place to stop bad ideas is in

---

[36]Viktor Frankl, *The Doctor and the Soul: Introduction to Logotherapy* (New York: Knopf, 1982), *xxi* (emphasis added).
[37]Op.cit., 240 (emphasis added).
[38]William J. Federer, *America's God and Country Encyclopedia of Quotations* (Coppel: FAME, 1994), 391.

the classroom *before* they become social and political ideologies.

We believe that positive law needs to be eliminated from education. As we explained earlier, positive law was built upon four influential thinkers: Darwin, Nietzsche, Bentham, and Mill. In previous chapters, we presented our arguments as to why Darwin's view of the origin of life (macroevolution) was wrong. We have also shown that atheism is unfounded and established theism as a credible worldview.[39]

Nietzsche's philosophy of life is false. His atheistic, nihilistic view of life negates all objective value but is self-defeating and inconsistent. Consider that as a nihilist, Nietzsche "values his right to negate all value. He values his freedom to hold his view and not to be forced to hold another position."[40]

With respect to the utilitarianism of Bentham and Mill, consider the following critique:

> The first problem with utilitarianism is that it implies that the end justifies any means necessary to attain it. If this were so, then Stalin's slaughter of some eighteen million could be justified in view of the communist utopia he hoped would eventually be achieved. Second, results alone do not justify any action. When the results come we must still ask whether they are good results or bad ones. The end does not justify the means; the means must justify themselves. Forced infanticide of all children thought to be carriers of genetic "impurities" is not justified by the goal of a purified genetic stock. Third, even utilitarians take the end as a universal good, showing that they cannot avoid a universal good. Otherwise from whence do they derive the concept of a good that should be desired for its own sake? Finally, desired results alone do not make something good. Often we desire what is wrong. Even desires for ends thought to be good are subject to the question, Are they good desires? So even here there must be some standard outside the desires by which they are measured.[41]

History has taught us some very important lessons about what a nation is capable of doing when it generates bad philosophy at the academic level and when its government embraces that philosophy. Some of the most powerful lessons history has tried to teach us about law happened during the war-crime trials of former Nazi leaders. In the next chapter we plan to show how the Nuremberg trials brought the debate between positive law and natural law to a head, setting the stage for the world to see upon which view a nation's legal system ought to be based.

---

[39]See the concluding paragraph of chapter 8.
[40]Norman L. Geisler, *Christian Ethics: Options and Issues* (Grand Rapids, Mich.: Baker, 1989), 39.
[41]Ibid., 37–38.

—10—
QUESTIONS ABOUT JUSTICE

I think the first duty of society is justice.

—ALEXANDER HAMILTON

IS IT WRONG TO PASS LAWS THAT DENY BASIC HUMAN RIGHTS?

The terror that the Nazis inflicted on innocent people stands out as one of the most repugnant memories in the annals of history. The war was one thing, but Hitler's death camps were unique in the sense that their central activity was a form of what came to be known as "industrialized murder." Coupling that with the "medical research" Dr. Josef Mengele and others carried out on prisoners, from babies all the way up to adults, makes this historical reality seem almost incomprehensible. When *Newsweek* ran a cover story on the fiftieth anniversary of the liberation of Auschwitz, they interviewed retired Lieutenant General Vasily Petrenko, who was the only surviving commander among the four Red Army divisions that encircled and liberated the camp. *Newsweek* reported that Petrenko was

> a hardened veteran of some of the worst fighting of the war. "I had seen many people killed," Petrenko says. "I had seen hanged people and burned people. But still I was unprepared for Auschwitz." What astonished him especially were *the children, mere infants,* who had been left behind in

the hasty evacuation. They were the *survivors of the medical experiments* perpetrated by the Auschwitz camp doctor, Josef Mengele, or the children of Polish political prisoners.[1]

The article went on to describe how the children were at Auschwitz either to be exterminated or to undergo torturous experiments under the authority of the sadistic scientific pursuits of Mengele. Much of his medical research was dedicated to "genetics" in an effort to gain a working knowledge of how to produce a "genetically pure race."

"The crimes that had been committed by the Nazis were unparalleled in human history. Auschwitz was something new on the earth. Its elaborate mechanisms for transporting, selecting, murdering and incinerating thousands of people a day constituted a kind of industrialized death."[2] Yet can America or any other country really charge the German officials with crimes against humanity? Especially since Germany felt it had a national obligation to achieve genetic purity? Let's take the time to examine what Germany did and why. This will help us gain a better understanding of the criminal charges that were brought against them after the war.

As social Darwinism and nationalism merged in Germany during the early twentieth century, the concept of fostering a genetically superior race called the *Volk* (the people) was established. The idea of the Volk was extended to various biological analogies, shaped by the contemporary beliefs of heredity, and designed to protect Germany from "racial inferiority."[3]

The Germans were trying to perfect *eugenics*,[4] the science that investigates methods involving the betterment of the genetic composition of the human race. (In this case, the Aryan race.) One of their goals was to eliminate the "inferior" races and offspring and preserve the "better" progeny. (This method is perfectly consistent with macroevolution and its central principle, the survival of the fittest.) If Nazi Germany could be successful in winning the upcoming war and in advancing their technology, they expected that one day genetically superior individuals would be cloned. Hence, the "super race" would emerge out of "blood and soil."

The Nazi death camps, therefore, became research laboratories for the advancement of "medical science." And it's not hard to imagine why many physicians and scientists were so overwhelmingly enticed by the Nazi paradigm:

---

[1]Jerry Adler, "The Last Days of Auschwitz," *Newsweek*, January 16, 1995, 47 (emphasis added).
[2]Ibid.
[3]George J. Annas and Michael A. Grodin, *The Nazi Doctors and the Nuremberg Code: Human Rights in Human Experimentation* (New York: Oxford University Press, 1992), 271.
[4]See the appendix for ethical analyses of eugenics and human cloning.

the biomedical emphasis, with its focus on genetically engineering a perfect Aryan race, played on their arrogance. They were given the best laboratories, the largest budgets, and the best working conditions—few could resist it. In the camps, they had all the human guinea pigs they needed. Some research objectives and techniques were as follows:

> To measure the limits of the human body, the Nazi physicians subjected concentration-camp inmates to high-altitude experiments, confining them in low-pressure chambers until their lungs exploded.
>
> To discover the most effective way of treating German pilots who had been downed in the North Sea, they [scientists] immersed prisoners in tanks of freezing water for hours, lowering their body temperatures to 26 degrees.
>
> To gain specimens for their Jewish skeleton collection, the Nazi physicians murdered and stripped the flesh from 100 Jewish prisoners.
>
> To compare the effectiveness of vaccines, they injected inmates with malaria, typhus, smallpox, cholera, and spotted fever. Physicians also broke their subjects' bones and then infected the wounds, fed them sea water until they had seizures and suffered cardiac arrest, [and] operated on them without anesthesia.
>
> To determine the physical causes of mental illness, some bodies were dissected, and their brains sent to research institutes, where scientists ran various tests.[5]

The research being conducted at the death camps was in accordance with Nazi law, and Nazi law defined what was right and just—in a word, what was *legal.* Looking at Germany's past as an example, one can see how quickly a nation can devalue human life and create laws that take away basic human rights. As long as naturalistic macroevolution and positive law are the dominating scientific and legal viewpoints both in theory (education) and in practice (law), we run the risk of returning to one of the darkest eras in the history of the human race. Educators must weigh the serious consequences of teaching students that humanity is merely of "blood and soil" and that human rights are not God-given, but rather determined by governments. If one believes governments determine human rights, we must ask "On what rationally consistent basis can a government declare another nation's laws to be unjust?"

DO GOVERNMENTS CREATE HUMAN RIGHTS OR DISCOVER THEM?

For both legal positivists and for supporters of natural law, this is the ultimate question, and the answer will influence other answers to fundamental

---

[5]Op. cit., 67–86.

questions concerning human rights. For example, what does it mean to be human, and what are human rights? If humans are essentially animals (as macroevolutionists believe) and governments create laws (as positivists believe), then who defines what a person is and what human rights are? Who says that all humans must have rights? Furthermore, how can one nation (the United States) accuse another nation (Nazi Germany) of violating human rights if *governments* decide what a person is and determine what human rights are (if they are to be at all)?

During the nineteenth century, America was so strongly divided over the issue of slavery that it became involved in the great military conflict between the United States of America (the Union) and the Confederate States of America (the Confederacy). The Civil War began on April 12, 1861, and lasted until May 26, 1865, when the last Confederate army surrendered. The war claimed over 600,000 lives—the dead and wounded combined totaled about 1.1 million. More Americans were killed in the Civil War than in all other American wars combined from the colonial period through the later phase of the Vietnam War (1959–1975). The Civil War destroyed property valued at $5 billion, brought freedom to four million black slaves, and opened wounds that have not yet completely healed even after nearly a century and a half. Why? What principle was under attack? What issue was at stake?

President Lincoln answered these questions on November 19, 1863, at Gettysburg, Pennsylvania, in an address dedicated to honoring those who had died there earlier that year. Most who have studied American history remember part of that address: "Fourscore and seven years ago our fathers brought forth on this continent, a new nation, conceived in Liberty, *and dedicated to the proposition that all men are created equal*" (emphasis added). Yet the import of Lincoln's first statement is often overlooked. "Fourscore and seven years ago" (eighty-seven years) puts the birth of the United States in 1776, the year the Declaration of Independence was written. (The Constitution was later drafted [1787] and ratified [1788], and George Washington took the oath of office to become the first U.S. president in 1789.) Mortimer J. Adler shed some light on Lincoln's reasons for dating the birth of the United States in 1776. He writes,

> In his years of argument against the extension of slavery to new territories, Lincoln repeatedly appealed to the Declaration of Independence. His opponents resorted to the Constitution, with its covert references to the institution of slavery, as decisive for issues of policy regarding the extension of slavery. In effect they took the adoption of the Constitution as the juridical birth date of the nation.... Consider his [Lincoln's] im-

promptu remarks in Independence Hall in Philadelphia on February 22, 1861, shortly before his inauguration.

"I have never had a feeling politically that did not spring from the sentiments embodied in the Declaration of Independence. I have often pondered over the dangers which were incurred by the men who assembled here and adopted that Declaration of Independence—I have pondered over the toils that were endured by the officers and soldiers of the army that achieved that independence. *I have often inquired of myself, what great principle or idea it was that kept this Confederacy so long together.* It was not the mere matter of separation of the colonies from the mother land; *but something in that Declaration giving liberty, not alone to the people of this country, but hope to all the world.* It was that which gave promise that in due time the weights would be lifted from the shoulders of all men, and that all should have an equal chance. . . . I would rather be assassinated on this spot than surrender it."[6]

Why continue the Civil War? Because Lincoln was committed to the proposition that all men are created equal. He often pondered the price the patriots paid for freedom, and he was willing to die for it. Moreover, he saw the Declaration as the instrument of liberty and justice not only for the United States of America but for the whole world. Positivists must shrink back from this view of hope, however, for *it is only the natural-law view that is consistent with the great second paragraph of the Declaration of Independence and the "self-evident" truths found therein.*

Natural-law supporters understand that governments are instituted on God's moral law in order to *secure* human rights, while the positivists believe governments *create* them. What then do positivists think of the Declaration?

On the positivist view, it is, as Jeremy Bentham claimed at the time, a piece of flamboyant rhetoric, aimed at winning converts to the cause of the rebellion, but without an ounce of truth in its pious proclamations about unalienable rights and how governments, which derive their just powers from the consent of the governed, are formed to make preexisting natural rights more secure.[7]

If the positivist position is true and Bentham (a utilitarian) is right, then our Founding Fathers drafted a document for no other reason than to serve their own ends. In fact, shortly after the Dred Scott decision, which declared that blacks were not persons under the Constitution, Judge Stephen A. Doug-

---

[6]Mortimer J. Adler, *Haves Without Have-Nots* (New York: Macmillan, 1991), 219–20.
[7]Ibid., 198.

las claimed that the Declaration of Independence referred to the white race alone and not to the African, in declaring all men to have been created equal. He said that the Founding Fathers were merely proclaiming that British subjects on this continent were equal to British subjects residing in Great Britain. Lincoln responded with the following sardonic words:

> I had thought the Declaration contemplated the progressive improvement in the condition of all men everywhere; but no [according to Douglas], it merely "was adopted for the purpose of justifying the colonists in the eyes of the civilized world in withdrawing their allegiance from the British Crown." . . . Why, that object having been effected some eighty years ago, the Declaration is of no practical use now—mere rubbish—old wadding left to rot on the battlefield after the victory is won.[8]

The positivists must logically align themselves with Douglas and not Lincoln, because for them there is no clear distinction between human (natural) and civil (legal) rights. Civil (or legal) rights are rights that were embraced as amendments to our constitution and rights that are explicitly defined in constitutions and in positive laws enacted by legislatures. *These rights can and have changed with time in our own country, and they vary significantly from culture to culture.* However, those who uphold natural law align themselves with both Lincoln and the Founding Fathers, understanding human or natural rights to be clearly distinguished from civil or legal rights. They also understand the significance of the term *unalienable* when added to the adjectives "human" and "natural" with respect to rights. Natural law supporters believe that these rights are not established by the positive enactments of governments and are "unalienable" in the sense that governments cannot take away what they do not bestow. Such was the understanding of law and human rights that gave birth to these United States of America, and such was the understanding of law and human rights that served as the basis for justice at Nuremberg.

ARE THE CONCEPTS OF LEGAL THEORY AND PERSONAL MORALITY RELATED?

Take a long, hard look at this next page of history and decide for yourself whether or not positive law is intellectually and legally credible with respect to justice and human rights. At the beginning of the chapter on law, we said that the most substantial body of thought in the discipline of jurisprudence (the

---

[8]Ibid., 221.

philosophy of law) is focused on the meaning of the concept of law itself (legal theory) and the relationship between this concept and the concept of morality. We believe that the priority and relationship between morality and law was decided, with the consent of an outraged world, at the Nuremberg trials.

The war-crime trials at Nuremberg, Germany, were some of the most significant trials of the twentieth century. In 1945 an international court of judges from the United States, England, France, and the Soviet Union tried top Nazi leaders, including Hermann Goering and Rudolf Hoess. The defendants were charged with conspiracy, crimes against peace, war crimes, and crimes against humanity. The prosecution presented horrifying films and photographs of concentration camps, which were seen by many for the first time.

President Harry S. Truman appointed Associate Justice Robert H. Jackson of the U.S. Supreme Court as the chief counsel to prosecute on behalf of the United States. Jackson was also the U.S. representative responsible for helping to establish an international military tribunal. This was something new; there had never been an international criminal court in all of history, and this event would set a precedent for the future. Jackson said,

> The war-weary people of the world insisted that the war criminals be dealt with—and speedily. . . . "Line them up and shoot them," was the solution from many quarters. . . . We could then wash our hands and write "finis" to the whole bloody chapter. We could go back to peaceful purposes and forget it all. *It was just this fear that we might "forget it all" that led some to believe that the guilt of the German leaders should be carefully documented; indeed, documented so painstakingly and with such clarity that the world could never forget.*[9]

For that and other reasons, on October 18, 1945, the chief prosecutors lodged an indictment with the tribunal charging twenty-four individuals with a variety of crimes and atrocities. Those charges included the deliberate instigation of aggressive wars, extermination of racial and religious groups, murder and mistreatment of prisoners of war, and the deportation to slave labor, the mistreatment, and the murder of hundreds of thousands of inhabitants of countries occupied by Germany during the war. On November 21, 1945, Robert H. Jackson delivered the opening statement on behalf of the prosecution and initiated trials that would shake the annals of jurisprudential history.

The strategy of the defense attorneys was to take the position that the defendants were simply loyal people obeying orders under a government operat-

---

[9]Robert H. Jackson, *The Case Against the Nazi War Criminals* (New York: Knopf, 1946), *v-vi* (emphasis added).

ing within the paradigm of positive law. The laws of Nazi Germany were considered to be instruments of social, economic, and political domination, both in the sense of furthering the concrete interests of the Nazis and sanctioning the existing order. The defense basically argued that law was nothing but regulations made by human legislators. Therefore, according to a positive view of law, the defendants were not guilty of violating any laws. (Their position was similar to Senator Joseph Biden's claim that "good natural law" is "subservient to the Constitution" of the United States.[10]) Germany considered their laws to be good because their laws were subservient to their constitution, *Mein Kampf,* and the overall welfare of the State. That is, German laws were based on a naturalistic macroevolutionary understanding of human nature, and they understood "good natural law" to be subordinate to the positive man-made laws of National Socialism.

The evidence presented by the prosecution at Nuremberg "stunned" the world. Eyewitnesses, film clips, and official papers (the Nazis documented most of the Holocaust) revealed repugnant and unimaginable horrors. The real question before the courts was "Was it illegal?" Affidavits such as the following were submitted as evidence against the defendants.

> I watched a family of about 8 persons, a man and a woman, both about 50 with their children of about 1, 8 and 10, and two grown-up daughters of about 20 and 24. An old woman with snow white hair holding the one-year-old child in her arms and singing to it, and tickling it. . . . The father was holding the hand of a boy about 10 years old and speaking to him softly; the boy was fighting his tears. The father was pointing toward the sky, stroked his head, and seemed to explain something to him. At that moment the SS-man at the pit shouted something to his comrade. The latter counted off about 20 persons and instructed them to go behind the earth mound. Among them was the family I have mentioned. . . . I walked around the mound, and found myself confronted by a tremendous grave. People were closely wedged together and lying on top of each other so that only their heads were visible. Nearly all had blood running over their shoulders from their heads. Some of the people shot were still moving. Some were lifting their arms and turning their heads to show that they were still alive. The pit was already two-thirds full. I estimated that it contained about 1,000 people. . . . The next batch were approaching already. They went down to the pit, lined themselves up against the previous victims and were shot.[11]

[10]Phillip E. Johnson, *Reason in the Balance* (Downers Grove, Ill.: InterVarsity, 1995), 134.
[11]Affidavit of Dr. Wilhelm Hoettl (November 5, 1945) in Robert H. Jackson, *The Nuremberg Case* (New York: Cooper Square, 1971), 169–70.

Even more astounding is the testimony of German leaders. One of the most notorious defendants, Rudolf Franz Ferdinand Hoess, actually took pride in the efficient manner in which he ran his death camp. His own words manifest his disposition:

> I commanded Auschwitz until December 1, 1943 and estimate that at least 2,500,000 victims were executed and exterminated there by gassing and burning, and at least another half million succumbed to starvation and disease making a total dead of about 3,000,000. . . . I used Cyclon B [deadly gas] . . . [and] it took from 3 to 15 minutes to kill the people in the death chambers. . . . After the bodies were removed our special commandos took off the rings and extracted the gold from the teeth of the corpses.
>
> Another improvement we made over Treblinka was that we built our gas chambers to accommodate 2,000 people at one time. . . . The way we selected our victims was as follows: we had two SS doctors on duty at Auschwitz to examine the incoming transports of prisoners. The prisoners would be marched by one of the doctors who would make spot decisions as they walked by. Those who were fit for work were sent into the camp. Others were sent immediately to extermination plants. *Children of tender years were invariably exterminated* since by reason of their youth they were unable to work. At Auschwitz we endeavored to fool the victims. . . . *Very frequently the women would hide their children under their clothes but of course when we found them we would send the children to be exterminated.*[12]

To better understand the dilemma these trials raise for those who uphold positive law, imagine that you are Robert H. Jackson, chief council for the United States, standing before an international court of law. You know that it is a fundamental principle of American law that a person cannot be tried under *ex post facto* statutes (laws made up after the fact), and a legal act cannot be made a crime retrospectively.

Legal positivists must logically agree that according to their view of law the defendants were technically acting in a legal manner and that there were no rational or legal grounds on which to prosecute the defendants. Mortimer J. Adler has said that if the positivist view concerning the relationship between law and justice is correct, it follows

- that *might makes right;*
- that there can be *no such thing as the tyranny of the majority;*

---

[12]Affidavit of Rudolf Franz Ferdinand Hoess (April 5, 1946) in Jackson, 171–73.

- that there are *no criteria for judging laws* or constitutions as unjust and in need of rectification or amendment;
- that *justice is local and transient,* not universal and immutable, but different in different places and at different times;
- that *positive laws have force only,* no authority, eliciting obedience only through the fear of the punishment that accompanies getting caught in disobeying them; and
- that there is *no distinction* between *mala prohibita* and *mala in se,* namely, between

    acts that are wrong simply because they are legally prohibited (such as breaches of traffic ordinances) and

    acts that are wrong in themselves, whether or not they are prohibited by positive law (such as murdering or enslaving human beings).[13]

As Robert H. Jackson, you are now standing in a court that has no jurisdiction under any body of positive law, and you are trying to prosecute men who were supposedly guilty of "crimes against humanity." The phrase "crimes against humanity" refers

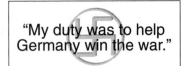

"My duty was to help Germany win the war."

to the violation of human rights. Yet, "if there are no natural rights, there are no human rights; if there are no human rights, there cannot be any crimes against humanity."[14] Moreover, you know that the defense will argue along those lines. If you hold to a positive view of law, on what ultimate and logically consistent basis would you begin to establish grounds to prosecute the defendants? In fact, this was the position the defense took.

A simple example of what Jackson was up against appears in a postwar transcript of an interrogation of two German engineers by Red Army officials. These two were senior engineers at a company called Topf, which manufactured cremation furnaces used at concentration camps in Buchenwald, Dachau, Mauthausen, Gross-Rosen, and Auschwitz-Birkenau. The following was excerpted from transcripts of the Red Army's military intelligence branch,[15] and the interchange is between a Soviet interrogator and Kurt Pfufer, responsible for the design and proper operation of the crematoriums.

---

[13]Adler, *Haves Without Have-Nots,* 197 (emphasis added).
[14]Ibid., 200.
[15]This documentation was discovered in May of 1993 by Gerald Fleming, who was doing research at the time. He was given permission by the Soviet authorities to study detailed files of the Red Army's intelligence branch. This interrogation transcript was excerpted from file 19/7, located in the Russian Central State archives. Prior to Gerald Fleming's research, it had never been made available to any historian.

Q: Did you know that [in] the gas chambers and in the crematoriums there [at Auschwitz] took place the liquidation of innocent human beings?

A: I have known since 1943 that *innocent human beings were being liquidated* in Auschwitz gas chambers and that their corpses were subsequently incinerated in the crematoriums. . . .

Q: Although you knew about the mass liquidation of innocent human beings in crematoriums, you devoted yourself to designing and creating higher capacity incineration furnaces for crematoriums—and *on your own initiative.*

A: I was a German engineer and key member of the Topf works and *I saw it as my duty* to apply my specialist knowledge in this way to help Germany win the war, just as an aircraft engineer builds airplanes in wartime, which are also connected with the destruction of human beings.[16]

The following interchange was between the other Topf engineer, Karl Schultze, and his Soviet interrogator. Schultze's response raises the essential question that needs to be posed to positivists who believe "good natural law" is subservient to human constitutions.

Q: How did you participate in its [crematoriums] setting up?

A: I am a German and supported and am supporting the Government in Germany and the laws of our government. Whoever opposes our laws is an enemy of the state because our laws established him as such.[17]

Positivists must logically sanction the principles used by the defense attorneys at Nuremberg. They must also accept the fact that Hitler and the Nazis took the guiding principle of naturalistic macroevolution—"the survival of the fittest"—and made the laws of their land subservient to their constitution, *Mein Kampf.* Anyone holding to legal positivism ought to be rationally consistent and agree that the defense was right and that the Nazis were not committing any illegal acts according to the laws of their land, nor could they be found guilty by the constitution of some other country.

We realize that not everyone who upholds the positive law view would agree with our conclusion about positivists aligning themselves with the defense attorneys at Nuremberg. The point we are making, however, is that all positivists are *logically connected* to the proposition that there are no higher laws than those laws created by human governments. The only rational way positivists could condemn the Nazis as being wrong would be to acknowledge that they

---

[16]Gerald Fleming, "Engineers of Death," *The New York Times*, Sunday, July 18, 1993, E19 (emphasis added).

[17]Ibid.

were *morally* wrong. But if positivists were to believe that the Nazis were immoral, then they must also admit that there exists a standard of morality beyond human governments. As C. S. Lewis said,

> If your moral ideas can be truer, and those of the Nazis less true, there must be something—some Real Morality—for them to be true about. . . . If the Rule of Decent Behavior meant simply "whatever each nation happens to approve," there would be no sense in saying that any one nation had ever been more correct in its approval than any other; no sense in saying that the world could ever grow morally better or morally worse.[18]

Without a standard of justice outside the world, how can someone logically point out injustice in the world? Positive law has no logically or legally consistent grounds for bringing justice to Nuremberg or any other international court, for that matter. Apart from an appeal to an objective, universal standard (natural law) that measures the laws of human governments, justice could not be served.

At the time, legal positivists in the United States protested the Nuremberg trials, claiming that they were illegal according to U.S. law. They argued that the idea that a legal act can be made a crime retrospectively is alien to the laws of many countries, including the U.S. Yet Jackson knew that the very foundation of law and justice rested upon a first principle of jurisprudence that would prevail and prove legal positivists wrong. For Jackson and for everyone who believes in the classical understanding of natural law, it follows

- that *might is not right*;
- that majorities *can be* tyrannical and unjust;
- that principles of justice and of natural right *enable us to assess* the justice or injustice of man-made laws and constitutions. . . .
- that *justice is universal and immutable,* always the same everywhere and at all times, whether or not recognized at a given time or place;
- that *positive laws have authority as well as force,* obeyed by criminals only because of fear of punishment if caught disobeying them, but obeyed by just individuals by virtue of the authority they exercise when they prescribe just conduct;
- that there are *mala in se* as well as *mala prohibita,* that is, *acts that are wrong in themselves whether or not they are prohibited by positive, man-made laws.*[19]

[18]C. S. Lewis, *Mere Christianity* (New York: Macmillan, 1952), 25.
[19]Adler, *Haves Without Have-Nots,* 198 (emphasis added).

One great lesson the world needs to learn from the Nuremberg trials is that positive law cannot provide the logical or moral basis for the protection of human rights; only natural law does. Also, the positivist cannot logically agree with the following remarks extracted from Robert H. Jackson's closing statement at Nuremberg:

> These two-score years in the twentieth century will be recorded in the book of years as one of the most bloody in all annals. . . . These deeds are the overshadowing historical facts by which generations to come will remember this decade. If we cannot eliminate the causes and prevent the repetition of these barbaric events, it is not an irresponsible prophecy to say that this twentieth century may yet succeed in bringing the doom of civilization. . . . We should not overlook the unique and emergent character of this body as an International Military Tribunal. It is no part of a constitutional mechanism of internal justice of any Signatory nations. . . . *As an International Military Tribunal, it rises above the provincial and transient and seeks guidance not only from International Law*[20] *but also from the basic principles of jurisprudence which are assumptions of civilization.*[21]

Philosophically speaking, without an objective standard of right and wrong against which morality and law can be measured, Jackson's argument is groundless. The first principles of law he referred to as "basic principles of jurisprudence" and "assumptions of civilization" are only ultimately and rationally justified if there exists a *transcendent moral law.* C. S. Lewis clearly points out the philosophical absurdity of trying to point to injustice in the world without a transcendent standard of justice. He said,

> My argument against God was that the universe seemed so cruel and unjust. But how had I got this idea of just and unjust? A man does not call a line crooked unless he has some idea of a straight line. What was I comparing this universe with when I called it unjust?

---

[20]Hugo Grotius, the "father of international law," based it upon natural law. He viewed it as a rational "method for arriving at a body of propositions underlying political arrangements and the provision of the positive [civil] laws."

[21]Robert H. Jackson, *The Nuremberg Case* (New York: Cooper Square, 1971), 120–22 (emphasis added).

If the whole show was bad and senseless from A to Z, so to speak, why did I, who was supposed to be part of the show, find myself in such violent reaction against it? A man feels wet when he falls into water, because man is not a water animal: a fish would not feel wet. . . . Thus in the very act of trying to prove that God did not exist—in other words, that the whole of reality was senseless—I found I was forced to assume that one part of reality—namely my idea of justice—was full of sense.

Consequently atheism turns out to be too simple. If the whole universe has no meaning, we should never have found out that it has no meaning: just as, if there were no light in the universe and therefore no creatures with eyes, we should never know it was dark. Dark would be without meaning.[22]

The analogy holds: If this universe had no light (no unchanging moral standards) and as a result creatures had no eyes (no sense of morality), the word *dark* (injustice) would ultimately be a meaningless term. Trials like those at Nuremberg only make sense if there exists a Divine Judge who sits in judgment on human (positive) law. Accordingly, Jackson appealed to objective and universal natural law with respect to personal moral accountability. *This appeal not only linked morality to law but also placed morality prior to human legislation. By doing so, Jackson was arguing for the existence of higher moral laws that transcended governments.* Consequently, Nazi leaders were found guilty of "crimes against humanity."

Nuremberg established a precedent with respect to governments creating laws (positive law) that oppose higher laws (natural law). If the citizens of a government are legally called to act in a manner that opposes natural law, they are morally obligated to disobey that government and to keep the higher law. On that basis, and on that basis alone, justice was served at Nuremberg.

In 1992, forty-seven years later, a similar trial was held. In February 1989, Ingo Heinrich, an East German border guard, killed a man who was attempting to gain his freedom by escaping to West Berlin. Within three years, after the elimination of the wall dividing East and West Berlin, Heinrich was tried for killing an innocent man, charged with manslaughter—natural law being the basis. *Time* magazine reported:

"Not everything that is legal is morally right."

Heinrich was just following orders. "Shoot to kill" was the command for dealing with people who tried to escape across the border, and in the

---

[22]Lewis, *Mere Christianity*, 45–46.

eyes of Heinrich's supervisors *his actions were not only legal but commendable.* Three years later, Heinrich, 27, lives in the same Berlin, but a different government holds sway and new laws prevail. Now he is, retroactively, a felon. . . . He was convicted of manslaughter . . . specifically, the trial judge said, for following the laws of his country rather than *asserting his conscience.* Said Judge Theodor Seidel: *"Not everything that is legal is [morally] right. The principle that an individual may be bound by a higher moral authority, beyond what the statutes provide, was established in West Germany decades ago, during trials of former Nazi leaders."*[23]

As previously noted, the most substantial body of thought in jurisprudence focuses on the meaning of the concept of law itself (legal theory) and the relationship between this concept and the concept of morality. Simply stated, *the implication of Nuremberg's establishment of the primacy of moral law is that governments and individuals have a responsibility to know this moral law and to derive positive laws from it to help secure human rights.*

The justice rendered at Nuremberg and Berlin was based on the same founding principle that the United States is based upon: the God-given value of the human race, bestowed upon humanity by the Creator. It only makes sense that laws cannot proceed from humanity itself; humans are self-centered and develop laws that reflect their own interests. Otherwise, we would need to have a legislator who is able to behold all the passions of humanity without being subject to them, and also be able to look across all of time in order to provide laws that would be suitable for all people through all ages.

In a commencement speech at Duke University, Ted Koppel, host of *Night Line,* pointed to what he considered the "moral compass that points in the same direction, regardless of fashion or trend." Commenting on the moral climate of a nation bombarded by the television image, he said,

> In the place of Truth we have discovered facts; for moral absolutes we have substituted moral ambiguity. We now communicate with everyone and say absolutely nothing. We have reconstructed the Tower of Babel and it is a television antenna. A thousand voices producing a daily parody of democracy in which everyone's opinion is afforded equal weight, regardless of substance or merit.
>
> Indeed, it can even be argued that opinions of real weight tend to sink with barely a trace in television's ocean of banalities. Our society finds Truth too strong a medicine to digest undiluted. In its purest form Truth is not a polite tap on the shoulder; it is a howling reproach. What Moses

---

[23]William A. Henry III, "The Price of Obedience," *Time,* February 3, 1992, 23 (emphasis added).

brought down from Mt. Sinai were not the Ten Suggestions, they are Commandments. . . . The sheer brilliance of the Ten Commandments is that they codify, in a handful of words, acceptable human behavior. Not just for then, or now, but for all time. Language evolves, power shifts from nation to nation and messages are transmitted with the speed of light. Man erases one frontier after another; and yet we and our behavior—and the Commandments, which govern that behavior—remain the same.[24]

Some argue that to teach timeless and un-changing moral laws is to introduce religious views into the classroom. How-ever, that argument is im-material because *the origin of an idea is irrelevant to its truth, historical accuracy, and academic credibility. It really doesn't matter whether*

or not an idea is religious in origin; what matters is if it is true. Education ought to be based upon truth, both philosophically and historically, and be free from all forms of prejudice. Neither does the allegation that an idea involves a Moral Law-giver make it unconstitutional; the very founding document of our country refers to "Nature's God" and "Nature's Laws" that come from Him.*

Some educators believe that to teach students about the basis for unalienable values and human rights is tantamount to trying to convert students and would lead to disunity and bigotry in the classroom, school, and country. Such a belief is not true. Time had a cover story titled, "What Ever Happened to Ethics? As-saulted by Sleaze, Scandals and Hypocrisy, America Searches for Its Moral Bearings." The leading article, "Looking to Its Roots," pointed out the disunity and moral disarray in America and what needs to be done in order to bring unity and rebuild a structure of values.

Time isolated the root cause of the collapse of private and public morality in America as being the protective obsession with self and image. The article went on to describe the average American home as becoming "a less stable and more selfish place." It went on to say, "Many people have begun to blame the

---

[24]Ted Koppel, Commencement speech, Duke University, May 10, 1987.

[25]There were two tables of the law, and there are differing views with regard to how many laws were on each table. But there is general agreement that the first table reflected duty to God and that the second table reflected duty to other human beings.

schools for not taking over the traditional family task of inculcating values."[26] The author cited a survey that indicated 90 percent of the respondents pointed their finger at the failure of parents to teach their children decent moral standards. The article then shifted to the idea of educational institutions being given the responsibility to teach ethics. Hence, the focal point of the article: "Who is to decide what are the right values?" After three pages of interviews with some of the finest legal, political, and academic minds of our nation, the author concluded,

> Interestingly, and perhaps reassuringly, some of the most thoughtful ethicists feel that the elements for an enduring moral consensus are right at hand—in the Constitution and the Declaration of Independence, with their combination of Locke's natural rights and Calvin's ultimate right. "It's all there, it's all written down," says Colgate Philosopher Huntington Terrell. "We don't have to be converted. It's what we have in common." Terrell calls for a move "forward to the fundamentals," in which people put their lives where their mouths have been: in line with the country's founding principles.[27]

As noted above, John Locke's view of natural rights was essential to establishing the infrastructure for the Declaration of Independence and the Constitution of the United States. In his book *Written on the Heart: The Case for Natural Law*, professor J. Budziszewski explains Locke's reasoning for God as the basis of equality in the sense that He has conferred value upon every human being. Budziszewski then cites Locke's second treatise (sections four through six), where Locke said,

> God has made us equal. And if we are equal, then we must be free: that is, God must intend us to serve only His purposes, not the purposes of one another. From this it follows that each of us is obligated to preserve not only himself but also, so far as possible, *every other human being*, and that therefore every human being has rights against all the others. Except to deal out justice to aggressors, no one may rightly take away or impair either the life or the means of living of another.[28]

Budziszewski comments on Locke's view, saying,

> You can see that Locke stakes his entire argument on natural law and

---

[26]Ezra Bowen, "Looking to Its Roots," *Time*, May 25, 1987, 27.
[27]Ibid., 29.
[28]J. Budziszewski, *Written on the Heart: The Case for Natural Law* (Downers Grove, Ill.: InterVarsity, 1997), 105.

natural rights on the existence of God. But how do we know God exists? Locke answers in his other writings that we know him by his works. The universe shows magnificent order and design; however, design presupposes a designer. . . . In our own century many theorists of rights try to do without God, or at least (as one of my colleagues once proposed) to shove him offstage. For Locke, however, *no God means no rights*, because our dignity is founded solely on our being made by his hand. But if you accept God, you have to accept the whole package: not only rights but law too.[29]

Supporters of the natural-law view put the moral law above human law for all the reasons we have stated. A person may have a legal right to do something, but if there is a conflict his or her moral obligation takes priority over it. "Human 'rights are the special objects of justice.' There are two kinds of rights: natural and positive. The former is a right 'from the very nature of things.' The other is a right 'from agreement, either private or public.' "[30]

We have given sufficient evidence and sound arguments as to why natural rights make sense and have priority over positive rights; it is up to you to decide for yourself which view of law is the most intellectually and legally credible. The Allied governments believed that individuals are personally accountable to keep natural law over positive law, and as such the Nazis were not on trial at Nuremberg—individual men were. The same is true of the border guard in Berlin. Indeed, *everyone* has a sense of this always-present moral law that speaks to our consciences even when no one else is watching! Concerning natural law, C. S. Lewis said,

These, then, are the two points I want to make. First, that human beings all over the earth have this curious idea that they ought to behave in a certain way, and cannot really get rid of it. Secondly, that they do not in fact behave in that way. They know the Law of Nature; they break it. These two facts are the foundation of all clear thinking about ourselves and the universe we live in.[31]

Engraved on the east wall of the U.S. Supreme Court, under the inscription "The Power of Government," one can find the basis for judicial law: the Ten Commandments. It is the law spoken of in the New Testament (Romans 2:14–15), the law whose moral principles are written on the hearts and consciences of all people, the law of God. There is another inscription in Washington, D.C., that's worth pondering. It is located on the northeast wall of the

---

[29]Ibid.
[30]Norman L. Geisler, *Thomas Aquinas: An Evangelical Appraisal* (Grand Rapids, Mich.: Baker, 1991), 172.
[31]Lewis, *Mere Christianity*, 1952, 21.

Jefferson Memorial. Jefferson himself warned us not to forget the basis of life and liberty. He said, "God who gave us life, gave us liberty. Can the liberties of a nation remain secure when we have removed a conviction that these liberties are the gift of God? Indeed, I tremble for my country when I reflect that God is just, that his justice cannot sleep forever." Amen!

WHICH WORLDVIEW IS TRUE (BEST CORRESPONDS TO REALITY)?

Once again, we want to review the cumulative conclusions that have been drawn thus far. The test method[32] being used to discover the truth about reality is based on utilizing the principle of the unity of truth (*the coherence principle*) and identifying and prioritizing the *first principles* of

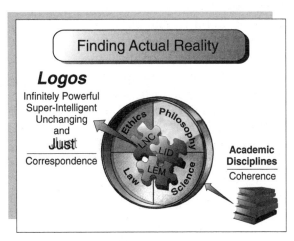

the academic disciplines that make up the various parts of the intellectual lens (worldview). As the first three parts (first principles)[33] of the intellectual lens were set into place in a coherent manner, we observed a *correspondence* among the conclusions reached and the most essential characteristics of reality.

The theistic worldview is the interpretive framework by which the facts of this world can be explained. The conclusions drawn from the first principles of logic, philosophy, cosmology, molecular biology, and information theory have ruled out atheism and pantheism as viable worldviews. As we continue to learn more about reality from the first principles in the forthcoming chapters, we must make every effort to see that the *priority, coherence,* and *correspondence* of previous first principles and their conclusions are protected.

Only the theistic conclusions agree with the first principles related to the nature of truth, the nature of the cosmos, and the existence and knowability of

---

[32]See chapter 2 to review the method of testing the truth claims of worldviews.

[33]The law of noncontradiction in logic, the unchanging reality in philosophy, and the principle of causality in science.

an infinitely powerful, intelligent, and unchanging Being (God/*Logos*). In applying the first principles of law to reality, we have concluded that there are absolute moral laws that exist and are objectively discoverable. Hence, we can now add the first principles associated with law to our list because they are consistent with and based upon theistic conclusions concerning the nature and attributes of God. In the chapters that follow, we will show that only theism in general (and Christian theism in particular) offers a rational justification for, and coherent explanation of, the questions surrounding the topics of evil and ethics.

	Atheism	Pantheism	Theism
Truth	Relative, No Absolutes	Relative to This World	Absolute Truth Exists
Cosmos	Always Existed	Not Real– Illusion	Created Reality
Logos	Does Not Exist	Exists, Unknowable	Exists, Knowable
Law	Relative, Determined by Humanity	Relative to This World	Absolute, Objective, Discovered

Furthermore, we will offer reasons as to why atheism and pantheism violate the first principles associated with these topics and how they fail to offer meaningful answers to these and other significant questions.

—11—
QUESTIONS ABOUT GOD AND EVIL

There is nothing more pointless than an answer to a question that is not fully understood, fully posed. We are far too impatient with questions, and therefore, far too shallow in appreciating answers.

—PETER KREEFT

WHY EVIL?

There is an immense quantity of books that have been written through the centuries in an effort to present an explanation for the origin of evil, its effect on humanity, and how to rectify it. The recommendations suggesting various ways to account for and solve the problem of evil are as diverse as the philosophers and theologians who have proffered them. In this chapter we will focus on the question of evil with respect to the existence of God: "If God, why evil?" To further narrow our focus, we are not referring to just any kind of God, but specifically to the theistic God described in the Bible.

In previous chapters we provided arguments and evidence for the existence of an infinitely powerful, eternal, intelligent, and moral Being. Yet it seems to be the case that if this God created all things, and if evil is something real, then He must be the author of evil. Therefore, when we consider that this God is infinitely powerful and He *could* stop evil, and that He is infinitely good and He *should* stop evil, it appears to make no sense that evil exists. In fact, this perceived quandary becomes more intense in light of the Bible's claim that God is also loving and just. If so, why doesn't He stop evil?

The existence of evil seems to contradict the Bible's description of the nature and attributes of God. Consequently, it is our task to show that the Bible correctly affirms both the existence of evil *and* God, and accurately describes both the nature of evil as real and the nature of God as all-powerful, good, loving, and just. So if this God exists, as theists claim, then why is there evil? And if there is evil, where is this theistic God when evil is running rampant, and why doesn't He do something about it?

WHERE IS GOD?

In his bestselling book *When Bad Things Happen to Good People,* Rabbi Harold Kushner raises the following questions regarding the God of the Bible and the Holocaust:

> *Where was God* while all this was going on? *Why* did He not intervene to stop it? *Why* didn't He strike Hitler dead in 1939 and spare millions of lives and untold suffering, or *why* didn't He send an earthquake to demolish the gas chambers? *Where was God?* [1]

Rabbi Kushner concludes that the essential problem with God is His imperfect and finite nature. He says,

> There are some things God does not control. . . . Are you capable of forgiving and loving God even when you have found out that *He is not perfect?* . . . Can you learn to love and forgive Him despite *His limitations?* [2]

Does God really lack the power to strike down a Hitler? Does He not have the wherewithal to demolish buildings fitted with gas chambers? Does not the Creator of the universe have the power to stop an army of Nazis? Why did God allow such carnage to occur in the first place? Before we address these questions, allow us to show why it is that only theism can even begin to provide meaningful answers.

---

[1] Harold S. Kushner, *When Bad Things Happen to Good People* (New York: Avon, 1981), 84 (emphasis added).
[2] Ibid., 45, 148 (emphasis added).

WHO CAN ANSWER?

It must be remembered that theism is not the only worldview that must provide credible answers to the questions surrounding the problem of evil. Atheism and pantheism must also consistently explain the origin and nature of evil within the framework of their respective worldviews. Pantheism affirms God and denies evil. Atheism affirms evil and denies God. The problem for theism is that it affirms both God and evil—which seems to be incompatible.

If God did not exist (atheism), or if evil were not real (pantheism), there would be no need for a chapter such as this. It is only when one claims that evil is real and that an all-good and all-powerful God exists that an explanation must be given. We intend to show that it is self-defeating to acknowledge evil and claim that there is no God. We will also explain why it is that atheists and pantheists cannot offer intellectually credible responses to the questions surrounding the problem of evil.

Pantheists ignore the problem of evil by calling it an illusion. Yet if it is, where did the illusion come from and why does it seem so real? Pain and evil are aspects of life that all people on this planet have experienced to one degree or another. It could more easily be said that in light of the universal persistence of the reality of evil, it is an illusion to believe that evil is just an illusion. Pantheists offer neither substantial explanation for the problem of evil nor intelligent justification for calling evil an illusion. We conclude, therefore, that pantheism lacks explanatory power with respect to addressing the problem of evil.

Atheists (and naturalists) must also explain why evil exists and why they consider it a problem that needs to be addressed. *The very fact that evil is troubling to atheists or naturalists logically leads to a standard of good or justice beyond the world.* In the previous chapter we explained the dilemma associated with atheism or naturalism in trying to define injustice; it is important to remember that the same dilemma exists with the problem of evil. Let's look again at what C. S. Lewis, as an atheist, struggled with—the rational credibility of fitting evil and injustice into his atheistic worldview.

> My argument against God was that the universe seemed so cruel and unjust. But how had I got this idea of just and unjust? A man does not call a line crooked unless he has some idea of a straight line. What was I comparing this universe with when I called it unjust?
>
> If the whole show was bad and senseless from A to Z, so to speak, why did I, who was supposed to be part of the show, find myself in such violent reaction against it? A man feels wet when he falls into water, because man

is not a water animal: a fish would not feel wet. . . .

Consequently atheism turns out to be too simple. If the whole universe has no meaning, we should never have found out that it has no meaning: just as, if there were no light in the universe and therefore no creatures with eyes, we should never know it was dark. Dark would be without meaning.[3]

Imagine once more a universe with no light (no ultimate standard of what is good or just) and creatures without eyes (no inherent concept of what is good or evil); in this theoretical atheistic reality, the concept of darkness (evil or injustice) is ultimately meaningless. If, as atheists suggest, evil is ultimately meaningless, then what is the problem? If we are merely part of a blind molecular process, how is it that atheists can rise above that process and say that some aspects of it are evil and some are good? Atoms are simply atoms; there are no evil atoms in the universe. Therefore, *atheism cannot logically offer a definition of evil without appealing to an ultimate standard of good.* If atheists try to do so, they end up affirming the very existence of that which they claim does not exist—the ultimate good (God).

In light of the claims of atheism and pantheism, it is clear that if people are honestly searching for an explanation to the origin and nature of evil, then they need to give theism a fair hearing. Among the three worldviews under consideration in this book—atheism (or naturalism), pantheism, and theism—only theism is able to deal with these questions in a sufficient manner. This truth must always be kept in the foreground as we attempt to account for the presence and persistence of evil in a theistic universe.

As Christian theists, we are not claiming that we know every answer to every question. However, we are claiming to know the answers to some of the most essential questions in this life. There are some questions that cannot be answered, but there are also some answers that cannot be questioned!

WHAT IS EVIL?

Questions are easy to ask, but answers can often be shallow or misunderstood if the depth of the question is not fully grasped. This is true for both the questioner and the one responding to the question. As we heard from Peter Kreeft, "There is nothing more pointless than an answer to a question that is not fully understood, fully posed. We are far too impatient with questions, and therefore, far too shallow in appreciating answers."[4]

---

[3]Lewis, *Mere Christianity*, 45–46.
[4]Peter Kreeft, *Making Sense Out of Suffering* (Ann Arbor, Mich.: Servant, 1986), 27.

Since this chapter is dedicated to answering questions concerning the problem of evil and the existence of God, it is incumbent upon us to probe more deeply into the implications and inferences of such questions. Without a proper definition and understanding of the nature of evil, the answers we give may appear to be shallow. Therefore, we plan not only to answer the questions associated with evil but to analyze what is meant by the concept as well. Furthermore, in subsequent chapters we will argue for the unique Christian analysis of the root cause of evil and the prescription it offers for evil's permanent cure. At that time, we will also show how a sovereign God is able to redeem all evil for a greater good.

On a superficial level it seems to make sense to believe that if God created everything, and if evil is something real, then God created evil. But it isn't true. God did not create evil things; things in themselves are not evil. When God created everything, He said that all of His creation was good. As we mentioned, there are no evil molecules or atoms in the world; when we think about evil people, we do not believe that their evil actions are a result of an evil molecular structure.

So what *is* evil? Evil can be real without being a substance, in the sense that it is a real lack or loss of something that ought to be there. Blindness is not a substance; it is a real lack of sight. A person who is blind lacks physical wholeness, and we look upon this loss of wholeness as bad or negative because people are meant to see. Nevertheless, we would not conclude that blind people are morally evil because they lack sight. In order for someone to be morally evil, she would have to lack moral wholeness or goodness. Evil, then, is *a lack or privation of what ought to be present and is not.* For example, if a father abuses his child when he ought to love her, we call him evil because abuse is present and love is missing when love ought to be present. This example helps us to define evil in relational terms.

Good things in the wrong relationship can result in what we call evil. Certain forms of cancer are the result of uncontrolled cell growth. Cells are good for our bodies, but when their relationships get out of control, and they do not relate to one another as they should, we consider that to be a form of evil. In the same way, nuclear power can be used by engineers to generate electricity and light up a city (a good relationship) or be used by terrorists to destroy a city filled with innocent people (a bad relationship).

When people use their free will, their ability to make an unforced decision between two or more alternatives, they actualize their potential to do good or evil. When one person uses his or her freedom to mistreat another, we call that evil. Think about it: What is it that bothers us when we hear about or see a parent abusing a child or a person shooting someone over something as petty as a parking space? Why do we feel a sense of outrage when we read about such merciless and barbaric behavior as the murder of innocent men, women, and children at places like Auschwitz and Treblinka? We don't hesitate to label those actions as evil; we innately believe that people ought not to treat other people in such a manner. When people visit a place like the Holocaust Museum—when they genuinely examine what the Nazis did to innocent people—they mostly experience a deep sense of injustice and loss. Something within each of us cries out about the inhumanity of such acts. Therefore, moral evil can be thought of as a corrupted relationship between two or more human beings—a relationship that is not what it ought to be. Don't miss the significance of this: *in order for moral evil to be present, a moral agent and a moral law must also exist.*

To summarize, we consider evil to be a real lack or privation in a good thing. Evil is not a substance, but a corruption of a substance. Just as when we turn off a light in a room darkness appears, so too does evil appear when good is not where it ought to be. Evil is analogous to rust on a car or moth holes in a garment. The rust corrodes the good metal that

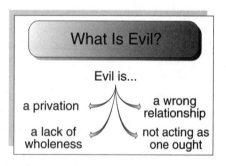

ought to be there, and the lack of that good metal can be thought of as evil. The holes in a garment eaten by a moth made the garment lack wholeness, or good fabric, resulting in evil. Evil, then, is an ontological[5] parasite and does not exist in and of itself. *Evil can only exist in something as a corruption of what ought to be there.* In relational terms, a corrupted understanding of human nature (who we are) and a rejection of moral obligations (how we ought to behave) are the primary causes of what we call evil.

DID GOD CREATE EVIL?

As Christian theists, we believe that the greatest good in all of reality is God. Furthermore, we know that we are finite beings, and since it is intrinsically impossible for finite beings to become the greatest good (an infinite God), the next best experience we can have is to be in a loving relationship with God

---

[5] *Ontology* is the discipline that deals with the nature of being or reality.

(Matthew 22:36–37). For that reason, God offers all people His love; it is His love that brings wholeness and holiness into human lives. Conversely, the greatest evil that anyone is capable of experiencing is being separated from that loving relationship with God. However, in order for us to engage in a loving relationship with God, we must be free to reject His love, for true love is always persuasive and never coercive. Therefore, the essential component of any loving relationship, including a relationship with God, is freedom. In order for God to make a universe where the greatest good (a loving relationship with Him)[6] was feasible, He would also have to create free creatures who would be capable of choosing or rejecting that greatest good.

Yet couldn't God create some other type of world where love is still possible and there is no evil or free choice—a better world than the theistic world? However, once this idea is raised, as C. S. Lewis pointed out, it necessarily implies a standard by which the world must be measured. Once the standard is put back into the equation, so is theism.[7] The God of the Bible has revealed in creation that *this world*, with free creatures capable of accepting or rejecting His love, is not the best world, but *is the best way to the best possible world—heaven*. There is no way to create a world where people are free to love God in order to experience the greatest good but are not free to reject God's love—the greatest evil. God created freedom as a good thing, yet evil can arise from that good thing. Therefore, God is not the direct author of evil; He created the potential for evil when He created free creatures, which also made it possible for them to experience His love (the greatest good).

God did not create robots; He created human beings with the power to freely choose between good and evil. If He created humans already predisposed (beyond their control) to love Him, that would not be true love. If we programmed our computer to tell us it loved us every time we turned it on, we would really be telling ourselves that we loved ourselves. The computer would only be mimicking our own thoughts, not being free to tell us otherwise. We would not be engaged in a love relationship but rather a severe form of narcissism. A love relationship must leave open the possibility of love being rejected—and, therefore, evil being chosen. When people reject God's love, they actualize the evil potential within themselves, which affects every other relationship into which they enter.

To say it would be better if God created nothing, rather than something,

---

[6]This is not contrary to the claim that our chief end is to glorify God and enjoy Him forever (*The Westminster Confession of Faith*)—this is what our love for Him will do (Matthew 22:37; Psalm 16:11).
[7]This is because such a standard must transcend this world, must be unchanging (to make measurement possible), and must be eternal. Only the theistic worldview corresponds.

doesn't make sense because there is no common ground to compare nothing with something. God could have created creatures that were not free; this would make the greatest good, a loving relationship with Him and others, impossible. If sin (one kind of evil) is defined as essentially choosing to reject the good that ought to be (in this case loving God), it is impossible for God to have created a world where people were free and sin

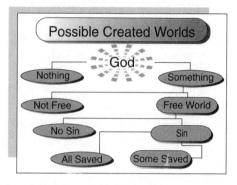

was not possible. Finally, if "salvation" is defined as God freely offering people a way back to a loving relationship with Him after they have rejected that relationship (sinned), and if love requires free choice, then it is also impossible to save people against their will. God cannot force His love on anyone because forced love is not love; it is a contradiction in terms.

It is plain, then, that creating free creatures has the inherent potential for evil occurring. C. S. Lewis aptly addressed the issue of free will and the utter futility of trying to outreason God by thinking that God could have created a better world:

> Some people think they can imagine a creature which was free but had no possibility of going wrong; I cannot. The happiness which God designs for His creatures is the happiness of being freely, voluntarily united to Him and to each other.
>
> Of course God knew what would happen if they used their freedom the wrong way: apparently He thought it worth the risk. Perhaps we feel inclined to disagree with Him. But there is a difficulty in disagreeing with God. He is the source from which all reasoning power comes: you could not be right and He wrong any more than a stream can rise higher than its own source. When you are arguing against Him you are arguing against the very power that makes you able to argue at all: it is like cutting off the branch you are sitting on. If God thinks this state of war in the universe a price worth paying for free will—that is, for making a live world in which creatures can do real good or harm and something of real importance can happen, instead of a toy world which only moves when He pulls the strings—then we may take it that it is worth paying.[8]

---

[8]Lewis, *Mere Christianity*, 52–53.

WHY DOESN'T GOD STOP EVIL?

If God must allow for the potential and actualization of evil, then why doesn't He stop evil when it is actualized? Because freedom enables us to reject God's love and to abuse and reject other people as well. Thus God is not the one who actualizes the potential for evil—we do when we freely choose to reject His love. The maximum latent power of evil resides in our capacity to refuse the love of God. For God to stop evil requires the elimination of that capacity: our free choice. But the elimination of our free choice would mean that we would not be capable of experiencing the greatest good, His love. *For God*

Stop Evil—Stop Good?

Love is
- the greatest good
- requires free choice

Free choice
implies the possibility of the opposite choice

God
alone is love, the greatest good

Greatest good for humanity
is God's love

Greatest evil for humanity
is rejecting God

To Stop
- evil is to stop free choices
- free choices is to stop love
- love is to stop the greatest good
- the greatest good is the greatest evil

to stop us from having the capability of experiencing the greatest good would be the greatest evil. The real question, then, is "Do we really want God to eliminate our free will?"

Taking this request to its practical dimension, consider the following scenarios.

Let's say that you decide to take up smoking. But since God knows that it's best if you don't, He decides that you aren't free to smoke. Every time you go to smoke, God turns your cigarette into a bubble blower. Instead of smoke filling the house, bubbles abound!

Or maybe you are a little too heavy-footed when it comes to driving. Knowing that you frequently exceed the speed limit, even if only a little, God makes sure there is a police officer there who is guaranteed to give you a ticket until you either stop speeding or lose your license.

Or perhaps you enjoy having a beer or two or more now and then. However, since God knows that you cannot hold your liquor, He decides to transform each beer you are about to drink into a large glass of milk.

The point we are trying to make is that almost all of us, if not all of us, have a problem with the evil brought about by the free choices others make and not with the evil that occurs as a result of our own free choices. In complaining about the evil that comes from free will, are we not in essence saying that God should stop the free choices of others, but that He should leave our own free choices alone?

Luke 13 records a verbal exchange between Jesus and a small group of people who approached Him, inquiring about the slaughter of innocent people at the hands of Pilate. They also wondered about a tragic event involving a tower that had fallen and killed eighteen people.[9] Jesus responded, but not in the way they expected. He did not explain why those events occurred; instead, He redirected the question back to the questioners. His brief comments to them imply a warning concerning the impending danger they would face if they did not acknowledge and address the evil *in their own hearts*. In essence He said, "Does the evil out there in the world really disturb you? If you are troubled by evil, start with the evil that is closest to you—the evil in your own heart. Leave the rest of the world to God and be more concerned about your own evil ways and the consequences you will face if you do not confess and turn to Him!" *If we want to see God stop evil, we should ask Him to begin with us.*

WHAT IS THE PURPOSE OF EVIL AND SUFFERING?

When Rabbi Harold Kushner concludes that God is imperfect, he automatically assumes some standard of perfection against which he measures God. However, Kushner fails to acknowledge the philosophical problem that kind of conclusion raises. It is essentially the same one that C. S. Lewis faced in his struggle to be intellectually honest as an atheist in addressing the problem of evil. When Lewis recognized that the world was unjust, he was forced to posit a standard of justice beyond the world. The same principle applies to Rabbi Kushner's conclusion. In order to say that God is imperfect, Kushner must posit a standard of perfection beyond God. However, the standard that Kushner alludes to is the perfect Being he denies exists. That leads us back to the position we took at the start—if this perfect Being does exist, why is there evil and suffering in the world?

In considering the full breadth and depth of the problem of evil, we agree with Peter Kreeft when he said that the existence of evil and suffering is more of a mystery than a problem. He likened it to love and said that since we are subjectively involved, we would find it hard to fully comprehend all of the reasons as to why it happens. As C. S. Lewis once suggested, "If only this

---

[9]We recognize that we have not yet defended the historical reliability of the New Testament documents. We will offer evidence and argue for that position in chapter 12. We merely want to introduce some related ideas here to give a deeper insight with respect to the Christian response to evil and suffering.

toothache would go away, I could write another chapter on pain." It is one thing to theorize about pain when you are fine, but it is quite another thing to do it when you are experiencing pain. Therefore, we acknowledge our incomplete explanation to account for all of the purposes that evil and pain may have in an individual's life. We do, however, know some of the good purposes produced by pain and suffering. Before we state some of these, we want to address the criticism that not knowing of purposes for evil and pain implies that God has no good purpose for why people suffer.

AN IMPORTANT DISTINCTION

Our not knowing all of the good purposes God has for pain and suffering doesn't mean that there are no good purposes. Our not knowing doesn't mean that God (an infinite Being) doesn't know. The only logical conclusion one can reach is that if God is all-good and all-knowing, then He must know good purposes for all pain and suffering in this world. It does not follow that evil proves that God is imperfect and limited; what follows is that we are imperfect and limited.

When it comes to evil and suffering, we may not know about all of God's purposes, but we do know some of them. *Some physical pain is necessary to develop character.* For example, sympathy is not achievable without misery, or patience without tribulation. Courage is unobtainable without fear, and endurance is occasioned only by hardship. In brief, some virtues would be totally absent without physical evil.[10] Character building is only accomplished through affliction. It was Helen Keller who said, "Character cannot be developed in ease and quiet. Only through experience of trial and suffering can the soul be strengthened, vision cleared, ambition inspired, and success achieved."

Of the four cardinal virtues (wisdom, courage, temperance, and justice), C. S. Lewis considered courage to be a form not only of each of the other three but of every virtue as well. He said,

> Courage is not simply one of the virtues, but the form of every virtue at the testing point, which means, at the point of highest reality. A chastity or honesty or mercy which yields to danger will be chaste or honest or merciful only on conditions. Pilate was merciful till it became too risky.[11]

---

[10]See Norman L. Geisler, *Philosophy of Religion* (Grand Rapids, Mich.: Zondervan, 1974), 389.
[11]C. S. Lewis, *Screwtape Letters* (Springdale, Pa.: Whitaker, 1984), 137.

Courage would be unnecessary without the presence of evil or danger. Consequently, the greater good of the development of virtue is impossible without the presence of evil. It may seem a high price to pay, but when the end product emerges in the form of personal integrity of character, it is worth the price of the pain endured.

Some physical pain is necessary to teach individuals that certain types of behavior are wrong and have physical or moral consequences. The decision to habitually choose vices like pride, anger, envy, greed, gluttony, lust, and sloth are manifestations of a person's refusal to master his or her physical and psychological impulses. A failure to learn how to develop and use self-control will end up reducing interest in virtue and the desire to cultivate good character. Teaching children how to deal with these vices at home, at school, and in society involves a particular level of suffering called discipline. Punishments are often necessary to teach individuals that they are stepping onto morally dangerous grounds. Only through the pain of discipline can a child learn self-control.

Some pain is necessary to warn us of an impending greater danger. Pain is used as a warning system to help us stay alive. People who have leprosy have participated in experiments in an effort to help keep them from causing themselves greater harm. One of the effects of leprosy is the loss of sensation at the extremities, and when someone with leprosy inadvertently touches a scorching hot plate or cuts off the tip of his finger with a saw, he will not feel the pain associated with these acts and may end up burning or mutilating himself.

In order for researchers to help people with leprosy, they put little electrical sensors and transmitters on them in an effort to warn them of impending danger. For example, when they got too close to some hot surface, the electrical unit gave them a shock that warned them not to touch that object. Yet after a while, the people who participated in these experiments did not like getting the shock treatment and turned down the intensity of the electrical discharge unit—the source of pain. As a result of these experiments, researchers learned that *in order for pain to properly serve its purpose and warn someone of danger, it had to be of the right intensity and out of that individual's control.* This kind of research is an encouragement to see pain as a blessing rather than an affliction.

> **Some Purposes for Pain**
>
> - To Develop Character
> - To Teach Moral Consequences
> - To Warn of Impending Danger
> - To Avoid Greater Suffering
> - To Get Our Moral Attention

Some pain is necessary to help us avoid greater suffering. The pain of enduring sitting in the dentist's chair is often needed to keep a person from suffering even greater pain. When someone ignores his or her health needs (proper rest, diet, exercise, etc.), it is good that the body reacts in a painful manner to let that individual know before the situation gets worse that something is wrong.

Finally, *some pain is used by God to get our moral attention.* Just as a parent who loves her child disciplines him in order to get his attention, God does the same. Some people have to be stretched out on their backs before they will ever look up to God. Most people turn to God in times of suffering, not when everything is going along just fine. Lewis said,

> God whispers to us in our pleasures, speaks to us in our conscience, but shouts to us in our pains: it is His megaphone to rouse a [morally] deaf world. . . . Until the evil man finds evil unmistakably present in his own existence, in the form of pain, he is enclosed in illusion. . . . No doubt Pain as God's megaphone is a terrible instrument; it may lead to final and unrepented rebellion. But it gives the only opportunity the bad man can have for amendment. It removes the veil; it plants the flag of truth within the fortress of a rebel soul.[12]

WHY IS THERE SO MUCH EVIL AND SUFFERING?

We have shown some of the good purposes for pain and suffering, but why does God allow *so much* of it to exist in the world? Couldn't there be less starvation, child abuse, rape, violence, killing, etc.? In one sense we have already addressed this question by pointing out that to stop evil, God must stop free will, and to stop free will is to stop the greatest good—which is the greatest evil. But let's consider another approach to answering this question.

Imagine that you are about to go to a party, and before you leave home, you come down with a toothache.[13] Although you feel a bit uncomfortable, you decide to go to the party anyway. However, when you get to the party and the evening begins to wear on, your toothache worsens and the pain intensifies. Now, let's put some quantitative values to this pain you are experiencing. Let's say the minimum pain level anyone can experience before the brain registers the pain caused by a toothache is equal to five units of pain. Let's also say that the maximum pain intensity that a person can experience is one hundred units of pain. When you entered the party your brain registered your pain level at fifteen units. Two hours later, it shot up to seventy-five units. After thirty more

---

[12]C. S. Lewis, *The Problem of Pain* (New York: Macmillan, 1962), 93, 95.

[13]This illustration is a variation and extension of the one C. S. Lewis presented in *The Problem of Pain*, (New York: Macmillan, 1962), 115.

minutes you hit the limit, registering one hundred units of pain. Let's also say that there are twenty-five people at the party (including yourself), and by some strange coincidence the other twenty-four individuals get toothaches that eventually max out at one hundred units of pain. Our question is "How much pain is being experienced in the room at this time?"

In one sense, the total amount of pain in the room is twenty-five times one hundred units, or 2,500 units, but it would be wrong to say that 2,500 units of pain are being experienced by any one person in the room. You must remember that no one is experiencing the suffering at an intensity of 2,500 units of pain. That composite pain is not in any one individual's consciousness. Adding twenty-five, twenty-five thousand or twenty-five million sufferers to this scenario doesn't add more pain, only more who suffer it. For that reason, the proper question to ask is not "Why is there so much pain and suffering?" but rather "Why do so many people experience it?"

Please understand that we are not making light of the amount of suffering in the world. We merely want to show that as horrible as it is to see an individual suffer the maximum pain that a single person can suffer, it still reflects the fact that pain and suffer-

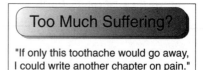

Too Much Suffering?

"If only this toothache would go away, I could write another chapter on pain."

C. S. Lewis

ing is limited to the experience of only one person, and only while that person is suffering. The interesting thing about the solidarity of human suffering is the positive psychological effect it has on the ones who suffer: the more people there are who share the same kind of pain, the easier it is for them to cope. Pain can become unbearable when there is no one around who truly understands and can relate to the sufferer. Ironically, the intensity of suffering is actually lessened when more than one person experiences it.

WHAT ABOUT FLOODS, TORNADOES, CANCER, AIDS, ETC.?

Christian theism does not claim that God created the best world possible. It does claim, however, that God created the best way to the best possible world. It follows, then, that the kind of physical world we live in, with natural evils in it, is compatible with the "best way" to obtain the best possible world. In this best way to the best possible world, physical evil results either directly or indirectly from the laws that govern the physical universe and the decisions of moral agents. God created the world in such a way that the natural laws work for the overall benefit of humanity. Yet natural evil can result from the overlapping of systems in the spatio-temporal continuum. Whenever two or more things compete for the same place at the same time, there will be conflicts. If a truck and a car pass through an intersection along the same trajectory, but traveling in opposite directions, there will be a collision if at least one of the vehicles does not stop or swerve out of the way. The end result will take the form of physical pain. Such is indigenous to a world of physical forces.

Physical evil can also result from natural by-products of processes that keep the overall balance of nature in place. When hot and cold air mix, they sometimes produce lightning as a good by-product of a thunderstorm. Thunderstorms are very good for lawns and crops. As the lightning travels through the air, it produces nitric oxide (a form of fertilizer). This is good because the rain will pour down nitric oxide (fertilizer) and help produce healthy lawns and crops. However, the same lightning will sometimes strike people or buildings and other objects, which could produce physical evil.

Likewise, earthquakes are a necessary part of a physical world. The relief of the earth's internal pressure is what keeps this planet from exploding. The balance of forces is also needed to keep the oceans and the mountains in place. Furthermore, the movement of the earth's tectonic plates recycles nutrients that collect in the ocean and returns them back to the continents.

None of these evil by-products are the intended result of the natural process, but they are the necessary result of the achievement of other natural goods. It is possible that floods, droughts, earthquakes, tornadoes, and other natural disasters are all necessary by-products of this physical world—and that this physical world is necessary for the best moral achievement.

Another cause of physical evil is the consequences of the free choices of moral agents. We have already addressed this issue, but here we would like to stress the principle of the solidarity of humanity in a *negative* manner. Our moral choices do not affect us alone; they affect others too. If two "consenting adults" decide to have an ongoing affair and one of them is married with children, the results affect the whole family. Other examples of the solidarity of humanity are sex-

What About Physical Evil?

- The direct/indirect result of freedom
- The by-product of good things
- Our own neglect/choices (diet, etc.)
- Others who influence/hurt us
- Freedom of choice
- Solidarity of humanity

God does not necessarily intervene but is always capable of redeeming

ually transmitted diseases, drug and alcohol abuse, pornography, etc. Regardless of the cause, the effect of individual choices on society as a whole has been, and continues to be, devastating.

In considering such things as birth defects, cancer, heart disease, and the like, we turn back to science and the second law of thermodynamics. According to this universal law of physics, everything in the universe is in a state of increasing deterioration. Unfortunately, that includes living organisms. Therefore, as time increases, so does deterioration. According to Christian theism, when God created the first human beings, they were genetically pure. After they chose to break their relationship with Him, the consequences of their free choice resulted in a progressive deterioration of the entire physical realm, including their bodies.

One way to illustrate the effect of the progressive deterioration of the physical realm is to point out what happens when a copy of a copy is made. Let's say that the page you are reading from is the original page that came out of the printer. Imagine that you take this original page and photocopy it. Take that copy and copy it. If you continue to make a copy of the preceding copy, after a while you will be able to see how deteriorated the copy has become when you compare it to the original. Now apply that illustration to genetics. From the first human beings to those living today, many copying distortions and errors were made. Couple that fact to the ever-increasing deterioration of the ecosystem, and you wind up with all kinds of genetic difficulties that can result in various physical afflictions.

Finally, we would be remiss if we did not include one of the primary explanations for the cause of physical evil. According to biblical (Christian) theism, God has allowed this world to be occupied by evil spiritual beings that possess free wills. Their decisions and actions must also be factored into the equation with respect to accounting for the problem of physical evil. Some physical evil results from the free choices of evil spiritual beings. As long as there are free beings (human or spiritual) committing evil deeds, there will be physical and/ or moral consequences for their behavior that affect this world.

Natural evils are an inevitable part of a natural world, and a natural world is essential for (or at least not incompatible with) the conditions of full freedom that are necessary for the attaining the best world achievable. Only biblical theism can adequately account for the presence of evil in this world. "Physical evil is essentially connected with moral evil. Moral evil is the best way to produce the optimally perfect moral world. Physical evil is necessitated in several ways: it is a condition, consequence, component, and warning in a morally free world. The evil that is not directly or indirectly traceable to human freedom is attributed to evil spirits."[14]

Therefore, we conclude that "physical evils are a necessary and concomitant dimension of the best kind of world for achieving the best of all moral worlds."[15] It is a sovereign God who allowed humanity to exercise freedom. God sovereignly willed that humans would have control over their own moral choices. In doing so, He provided for the greatest good but also gave us the power to commit acts of evil.

CAN GOD BE SOVEREIGN AND STILL ALLOW FOR HUMAN FREEDOM?

Now that we hopefully have a better understanding of the problem of evil, we can return to Rabbi Harold Kushner's conclusion mentioned earlier. Kushner believes that God is not in control of all things; thus he infers that God's sovereignty cannot coexist with human freedom, seeing human freedom as God's giving up His control over the world. In a previous work, the fallacy of Kushner's kind of thinking was exposed, and it was pointed out that

> . . . every moral action [must] be either (a) caused from without, (b) not caused, or (c) self-caused. But to cause a moral action from without would be a violation of freedom. It would be determinism, and it would eliminate individual responsibility for the action. Ultimately, it would make God directly responsible for performing evil acts. And not to be caused at all would make the act gratuitous, arbitrary, irresponsible, and unpredictable. But human acts are predictable and responsible (God knows what men will do with their freedom and holds them responsible for it). Hence, human moral acts must be self-caused or self-determined. . . .[16]

> Self-determination is neither contradictory nor irresponsible. A man is responsible for what he by moral choice comes to be. That is to say, he is responsible for his own free moral determination. . . . God determined that man would be a self-determining creature. God caused the man to have self-causality of moral thought and action. Human freedom is delegated sovereignty. The Sovereign made man sovereign over his own moral destiny. Nevertheless, God is in control of the whole process because, (1) God by His own foreknowledge sees what freedom will do and He can bring a

[14]Norman L. Geisler, *Philosophy of Religion* (Grand Rapids, Mich.: Zondervan, 1974), 402.
[15]Ibid., 403.
[16]Self-caused *acts* are not a contradiction, as is the case with self-caused *beings*. It is possible for someone to cause his or her own *becoming* (which is what free choice does), but it is impossible for someone to cause his or her own *being*. Or better, we can cause our own *actions* but not our own *being*.

greater good out of it; (2) God is in sovereign control of the end in which men's free choices will be permanentized according to their own will so that free choice to do evil will bring eternal bondage to the autonomy of one's own evil will, and freedom to do the good will bring eternal liberation to an infinite good. In brief, God (the primary Cause) is working in and through the self-causality of human freedom (the secondary cause) to produce the greatest good for the greatest number (the final cause) in accordance with the absolute perfection of His own nature (the exemplar cause).[17]

In an effort to illustrate what we are saying, consider this visual aid. We have placed God *outside* of the space-time continuum and show Him, as He is, existing in eternity and sovereign over all things. God is the only totally free and independent being that exists; all human beings are dependent and contingent by their very nature. *Inside* the space-time

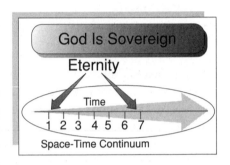

continuum free creatures exist and freely act upon their own will. The arrow moving toward the right represents the progression of time with a scale marked by days of the week. The arrows emerging out of eternity and showing up in time represent God's eternal proclamations. He decrees from eternity, but the results of those decrees take place in time. For example, a doctor who prescribes a certain medication for ten days issues one prescription (decree), and that one prescription takes place over time. In a similar manner, God prescribes from all eternity and His prescriptions take place over time.

Now let's say that the seven days in our illustration represent the events that took place during the week that Jesus Christ was crucified. During that week, certain individuals made specific free choices that affected their own destiny and caused the death of Jesus. Judas freely chose to betray Jesus to the authorities for thirty pieces of silver. The disciples of Jesus

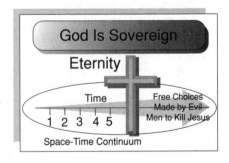

freely chose to abandon Him. The religious authorities freely chose to turn

---

[17]Op. cit., 401–402.

Him over to the Roman authorities and demand that He be executed. The mob freely chose to have Pilate release Barabbas and crucify Jesus. Pilate freely chose to condemn Jesus to death by crucifixion. That takes us to day five, the day Jesus was crucified.

After the death of Jesus, He is buried in a tomb. His friends mourn His death, and those who freely chose to take part in killing Him have accomplished the task they set out to do. Time has passed and the crucifixion, death, and burial of Jesus has taken place. Nothing and no one on the earth can go back and change the events that led to the death of Jesus

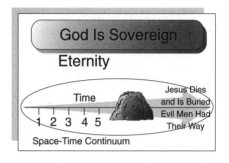

Christ. From a human perspective, it seems as though God was absent and failed to take control in order to save His own Son from the suffering He endured at the hands of evil men.

However, God will have the final word in this situation, as in all matters! As always, Jesus submitted Himself to the plan of His Father and obeyed the earthly authority over Him. They freely chose to kill Jesus by crucifixion, thinking that they had control of His final destiny. They made their choices, and God will hold them responsible for their actions.

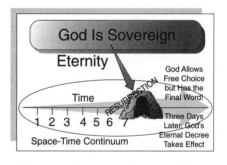

However, since God is sovereign over all things, He has the final word and had decreed from eternity that Jesus would rise from the dead three days after they crucified Him. With the Resurrection, God controls the final destiny of Jesus without violating the freedom of the evil individuals who sentenced Jesus to death by crucifixion. Both the sovereignty of God and the responsibility of human beings exist without contradiction.

The key to all this is that *God is outside of time but can act in time.* God uses the free choices of evil humans to accomplish His purposes. Even when evil people commit cruel and unjust acts by way of their freedom, they can never obstruct the purposes of a sovereign God. As C. S. Lewis said,

The crucifixion itself is the best, as well as the worst, of all historical events, but the role of Judas remains simply evil. We may apply this first to the problem of other people's suffering. A merciful man aims at his neighbor's good and so does "God's will," consciously co-operating with "the simple good." A cruel man oppresses his neighbor, and so does simple evil. But in doing such evil, he is used by God, without his own knowledge or consent, to produce the complex good—so that the first man serves God as a son, and the second as a tool. For you will certainly carry out God's purpose, however you act, but it makes a difference to you whether you serve like Judas or like John.[18]

A simpler, yet accurate, way to understand how something can be determined and still be freely chosen is the example of watching a videotape. Let's say that for some reason you weren't able to watch the Super Bowl live, so you asked your friend to videotape it. When you finally have the time to sit down and watch it, you are watching a game that is determined. But every play and action that you are observing was freely chosen.

After considering the nature of the God of Christian theism and the logical options with respect to evil, we conclude that God has the capability of intervening if and/or when He determines. If He decides not to intervene, we can assume He is allowing evil to persist in order to achieve a greater good, even if we have no knowledge of that greater good. Furthermore, God is capable of redeeming our evil choices, or the evil others choose to do to us, as part of His sovereign plan to bring about the greater good. God allowed evil to have its way with His Son, and yet He had

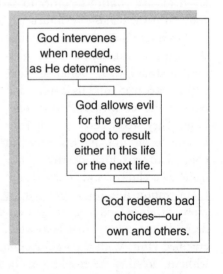

God intervenes when needed, as He determines.

God allows evil for the greater good to result either in this life or the next life.

God redeems bad choices—our own and others.

the final word at the end when He accomplished His purposes to bring about a greater good in the life of Jesus and all who believe in Him. This victory over evil is the central theme of the Christian message, referred to as the gospel or Good News.

As we have seen, atheism and pantheism fail to provide credible answers to the questions surrounding the problem of evil within the framework of their

---

[18]Lewis, *The Problem of Pain*, 111.

respective worldviews.[19] If God does not exist (atheism), or if evil is not real (pantheism), then why bother with evil? For atheists, evil is merely a matter of human ignorance, and the answer to the problem is education. For pantheists, evil is an illusion and needs no answer because evil is not really a problem. It is only when one claims that evil is real, and that an all-good, all-knowing, and all-powerful God exists, that an explanation must be given. Christian theism acknowledges that evil is anchored in every human heart and manifested by a self-centered lifestyle. We will speak directly to that problem and look at what can be done about it in the chapter on

	Atheism	Pantheism	Theism
Truth	Relative, No Absolutes	Relative to This World	Absolute Truth Exists
Cosmos	Always Existed	Not Real— Illusion	Created Reality
God (Logos)	Does Not Exist	Exists, Unknowable	Exists, Knowable
Law	Relative, Determined by Humanity	Relative to This World	Absolute, Objective, Discovered
Evil	Human Ignorance	Not Real— An Illusion	Selfish Heart

ethics and morals.

Although we have given an account for the problem of evil from a Christian theistic perspective, some questions still remain: "What has God done about evil? What is God's ultimate answer to defeating the problem of evil? How does God plan to redeem all evil for His purpose of producing the greatest good?" In order to answer these questions, we need to examine the claims of Jesus Christ as documented in the New Testament.

However, before we look at the root cause of evil behavior and the permanent cure offered by Jesus, we must address the issue of the historical reliability of the New Testament documents. In fact, with the postmodern understanding of history and the meaning of any historical text being called into question, we must first establish the credibility of the notion that history is objectively knowable. We will address these issues in the next chapter.

---

[19]See chapter 2 in order to review the method of testing the truth claims of worldviews.

─12─
QUESTIONS ABOUT HISTORY AND JESUS

If one judged a person's greatness by historical standards, Jesus stands first.

—H. G. WELLS

WHAT IS HISTORY?

Christianity's central teaching—the gospel—claims that the death and resurrection of Jesus Christ are historical facts, that Christianity is an historically verifiable religion. Indeed, the apostle Paul affirms that if Christ did not rise from the dead, then Christianity is simply false (1 Corinthians 15:12–15). But before we can know whether the Resurrection is an objective fact of history, we must know whether there is any such thing as objective history.

First, let's define it. History can be thought of as "that which has happened as well as the record of it."[1] Moreover, the word *history*

> . . . refers to a kind of knowledge. It refers to a type of literature. It means an actual sequence of events in time, which constitutes a process of irreversible change. . . . In its original Greek root, the word "history" means research, and implies the act of judging the evidences in order to separate fact from fiction. . . . Originally, research set the historian apart from the poet and the maker of myths or legends. They told stories, too;

---

[1]Mortimer J. Adler, *The Great Ideas: A Lexicon of Western Thought* (New York: Macmillan, 1992), 307.

but only the historian restricted himself to telling a story based on the facts ascertained by inquiry of research.[2]

The historian tries to make credible statements about particular past events. The historical method is similar to the scientific method when applied to investigations concerning unobserved and unrepeatable events from the past—both history and origin science attempt to make accurate statements about them. History is also similar to forensic science in its endeavor to "reconstruct" past singular events. The question we now want to pose is "Can a miraculous event be known in an historical context?"

ARE MIRACLES POSSIBLE?

Some discount the New Testament as a reliable source of history based on the fact that it contains miracles. They usually refer to David Hume's dictum that there is "uniform experience against miracles." Hume argued that miracles are a violation of natural law and are therefore disqualified. He also said, "The wise man should never believe that which is based on the lowest degree of probability." Is Hume correct to state that miracles cannot be considered a part of true history?

In his book titled *Miracles*, C. S. Lewis responded to Hume, saying, "If there is absolutely 'uniform experience' against miracles, if in other words they have never happened, why then they never have [happened]? Unfortunately we know the experience against them to be uniform only if we know that all the reports of them are false. And we can know that all reports of them to be false only if we know already that miracles have never occurred. In fact, we are arguing in a circle."[3]

As we have seen, someone who uses this type of argument winds up committing one of the most basic fallacies of logic—*begging the question.* Question begging is circular reasoning; in this case the conclusion, "there is uniform experience against miracles," is covertly used as the premise, "miracles never happen."

We said that the historical method and the scientific method are similar with respect to their goals—both endeavor to verify the truth or falsehood of singular events from the past. However, they are different with respect to their methodologies and verification processes. Lewis explained:

[2]Ibid., 308.
[3]C. S. Lewis, *Miracles* (New York: Macmillan, 1960), 102.

This point of scientific method merely shows (what no one to my knowledge ever denied) that if miracles did occur, science, as science, could not prove, or disprove, their occurrence. What cannot be trusted to recur is not material for science: that is why history is not one of the sciences. You cannot find out what Napoleon did at the battle of Austerlitz by asking him to come and fight it again in a laboratory with the same combatants, the same terrain, the same weather, and in the same age. You have to go to the records. We have not, in fact, proved that science excludes miracles: we have only proved that the question of miracles, like the innumerable other questions, excludes laboratory treatment.[4]

IF GOD IS, THEN MIRACLES ARE POSSIBLE

Miracles are special acts of God, and acts of God are only possible if there is a God who can act. We have already shown in previous chapters that theism is credible and that the most spectacular miracle of all—creation—is scientifically and philosophically sound. Therefore, it makes sense that there can be acts of God. If, however, you are still inclined to reject this conclusion, consider once more this statement by Lewis:

> If the "natural" means that which can be fitted into a class, that which obeys a norm, that which can be paralleled, that which can be explained by reference to other events, then Nature herself as a whole is *not* natural. If a miracle means that which must simply be accepted, the unanswerable actuality which gives no account of itself but simply *is*, then the universe is one great miracle.[5]

Since miracles make sense in a theistic universe, we can concentrate on the logical and evidential aspects of the New Testament documents that record miracles as a part of history. To do so, however, we must first show that the documents themselves are historically reliable. In order to accomplish this task, we must identify generally acceptable test criteria that could be applied to any document from antiquity.

HOW CAN WE TEST THE RELIABILITY OF ANCIENT DOCUMENTS?

Once again we note that history is similar to origin science (see chapter 4) in its goal of establishing the probability of singular events from the past. The

---

[4]C. S. Lewis, *God in the Dock* (Grand Rapids, Mich.: Eerdmans, 1970), 134.
[5]Ibid., 36.

parameters of history are philosophical in nature with respect to the intellectual lens (worldview) through which the historian views (interprets) past events. The verification process of the historical method is legal in nature in that the investigation involves establishing the truth or falsehood of eyewitness accounts. There are other important factors that we will point out, but for now these intellectual dimensions of the historical method will hopefully help us to understand the basis for developing a reliable historical methodology.

There is an essential difference between *statements made about God* and *statements claiming that God acted at a certain point in time*—in history. The claims of the New Testament place the events squarely in the continuum of secular history. Unlike many other religions, Christianity is based on historical evidence that can be tested and found to be true or to be false. One essential legal rule, known to every lawyer, is that *declarations must give the time and place*. The New Testament does so with the utmost precision. For example, in Luke 3:1–2 we read,

> In the fifteenth year of the reign of Tiberius Caesar—when Pontius Pilate was governor of Judea, Herod tetrarch of Galilee, his brother Philip tetrarch of Iturea and Traconitis, and Lysanias tetrarch of Abilene—during the high priesthood of Annas and Caiaphas, the word of God came to John son of Zechariah in the desert.

These New Testament events are open to examination. If someone can demonstrate that these people or places never existed or that these events did not happen, the reliability of the New Testament documents would be put at risk. However, sufficient evidence to support the accuracy of this report would argue for the reliability of the New Testament documents.

Of course, the question is "How much evidence is enough evidence?" In his book *Introduction to Research in English Literary History*, military historian Dr. C. Sanders offers criteria for establishing the reliability and accuracy of any piece of literature from antiquity.[6] There are three basic tests that Sanders identified for deciding if an ancient document is reliable:

- *Bibliographical Test:* Since we do not have the original documents (autographs), how reliable and accurate are the copies we have in regard to the number of manuscripts (MSS),[7] and what is the time interval between the original and the copy/copies in existence?

---

[6]C. Sanders, *Introduction to Research in English Literary History* (New York: Macmillan, 1952), 143ff.

[7]A manuscript is a handwritten literary composition, in contrast to a printed copy. An original manuscript is the first one produced, usually referred to as an autograph. There are no known autographs of the New Testament; in fact, none are needed because of the abundance of manuscript copies.

- *Internal Test:* What is in the text? Is the text internally consistent?
- *External Test:* What is outside the text? What pieces of literature or other data are extant (in existence), apart from the one being studied, that confirm the accuracy of the inner testimony of the document? (In other words, is there literature apart from the document that supports what's in it?)

DOES THE NEW TESTAMENT PASS THE BIBLIOGRAPHICAL TEST?

Again, there are two basic questions: (1) Not having the original documents, how reliable are the copies we have in regard to the number of manuscripts? and (2) What is/are the time interval(s) between the original and the extant copy/copies? In response to these questions, one must understand that there is more abundant and accurate manuscript evidence for the New Testament than for any other book from the ancient world. Furthermore, there are more manuscripts copied with greater accuracy and earlier dating than for any secular classic from antiquity.

In his book *History and Christianity*, John Warwick Montgomery presents a strong case for the historical Jesus. In the beginning of his work, Montgomery cites a lecture by Professor Avrum Stroll, delivered at the University of British Columbia, titled "Did Jesus Really Exist?" Professor Stroll's position is summarized in the closing sentence of his lecture.

> An accretion of legends grew up about this figure [Jesus], was incorporated into the gospels by various devotees of the movement, was rapidly spread throughout the Mediterranean world by the ministry of St. Paul; and that [sic] because this is so, it is impossible to separate these legendary elements in the purported descriptions of Jesus from those which in fact were true of him.[8]

In responding to this hypothesis, and others of a similar nature, we need only point out a few facts about the manuscript evidence. One fact is located in the John Rylands Library in Manchester, England, and is known as the *John Rylands Fragment.* This papyrus contains five verses from the Gospel of John (18:31–33, 37–38). It was found in Egypt and is dated between A.D. 117 and 138. The great philologist (a person who studies written texts to establish their authenticity) Adolf Deissmann argued that it may have been even earlier.[9] This discovery destroyed the idea that the New Testament was written down during

---

[8]John Warwick Montgomery, *History and Christianity* (Minneapolis: Bethany House, 1964), 14.
[9]Norman Geisler and William Nix, *A General Introduction to the Bible* (Chicago: Moody, 1982), 268.

the second century in order to provide time for myths to grow around the truth.

The following table is a small sample of the abundant manuscript evidence available in support of giving the New Testament documents a superior passing grade on the bibliographical test. This table features New Testament manuscripts, dates, content, and locations of some of the most important manuscripts.[10, 11]

THE NEW TESTAMENT MANUSCRIPTS

Manuscript	Date	Content	Present Location
John Rylands Fragment	C. A.D. 125	John's gospel 18:31–33, 37–38	John Rylands Library Manchester, England
Bodmer Papyri	C. A.D. 200	Fragments: 40 pages of John, Jude, Luke, 1 & 2 Peter	Peter Bodmer Library, Cologny, Switzerland (near Geneva)
Chester Beatty Papyri	C. A.D. 250	Major portions of Matthew, John, Mark, Luke, Acts	C. Beatty Museum, Dublin, Ireland
Codex Vaticanus	C. A.D. 325	Most of the Old Testament (OT) and New Testament (NT)	Vatican Library, Rome
Codex Sinaticus	C. A.D. 340	Half of OT, most of NT	British Museum, London
Codex Ephraemi Rescriptus	C. A.D. 350	All of NT except 2 John and 2 Thessalonians	National Library, Paris
Codex Bezae (D) Codex Cantabrigiensis	C. A.D. 500	Four Gospels, Acts, 3 John 11–15	Cambridge University Library, England
Codex Claromontanus	C. A.D. 550	Pauline Epistles, Hebrews	National Library, Paris
Codex Coislinianus	c. 6th cent.	Pauline Epistles	Various Libraries (Paris, Moscow, Kiev)

Again, this is only a small sample of the empirical evidence in support of the reliability of the New Testament documents. The sum total of Greek MSS alone now is 5,686—and counting. In addition there are 10,000+ MSS in

[10]Ibid., 268–80.
[11]Bruce Metzger, *The Text of the New Testament* (New York: Oxford University Press, 1964), 30–54.

Latin, 4,100 in Slavic, 2,500+ in Armenian, 2,000+ in Ethiopic, etc. That's 24,286, plus hundreds in other languages.[12]

The chart below shows that the only other ancient text that can even try to compare to the MSS evidence for the New Testament (5,686 Greek) is Homer's *Iliad*, with a mere 643 copies.

The time span between the original text and the earliest extant manuscript copy is very significant. The larger the time span, the less data there is for scholars to work with to reconstruct the original. *The average time span between the original and earliest copy of the other ancient texts is over 1,000 years.*[13] However, the New

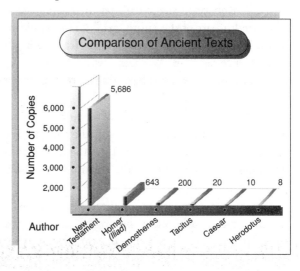

Testament has a fragment within one generation of its original composition. Whole books appear within 100 years of the original, most of the New Testament within 200 years, and the entire New Testament within 250 years from the date of its completion.

Furthermore, the degree of accuracy is greater for the New Testament than for other documents that can be compared—approximately 99 percent accurately copied. The fact is that "most books do not survive with enough manuscripts that make comparison possible. A handful of copies that are 1,000 years old after the fact do not provide enough links in the missing chain nor enough variant readings in the manuscript to enable textual scholars to reconstruct the original."[14] How significant, in contrast, are the New Testament variant readings?

---

[12]For more details on these texts, see Norman Geisler and William Nix, *A General Introduction to the Bible* (Chicago: Moody, 1982), 285, 366; Bruce Metzger, *The Text of the New Testament* (New York: Oxford University, 1964), 30–54; and Archibald T. Robertson, *An Introduction to the Textual Criticism of the New Testament* (Nashville: Broadman, 1925), 70.

[13]1,000 years for Tacitus and Caesar, 1,300 years for Herodotus, and 1,500 years for Demosthenes. The time span for Homer's *Iliead* is not known.

[14]Norman Geisler, *Christian Apologetics* (Grand Rapids, Mich.: Baker, 1976), 308.

Westcott and Hort estimated that only about one-eighth of all the variants have any weight, as most of them are merely mechanical matters such as spelling or style. Of the whole, then, only about one-sixtieth rise above "trivialities," or can in any sense be called "substantial variations."[15] Mathematically this would compute to a text that is 98.33 percent pure.

A. T. Robertson suggested that the real concern of textual criticism is of a "thousandth part of the entire text."[16] This would make the reconstructed text of the New Testament 99.9 percent free from substantial or consequential error. Hence, as B. B. Warfield observed, "The great mass of the New Testament, in other words, has been transmitted to us with no, or next to no variations."[17]

At first, the great multitude of variants would seem to be a liability to the integrity of the biblical text. But just the contrary is true, for the larger number of variants supplies at the same time the means of checking on those variants. As strange as it may appear, the corruption of the text provides the means of its own correction.[18]

An honest comparison of three observations: (1) the number of MSS, (2) the time span between the original and the earliest copy, and (3) the accuracy of the New Testament, all bear witness that the New Testament is the most historically accurate and reliable document from all of antiquity. If one cannot trust the New Testament at this point, then one must reject all of ancient history, which rests on much weaker evidence. So definite is the evidence for the New Testament that no less a scholar than the late Sir Frederic Kenyon could write,

> The interval then between the dates of original composition and the earliest extant evidence becomes so small as to be in fact negligible, and the last foundation for any doubt that the Scriptures have come down to us substantially as they were written has now been removed. Both the *authenticity* and the *general integrity* of the books of the New Testament may be regarded as finally established.[19]

---

[15]B. F. Westcott and F. J. A. Hort, eds., *The New Testament in the Original Greek*, 2nd ed. (New York: Macmillan, 1928), vol. II, no. 2.

[16]Archibald T. Robertson, *An Introduction to the Textual Criticism of the New Testament* (Nashville: Broadman, 1925), 22.

[17]Benjamin B. Warfield, *An Introduction to the Textual Criticism of the New Testament* (London: n.p., 1886), 154.

[18]Norman Geisler and William Nix, *A General Introduction to the Bible* (Chicago: Moody, 1982), 365–66.

[19]Ibid., 285.

DOES THE NEW TESTAMENT PASS THE INTERNAL TEST?

The internal test utilizes one of Aristotle's dictums from his *Poetics*. He said,

> They [the critics] start with some improbable presumption; and having
> so decreed it themselves, proceed to draw inferences, and censure the poet
> as though he had actually said whatever they happen to believe, if his state-
> ment conflicts with their notion of things. . . . Whenever a word seems to
> imply some contradiction, it is necessary to reflect how many ways there
> may be of understanding it in the passage in question. . . . So it is probably
> the mistake of the critics that has given rise to the Problem. . . . See
> whether he [the author] means the same thing, in the same relation, and
> in the same sense, before admitting that he has contradicted something he
> has said himself or what a man of sound sense assumes as true.[20]

In other words, *if it can be shown that the author has not contradicted himself,
the benefit of the doubt is to be given to the author of the document itself, and not
arrogated by the critic.* As John Warwick Montgomery insists, "One must listen
to the claims of the document under analysis, and not assume fraud or error
unless the author disqualified himself by contradictions or known factual inaccuracies."[21] In the New Testament, no *real* contradictions have been proven,
and *apparent* discrepancies are expected in independent reliable testimony.
There have been many alleged contradictions in the Bible, most of which have
been cleared up by proper jurisprudential procedures, accurate principles of
interpretation, and noteworthy archaeological discoveries.

To help gain a better understanding of what we mean, we have summarized
some of the principles that ought to be applied to the interpretation of any
document written in the past. This is by no means an exhaustive list, but it is
sufficient for the scope of this work. (For a more comprehensive study, we refer
you to *When Critics Ask.*[22] We also recommend Gleason Archer's *Encyclopedia
of Biblical Difficulties.*[23]) Before an intellectually honest person concludes that
a document is internally inconsistent, he should first make sure the following
principles have been correctly applied to the text.

Consider the language, culture, geography, and history of the time in which
the document was written. The Bible has been around for many years, parts of

---

[20]Richard McKeon, ed., *The Basic Works of Aristotle* (New York: Random, 1941), 1485–86.

[21]John Warwick Montgomery, *History and Christianity* (Minneapolis: Bethany House, 1964), 29.

[22]Norman L. Geisler and Thomas Howe, *When Critics Ask: A Popular Handbook on Bible Difficulties* (Grand Rapids, Mich.: Baker, 1992).

[23]Gleason L. Archer, *Encyclopedia of Biblical Difficulties* (Grand Rapids, Mich.: Zondervan, 1982).

it for as long as four millennia. How are we going to understand what the authors were saying and the various circumstances in which they lived? We must bridge these four gaps.

THE LANGUAGE GAP

Gleason Archer is uniquely gifted in his command of ancient languages. In *Encyclopedia of Biblical Difficulties*, he reminds his readers to

> consider how confused a foreigner must be when he reads in a daily newspaper: "The prospectors made a *strike* yesterday up in the mountains." "The union went on *strike* this morning." "The batter made his third *strike* and was called out by the umpire." "*Strike* up with the Star Spangled Banner." "The fisherman got a good *strike* in the middle of the lake." Presumably each of these completely different uses of the same word go back to the parent and have the same etymology. But complete confusion may result from misunderstanding how the speaker meant the word to be used. . . . We must engage in careful exegesis in order to find out what he meant in light of contemporary conditions and usage.[24]

We speak English, but the Bible was written in Hebrew and Greek (and a few parts in Aramaic, which is similar to Hebrew). Therefore, we have a language gap; if we don't bridge it, we won't fully be able to understand the Bible.

THE CULTURE GAP

If we don't understand the various cultures of the time in which the Bible was written, we'll never comprehend its meaning. For example, if we did not know anything about the Jewish culture at the time of Christ, the Gospel of Matthew would be very difficult to grasp. Concepts such as the Sabbath, Jewish rituals, the temple ceremonies, and other customs of the Jews must be understood within cultural context in order to gain the true meaning of the author's ideas.

THE GEOGRAPHY GAP

A failure to be familiar with geography will hinder learning. For instance, in 1 Thessalonians 1:8 we read, "For from you sounded out the word of the Lord not only in Macedonia and Achaia, but also in every place your faith [toward] God is spread abroad." What is so remarkable about this text is that the message traveled so quickly. In order to understand how, it is necessary to know the geography.

---

[24]Ibid., 16.

Paul had just been there, and when he wrote the letter, very little time had passed. Paul had been with them for a couple of weeks, but their testimony had already spread far. How could that happen so fast? If you study the geography of the area you'll find that the Ignatian Highway runs right through the middle of Thessalonica. It was the main concourse between the East and West, and whatever happened there was passed all the way down the line.[25]

THE HISTORY GAP

Knowing the history behind a passage will enhance our comprehension of what was written. In the Gospel of John, the whole key to understanding the interplay between Pilate and Jesus is based on the knowledge of history.

> When Pilate came into the land with his emperor worship, it literally infuriated the Jews and their priests. So he was off to a bad start from the very beginning. Then he tried to pull something on the Jews, and when they caught him, they reported him to Rome, and he almost lost his job. Pilate was afraid of the Jews, and that's why he let Christ be crucified. Why was he afraid? Because he already had a rotten track record, and his job was on the line.[26]

Consider something known as the psychology of testimony. This refers to the way witnesses of the same event recall it with a certain level of discrepancy, based on how they individually observe, process, store, and retrieve the memories of an event.

One person may recall an event in strict chronological order; another may testify according to the principle of the association of ideas. One person may remember events minutely and consecutively, while someone else omits, condenses, or expands. These factors must be considered in comparing eyewitness accounts, and this is why history expects a certain amount of variability in human testimony. For example, let's say that twelve eyewitnesses observed the same event—a car accident. If those witnesses were called to testify in a court of law, what would the judge think if all twelve witnesses gave the same exact testimony of the event, with every detail being identical? Any good judge would immediately conclude they were in collusion and reject their accounts. The variations of the observations of the eyewitness testimonies actually add to the integrity of their recall. What are the most essential guidelines used as criteria for deciding if the testimonies are true?

---

[25]John MacArthur, *How to Study the Bible* (Chicago: Moody, 1982), 72.
[26]Ibid.

COMPLETE AGREEMENT ON THE MAIN POINTS

For instance: (1) The car accident occurred at a specific time and at a certain place; (2) a general description of the two vehicles involved; and (3) the drivers were both males, etc. Let's say all twelve witnesses agreed on the time and place and said the accident involved a red Ford Escort and a black Dodge truck. They all testify that the Escort driver was a younger man and the Dodge driver was an older man. They are in agreement on the main points. With respect to the New Testament and the person of Jesus, the eyewitnesses reached a clear consensus on the main points of His miraculous life, how He died, and His resurrection from the dead.

COMPLETE AGREEMENT ON SIGNIFICANT DETAILS SUPPORTING THE MAIN POINTS

A good judge looks for agreement on crucial facts that support the main event. In our example, the weather, the road conditions, and the impact that occurred would be considered to be some of the essential supporting facts relevant to the case. The type of accident that occurred is also important—was it a head-on collision, a sideswipe, a rear-end?

In the New Testament, the Gospel accounts all agree on the significant details that support Jesus' virgin birth, the calling of His twelve disciples, and His teachings about the nature of God, humanity, good and fallen angels, salvation, etc. They also agree on the reactions of the religious and political leaders, which led to His death. They all agree that Jesus had both a religious and political trial and was sentenced to death by the Roman governor, Pontius Pilate. They all agree that Jesus was beaten, crucified, buried, and raised from the dead on the third day after His death.

APPLICATION OF ARISTOTLE'S DICTUM

Earlier, we mentioned Aristotle's dictum involving the principle of giving the benefit of the doubt to the author of the document and not allowing it to be arrogated by the critic. In *Poetics* Aristotle outlined twelve responses to critics who hunt for various kinds of defects when examining the work of authors from the past. He divided the critics' mistakes into five categories.

The objections, then, of critics start with faults of five kinds: the allegation is always that something is either (1) impossible, (2) improbable, (3) corrupting, (4) contradictory, or (5) against technical correctness. The answers to these objections must be sought under one or other of the above-mentioned heads, which are twelve in number.[27]

Before we apply this to the New Testament, allow us to illustrate it. One of us has a friend—let's call him Ken—who lives in the Midwest. Ken had three very good friends—let's call them Jim, John, and Mark—who live on the East Coast. One day Ken received a note from John saying that Jim was involved in a terrible automobile accident and *died instantly*. The following day, Ken received a letter from Mark saying that Jim was in an automobile accident and survived but *died some time later*. At first glance, these two accounts seem to contradict each other. Either Jim died instantly in the accident or he did not.

Now, Ken knew that John and Mark were reliable sources, and he trusted them to give him an accurate account of the events surrounding their mutual friend's death. As it turned out, John and Mark were both right, but there was missing information. Jim was actually involved in two automobile accidents on the same day. In the first accident, Jim was badly injured but survived. A "Good Samaritan" stopped to help him, taking him to the nearest emergency room. However, on the way to the hospital, the driver of that vehicle was involved in a very serious accident, and as a result Jim was instantly killed. Hence, both accounts were correct. John was not aware of the first accident; he only knew about the second one that instantly killed Jim. Mark was only aware of the details of the first accident in which Jim survived, and not the second; he only knew that Jim died later that day. The apparent contradiction was solved when the rest of the truth was discovered.

Aristotle's dictum applies to the New Testament as well, as this next example shows. In the Gospel according to Matthew, he records the death of Judas as suicide by hanging (Matthew 27:5). However, in Acts 1:18 Luke records the death of Judas as having occurred when he fell down and his body "burst open." Some scholars have determined that these two divergent accounts are irreconcilable; they assume that one or even both of these accounts are incorrect. If Matthew and Luke are trustworthy in giving an accurate accounts of the events, it certainly seems as if at least one of them is in error: Judas either fell down or he hung himself. Or is there another option?

If the branch from which Judas hung himself was dead and dry—and there are many trees that match this description even to this day on the brink of the canyon that tradition identifies as the place where Judas died—it would take only one strong gust of wind to yank the heavy corpse

[27]Richard McKeon, ed., *The Basic Works of Aristotle* (New York: Random, 1941), 1486.

and split the branch to which it was attached and plunge both with great force into the bottom of the chasm below. There is indication that a strong wind arose at the hour Christ died and ripped the great curtain inside the temple from top to bottom (Matthew 27:51).[28]

These accounts are not contradictory, but mutually complementary. Judas hung himself exactly as Matthew affirms that he did. The account in Acts simply adds that Judas fell, and his body opened up at the middle and his intestines gushed out. This is the very thing one would expect of someone who hanged himself from a tree over a cliff and fell on sharp rocks below.[29]

The integrity of the testimonies given by the New Testament authors is crucial because they testified before the world, including some of their most severe antagonists. They proclaimed their message as eyewitnesses and were exposed to criticism and correction by their opponents (Acts 2:22). That kind of pressure to keep the facts straight happens to very few people in history; these authors could not afford to risk inaccuracies. Any manipulation of the facts would at once be exposed, for there were many living eyewitnesses who would have stepped forward immediately had they misrepresented the truth. Consequently, we conclude that the New Testament passes the internal consistency test.

DOES THE NEW TESTAMENT PASS THE EXTERNAL TEST?

"What sources are there, apart from the writings under analysis, that confirm the document's accuracy, reliability, and authenticity?" In other words, is there literature or other evidence, apart from the New Testament, that confirms the inner testimony of the New Testament authors? In response to this question we offer the following objective evidence, extracted from the various noted sources, to confirm the general outline of the New Testament.

THE TESTIMONY OF FLAVIUS JOSEPHUS, JEWISH HISTORIAN (A.D. 37–100)[30]

The Jewish historian Josephus was born of a priestly family in A.D. 37. At the age of nineteen he joined the Pharisaic party. . . . On the outbreak

[28]Archer, *Encyclopedia of Biblical Difficulties*, 344.
[29]Geisler and Howe, *When Critics Ask: A Popular Handbook on Bible Difficulties*, 361.
[30]F. F. Bruce, *The New Testament Documents, Are They Reliable?* (Grand Rapids, Mich.: Eerdmans, 1985), 102–12.

of the Jewish War in A.D. 66 he was made commander of the Jewish forces in Galilee, and defended the stronghold of Jotapata against the Romans until further resistance was useless. . . . Josephus found himself one of the last two survivors. He persuaded his fellow-survivor that they might as well give themselves up to the Romans. . . .

Josephus was attached to the Roman general headquarters during the siege of Jerusalem, even acting as an interpreter for Titus, Vespasian's son and successor in the Palestinian command. . . . After the fall of the city and crushing of the rebellion, Josephus settled down comfortably in Rome as a client and pensioner [assistant] of the emperor, whose family name Flavius he assumed, being thenceforth known as Flavius Josephus. . . . He employed his years of leisure in Rome in such a way as to establish some claim upon their gratitude, by writing a history of their nation. His literary works include a *History of the Jewish War* . . . an *Autobiography* . . . and twenty books of *Antiquities of the Jews,* in which he recorded the history of his own nation from the beginning of Genesis down to his own day. . . .

Here, in the pages of Josephus, we meet many figures who are well known to us from the New Testament: the colorful family of the Herods; the Roman emperors Augustus, Tiberius, Claudius, and Nero; Quirinius, the governor of Syria; Pilate, Felix, and Festus, the procurators of Judea; the high priestly families—Annas, Caiaphas, Ananias, and the rest; the Pharisees and the Sadducees; and so on. Against the background which Josephus provides we can read the New Testament with greater understanding and interest.

The sudden death of Herod Agrippa I, narrated by Luke in Acts 12:19–23, is recorded also by Josephus (*Antiquities,* xix.8.2) in a form agreeing with Luke's general outline, though the two accounts are quite independent of each other. . . . More important still, Josephus makes mention of John the Baptist and of James the brother of our Lord, recording the death of each in a manner manifestly independent of the New Testament. . . . In *Antiquities* xviii.5.2 we read how Herod Antipas, tetrarch of Galilee, was defeated in battle by Aretas, king of the Nabataean Arabs, the father of Herod's first wife, whom he deserted for Herodias. Josephus goes on to say,

> Now some of the Jews thought that Herod's army had been destroyed by God, and that it was a very just penalty to avenge John, surnamed the Baptist. For Herod had killed him, though he was a good man, who bade the Jews practice virtue, be just one to another and pious towards God, and come together in baptism. . . . Herod feared that his persuasive power over men, being so great, might lead to a rising, as they seemed ready to follow his counsel in everything. . . . Because of this suspicion of Herod, John was sent in

chains to Machaerus . . . and there put to death.

Later in *Antiquities* (xx.9.1), Josephus describes the high-handed acts of the high priest Ananus after the death of the procurator Festus (A.D. 61) in these words:

> Ananus . . . was of a bold disposition and exceptionally daring; he followed the party of the Sadducees, who are severe in judgment above all the Jews. . . . Ananus was of such disposition, he thought he had now a good opportunity, as Festus was now dead, and Albinus was still on the road; so he assembled a council of judges, and brought before it the brother of Jesus the so-called Christ, whose name was James, together with some others, and having accused them as law-breakers, he delivered them over to be stoned.

The account of Josephus is chiefly important because he calls James "the brother of Jesus the so-called Christ," in such a way as to suggest that he has already made some reference to Jesus. And we do find reference to Him in all extant copies of Josephus, the so-called *Testimonium Flavianum* in *Antiquities* xviii.3.3. There Josephus narrates some of the troubles which marked the procuratorship of Pilate, and continues:

> And there arose about this time Jesus, a wise man, *if indeed we should call him a man;* for he was a doer of marvelous deeds, a teacher of men who receive the truth with pleasure. He led away many Jews, and also many of the Greeks. *This man was the Christ.* And when Pilate had condemned him to the cross on his impeachment by the chief men among us, those who had loved him at first did not cease; *for he appeared to them on the third day alive again, the divine prophets having spoken these and thousands of other wonderful things about him:* and even now the tribe of Christians, so named after him, has not yet died out.

This is a translation of the text of this passage as it has come down to us, and we know that it was the same in the time of Eusebius [about A.D. 263–about A.D. 339], who quotes it twice. One reason why many have decided to regard it as a Christian interpolation is that Origen says that Josephus did not believe Jesus to be the Messiah nor proclaim Him as such. That Josephus was no Christian is certain in any case. But it seems unlikely that a writer who was not a Christian should use the expressions printed above in italics. Yet there is nothing to say against the passage on the ground of textual criticism; the manuscript evidence is as unanimous and ample as it is for anything in Josephus. . . . If, however, we look more closely at these italicized sections, it may occur to us to wonder if it is not possible that Josephus was writing with his tongue in his cheek. *"If indeed we should call him a man"* may be a sarcastic reference to the Christians' belief in Jesus as the Son of God. *"This man was the Christ"* may mean no more than that this was the Jesus commonly called the Christ. . . . As for the third italicized section, the one about the resurrection, this may simply be intended to record what the Christians averred. Some acute critics have found no difficulty in accepting the *Testimonium Flavianum* as it stands. . . .

Two other emendations [revisions of the same section of Josephus cited above] have much to commend them. . . . If, then, we adopt these emendations of the text, this is what we get as a result:

> And there arose about this time *a source of new troubles*, one Jesus, a wise man. He was a doer of marvelous deeds, a teacher of men who receive *strange things* with pleasure. He led away many Jews, and also many of the Greeks. This man was the *so-called* Christ. And when Pilate had condemned him to the cross on his impeachment by the chief men among us, those who had loved him at first did not cease; for he appeared to them, *as they said*, on the third day alive again, the divine prophets having spoken these and thousands of other wonderful things about him: and even now the tribe of Christians, so named after him, has not yet died out.

The italics this time mark the emendations. This version of *Testimonium* has got rid, by one or two very simple devices, of the difficulties of the traditional text, while it preserves (or even enhances) the worth of the passage as a historical document. The flavor of contempt is a little more marked as a result of the additions; and the closing reference to "the tribe of Christians" is not inconsonant with a hope that though they have not yet died out, they soon may.

We have therefore very good reason for believing that Josephus did make reference to Jesus, bearing witness to (a) His date, (b) His reputation as a wonder-worker, (c) His being the brother of James, (d) His crucifixion under Pilate at the information of the Jewish rulers, (e) His messianic claim, (f) His being the founder of "the tribe of Christians," and probably (g) the belief in His rising from the dead.

THE TESTIMONY OF EARLY GENTILE WRITERS[31]

The first Gentile writer who concerns us seems to be one called Thallus, who about A.D. 52 wrote a work tracing the history of Greece and its relations with Asia from the Trojan War to his own day. He has been identified with a Samaritan of that name, who is mentioned by Josephus (*Antiquities* xviii.6.4) as being a freedman of the Emperor Tiberius. Now Julius Africanus, a Christian writer on chronology about A.D. 221, who knew the

---

[31]Ibid., 113–20.

writings of Thallus, says when discussing the darkness which fell upon the land during the crucifixion of Christ:

"Thallus, in the third book of his histories, explains away this darkness as an eclipse of the sun—unreasonably, as it seems to me" (unreasonably, of course, because a solar eclipse could not take place at the time of the full moon, and it was at the season of the Paschal full moon that Christ died).

From this reference in Julius Africanus it has been inferred (a) that the Gospel tradition, or at least the traditional story of the passion, was known in Rome in non-Christian circles towards the middle of the first century; and (b) that the enemies of Christianity tried to refute this Christian tradition by giving a naturalistic interpretation to the facts which it reported. . . .

The greatest Roman historian in the days of the Empire was Cornelius Tacitus, who was born between A.D. 52 and 54 and wrote the history of Rome under the emperors. About the age of sixty, when writing the history of the reign of Nero (A.D. 54–68), he described the great fire which ravaged Rome in A.D. 64 and told how it was widely rumored that Nero had instigated the fire, in order to gain greater glory for himself by rebuilding the city. He goes on:

Therefore to scotch the rumor, Nero substituted as culprits, and punished with the utmost refinements of cruelty, a class of men, loathed for their vices, whom the crowd styled Christians. Christus, from whom they got their name, had been executed by sentence of the procurator Pontius Pilate when Tiberius was emperor; and the pernicious superstition was checked for a short time, only to break out afresh, not only in Judaea, the home of the plague, but in Rome itself, where all the horrible and shameful things in the world collect and find a home.

This account does not strike one as having been derived from Christian sources nor yet from Jewish informants, for the latter would not have referred to Jesus as Christus. For the pagan Tacitus, Christus was simply a proper name; for the Jews, as for the first century Christians, it was not a name but a title, the Greek equivalent of the Semitic *Messiah* ("Anointed"). . . .

In A.D. 112, C. Plinius Secundus (Pliny the Younger), governor of Bithynia in Asia Minor, wrote a letter to the Emperor Trajan, asking his advice on how to deal with the troublesome sect of Christians, who were embarrassingly numerous in his province. According to evidence he had secured by examining some of them under torture,

They were in the habit of meeting on a certain fixed day before it was light, when they sang an anthem to Christ as God, and bound themselves by a solemn oath (*sacramentum*) not to commit any wicked deed, but to abstain from all fraud, theft and adultery, never to break their word, or deny a trust when called upon to honor it; after which it was their custom to separate, and then meet again to partake of food of an ordinary and innocent kind.

Whatever else may be thought of the evidence from early Jewish and Gentile writers . . . it does at least establish, for those who refuse the witness of Christian writings, the historical character of Jesus Himself. Some writers may toy with the fancy of a "Christ-myth," but they do not do so on the ground of historical evidence. The historicity of Christ is as axiomatic for an unbiased historian as the historicity of Julius Caesar. It is not historians that propagate the "Christ-myth" theories.

Combining these historical non-Christian testimonies about Christ, we get the following picture:[32]

(1) Jesus was from Nazareth; (2) he lived a wise and virtuous life; (3) he was crucified in Palestine under Pontius Pilate during the reign of Tiberius Caesar at Passover time, being considered the Jewish king; (4) he was believed by his disciples to have been raised from the dead three days later; (5) his enemies acknowledged that he performed unusual feats they called "sorcery"; (6) his small band of disciples multiplied rapidly, spreading even as far as Rome; (7) his disciples denied polytheism, lived moral lives, and worshiped Christ as Divine. This picture confirms the view of Christ presented in the New Testament Gospels.

This general outline is perfectly congruent with that of the New Testament. To further substantiate the historicity of the New Testament, consider the following archaeological and historical evidence.[33]

THE TESTIMONY OF ARCHAEOLOGY

EVIDENCE RELATED TO JESUS' DEATH[34]

Two fascinating discoveries illuminate the death of Christ and, to some degree, His resurrection. The first is an unusual decree; the second is the body of [a] crucifixion victim.

---

[32]Norman L. Geisler, *Baker Encyclopedia of Christian Apologetics*, (Grand Rapids, Mich.: Baker, 1999), 385.

[33]The archaeological evidence summarized here is for the New Testament only. For a summary of the evidence with respect to the Old Testament, see Ibid., 48–52.

[34]Ibid., 48.

The Nazareth Decree. A slab of stone was found in Nazareth in 1878, inscribed with a decree from Emperor Claudius (A.D. 41–54) that no graves should be disturbed or bodies extracted or moved. This type of decree is not uncommon, but the startling fact is that here "the offender [shall] be sentenced to capital punishment on [the] charge of violation of [a] sepulchre." Other notices warned of a fine, but death for disturbing graves? A likely explanation is that Claudius, having heard of the Christian doctrine of resurrection and Jesus' empty tomb while investigating the riots of A.D. 49, decided not to let any such report surface again. This would make sense in light of the Jewish argument that the body had been stolen (Matthew 28:11–15). This is early testimony to the strong and persistent belief that Jesus rose from the dead.

Yohanan—A Crucifixion Victim. In 1968, an ancient burial site was uncovered in Jerusalem containing about thirty-five bodies. It was determined that most of these had suffered violent deaths in the Jewish uprising against Rome in A.D. 70. One of these was a man named Yohanan Ben Ha'galgol. He was about twenty-four to twenty-eight years old, had a cleft palate, and a seven-inch nail was driven through both his feet. . . . The nail had gone through a wedge of acacia wood, then through the heels, then into an olive wood beam. There was also evidence that similar spikes had been put between the two bones of each lower arm. These had caused the upper bones to be worn smooth as the victim repeatedly raised and lowered himself to breathe (breathing is restricted with the arms raised). Crucifixion victims had to lift themselves to free the chest muscles and, when they grew too weak to do so, died by suffocation. Yohanan's legs were crushed by a blow, consistent with the common use of Roman *crucifragium* (John 19:31–32). Each of these details confirms the New Testament description of crucifixion.

Archaeological discoveries bear witness to the places described in the New Testament. Some of those discoveries include

- The Pavement of John 19:13
- The pool of Bethesda
- Jacob's well
- The pool of Siloam
- The ancient cities of Bethlehem, Nazareth, Cana, Capernaum, and Chorazin
- The residence of Pilate in Jerusalem.

Much more textual and archaeological evidence supports the accuracy of the New Testament. But even these examples reveal the extent to which archaeology has confirmed the truth of the Scriptures. Archaeologist Nelson Glueck has boldly asserted that "it may be stated categorically that no archaeological discovery has ever controverted a biblical reference. Scores of archaeological findings have been made which confirm in clear outline or exact detail historical statements in the Bible" (*Rivers in the Desert* [Philadelphia: Jewish Publication Society, 1969], 31).

THE TESTIMONIES OF EXPERT ARCHAEOLOGICAL WITNESSES[35]

World-class biblical archaeologist *William F. Albright* has said,

The excessive skepticism shown toward the Bible by important historical schools of the eighteenth and nineteenth centuries, certain phases of which still appear periodically, has been progressively discredited. Discovery after discovery has established the accuracy of innumerable details, and has brought increased recognition to the value of the Bible as a source of history" (*The Archaeology of Palestine* [Baltimore: Penguin, 1949], 127–28).

Professor F. F. Bruce notes,

Where Luke has been suspected of inaccuracy, and accuracy has been vindicated by some inscription evidence, it may be legitimate to say that archaeology has confirmed the New Testament record" (*Archaeological Confirmation of the New Testament*, 331).

Yale archaeologist *Millar Burrows* states,

On the whole, archaeological work has unquestionably strengthened confidence in the reliability of the Scriptural record. More than one archaeologist has found his respect for the Bible increased by the experience of excavation in Palestine (*What Mean These Stones?* [New Haven, Conn.: American Schools of Oriental Research, 1941], 1).

Sir William Ramsey is regarded as one of the great New Testament archaeologists. After reading criticism about the book of Acts, he became convinced that it was not a trustworthy account of the facts of that time (A.D. 50) and therefore was unworthy of consideration by a historian. In his research on the history of Asia Minor, Ramsey was eventually compelled to consider the writings of Luke. He observed the meticulous accuracy of the historical details and gradually reconsidered his position. After thirty years of study, he concluded,

Luke is a historian of the first rank; not merely are his statements of fact trustworthy . . . this author should be placed along with the

---

[35]Ibid.

very greatest of historians (*The Bearing of Recent Discovery on the Trust-worthiness of the New Testament*, 222).

THE TESTIMONY OF HISTORY: THE BOOK OF ACTS AND THE GOSPEL OF LUKE[36]

Besides the general outline of New Testament history being confirmed by non-Christian sources close to Christ, there is *specific* confirmation of specific facts of New Testament history from archaeology. We will focus our attention on the history recorded by Luke in the book of Acts. The following outline was extracted from the *Baker Encyclopedia of Christian Apologetics*.[37]

> If Acts was written before A.D. 70 while the eyewitnesses were still alive, then it has great historical value in informing us of the earliest Christian beliefs.
>
> If Acts was written by Luke, the companion of the apostle Paul, it brings us right to the apostolic circle, those who participated in the events reported.
>
> If Acts is shown to be accurate history, then it brings credibility to its reports about the most basic Christian beliefs of miracles, the death (Acts 2:23), resurrection (Acts 2:23, 29–32), and ascension of Christ (Acts 1:9–10).
>
> If Luke wrote Acts, then his "former treatise" (Acts 1:1), the Gospel of Luke, should be extended the same early date (within the lifetime of apostles and eyewitnesses) and credibility.

The evidence in support of the date and authenticity of the Acts of the Apostles includes Roman history, traditional arguments, general and specialized knowledge of the author, and specific local knowledge of the author (names of numerous places and people, conditions, customs, and circumstances). We refer you to the *Baker Encyclopedia of Christian Apologetics* for the evidence available under each of these headings. For our purposes, we will list the facts with respect to Roman history and Luke's knowledge of specific local information.

THE TESTIMONY OF A ROMAN HISTORIAN

While New Testament scholarship, long dominated by higher criticism, has been skeptical of the historicity of the Gospels and Acts, this has not

---

[36]The author of the book of Acts (1:1) also wrote the Gospel of Luke (cf. Luke 1:1).
[37]Op. cit., 4–5.

been true of Roman historians of the same period. Sherwin-White is a case in point.[38]

Another historian added the weight of his scholarship to the question of the historicity of the book of Acts. Colin J. Hemer lists seventeen reasons to accept the traditional early date that would place the research and writing of Acts during the lifetime of many participants.[39] These strongly support the historicity of Acts and, indirectly, the Gospel of Luke (cf. Luke 1:1–4; Acts 1:1):

1. There is no mention in Acts of the fall of Jerusalem in A.D. 70, an unlikely omission, given the content, if it had already occurred.

2. There is no hint of the outbreak of the Jewish War in A.D. 66, or of any drastic or specific deterioration of relations between Romans and Jews, which implies it was written before that time.

3. There is no hint of deterioration of Christian relations with Rome involved in the Neronian persecution of the late 60s.

4. The author betrays no knowledge of Paul's letters. If Acts were written later, why would Luke, who shows himself so careful of incidental detail, not attempt to inform his narrative by relevant sections of the Epistles? The Epistles evidently circulated and must have become available sources. This question is beset with uncertainties, but an early date is suggested by the silence.

5. There is no hint of the death of James at the hands of the Sanhedrin in ca. 62, recorded by Josephus (*Antiquities* 20.9.1.200).

6. The significance of Gallio's judgment in Acts 18:14–17 may be seen as setting a precedent to legitimize Christian teaching under the umbrella of tolerance to Judaism.

7. The prominence and authority of the Sadducees in Acts belongs to the pre–70 era, before the collapse of their political cooperation with Rome.

8. Conversely, the relative sympathetic attitude in Acts to Pharisees (unlike that in Luke's Gospel) does not fit well in the period of Pharisaic revival after scholars of Jamnia met, ca. 90. As a result of that meeting, a phase of escalated conflict with Christianity was led by the Pharisees.

9. Some have argued that the book antedates the coming of Peter to Rome, and also that it uses language which implies that Peter and John, as well as Paul himself, were still alive.

10. The prominence of "God-fearers" in the synagogues in Acts would seem to point to the pre–Jewish War situation.

11. The insignificant cultural details are difficult to place with precision,

---

[38]A. N. Sherwin-White, *Roman Society and Roman Law in the New Testament* (Oxford: Clarendon, 1963).
[39]Colin J. Hemer, *The Book of Acts in the Setting of Hellenistic History* (Winona Lake, Ind.: Eisenbrauns, 1990).

but may best represent the cultural milieu of the Julio-Claudian Roman era.

12. Areas of controversy within Acts presuppose the relevance of the Jewish setting during the temple period.

13. Adolf Harnack argued that the prophecy placed in Paul's mouth at Acts 20:25 (cf. 20:38) may have been contradicted by later events. If so, it presumably was penned before those events occurred.

14. Primitive formulation of Christian terminology is used in Acts that fits an early period. Harnack lists christological titles, such as *Insous* and *ho kurios*, that are used freely, whereas *ho Christos* always designates "the Messiah," rather than a proper name, and *Christos* is otherwise used only in formalized combinations.

15. Rackham draws attention to the optimistic tone of Acts, which would not have been natural after Judaism was destroyed and Christians martyred in the Neronian persecutions of the late 60s (Hemer, 376–82).

16. The ending of the book of Acts. Luke does not continue Paul's story at the end of the two years of Acts 28:30. "The mention of this defined period implies a terminal point, at least impending" (Hemer, 383). He adds, "It may be argued simply that Luke had brought the narrative up to date at the time of writing, the final note being added at the conclusion of the two years" (ibid., 387).

17. The "immediacy" of Acts 27–28: "This is what we have called the 'immediacy' of the later chapters of the book, which are marked in a special degree by the apparently unreflective reproduction of insignificant details, a feature which reaches its apogee in the voyage narrative of Acts 27–28. . . . The vivid 'immediacy' of this passage in particular may be strongly contrasted with the 'indirectness' of the earlier part of Acts, where we assume that Luke relied on sources or the reminiscences of others, and could not control the context of his narrative" (ibid., 388–89).

SPECIFIC LOCAL KNOWLEDGE

Luke manifests an incredible array of knowledge of local places, names, conditions, customs, and circumstances that befits an eyewitness contemporary recording the time and events. Acts 13–28, covering Paul's travels, particularly shows intimate knowledge of local circumstances. . . . Numerous things are confirmed by historical and archaeological research. (We have listed twenty-five out of the forty-three in the *Baker Encyclopedia of Christian Apologetics*.)

1. A natural crossing between correctly named ports (13:4–5). Mount Casius, south of Seleucia, stands within sight of Cyprus. The *name* of the procon-

sul in 13:7 cannot be confirmed, but the *family* of the Sergii Pauli is attested.

2. The proper river port, Perga, for a ship crossing from Cyprus (13:13).

3. The proper location of Lycaonia (14:6).

4. The unusual but correct declension of the name *Lystra* and the correct language spoken in Lystra. Correct identification of the two gods associated with the city, Zeus and Hermes (14:12).

5. The proper port, Attalia, for returning travelers (14:25).

6. The correct route from the Cilician Gates (16:1).

7. The proper form of the name *Troas* (16:8).

8. The proper identification of Philippi as a Roman colony. The right location for the river Gangites near Philippi (16:13).

9. Association of Thyatira with cloth dyeing (16:14). Correct designations of the titles for the colony magistrates (16:20, 35, 36, 38).

10. The proper locations where travelers would spend successive nights on this journey (17:1).

11. The presence of a synagogue in Thessalonica (17:1), and the proper title of *politarch* for the magistrates (17:6).

12. The correct explanation that sea travel is the most convenient way to reach Athens in summer with favoring east winds (17:14).

13. The abundance of images in Athens (17:16), and reference to the synagogue there (17:17).

14. Depiction of philosophical debate in the *agora* (17:17). Use in 17:18–19 of the correct Athenian slang epithet for Paul, *spermologos*, and the correct name of the court (*areios pagos*). Accurate depiction of Athenian character (17:21). Correct identification of altar to "an unknown god" (17:23). Logical reaction of philosophers who deny bodily resurrection (17:32). *Areopogites*, the correct title for a member of the court (17:34).

15. Correct identification of the Corinthian synagogue (18:4). Correct designation of Gallio as proconsul (18:12). The *bema* (judgment seat) can still be seen in Corinth's forum (18:16).

16. The cult of Artemis of the Ephesians (19:24, 27). The cult is well attested, and the Ephesian theater was the city meeting-place (19:29).

17. Correct title *grammateus* for the chief executive magistrate and the proper title of honor, *Neokoros* (19:35). Correct name to identify the goddess (19:37). Correct designation for those holding court (19:38). Use of plural *anthupatoi* in 19:38 is probably a remarkably exact reference to the fact that two men jointly exercised the functions of proconsul at this time.

18. Use of precise ethnic designation *Beroiaios* and the ethnic term *Asianos* (20:4).

19. The permanent stationing of a Roman cohort in the Fortress Antonia to suppress disturbances at festival times (21:31). The flight of steps used by guards (21:31, 35).

20. The correct identifications of Ananias as high priest (23:2) and Felix as governor (23:24).

21. Explanation of the provincial penal procedure (24:1–9).

22. Agreement with Josephus of the name *Porcius Festus* (24:27).

23. Note of the right legal appeal by a Roman citizen (25:11). The legal formula of *de quibus cognoscere volebam* (25:18). The characteristic form of reference to the emperor (25:26).

24. Precise name and place given for the island of Cauda (27:16). Appropriate sailors' maneuvers at the time of a storm (27:16–19). The fourteenth night judged by experienced Mediterranean navigators to be an appropriate time for this journey in a storm (27:27). The proper term for this section of the Adriatic Sea at this time (27:27). The precise term, *bolisantes*, for taking soundings (27:28). The position of probable approach of a ship running aground before an easterly wind (27:39).

25. The proper title *protos* (*tes nesou*) for a man in Publius's position of leadership on the islands (28:7).

CONCLUSION[40]

The historicity of the book of Acts is confirmed by overwhelming evidence. Nothing like this amount of detailed confirmation exists for another book from antiquity. This is not only a direct confirmation of the earliest Christian belief in the death and resurrection of Christ, but also, indirectly, of the Gospel record, since the author of Acts (Luke) also wrote a detailed Gospel. This Gospel directly parallels the other two Synoptic Gospels. The best evidence is that this material in Luke was composed by A.D. 60, only twenty-seven years after the death of Jesus. This places the writing during the lifetime of the eyewitnesses to the events recorded (cf. Luke 1:1–4). This does not allow time for an alleged mythological development by persons living generations after the events. The Roman historian [A. N.] Sherwin-White has noted that the writings of Herodotus enable us to determine the rate at which legends develop. He concluded that "the tests suggest that even two generations are too short a span to allow the mythical tendency to prevail over the hard historic core of the oral tradition"

---

[40]Geisler, *Baker Encyclopedia of Christian Apologetics*, 7–8.

(Sherwin-White, 190). Julius Müller (1801–1878) challenged the scholars of his day to produce even one example in which a historical event developed many mythological elements within one generation (*The Theory of Myths* [London: John Chapman, 1844], 29). None exist.

Both the authenticity and the historicity of the New Testament documents are firmly established today. *The authentic nature and vast amount of manuscript evidence is overwhelming, and even more so when compared to the classical texts from antiquity.* Furthermore, many of the original manuscripts date from within twenty to fifty years of the events in Jesus' life, that is, *from contemporaries and eyewitnesses.*

The historicity of these contemporary accounts of Christ's life, teaching, death, and resurrection is also established on *firm historical grounds.* As to the accuracy of the eyewitness reports, there is support in general from the secular history of the first century and, in particular, from *numerous archaeological discoveries supporting specific details* of the New Testament account.

The integrity of the New Testament writers seems to be established by the quantity and independent nature of their witness. However, we need to examine the character of these witnesses as well. We may have an accurate record from history, but how do we know that the witnesses are not lying?

ARE THE NEW TESTAMENT AUTHORS RELIABLE EYEWITNESSES?

Simon Greenleaf (1783–1853), the famous Royall Professor of Law at Harvard University, is considered one of the academicians most responsible for helping Harvard Law School gain an eminent standing among the legal schools in the United States.

> Greenleaf produced a famous work titled *A Treatise on the Law of Evidence* which is still considered the greatest single authority on evidence in the entire literature of legal procedure. In 1846, while still Professor of law at Harvard, Greenleaf wrote a volume entitled *An Examination of the Testimony of the Four Evangelists by the Rules of Evidence Administered in the Courts of Justice.*[41]

SIMON GREENLEAF'S RULES FOR CREDIBILITY

John Warwick Montgomery, in the appendix of his work, *The Law Above the Law,*[42] summarized Simon Greenleaf's criteria for determining the credibil-

---

[41]John Warwick Montgomery, *The Law Above the Law* (Minneapolis: Bethany House, 1975), 191.
[42]Ibid.

ity of witnesses. These are the five main points.

First, *their honesty.* A person ordinarily speaks the truth when there is no prevailing motive or inducement to the contrary. This presumption is applied in courts of justice, even to witnesses whose integrity is not wholly free from suspicion. Therefore, it is all the more applicable to the evangelists, whose witness went against all their worldly interests. They were willing to (and many did) die for their testimony.

Had not Jesus actually risen from the dead, and had His disciples not known this fact as certainly as they knew any other fact, it would have been impossible for them to have persisted in affirming the truths they narrated. To have persisted in so gross a falsehood after it was known to them was not only to encounter, for life, all the evils that man could inflict from without, but also to endure the pangs of inward and conscious guilt, with no hope of future peace, no testimony of a good conscience, no expectation of honor or esteem among the people, and no hope of happiness in this life or in the world to come. There is no plausible motivation for believing their testimony was false. It is impossible to read their writings and not feel that we are conversing with men of holiness and of tender conscience, with men acting under an abiding sense of the presence and omniscience of God, and of their accountability to Him, living in His fear, and walking in His ways.

Second, *their ability.* We must concur that the ability of a witness to speak the truth depends on the opportunities that he has had for observing the fact, the accuracy of his powers of discernment, and the faithfulness of his memory in retaining the facts once they are observed and known. Until the contrary is shown by an objector, it is always to be presumed that people are honest and of sound mind, and of the average and ordinary degree of intelligence. This is not just the judgment of mere charity; it is also the uniform presumption of the law of the land. It is a presumption that is always allowed freely and fully to operate until the fact is shown to be otherwise by the party who denies the applicability of this presumption to the particular case in question. Whenever an objection is raised in opposition, the burden of proof is on the objector by the common and ordinary rules of evidence and by the law and practice of the courts.

Matthew was trained by his calling to habits of severe investigation and suspicious scrutiny; Luke's profession demanded an exactness of observation equally close and searching. The other two evangelists, it has been well remarked, were too unlearned to forge the story of their Master's life. This, of course, assumes they were eyewitnessed and/or were eyewitnesses of the events (a point addressed below).

Third, *their number and the consistency of their testimony.* The discrepancies between the narratives of the several evangelists, when carefully examined, will not be found sufficient to invalidate their testimony. Many seeming contradictions prove, upon closer scrutiny, to be in substantial agreement, as we have already noted.[43]

Fourth, *the conformity of their testimony with experience.* David Hume stated that the existence of natural laws from the uniform course of human experience is our only guide in reasoning concerning matters of fact; whatever is contrary to human experience, he pronounced incredible. His remark contains this fallacy: it excludes all knowledge derived by inference or deduction from facts. In other words, man is limited to the results of his own sensory experience. (We have already confronted Hume's beliefs.)

Fifth, *the coincidence of their testimony with collateral and contemporaneous facts and circumstances.* All that Christianity asks of honest inquirers on this subject is that they would be consistent with themselves, that they would treat the evidences for the faith as they treat the evidence of other things, and that they would examine its actors and witnesses. The witnesses should be compared with themselves, with each other, and with surrounding facts and circumstances, and their testimony should be sifted as if it were given in a court of justice on the side of the adverse party, the witness being subjected to a rigorous cross-examination. The result, it is confidently believed, will be a firm conviction of their integrity, ability, and truth.[44]

CONTEMPORARIES AND EYEWITNESSES

While much of ancient history was not recorded by eyewitnesses or contemporaries, it is nonetheless considered sufficiently reliable to inform us about the major events that *were* recorded. For example, our knowledge of Alexander the Great is based on biographies written three- to five-hundred years after his death. In contrast, in the case of the New Testament documents that inform us about the death and resurrection of Christ, even Bible critics admit some of them date from the lifetime of contemporary eyewitnesses. For example,

1. Most critics agree Paul wrote 1 Corinthians around A.D. 55–56. In it, he speaks of over 500 eyewitnesses of the resurrection of Jesus Christ— most of whom were still living (1 Corinthians 15:6).
2. A noted Roman historian, Colin J. Hemer, has established that Acts [as shown above], which has been confirmed as historically accurate in

---

[43]For a detailed examination of this, see Geisler and Howe, *When Critics Ask.*
[44]Montgomery, *The Law Above the Law,* 118–39.

hundreds of details, was written between A.D. 60 and 62. Yet Acts 1:1 refers to a "former book" [the Gospel of Luke] that this same accurate historian wrote. Indeed, the Gospel of Luke not only claims to be accurate history based on eyewitness and documentary evidence (Luke 1:1–4), but has been verified to be so. Again, consider this pinpoint historical reference that has been confirmed to be true: "In the fifteenth year of the reign of Tiberius Caesar—when Pontius Pilate was governor of Judea, Herod tetrarch of Galilee, his brother Philip tetrarch of Iturea and Traconitis, and Lysanias tetrarch of Abilene—during the high priesthood of Annas and Caiaphas, the word of God came to John son of Zechariah in the desert" (Luke 3:1–2).

3. William F. Albright wrote, "We can already say emphatically that there is no longer any solid basis for dating any book of the New Testament after about A.D. 80, two full generations before the date between A.D. 130 and A.D. 150 given by the more radical New Testament critics of today" (*Recent Discoveries in Bible Lands* [New York: Funk and Wagnalls, 1956], 136). Elsewhere Albright said, "In my opinion, every book of the New Testament was written by a baptized Jew between the forties and the eighties of the first century (very probably sometime between A.D. 50 and A.D. 75)" ("Toward a More Conservative View," *CT*, 18 January 1993, 3).[45]

4. John A. T. Robinson, known for his role in launching the "Death of God" movement, wrote a revolutionary book titled *Redating the New Testament*, in which he posited revised dates for the New Testament books that place them earlier than the most conservative scholars ever held. Robinson places Matthew at 40 to after 60, Mark at about 45 to 60, Luke at before 57 to after 60, and John at from before 40 to after 65. This would mean that one or two Gospels could have been written as early as seven years after the crucifixion. At the latest they were all composed within the lifetimes of eyewitnesses and contemporaries of the events. Assuming the basic integrity and reasonable accuracy of the writers, this would place the reliability of the New Testament documents beyond reasonable doubt."[46]

CONCLUSION

It should be remembered that very little of the literature of the evangelists' time and place has come down to us; the collateral sources and means of corroborating and explaining their writings are proportionally limited. The contemporary writings and works of art that have reached us have invariably been

[45]Geisler, *Baker Encyclopedia of Christian Apologetics*, 529.
[46]Ibid.

found to confirm their accounts, to reconcile what was apparently contradictory, and to supply what seemed defective or imperfect. In conclusion, if we had access to more of the same, all other similar difficulties and imperfections would vanish.

Had the evangelists been false historians, they would not have committed themselves upon so many particulars. They would not have furnished the vigilant inquirers of that period with such an effectual instrument for bringing them into discredit with the people, nor would they have foolishly supplied, in every page of their narrative, so many materials for a cross-examination, which would infallibly have disgraced them.

There is also a striking naturalness in the characters exhibited in the sacred historians, rarely if ever found in works of fiction, and probably nowhere else to be collected in a similar manner from fragmentary and incidental allusions and expressions in the writings of different persons.

There are other internal marks of truth in the narratives of the evangelists that only need be alluded to here, as they have been treated with great fullness and force by able writers whose works are familiar to all. Among these are the nakedness of the narratives—the absence of all parade by the writers about their own integrity, of all anxiety to be believed or to impress others with a good opinion of themselves or their cause, of all marks of wonder, or of desire to excite astonishment at the greatness of the events they record, and of all appearances of design to exalt their Master. On the contrary, there is the most perfect indifference on their part whether they are believed or not; or rather, the evident consciousness that they are recording events well known to all, in their own time and place, and undoubtedly to be believed.

Their simplicity and artlessness should not pass unnoticed in readily stating even those things most disparaging to themselves. Their want of faith in their Master, their dullness of apprehension of His teachings, their strife for preeminence, their inclination to call fire from heaven upon their enemies, their desertion of their Lord in His hour of extreme peril—these and many other incidents tending directly to their own dishonor are, nevertheless, set down with all the directness and sincerity of truth, as by men writing under the deepest sense of responsibility to God.[47]

WHAT CAN WE CONCLUDE ABOUT THE NEW TESTAMENT DOCUMENTS?

You may not have been aware of the amount of overwhelming evidence that supports the historicity of the New Testament documents. If so, perhaps

---

[47]Montgomery, *The Law Above the Law*, 138–39.

you can now have an appreciation for why C. S. Lewis, the great Oxford and Cambridge scholar, in describing his change of worldviews from atheism to theism in general and Christianity in particular, said,

> Early in 1926 the hardest boiled of all the atheists I ever knew sat in my room on the other side of the fire and remarked that the evidence for the historicity of the Gospels was really surprisingly good. . . . "It almost looks as if it had really happened once." To understand the shattering impact of it [his remark], you would need to know the man (who has certainly never since shown any interest in Christianity). If he, the cynic of cynics, the toughest of the toughs, were not—as I would have put it—"safe," where could I turn? The odd thing was that before God closed in on me, I was in fact offered what now appears a moment of wholly free choice. . . . I could open the door or keep it shut. . . . The choice appeared to be momentous but it was also strangely unemotional. I was moved by no desires or fears. In a sense I was not moved by anything. I chose to open, to unbuckle, to loosen the rein.[48]

Lewis described the evidence in favor of the historical reliability of the New Testament as the closing in of God on him. This "closing in" is *coming to intellectually honest terms with who the person of Jesus Christ really is.* Jesus was especially concerned about bringing His contemporaries to an accurate conception of Himself. We believe that is a fair request; no one wants to be misunderstood, and no intellectually honest person should want to have a false impression of who someone is. It is essential in the case of Jesus, who has had such an influence on world history, that any misconception be eliminated at all costs. Consider who this Jesus of history really is, but consider it in light of the primary source—the New Testament documents. These documents give an accurate portrait of Jesus Christ that cannot be erased by any credible investigator.

Since the reliability of the New Testament documents and the integrity of the authors have been established as historically reliable and credible, we can conclude that we have an accurate record of the events and the claims that Jesus Christ made about Himself and others. We can also examine the evidence given by Him to support those claims, specifically that He was God-incarnate. We will do so in the next chapter.

[48]C. S. Lewis, *Surprised by Joy* (New York: Harcourt Brace & Co., 1955), 223–24.

13
QUESTIONS ABOUT THE DEITY OF JESUS CHRIST

*"Who do you say I am?" "You are the Christ,
the Son of the living God."*

—MATTHEW 16:15–16

WHO IS JESUS CHRIST?

By any standard Jesus is one of the greatest figures in history. He is the founder of the world's largest religion—Christianity—which claims nearly two billion followers. When inquiring as to the identity of Jesus, it only makes sense to go directly to the primary source, the New Testament, and read for ourselves what He said. We have already argued for the historical reliability of the New Testament documents and for the integrity of its authors; we have demonstrated that we have an accurate record of the events therein. We can also examine the evidence given to support the claims that Jesus Christ made about Himself and others—specifically that Jesus was God-incarnate. This evidence includes three things: (1) His fulfillment of messianic prophecy, (2) His miraculous and sinless life, and (3) His resurrection from the dead.

Orthodox Christianity claims that Jesus of Nazareth was God in human flesh, a doctrine that is absolutely essential to the historical faith. If it is true, then Christianity is unique and authoritative above all other religions, including Judaism and Islam. If it is not, then Christianity does not differ in *kind* from these others but only in *degree*. Therefore we will begin with the claims that Jesus made about Himself, for if we want to know about a certain man, it makes the most sense to (1) go to him and ask him who he is, and (2) go to his closest friends and ask what he said about Himself. (It is essentially irrelevant to consider present opinions about the identity of Jesus, since almost all—if not all—of what we know about Jesus is directly derived from the primary documents themselves, meaning the New Testament. This approach is fair and scholarly in attempting to answer the question regarding the identity of Jesus Christ.)

WHO DID JESUS CHRIST CLAIM TO BE?

Let's begin answering this question by summarizing what we have concluded about the nature of God from previous chapters. Based on the first principles of logic, philosophy, science, and law, we established that God is the uncaused, eternal, unlimited, and unchanging Being who caused all finite things to come to be. As the First Cause of all that exists, God is the only true sovereign and independent (free) Being. Moreover, God is a personal being; He possesses intelligence, a will, and emotions, and He is moral. We can divide God's attributes into two fundamental categories: transferable and nontransferable.

God's nontransferable attributes are those that cannot be bestowed on another, such as His aseity (self-existence), sovereignty (ruling power), infinity (limitlessness), immutability (unchangeability), and eternality (timelessness). God alone possesses these qualities because they are essential to His nature (*what* He is—divine). Angels and humans do not and cannot have these qualities because they are not essential to their nature.[1]

Now let's go to the New Testament and examine the claims of Jesus to see if He either directly or indirectly claimed any of the nontransferable attributes of God.[2]

(1) In the gospel of John, Jesus refers to Himself as YHWH ("I AM"). The name YHWH, "Yahweh," was so sacred that devout Jews would not even pronounce it. Yahweh is the *I AM* of Exodus 3:14, the name that God called Himself—and for the Jews, *He alone is God*. In John 8:56–59 Jesus claimed to

---

[1] Examples of God's transferable attributes are goodness, justice, love, and mercy. Also, as we are made in God's image, we have rational, moral, volitional, and emotional capabilities, among other things.

[2] It is worth taking the time to look up the verses we have referenced in order to understand the context in which they appear.

be this *I AM*: "I tell you the truth . . . before Abraham was born, I am!" When the Jews heard His claim, they became so outraged that they immediately "picked up stones to stone him."

Jesus used the name Yahweh at other times as well: "I told you that you would die in your sins; if you do not believe that *I AM* the one I claim to be, you will indeed die in your sins" (John 8:24). Jesus not only claims to be *I AM* but He also stresses that wrongly identifying who He is will result in eternal death—separation from God forever.

(2) In John 18:4–6 once again we find Jesus claiming the name *I AM*. This passage is of particular interest because of the response of the arrest party searching for Him. He asked them, "Who is it you want?" They replied, "Jesus of Nazareth." He answered, "I AM [He]."[3] At this, they drew back and fell to the ground. Under any other circumstances, this would be quite an odd reaction; however, the power of God was manifested in these words of Jesus that revealed His identity—Yahweh.

(3) In John 17:3–5 Jesus again emphasizes the link between knowing His true identity and being saved from eternal darkness. In one of His most intimate moments of speaking with His Father, Jesus said, "Now this is eternal life: that they may know you, the only true God, and Jesus Christ, whom you have sent." According to Jesus, to know Him is to know God, and in John 14:9 He said that to see Him was to see God: "Anyone who has seen me has seen the Father." In fact, not only did He assert that in order to know God one must know Him as well, and that to see God one can gaze upon Him, He also claimed that anyone wanting to begin a relationship with God must go through Him: "I am the way and the truth and the life. No one comes to the Father except through me. If you really knew me, you would know my Father as well" (John 14:6–7).

(4) Jesus also claimed that He should be honored in the same manner that the Father is honored (worshiped): "He who does not honor the Son does not honor the Father, who sent him" (John 5:23). The Father is God and is worshiped as Lord of the universe. When one of the disciples of Jesus worshiped Him as Lord and God, Jesus did not chastise Him for being mistaken. In fact, He not only accepted those titles but also commended others who believed in Him without having seen Him in the flesh. "Thomas said to him [Jesus], 'My Lord and my God!' Then Jesus told him, 'Because you have seen me, you have believed; blessed are those who have not seen and yet have believed'" (John 20:28–29).

---

[3]We put the "He" in brackets because it isn't there in the original Greek.

(5) In John 17:5 Jesus claimed to share God's glory from all eternity. Yet in Isaiah 42:8, Yahweh said, "I will not give my glory to another." *Jesus claimed to be God.*

(6) There are many additional passages where Jesus refers to Himself as God by way of the various titles that, in the Old Testament, are applied only to God. We have listed some of these below.

> Jesus said, "I am the good shepherd" (John 10:11); the Old Testament declared, "Yahweh is my shepherd" (Psalm 23:1).
> Jesus claimed to be judge of all men and all nations (John 5:27; Matthew 25:31); the prophet Joel, quoting Yahweh, wrote, "For there I will sit to judge all the nations round about" (Joel 3:12 KJV).
> Jesus said, "I am the light of the world" (John 8:12); the Old Testament proclaimed, "Yahweh shall be unto thee an everlasting light, and thy God thy glory" (Isaiah 60:19 KJV), and "Yahweh is my light" (Psalm 27:1).
> Jesus claimed to forgive sins (Mark 2:5), and the Jews reacted with, "Who can forgive sins but God alone?" (Mark 2:7). Jesus then proved His authority by His healing miracle (Mark 2:10–12); however, Jeremiah 31:34 states that "[God] will forgive."
> Jesus claimed to be the giver of life (John 5:21–23); God alone gives life (1 Samuel 2:6; Deuteronomy 32:39).
> Finally, Jesus said, "I and the Father are one" (John 10:30). The term *one* refers to the essence or nature of His being.

The declarations of deity that Jesus made to the monotheistic Jewish people of His day were self-evident. The Jews knew very well that *no mere man* should claim the same honor and titles due to God alone. They reacted with violence by trying harder to kill him because "he [Jesus] was even calling God his own Father, making Himself equal with God" (John 5:18). Jesus confronted their hearts, saying, "I have shown you many great miracles from the Father. For which of these do you stone me?" The Jews replied, "We are not stoning you for any of these, but for blasphemy, because *you, a mere man, claim to be God*" (John 10:32–33, emphasis added). The Jews, the leadership in particular, were outraged when Jesus spoke to them about His true identity. C. S. Lewis said,

> Then comes the real shock. Among the Jews there suddenly turns up a man who goes about talking as if He was God. He claims to forgive sins. He says He has always existed. He says He is coming to judge the world at the end of time. Now let us get this clear. Among Pantheists, like the Indians, anyone might say that he was a part of God, or one with God: there would be nothing very odd about it. But this man, since He was a Jew, could not mean that kind of God. God, in their language, meant the

being outside the world Who made it and was infinitely different from anything else. And when you have grasped that, you will see that what this man said was, quite simply, the most shocking thing that has ever been uttered by human lips.[4]

The Old Testament forbids worship of anyone or anything except for God alone (Exodus 20:1–4; Deuteronomy 5:6–8); the New Testament agrees (Acts 14:15; Revelation 22:8–9). Yet Jesus accepted worship on nine recorded occasions without ever rebuking those offering it, as documented in the following passages:

- A healed leper worshiped Him (Matthew 8:2).
- A ruler knelt before Him (Matthew 9:18).
- The disciples worshiped Him (Matthew 14:33).
- A Canaanite woman knelt before Him (Matthew 15:25).
- The mother of James and John worshiped Him (Matthew 20:20).
- A Gerasene demoniac fell to his knees in front of Him (Mark 5:6).
- A healed blind man worshiped Him (John 9:38).
- Again, all the disciples worshiped Him (Matthew 28:17).
- Thomas literally called Him "the Lord of me and the God of me" (John 20:28).

WHAT DID THE APOSTLES SAY ABOUT JESUS CHRIST?

Those who were the closest to Jesus, the apostles, accepted His claims and recorded their own opinions regarding His identity. We have noted some of these below.

"They will call him [Jesus] Immanuel—which means, 'God with us' "(Matthew 1:23).

"In the beginning was the Word, and the Word was with God, and the Word was God. . . . The Word became flesh and made his dwelling among us. We have seen his glory, the glory of the One and Only. . . . No one has ever seen God, but God the One and Only . . . has made him known" (John 1:1, 14, 18).

"Thomas said to him [Jesus], 'My Lord and my God!' " (John 20:28).

"For in Christ all the fullness of the Deity lives in bodily form" (Colossians 2:9).

[4]Lewis, *Mere Christianity*, 54–55.

" . . . the glorious appearing of our great God and Savior, Jesus Christ" (Titus 2:13).

"God our Savior" (Titus 1:3; 2:10; cf. 2 Peter 1:1; Luke 1:47; 1 Timothy 4:10).

"The Son is the radiance of God's glory and the exact representation of his being" (Hebrews 1:3).

"He [Jesus] is before all things, and in him all things hold together" (Colossians 1:17).

"For God was pleased to have all his fullness dwell in him [Jesus]" (Colossians 1:19).

"All things were created . . . by him [Jesus] and for him" (Colossians 1:16; cf. John 1:3).

The other authors of the New Testament concur with and testify to the deity of Jesus Christ. In comparing the Old and New Testaments, it is very clear that the names and attributes of God were given to Jesus, identifying Him as God. Consider the following verses (emphasis added).

OLD TESTAMENT

- Isaiah 40:25—" 'Who is my equal,' *says the Holy One* [God]."
- Isaiah 42:8—"I am the LORD [Yahweh]. . . . I will not give *my glory to another*."
- Exodus 20:3—[God spoke and said,] "You shall have *no other gods* before me."
- Exodus 20:5—[God said,] "You *shall not* bow down to them or *worship* them [other gods]."

NEW TESTAMENT

- Luke 4:34—Jesus is confessed by the evil spirits to be "*the Holy One.*"
- Revelation 15:4—The song of the Lamb [Jesus] states, "For *you alone are holy.*"
- John 5:23—Jesus said that all people are to "*honor the Son* just as they honor the Father."
- John 17:5—Jesus prayed, "Father, glorify me in your presence with the *glory I had with you* before the world began."
- Hebrews 1:6—"Let all God's angels *worship him* [Jesus].
- Revelation 5:12–14—" 'Worthy is the Lamb [Jesus], who was slain, to receive power and wealth and wisdom and strength and honor and glory and praise. . . . *To the Lamb be praise and honor and glory and power,* for ever and ever!' . . . And the elders fell down and worshiped."

The table below is offered as a supplement to the known facts already given regarding the deity of Jesus Christ. As shown, God's nontransferable titles and attributes are used to describe the nature of Jesus Christ, and since God alone possesses these qualities, essential to His divine nature, we can rightly conclude that Jesus is God. This table can be found in *Jesus, a Biblical Defense of His Deity*, by Josh McDowell and Bart Larson.[5]

Title/Attribute	As Used of Yahweh	As Used of Jesus
YHWH (I AM)	Exodus 3:14 Deuteronomy 32:39 Isaiah 43:10	John 8:24 John 8:58 John 18:5
Giver of Life	Genesis 2:7 Deuteronomy 32:39 1 Samuel 2:6	John 5:21 John 10:28 John 11:25
Forgiver of Sin	Exodus 34:6–7 Nehemiah 9:17 Daniel 9:9	Mark 2:1–12 Acts 26:18 Colossians 2:13
Omnipresent	Psalm 139:7–12 Proverbs 15:3	Matthew 18:20 Matthew 28:20
Omniscient	1 Kings 8:39 Jeremiah 17:9–10, 16	Matthew 11:27 Luke 5:4–6 John 2:25; 16:30 John 21:17 Acts 1:24
Omnipotent	Isaiah 40:10–31 Isaiah 45:5–13, 18	Matthew 28:18 Mark 1:29–34 John 10:18
Preexistent	Genesis 1:1	John 1:15, 30 John 3:13, 31–32 John 6:62; 16:28 John 17:5
Eternal	Psalm 102:26–27 Habakkuk 3:6	Isaiah 9:6 Micah 5:2 John 8:58
Immutable	Numbers 23:19	Hebrews 13:8

In comparing the titles and attributes ascribed to both God and Jesus, the most logical conclusion is that Jesus has a divine nature—the nature of God.

[5]Josh McDowell and Bart Larson, *Jesus, a Biblical Defense of His Deity* (San Bernardino, Calif.: Here's Life, 1983), 62–64.

This is consistent with the clear claims of Jesus, the witnessed claims of His disciples, the historically verified claims of other New Testament authors, and, correspondingly, has been held as true throughout the history of orthodox Christianity. It's a fact: Jesus claimed to be God. But then Jesus asked of His listeners—and asks each of us—what is perhaps the ultimate question: "Who do you say that I am?"

WHAT ABOUT YOU—WHO DO YOU SAY JESUS CHRIST IS?

Here is a list of possible options that exist with respect to the true identity of the nature and person of Jesus Christ.

(1) Jesus was just God (only an infinite divine nature).
(2) Jesus was just a man (only a finite human nature).
(3) Jesus was just an angel (only a finite angelic nature).
(4) Jesus was an angel-man (both finite angelic and finite human natures).
(5) Jesus was and is God-incarnate (both finite human and infinite spirit natures).

OPTION #1—JESUS WAS JUST GOD (ONLY AN INFINITE DIVINE NATURE).

Jesus was born of a human mother (Galatians 4:4). He grew up like any other human being (Luke 2:52). He hungered (Matthew 4:4) and thirsted (John 19:28). He grew weary and needed rest (John 4:6). He sorrowed and cried (John 11:33–35). He suffered (John 19:1), died (John 19:33), and was buried (John 19:40–42). He was human in every sense that we are, yet He was without sin (Hebrews 4:15). For these reasons, we will disregard option #1.

OPTION #2—JESUS WAS JUST A MAN (ONLY A FINITE HUMAN NATURE)

It is quite clear that Jesus claimed to be more than merely a man. As previously mentioned, Jesus claimed to have existed before Abraham (John 8:58) and before the creation of time and the universe. He forthrightly said, "Now, Father, glorify me in your presence with the glory I had with you before the world began" (John 17:5). Therefore, option #2 can be eliminated as well.

OPTION #3—JESUS WAS JUST AN ANGEL (ONLY A FINITE ANGELIC NATURE)

Some people believe that Jesus was an angel. The following quote gives the basis for why the Jehovah's Witnesses, for example, insist that Jesus was actually Michael, the archangel:

> At 1 Thessalonians 4:16 the command of Jesus Christ for the resurrection to begin is described as "the archangel's call," and Jude 9 says that the archangel is Michael. Would it be appropriate to liken Jesus' commanding call to that of someone lesser in authority? Reasonably, then, the archangel Michael is Jesus Christ.[6]

First, the entire text of 1 Thessalonians 4:16 is not quoted. The complete verse reads, "For the Lord Himself will come down from heaven with a loud command, with the voice of the archangel and with the trumpet call of God." To be consistent with their interpretative method, they should also conclude that Jesus is a trumpet, for we are told that Jesus the Lord will be coming "with" the archangel Michael and "with" the trumpet call of God. If the Watchtower is correct and Jesus is coming "as" (and not "with") the archangel, then He must also be coming "as" (and not "with") the trumpet.[7]

Second, in the above quote, note how the Watchtower refers to its conclusion as "reasonable." They truly believe that it is *unreasonable* to conclude that God could become a man. Yet they believe it is *reasonable* that an angel could become a man. However, if Michael did take on a human nature and Jesus was really an angel, then how is it He was born of a virgin? Also, if Jesus was just an angel, He had many occasions to correct the Jews concerning His identity. For example, in John 10:33 Jesus asked the Jews why they wanted to stone Him and they said, "For blasphemy, because you, a mere man, claim to be God." Jesus could have easily set them straight by telling them He was not God but rather an angel, for on every scriptural occasion that worship is offered to an angel, it is refused.

Furthermore, during the trial before the Sanhedrin, the high priest said to Jesus, "I charge you under oath by the living God: Tell us if you are the Christ, the Son of God." Jesus responded by referring to Himself as the Son of God: "Yes, it is as you say. . . . But I say to all of you: In the future you will see the Son of Man sitting at the right hand of the Mighty One and coming on the

---

[6] *Reasoning From the Scriptures* (New York: Watchtower Bible and Tract Society, 1985), 218 (emphasis added).

[7] In addressing the view of Jehovah's Witnesses in particular, we will have addressed similar views pertaining to the identity of Jesus Christ as merely an angelic being.

clouds of heaven" (Matthew 26:63–64). In this passage Jesus claims, under oath, to be the Messiah, the Son of God. His future reference to Himself as the Son of Man sitting at the right hand of the Mighty One is significant for at least two reasons. First, the Watchtower teaches that when Jesus used the title "Son of Man," He was referring to His human or earthly state. But when Jesus referenced Daniel 7:13 (coming on the clouds) and applied it to Himself, He was claiming to be the Son of God, disallowing their interpretation. Second, Jehovah's Witnesses believe that when Jesus (the Son of Man) died, His death was the end of the human life of Jesus. For instance, from the Watchtower:

> What happened to Jesus' fleshly body? Did not the disciples find his tomb empty? They did, because God removed Jesus' body. Why did God do this? It fulfilled what had been written in the Bible (Psalm 16:10; Acts 2:31). Thus Jehovah saw fit to remove Jesus' body, even as he had done before with Moses' body (Deuteronomy 34:5, 6). Also, if the body had been left in the tomb, Jesus' disciples could not have understood that he had been raised from the dead, since at that time they did not fully appreciate spiritual things.[8]

If the Son of Man, Jesus, remained dead, and if God hid the body, why would Jesus say that He'd be returning? Matthew 26:63–64 only makes sense if Jesus was raised from the dead and would return as a resurrected man. Moreover, and more importantly, notice that when Jesus said He would return, He said He would be sitting at the right hand of the "Mighty One." Yet the Watchtower makes a significant distinction between the titles *Mighty* and *Almighty*. They believe that Jesus, as the angel Michael, is the *Mighty* One, and that God is the *Almighty* One: "Jesus is spoken of in the Scriptures as 'a god,' even as 'Mighty God' (John 1:1; Isaiah 9:6). But nowhere is he spoken of as being Almighty."[9]

If Matthew 26:63–64 is actually referring to Michael as the Mighty One, how can Jesus claim that in the future He would be sitting at the right hand of the Mighty One? The Watchtower claims that Jesus is Michael. If the Mighty One *is* Michael (and, therefore, Jesus) rather than the Father, would not Jesus be saying in Matthew 26:63–64 that He will be seen sitting at His own right hand? It is clear that Jesus can only be referring to Himself as the resurrected Son of God, who would be sitting at the right hand (position of power) of God the Father. We can rule out option #3: Jesus was not an angel.

[8] *You Can Live Forever in Paradise on Earth* (New York: Watchtower, 1984), 144.
[9] *Reasoning From the Scriptures*, 150 (emphasis added).

OPTION #4—JESUS WAS AN ANGEL-MAN (BOTH FINITE ANGELIC AND FINITE HUMAN NATURES)

First and foremost, it must be noted that Jesus referred to Himself as God and never as an angel. Indeed, He created all angels (Colossians 1:15–16) and all angels worship Him (Hebrews 1:6). Second, the New Testament emphatically denies that Jesus was an angel. Consider Hebrews 1:3–14:

(v. 3) The Son is the radiance of God's glory and the exact representation of his being, sustaining all things by his powerful word. After he had provided purification for sins, he sat down at the right hand of the Majesty in heaven. (v. 4) So he became as much superior to the angels as the name he has inherited is superior to theirs.

(v. 5) For to which of the angels did God ever say, "You are my Son; today I have become your Father"? Or again, "I will be his Father, and he will be my Son"?

(v. 6) And again, when God brings his firstborn into the world, he says, "Let all God's angels worship him." (v. 7) In speaking of the angels he says, "He makes his angels winds, his servants flames of fire."

(v. 8) But about the Son he says, "Your throne, O God, will last for ever and ever, and righteousness will be the scepter of your kingdom. (v. 9) You have loved righteousness and hated wickedness; therefore God, your God, has set you above your companions by anointing you with the oil of joy."

(v. 10) He also says, "In the beginning, O Lord, you laid the foundations of the earth, and the heavens are the work of your hands. (v. 11) They will perish, but you remain; they will all wear out like a garment. (v. 12) You will roll them up like a robe; like a garment they will be changed. But you remain the same, and your years will never end."

(v. 13) To which of the angels did God ever say, "Sit at my right hand until I make your enemies a footstool for your feet"? (v. 14) Are not all angels ministering spirits sent to serve those who will inherit salvation?

The letter to the Hebrews corrects faulty thinking about the identity of Jesus and clearly sets forth the superior nature and person of Jesus Christ. If Jesus was an angel and a man, then this passage should reflect both persons—Michael and Jesus. It doesn't.

The apostle Paul affirms in Romans 1:3–4 that "regarding his [God's] Son, who as to his human nature was a descendant of David [human nature], and who through the Spirit of holiness was declared with power to be the Son of God [divine nature] by his resurrection from the dead: Jesus Christ our Lord." What do these titles mean to the Watchtower? They believe "[the] evidence indicates that the Son of God was known as Michael before he came to earth and is known by that name since his return to heaven where he resides as the glorified spirit Son of God."[10] If this is the case, then why does Philippians 2:9–11 tell us that after His death on the cross, God exalted Jesus to the highest place and "gave him the name that is above every name, that at the name of Jesus [not Michael] every knee should bow, in heaven and on earth and under the earth, and every tongue confess that Jesus Christ [not Michael] is Lord, to the glory of God the Father"?

Referring back to Hebrews 1:6–8, even though the text clearly states that Jesus is to be worshiped by "all God's angels," including Michael, the Watchtower teaches that when Michael was brought into the world as a man, the "rest" of the angels worshiped him. This qualification is not in the text. If this view *were* correct, the contrast given in verse eight, "But about the Son he says, 'Your throne, O God' . . ." would seem to indicate that Michael is being called God. *Yet this is not what the Watchtower teaches.* So in order to explain this dilemma, they tell us that this verse should be translated, "God is your throne" and not "Your throne, O God." Now, it is possible to translate this verse in that manner, depending on the context of the passage. But *the context is clearly against it, since it attributes deity to Christ* (Hebrews 1:2–3, 8). Further, let's consider what the Watchtower teaches in light of Matthew 22:41–45:

> While the Pharisees were gathered together, Jesus asked them, "What do you think about the Christ? Whose son is he?" "The son of David," they replied. He said to them, "How is it then that David, speaking by the Spirit, calls him 'Lord'? For he says, 'The LORD said to my Lord: "Sit at my right hand until I put your enemies under your feet." ' If then David calls him 'Lord,' how can he be his son?" No one could say a word in reply, and from that day on no one dared to ask him any more questions.

Jesus' argument effectively silenced His critics, because in order for King David to call his own son (descendant) Lord, David's son had to be more than just a man. Now, the Watchtower would agree, saying that Michael is the one David referred to as Lord, because an angel is greater than a man. Suppose that they are right—that David is referring to Michael and not Jesus. At the same time, Jehovah's Witnesses affirm that God would never refer to an angel as "Lord" ("The LORD [*Yahweh* or *Jehovah*] said to my Lord" [*Adonai*]), and we wholeheartedly agree with them.

Based upon this line of reasoning, the Watchtower ought also to agree that

[10]Ibid., 218.

Jesus is Lord of both angels and men, based upon Hebrews 1:10: "He [Yahweh-God] also says, 'In the beginning, O LORD [Jesus], you laid the foundations of the earth, and the heavens are the work of your hands.'" Now, it's one thing for a man to call another man "LORD," or for a man to call an angel "LORD," but since when does Yahweh refer to an angel or a man as "LORD"? The answer fits squarely with the orthodox Christian position: the first person of the triune God, the Father, can only logically be referring to the second person of the triune God, Jesus His Son, who can properly be called "LORD" because they share the same divine nature. It is clear that we can discard option #4.

God exists as three divine persons; if Jesus is one of the three persons, then Jesus must possess both a human and a divine will. It makes sense, then, for Jesus to refer to Himself in the singular, since His dual nature does not imply separate persons. Therefore only two wills are interacting—the human will of Christ and the divine will of God. For example, when Jesus was praying to His Father, He said, "Yet not as I will, but as you will" (Matthew 26:39). Jesus is one person who has two wills, one operating through each nature—human and divine. His prayer reflects human will, not divine will. This point leads us to option #5.

OPTION #5—JESUS WAS AND IS GOD-INCARNATE (BOTH FINITE HUMAN AND INFINITE SPIRIT NATURES)

Orthodox Christianity holds to the belief that Jesus, the "Son of God," took on a finite human nature and became a man—God-incarnate. Passages such as Philippians 2:5–8 make more sense when taken in the context of the union of two natures found in the one person, Jesus Christ. The Bible states it plainly:

> (v. 5) Your attitude should be the same as that of Christ Jesus: (v. 6) Who, being in very nature God, did not consider equality with God something to be grasped, (v. 7) but made Himself nothing, taking the very nature of a servant, being made in human likeness. (v. 8) And being found in appearance as a man, he humbled Himself and became obedient to death—even death on a cross!

Notice this text does not say that God became man, i.e., that the infinite became finite. *It would be a logical contradiction to say that the infinite and the finite exist in the same nature.* We will examine this mystery below, but for now it is important to see that this doctrine is not a contradiction. We can understand this text to say that "Jesus Christ, the Eternal Son of God, *retaining all his divine attributes*, took to Himself a human volitional behavior pattern when He took to Himself all the essential attributes of human nature."[11] This understanding of the two natures of the one person of Jesus leads us to our next question.

HOW CAN JESUS CHRIST BE BOTH GOD AND MAN?

The New Testament clearly points to Jesus as being one person who has two natures, human and divine. A quick glance at this truth may bring about the misunderstanding that the often-touted phrase—"God became man"—means that the infinite became the finite. This is not a technically accurate description of the Incarnation. It may be okay to verbalize the Incarnation in that manner within the circle of like-minded believers—as long as the meaning is clearly understood by the speaker and listeners. Precisely, however, the Incarnation should be understood to mean that, "Jesus, God the Son, existing as the second person of the triune God, *united* His divine nature to a human nature and through it came into the world." Meaning, He didn't stop being God when He added humanity to Himself. Normally, the immediate response to this truth claim is, "How is this possible?"

As Athanasius taught us, *in the Incarnation there was no subtraction of deity but an addition of humanity.* To better explain, let us first consider the evidence from the Word of God, which reveals God existing as a different kind of Being—one with more than one person per nature. We human beings have one person per nature; in this sense, we could say that humans are "one-dimensional beings." It is dangerous to believe that God must be like us in our being—that He has human limitations. In Mark 12:28–30 we read,

> (v. 28) One of the teachers of the law came and heard them debating. Noticing that Jesus had given them a good answer, he asked him, "Of all the commandments, which is the most important?" (v. 29) "The most important one," answered Jesus, "is this: 'Hear, O Israel, the Lord our God, the Lord is one. (v. 30) Love the Lord your God with all your heart and with all your soul and with all your mind and with all your strength.'"

Jesus responds to this question with a verse from the Old Testament referred to by the Jewish people as the *Shema*. It is a direct quote from Deuteronomy 6:4, which literally reads, "Yahweh, our God, Yahweh is one." What is

[11]James Oliver Buswell, Jr., *A Systematic Theology of the Christian Religion*, vol. 2 (Grand Rapids, Mich.: Zondervan, 1962), 54.

not readily apparent in the English language is the specific use of the word *one*. To the mind of a Jew, *this* term *one* refers to a *plural* oneness, and Jesus' use of it was extremely strategic. Allow us to explain its significance.

In the Hebrew language there are two terms that are translated into English as the word *one*. The first is the word *yachid*, which denotes an *exclusive singularity*. The second is the word *echad*, which denotes a *plural unity*. The essential question is "Which term is used in the Shema?" The answer is *echad*. Therefore, if we translate Deuteronomy 6:4 into English with more clarity, it reads, "Yahweh, our God, Yahweh is a plurality within an indivisible unity." Anyone can easily verify this by looking up these words in an exhaustive concordance/dictionary (*Strong's*, for example).

Other references help us to further understand the use of *echad*. For example, in the familiar passage cited at weddings, the plural term *echad* is used to describe the unity of the husband/wife relationship. In Genesis 2:24 we read that "they will become one [*echad*] flesh."

In Numbers 13:23 *echad* is used to describe more than two as one unity. When Moses sent out a group of men to explore Canaan, they returned with some fruit. The cluster of grapes they brought back was so large that it took two men to carry "one" cluster. The text reads, "They cut off a branch bearing a single [*echad*] cluster of grapes." Here we have a group of grapes referred to as a singular cluster, but as a plural unity as well.

We are beginning to understand the significance of Jesus' including the Shema as part of the greatest commandment. *The law of God is based upon the nature of God.* For this reason, to understand the true meaning of the law of God, the true nature of God must be understood as well. The law is primarily concerned with relational harmony, that is, true unity within the diversity of a community. The plurality of God and the unity of God are both the standard and primary example of this truth. Therefore we believe it is not by accident that the passage immediately following this one in Mark 12 is the text where Jesus asks the teachers of the law about the identity of the Christ.... Once again:

> (v. 35) How is it that the teachers of the law say that the Christ is the Son of David? (v. 36) David himself, speaking by the Holy Spirit, declared: "The LORD said to my Lord: 'Sit at my right hand until I put your enemies under your feet.' " David himself calls him "Lord." How then can he be his son?

After considering the person and nature of Jesus, we have a better understanding of the point He was making by raising this question. Remember, the

Jews wanted to kill Him, not for the miracles He was doing, but for *who He claimed to be!* The declarations that Jesus made to the monotheistic Jewish people were self-evident in that society: this man was "making Himself equal with God" (John 5:18).

Biblically speaking, there is more than enough evidence to conclude that the fundamental nature of God is portrayed by the Scriptures as a plural oneness. With respect to theology, to speak of the nature or essence of God is to speak about *what* kind of Being God is, while to speak of the personhood of God is to speak about *who* God is. We can now conclude *what* God is: He is a plurality within unity. That is, He has one divine nature (what) shared by three persons (who)—the Father (who[1]), Son (who[2]), and Holy Spirit (who[3]).[12] It can also be said that God is one divine unity consisting of a plurality of persons. This three-personal Being's *whoness* is composed of an internal relationship containing three distinct individual persons—the Father, the Son, and the Holy Spirit.

Consider this illustration. It may now be a bit clearer that the infinite *what* (God) did not become a finite *what* (man); rather, God the Son (who[2]), having an infinite nature (what[1]), assumed in addition a finite nature—a finite *what* (what[2]). There are not three gods (three *whats*)—there is only one God (what[1]) and three persons (three *whos*) that possess this one divine nature. It was only the second person, Jesus (who[2]), who shares the divine nature (what[1]), who took on a second, human nature (what[2]).

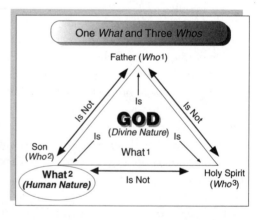

Consequently, Jesus, God the Son, came to earth by taking on—adding—a human nature. The union of the divine and human natures in the one person of Jesus Christ is called the *hypostatic union*. It was defined at the Council of Chalcedon in A.D. 451 and affirms the personal unity as well as the two natures of the Son of God. This truth is a divine mystery, revealed in the Holy Scrip-

---

[12]Earlier we noted that three essential characteristics denote personhood: intellect, emotions, and free will. The Holy Spirit is the third person in the Godhead. He has intellect (1 Corinthians 2:10–11—the Spirit knows and reveals); He possesses emotions (Ephesians 4:30—do not grieve the Holy Spirit of God); and He has free will (1 Corinthians 12:11—the Spirit gives gifts as He determines).

tures. Commenting on the two natures of Jesus Christ, one author said,

> The doctrine simply is that our Lord Jesus Christ as the eternal Son of God retained His entire complex of divine attributes, and always and under all circumstances conducted Himself in a manner perfectly consistent with His divine attributes. He took a complete complex of essential human attributes, and, during "the days of His flesh" (Hebrews 5:7) always and under all circumstances conducted Himself in a manner perfectly consistent with sinless human nature.[13]

Accordingly, when we read in the New Testament that Jesus hungered, thirsted, became tired, suffered in the flesh, and died, it is the human characteristics of Jesus being referenced, not the divine. This view of the deity of Jesus Christ was the dominant position of the early Christian church—namely, that human characteristics are to be predicated on Christ's humanity and not His deity.

IS THERE ANY WAY TO ILLUSTRATE THIS DIVINE MYSTERY?

We can now say with confidence that Jesus Christ has two natures; this is not the mystery. *The mystery is in understanding how the two natures of Christ relate.* It has been revealed to us that the two natures of Christ are in perfect union. However, the Bible does not offer us *exhaustive* knowledge on this truth, but rather *sufficient* knowledge. There is no perfect illustration that will completely capture and illuminate this mystery; the best we can do is to ponder the illustration God gives us in His Word. God refers to Himself as light, and Jesus called Himself the light of the world. Perhaps by gaining a better understanding of the nature of light, we can also better grasp this divine mystery.

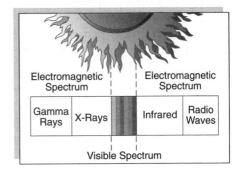

Through many years of experimenting with and studying light, scientists have learned that light has two apparently mutually exclusive natures: it behaves like a particle *and* like a wave. The particle

---

[13]Op. cit., vol. 2, 55.

nature of light manifests itself in packets of energy called *photons,* which are different from particles of matter in that they have no mass and always move at the constant speed of about 186,000 miles/second (the speed of light). At the same time, the wave nature manifests itself when light diffracts or bends as it passes around a corner (of an object). The waves associated with light are called *electromagnetic* waves because they consist of changing electric and magnetic fields.

This dual nature of light appears to be mutually exclusive—a contradiction—but in reality is not. If physicists were to claim that the wave nature of light *is* the particle nature of light, then *that* would be a contradiction. But they don't. Moreover, physicists do not claim that light has a particle nature on some days of the week and a wave nature on the others (different natures at different times). What physicists do claim is that *light has a dual nature*—a wave nature and a particle nature *at the same time.* The problem for physicists is not that light has a dual nature; *the mystery lies in understanding how the two natures of light relate to each other.* This is the same kind of mystery that exists with the relationship between the two natures of Jesus Christ. Let's consider approaching the mystery of the dual natures of light from the vantage point of the laws of physics. In doing so, we are analyzing how "higher" laws relate to "lower" laws.

Albert Einstein dedicated the last twenty-five years of his life endeavoring to formulate the *unified field theory.* Einstein's effort was considered to be a valiant attempt to discover a higher law of physics that subsumes the four basic (lower) laws of physics—the strong nuclear, weak nuclear, electromagnetic, and gravitational forces. Physicists believe that this one unifying force field would describe all of the fundamental forces in the space-time universe entirely in terms of fields. This superforce, described by a higher law, would not violate the lower laws of physics but would provide the missing information to explain how the lower laws are related in a unifying way.

One of the probable results of discovering this superforce would be in giving physicists a better understanding of how the two natures of light relate. This higher law of physics would transcend and unite the lower laws, including particle and wave physics. For instance, the two laws that operate with respect to the phenomenon of flight are the laws of aerodynamics and gravity. Yet the higher law, aerodynamics, does not *violate* or *negate* the lower law of gravity—instead, it *transcends* the law of gravity. For example, when a plane is at thirty thousand feet, gravity is not violated, nor does it go out of existence; it is in full operation with the higher law of aerodynamics at work. It was actually through the understanding of the lower law (gravity) that led scientists and engineers to discover the higher law (aerodynamics).

In a similar manner, we are told that it is through the study and understanding of the commandments of God that we are led to Christ. We are also told by the Word of God that the lower laws (the commandments) were put in charge to lead us to the higher law of Christ (Galatians 3:24). If it were not for the knowledge of the lower laws of God, we would not recognize our sinful nature and acknowledge the need for the higher law of life (Romans 7:7). Just as gravity binds us to the earth and aerodynamics frees us to soar, the lower laws of God bind us to death and the higher law of the Spirit of life sets us free from the law of sin and death (Romans 8:2).

It is possible that physicists will never discover the higher law that explains the dual nature of light, but through their motivation to do so they have found and will most probably continue to find many other treasures. It is often the case that during the quest to find such elusive knowledge, other vital discoveries are made—the quest itself is a rich source of enlightenment. Yet that enlightenment may never have been possible were it not for the mystery of the dual nature of light. Similarly, a study of the dual nature of Jesus Christ can, and often will, lead to a deeper and richer relationship with God through His Word and by His Spirit.

In his book *Alleged Discrepancies of the Bible*, John Haley discusses some of the reasons why God included mysteries and apparent discrepancies in His Word. Haley suggests that God included them by design and that they were "doubtless intended as a stimulus to the human intellect, as provocative of mental effort" and "serve to awaken curiosity and to appeal to the love of novelty."[14] We may never solve the mystery; then again, it could be that the Author of life never meant for it to be solved.

HOW DID JESUS CHRIST SUBSTANTIATE HIS CLAIM TO BE GOD?

It is one thing to claim to be God; it is quite another to back up the claim. Jesus offered at least three lines of evidence to support His claim to be the Son of God (Lord) and the Son of Man (Savior). The three proofs are

(1) His fulfillment of Old Testament prophecies
(2) His sinless life and miraculous deeds
(3) His resurrection from the dead.

The miracles associated with Christ's claim to be God are acts of God con-

---

[14]John Haley, *Alleged Discrepancies of the Bible* (Springdale, Pa.: Whitaker, 1992), 30.

firming Him to be the Son of God. The convergence of these three great miraculous happenings (fulfilled prophecy, sinless life/miraculous deeds, and resurrection) lead forthrightly to the conclusion that Jesus Christ is who He claimed to be—the unique Son of God. The following is offered as evidence in support of the claims of Jesus Christ.[15]

HIS FULFILLMENT OF OLD TESTAMENT PROPHECIES

The Old Testament predictions about Christ were made hundreds of years in advance. Even the most liberal critic of the Old Testament admits to the completion of the prophetic books by some four hundred years before Christ and the book of Daniel by about 165 B.C. And when there are dozens of these prophecies converging in the lifetime of one man, it becomes nothing less than miraculous. Consider the following sampling:

1. The Christ (Messiah) will be born of a woman (Genesis 3:15).
2. He will be born of a virgin (Isaiah 7:14).
3. He will be of the seed of Abraham (Genesis 12:1–3; 22:18).
4. He will be of the tribe of Judah (Genesis 49:10; Luke 3:23, 33).
5. He will be of the House of David (2 Samuel 7:12; Matthew 1:1).
6. His birthplace will be Bethlehem (Micah 5:2; Matthew 2:1).
7. He will be anointed by the Holy Spirit (Isaiah 11:2; Matthew 3:16–17).
8. He will be heralded by a messenger of God (Isaiah 40:3; Matthew 3:1–2).
9. He will perform miracles (Isaiah 35:5–6; Matthew 9:35).
10. He will cleanse the temple (Malachi 3:1; Matthew 21:12).
11. He will be rejected by His own people (Psalm 118:22; 1 Peter 2:7).
12. He will die some 483 years after 444 B.C. (Daniel 9:24).
13. He will die a humiliating death (Psalm 22; Isaiah 53; Matthew 27), involving:
    A. Rejection by Israel (Isaiah 53:3; John 1:10–11; 7:5, 48).
    B. Silence before His accusers (Isaiah 53:7; Matthew 27:12–19).
    C. Humiliation—being mocked (Psalm 22:7–8; Matthew 27:31).
    D. Piercing of His hands and feet (Psalm 22:16; John 20:25).
    E. Being crucified with thieves (Isaiah 53:12; Luke 23:33).
    F. Praying for His persecutors (Isaiah 53:12; Luke 23:34).
    G. Piercing of His side (Zechariah 12:10; John 19:34).
    H. Burial in a rich man's tomb (Isaiah 53:9; Matthew 27:57–60).
    I. Casting lots for His garments (Psalm 22:18; John 19:23–24).

---

[15]This section is based on a previous work by Norman Geisler, *Christian Apologetics*, 339–51.

14. He will rise from the dead (Psalm 16:10; Mark 16:6; Acts 2:31).
15. He will ascend into heaven (Psalm 68:18; Acts 1:9).
16. He will sit at the right hand of God (Psalm 110:1; Hebrews 1:3).

All these and many more prophecies (nearly two hundred!) were fulfilled in the person of Jesus of Nazareth, who claimed to be the Jewish Messiah—"the Christ, the Son of God" (Matthew 26:63–64). In fact, He claimed to be the central theme of the entire Old Testament, saying to two of His disciples, " 'How foolish you are, and how slow of heart to believe all that the prophets have spoken! Did not the Christ have to suffer these things and then enter his glory?' And *beginning with Moses and all the Prophets, he explained to them what was said in all the Scriptures concerning Himself*" (Luke 24:25–27, emphasis added).

Some have argued that psychics have made predictions like the Bible's. However,

> One test of a prophet was whether they ever uttered predictions that did not come to pass (Deuteronomy 18:22). Those whose prophecies failed were stoned (18:20)—a practice that no doubt gave pause to any who were not absolutely sure their messages were from God. Amid hundreds of prophecies, biblical prophets are not known to have made a single error. A study of psychics in 1975 and observed until 1981 showed that of the seventy-two predictions, only six were fulfilled in any way. Two of these were vague and two others were hardly surprising—the U.S. and Russia would remain leading powers and there would be no world wars. The People's Almanac (1976) did a study of predictions of twenty-five top psychics. The results: Of the total seventy-two predictions, sixty-six (92 percent) were totally wrong (Kole, 69). An accuracy rate around 8 percent could easily be explained by chance and general knowledge of circumstances. In 1993 the psychics missed every major unexpected news story, including Michael Jordan's retirement, the Midwest flooding, and the Israel-PLO peace treaty. Among their false prophecies were that the Queen of England would become a nun, and Kathie Lee Gifford would replace Jay Leno as host of "The Tonight Show" (*Charlotte Observer* 12/30/93).[16]

HIS SINLESS LIFE AND MIRACULOUS DEEDS

Simply living a sinless life, as difficult as that would be, wouldn't necessarily prove someone to be God. However, if someone both claims to be God *and* offers a sinless life as evidence, it is an entirely different matter. If a man lives

---

[16]Norman L. Geisler, *Baker Encyclopedia of Christian Apologetics*, 615.

an impeccable life and offers as the truth about himself that he is God-incarnate, his claim must at least be seriously considered. Of course, if someone claimed to be God and did not live a sinless life, it would prove that he was not God.

There are some who dare to claim perfection, but few take them seriously, least of all those who know them best. With Jesus it is quite different; those who knew Him best thought the most highly of Him. One of the most significant testimonies concerning a man's character comes from those who are closest to him. From the lips of Jesus' most intimate friends and disciples who had lived with Him for several years at close range came glowing testimonies:

- Peter—"A lamb without blemish or defect" (1 Peter 1:19).
- Peter—"No deceit was found in His mouth" (1 Peter 2:22).
- Paul—He "had no sin" (2 Corinthians 5:21).
- Author of Hebrews—". . . yet was without sin" (Hebrews 4:15).
- John—"He is pure" (1 John 3:3).
- Jesus—"Can any of you prove me guilty of sin?" (John 8:46). (He directed this question to those *looking for a reason* to convict Him.)

Jesus' life was not only sinless, but it was miraculous from the beginning:

1. He was born of a virgin (Matthew 1:21; Luke 1:27).
2. He turned water into wine (John 2:7).
3. He walked on water (Matthew 14:25).
4. He multiplied bread (John 6:11).
5. He opened the eyes of the blind (John 9:7).
6. He made the lame walk (Mark 2:3).
7. He cast out demons (Mark 1:34).
8. He healed the multitudes of all kinds of sickness (Matthew 9:35).
9. He raised the dead to life (John 11:43–44).
10. He knew what men were thinking in their hearts (John 2:25).

When Jesus was asked whether He was the Messiah, He offered His miracles as evidence, saying, "Go back and report to John what you hear and see: The blind receive sight, the lame walk, those who have leprosy are cured, the deaf hear, the dead are raised" (Matthew 11:4–5). Miracles such as these were accepted by the Jews of Jesus' day as an evident sign of divine favor on the person performing them. The messianic miracles were proof that the performer was the Messiah (Isaiah 35:5–6).

The Jews knew Jesus had performed miracles; they asked, "How can a sinner do such miraculous signs?" (John 9:16). One of the Jewish leaders, Nicodemus, stated the Jewish position well when he acknowledged to Jesus, "Rabbi, we know you are a teacher who has come from God. For no one can perform the miraculous signs you are doing if God were not with him" (John 3:2). Peter proclaimed, "Men of Israel, listen to this: Jesus of Nazareth was a man accredited by God to you by miracles, wonders and signs, which God did among you through him, as you yourselves know" (Acts 2:22). The author of Hebrews stated, "This salvation, which was first announced by the Lord, was confirmed to us by those who heard him. God also testified to it by signs, wonders and various miracles, and gifts of the Holy Spirit distributed according to his will" (Hebrews 2:3–4).

The person of God verifies the message of God through the one performing the act. And in Jesus Christ's case, the message was, and still is, "I am God; here are the acts of God to prove it." Of all the acts, the most critical act of God was Jesus' resurrection from the dead.

HIS RESURRECTION FROM THE DEAD

This is truly the grandest and greatest miracle of them all. The fact that both the Old Testament and Jesus predicted in advance that He would rise from the dead makes the miracle that much more powerful. Consider the following verses:

1. "You will not abandon me to the grave, nor will you let your Holy One see decay" (Psalm 16:10).
2. The Messiah will come and die (Isaiah 53; Psalm 22).
3. The Messiah will have enduring political reign from Jerusalem (Isaiah 9:6; Daniel 2:44). (For the Messiah to die, then reign, He would have to rise from the dead.)
4. "Destroy this temple [of Jesus' body], and I will raise it again in three days" (John 2:19–21).
5. "For as Jonah was three days and three nights in the belly of a huge fish, so the Son of man will be three days and three nights in the heart of the earth" (Matthew 12:40).
6. "The Son of man must suffer . . . and he must be killed and on the third day be raised to life" (Luke 9:22).
7. "No one takes [my life] from me, but I lay it down of my own accord. I have authority to lay it down and authority to take it up again" (John 10:18).

The evidence is there to be believed, but as Jesus said, "If they do not listen to Moses and the Prophets, they will not be convinced even if someone rises from the dead" (Luke 16:31). Josh McDowell raises a good point about the trustworthiness of the eyewitness account concerning the resurrection of Jesus Christ. He says,

> I can trust the apostles' testimonies because, of those twelve men, eleven died martyrs' deaths on the basis of two things: the resurrection of Christ, and their belief in him as the Son of God. They were tortured and flogged, and they finally faced death by some of the cruelest methods then known. . . . The response that is usually chorused back is this: "Why, a lot of people have died for a lie; so what does it prove?" Yes, a lot of people have died for a lie, but they thought it was the truth. Now if the resurrection didn't take place (i.e., was false), the disciples knew it. I find no way to demonstrate that they could have been deceived. Therefore [if it was a lie] these eleven men not only died for a lie—here is the catch—but they knew it was a lie.[17]

Consider also the other martyrs in the early Christian church. Paul, who fostered the execution of Christians before his own encounter with the resurrected Christ and his subsequent conversion to Christianity, claimed that there were over five hundred eyewitnesses of the resurrection of Jesus Christ (1 Corinthians 15:6). With numbers like that in mind, the odds of the resurrection not happening are highly improbable, if not impossible. You can find people throughout history who died for what they believed to be the truth, but you would be hard pressed to find over five hundred people who were willing to die for something they knew to be false.

On the basis of the historical reliability of the New Testament, therefore, we can be sure that we possess the essence of the teachings of Jesus Christ about Himself. The titles of deity He applied to Himself and the worship He accepted, as well as the other claims He made, lead the honest inquirer to conclude that Jesus thought of Himself as God-incarnate in human form. Moreover, an examination of His disciples' beliefs about Him reveals that they too taught that He was equal with and identical to God. Again, the evidence offered by Jesus to substantiate His claim to be God intersects with three great miraculous happenings: His fulfillment of prophecies made hundreds of years before His birth, His sinless and miracle-filled life, and His triumphant bodily resurrection out of the grave. Jesus Christ is who He claims to be: the one and only Son of God.

"What about you? What do you think about the Christ? Whose son is He?" If someone was still not convinced of the claims Jesus made about Himself, or the claims His disciples made about Him, they would have to consider the

---

[17]Josh McDowell, *More Than a Carpenter* (Wheaton, Ill.: Tyndale, 1973), 61–62.

alternatives. Some claims were nothing short of insane if Jesus isn't God. For example, consider His claim to forgive sins in Mark 2:1–12. A paralytic man was brought to Jesus by his friends—a man that Jesus had never seen before, lying on a mat, fully paralyzed—and the very first thing Jesus says to him is, "Son, your sins are forgiven." The religious leaders respond by saying, "Why does this fellow talk like that? He's blaspheming! Who can forgive sins but God alone?" Also notice how Jesus knew what they were thinking: "Immediately Jesus knew in his spirit that this was what they were thinking in their hearts, and he said to them, 'Why are you thinking these things? Which is easier: to say to the paralytic, "Your sins are forgiven," or to say, "Get up, take your mat and walk"? But that you may know that the Son of Man has authority on earth to forgive sins . . .' " With this statement Jesus healed the paralytic, and he got up and took his mat and walked out in full view of them all. Once again, Jesus substantiated His claim to deity with an act of God confirming Him to be God's Son.

In *Mere Christianity,* C. S. Lewis challenged his readers to take a close look at this particular claim of Jesus. The following is a rather lengthy quote, but it's worth reading, for it contains some of Lewis's amazing insights concerning the claim of Jesus to forgive sins. He said,

> One part of the claim tends to go unnoticed because we have heard it so often that we no longer see what it amounts to. I mean the claim to forgive sins: any sins. Now unless the speaker is God, this is really so preposterous as to be comic. We can all understand how a man forgives offences against himself. You tread on my toe and I forgive you, you steal my money and I forgive you. But what should we make of a man, himself unrobbed and untrodden on, who announced that he forgave you for treading on other men's toes and stealing other men's money? Asinine fatuity is the kindest description we should give of his conduct. Yet this is what Jesus did. He told people that their sins were forgiven, and never waited to consult all the other people whom their sins had undoubtedly injured. He unhesitatingly behaved as if He was the party chiefly concerned, the person chiefly offended in all offences. This makes sense only if He really was the God whose laws are broken and whose love is wounded in every sin. In the mouth of any speaker who is not God, these words would imply what I can only regard as a silliness and conceit unrivalled by any other character in history.

> Yet (and this is the strange, significant thing) even His enemies, when they read the Gospels, do not usually get the impression of silliness and conceit. Still less do unprejudiced readers. Christ says that He is "humble and meek" and we believe Him; not noticing that, if He were merely a

man, humility and meekness are the very last characteristics we could contribute to some of His sayings.

I am trying here to prevent anyone saying the really foolish thing that people often say about Him: "I'm ready to accept Jesus as a great moral teacher, but I do not accept His claim to be God." That is the one thing we must not say. A man who was merely a man and said the sort of things Jesus said would not be a great moral teacher. He would either be a lunatic—on a level with the man who says he is a poached egg—or else he would be the Devil of Hell. You must make your choice. Either this man was, and is, the Son of God: or else a madman or something worse. You can shut him up for a fool, you can spit at Him and kill Him as a demon; or you can fall at His feet and call Him Lord and God. But let us not come with any patronizing nonsense about His being a great human teacher. He has not left that open to us. He did not intend to.[18]

There is a very important consequence that follows from the conclusion that Jesus Christ is God: His divine authority. *Whatever Jesus Christ taught must be true, for God cannot lie or teach what is false.* In the next chapter, we will consider Jesus' ethical teachings.

---

[18]Lewis, *Mere Christianity*, 55–56.

—14—
QUESTIONS ABOUT ETHICS AND MORALS

All men alike stand condemned, not by alien codes of ethics, but by their own, and all men therefore are conscious of guilt.

—C. S. Lewis

WHAT ARE ETHICS AND MORALS?

The words *ethics* and *morals* are commonly used interchangeably. When we use the term *ethics*, we are referring to a fixed set of (moral) laws by which one can measure human behavior. Defining ethics in this way gives us a basis for making *moral* judgments. Ethics can be thought of as the standards, laws, or prescriptions that individuals are obligated to obey. Said another way, we can understand ethics as a set

MORALS (What Ought to Be)	MORES (What Is)
• A Prescription	• A Description
• The Law	• The Life
• The Standard	• The Behavior

of standards (what ought to be) by which one *evaluates* human behavior and judges it as morally right or morally wrong. The term *mores* is indicative of the kind of behavior in which a person engages—either good or bad—yet without moral *laws* (ethics) it makes no sense to speak of moral *evaluations*.

It must be seen that without an ethical standard, moral judgments would

309

not be possible. Moreover, if God did not exist, and the only objective laws in the universe were the laws of physics and chemistry, moral judgments would be senseless. We are not saying that atheists or naturalists cannot make a moral judgment; what we are saying is that they have no real *basis* for their moral judgments. C. S. Lewis describes how life would be if all behavior were to be reduced to following the laws of nature:

> If Naturalism is true, "I ought" is the same sort of statement as "I itch" or "I'm going to be sick." In real life when a man says "I ought" we may reply, "Yes. You're right. That is what you ought to do," or else, "No. I think you are mistaken." But in a world of Naturalists (if Naturalists really remembered their philosophy out of school) the only sensible reply would be, "Oh, are you?" All moral judgments would be statements about the speaker's feelings, mistaken by him for statements about something else (the real moral quality of actions) which does not exist.[1]

In other words, if all moral judgments are reduced to *descriptions of what is*, then there is no logical basis to offer *prescriptions for what ought to be*. The laws of nature simply describe what is— in the strictest sense they are merely descriptions of the way things work. Lewis develops this idea in a way that captures our main point.

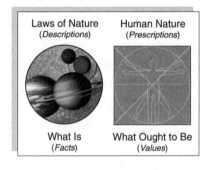

Laws of Nature (Descriptions)	Human Nature (Prescriptions)
What Is (Facts)	What Ought to Be (Values)

> When you say that falling stones always obey the law of gravitation, is not this much the same as saying that the law only means "what stones always do"? You do not really think that when a stone is let go, it suddenly remembers that it is under orders to fall to the ground. You only mean that in fact it does fall. In other words, you cannot be sure that there is nothing over and above the facts themselves, any law about what ought to happen, as distinct from what does happen. The laws of nature, as applied to stones or trees, may only mean "what Nature, in fact, does." But if you turn to the Law of Human Nature, the Law of Decent Behavior, it is a different matter. That law certainly does not mean "what human beings, in fact, do"; for as I said before, many of them do not obey this law at all, and none of them obey it completely. The law of gravity tells you what stones do if you drop them; but the Law of Human Nature tells you what human beings ought to do and do not. In other words, when you are

---

[1] C. S. Lewis, *Miracles* (New York: Macmillan, 1960), 36.

dealing with humans, something else comes in above and beyond the actual facts. You have the facts (how men do behave) and you also have something else (how they ought to behave).[2]

This distinction between "what is" and "what ought to be" is the essential difference between the fact of human behavior (mores) and the law of human nature or natural law (morals). Without this differentiation, "what ought to be" simply reduces to "what is" and the distinction between mores and morals disappears. Consequently, moral actions are no longer a matter of ethics. They become a matter of socially acceptable behavior; the *ethnic* defines ethics—the society determines what is morally right.

We plan to show how a belief in subjective or ethnic morality logically leads to a self-defeating position and to the destruction of all values. However, before we do so, we need to briefly review our position with respect to the conclusions we have drawn from our knowledge of first principles.

DO ABSOLUTE MORAL LAWS EXIST?

Academic Discipline	First Principle Conclusions
Logic (LNC)	The laws of logic must be objective and universal in nature. Objective reason is a necessary precondition for truth and the academic basis for all fields of knowledge.
Philosophy (Fixed Point)	Truth (knowledge of reality) is discovered by reason. A statement that matches (corresponds to) reality is true. Reality must be unchanging, the reference point that makes philosophical inquiry valid.
Science (Causality, Second Law)	Objective reason (the laws of logic) and the principle of causality are necessary preconditions for science. The 2nd Law of Thermodynamics holds the supreme position and demonstrates the credibility of positing an infinitely powerful and intelligent First Cause.
Law (Universal Standard)	Only persons have the natural and unalienable rights. Human rights are not based upon the arbitrary dictates of any government. Furthermore, justice requires an objective and universal moral law (standard) that transcends the laws of society.

---

[2]Lewis, *Mere Christianity*, 27–28.

We have already established the credibility of natural law, or what Lewis called "The Law of Human Nature." Now we want to take a more in-depth look at the same topic from a personal perspective. This table provides a summary of the conclusions we have drawn from the first principles presented in previous chapters. In light of what has already been stated, we want to bring the question of universal moral laws down to an individual level and discuss the existence of personal ethical obligations. People usually agree that the Nazis were morally wrong and guilty of committing "crimes against humanity." However, these same individuals can easily turn around and disagree with the belief that objective, binding moral laws exist. Their main argument is usually based on the belief that ethics are subjective and personal.

We have also made clear the validity of moral absolutes and the consequences of denying them. We concluded that justice at Nuremberg was based upon the self-evident truths and moral absolutes such as those set forth in the Declaration of Independence. As we saw, it was demonstrated at Nuremberg and Berlin that these moral absolutes existed as the basis of civil laws for all governments. Furthermore, every human being—through her conscience—is to be held accountable for violating these moral laws. Near the end of chapter 10 we included this quote from C. S. Lewis:

> These, then, are the two points I want to make. First, that human beings all over the earth have this curious idea that they ought to behave in a certain way, and cannot really get rid of it. Secondly, that they do not in fact behave in that way. They know the Law of [Human] Nature; they break it. These two facts are the foundation of all clear thinking about ourselves and the universe we live in.[3]

Lewis believed that all individuals are consciously aware of an impinging moral law that they ought to keep but, in fact, cannot keep and cannot get rid of. He also said that these two facts are the foundation of all clear thinking and later added, "If they are the foundation, I had better stop to make that foundation firm."[4] We have already firmed up this foundation with respect to showing how the moral law is not just a matter of social convention—like the educational system. As Lewis pointed out, that we learn something from our parents or teachers does not mean it must necessarily be merely a human invention. Just as the basic laws of logic or physics are taught by teachers in different cultures and do not change from one culture to another, so it is with respect to the universal moral law. This can easily be seen in moral judgments:

---

[3]Ibid., 21.
[4]Ibid.

When we judge actions as morally right or morally wrong, as in the case of the Nazis, we are, in fact, measuring them against the moral law. Therefore, universal moral laws necessarily exist.

We have also shown that if moral laws were not discoverable, there would be no sense in trying to make moral judgments and no such thing as moral progress. Moral progress means that change is occurring and that this change is moving toward—not away from—a better state of real morality. If this isn't true, there would be no sense in saying that some moral ideologies are better than others. It is only by using a moral standard that we are able to say that some moral ideas conform to that standard and are, therefore, better than other moral ideas.

Basing all judgments on social convention is only one attempt among many to eliminate the belief in objective values. Two other popular views try to reduce ethics to human instincts and/or human emotions. Lewis wrote a rebuttal to both views, and his arguments against instincts and emotions can be found in *Mere Christianity* and *The Abolition of Man*, respectively. Rather than trying to improve on the arguments presented by a great thinker such as Lewis, we have summarized his responses to human instincts and emotions below.

ISN'T ETHICS JUST HUMAN INSTINCTS?

Before we respond to this view of ethics, we must be clear about what is meant by human instinct. *Webster's* defines instinct as "an inborn tendency to behave in a way characteristic of a species; natural, unacquired mode of response to stimuli." With respect to psychoanalysis, it is "a primal biological urge, as hunger, impelling a response, as eating, which brings release of tension; the human instincts are conceived of as including the self-preservative, the sexual, and, sometimes, the aggressive."[5] Is this understanding of human instincts the same as the moral law? No! Lewis did suggest that sometimes we sense a desire to help another person, and that this desire could no doubt be due to the urge or instinct to preserve the human race—herd instinct. However, he also noted the following critical distinction between feeling *a desire to help* someone and *feeling that we ought to help* whether we want to or not.

> Suppose you hear a cry for help from a man in danger. You will probably feel two desires—one a desire to give help (due to herd instinct),

---

[5] D. Guralnik, ed., *Webster's New World Dictionary of the American Language* (New York: Simon & Schuster, 1982), 730.

the other a desire to keep out of danger (due to the instinct for self-preservation). But you will find inside you, in addition to these two impulses to help, a third thing which tells you that *you ought to* follow the impulse to help, and suppress the impulse to run away. Now this thing that judges between two instincts, that decides which should be encouraged, cannot itself be either of them. You might as well say the sheet of music which tells you, at a given moment, to play one note on the piano and not another, is itself one of the notes on the keyboard. The Moral Law tells us the tune we have to play: our instincts are merely the keys.[6]

Lewis went on to explain the difficulty we experience when two instincts are in conflict. When this happens, and there is nothing in our mind except the two conflicting impulses, then the stronger of the two must surely win. It is precisely at this moment of struggling between the two urges that we are most conscious of the moral law, because it usually seems to be telling us to choose the

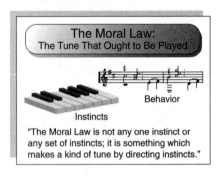

The Moral Law:
The Tune That Ought to Be Played

Behavior

Instincts

"The Moral Law is not any one instinct or any set of instincts; it is something which makes a kind of tune by directing instincts."

weaker of the two instincts. With respect to Lewis's illustration, we would probably want to be safe (self-preservation) much more than we would want to help the man in danger (herd instinct), yet the moral law tells us to help him all the same. Furthermore, Lewis noted that the moral law often tells us to try to make the right impulse stronger than it naturally is.

> We often feel it our duty to stimulate the herd instinct, by waking up our imagination and arousing our pity and so on, so as to get up enough steam for doing the right thing. But clearly we are not acting *from* instinct when we set about making an instinct stronger than it is. The thing that says to you, "Your herd instinct is asleep. Wake it up," cannot itself *be* the herd instinct. The thing that tells you which note on the piano needs to be played louder cannot itself be that note. . . . Strictly speaking, there are no such things as good and bad impulses. Think once again of the piano. It has not got two kinds of notes on it, the "right" notes and the "wrong" ones. Every single note is right at one time and wrong at another. The Moral Law is not any one instinct or any set of instincts: it is something

---

[6]Op. cit., 22 (emphasis added).

which makes a kind of tune (the tune we call goodness or right conduct) by directing the instincts.[7]

Lewis argued that the moral law is not merely another one of our instincts; if it were, we ought to be able to call one of those instincts "good." Yet this is not the case. There are no instincts that the moral law may not sometimes tell us to suppress and none that it may not sometimes tell us to encourage. Lewis also highlighted the danger in setting up one of the impulses of human nature as the thing that "ought to" be followed at all costs. We have shown that history confirmed this, for example, in the "survival of the fittest" instinct that Hitler integrated into Nazi dogma and acted upon in aggression. What logically followed was mass genocide. We conclude, then, that there is more to morality than mere human instinct. But why couldn't morals and ethics simply be a product of the human psyche?

ISN'T ETHICS JUST A MATTER OF EVINCING ONE'S FEELINGS?

The response to this question is rather long, so please follow the arguments presented carefully. The length of this response is necessary in light of the popular belief in subjective ethics and the emphasis contemporary psychology and sociology place on emotions and feelings rather than on moral responsibility. We are not condemning psychology and sociology in general, for they certainly have made many positive contributions with respect to understanding human nature and social actions. However, for the most part, these positive contributions have been outweighed by the damage they have done to our collective comprehension of moral responsibility and ethics—along with the proper understanding of human nature. The danger occurs when the people of a society embrace an erroneous view of human nature and dismiss ethics as purely emotive; when this happens, it's only a matter of time before that society begins to reap the bitter fruits of the beliefs it has sown. We plan to show how this is precisely the case in the United States.

In the following citation, Solomon Schimmel, author of *The Seven Deadly Sins*, gives a concise overview of the emphasis contemporary psychology places on feelings:

> Psychoanalysis shifts the burden of *moral responsibility* from the adult to his parents and childhood experiences. It recognizes *the power of lust* but

---

[7]Ibid., 22–23.

sees greater psychological danger in overcontrolling rather than under-controlling it. Behavior therapy focuses on what we do, not whether or not we should do it. . . . Adlerian, or individual, therapy appreciates the *pull of pride.* . . . However, because of its focus on overcoming feelings of inferiority it can err on the side of pride and fail to appreciate the value of humility. . . . Gestalt therapy focuses on the present rather than harping on the past or worrying about the future. *Its main concern is how we feel rather than what we think. It also encourages overt expressions of feelings, particularly anger and resentment.* In these respects gestalt therapy is at odds with much of the traditional moral approach to dealing with our emotional problems and flaws of character. . . . Rational-emotive and other cognitive therapies . . . say *our feelings of guilt and shame are basically our own doing,* the results of our distorted thoughts and irrationality; we should learn how to get rid of them.[8]

This tells the story of contemporary psychology, yet the appeal to subjective ethics is not new: a critique was written by C. S. Lewis in 1943 (*The Abolition of Man*). In that book Lewis examined a publication written by two authors who attempted to reduce all objective value statements to assertions about the speaker's subjective feelings or emotional state. Out of professional respect for the authors, Lewis kept their names and the book title confidential. He used a fictitious title—*The Green Book*—and identified the authors by imaginary names—Gaius and Titius. Lewis felt the need to respond to *The Green Book* because it was supposed to be used as a textbook in the upper grades to teach the art of English composition, but it was teaching much more! He warned that "the very power of Gaius and Titius depends on the fact that they are dealing with a boy: a boy who thinks he is 'doing' his 'English prep' and has no notion that ethics, theology, and politics are all at stake."[9]

Lewis further explained how the students who used *The Green Book* in class were not being taught a theory, per se, but were being exposed to the authors' basic assumption. That assumption was their belief that all value statements were subjective, unimportant, and "nothing but" an individual's projection of his or her own feelings. Lewis saw the pending danger in that the students in the classroom who assimilated the authors' assumption into their own way of thinking would ultimately be influenced by it. He said, "An assumption, which ten years hence, its origin forgotten and its presence unconscious, will condition him to take one side in a controversy which he has never recognized as a

[8]Solomon Schimmel, *The Seven Deadly Sins: Jewish, Christian, and Classical Reflections on Human Psychology* (New York: Oxford University Press, 1997), 7–8 (emphasis added).
[9]C. S. Lewis, *The Abolition of Man* (New York: Macmillan, 1955), 16.

controversy at all."[10] Lewis cited an example of one of the lessons in *The Green Book* and how it went beyond the subject of English composition. He said, "That is their day's lesson in English, though of English they have learned nothing. Another little portion of the human heritage has been quietly taken away from them before they were old enough to understand."[11]

Lewis pointed out the serious responsibility educators have with respect to teaching the correct view of ethics: "Aristotle says that the aim of education is to make the pupil like and dislike *what he ought*. When the age for reflective thought comes, the pupil who has been thus trained in 'ordinate affections' or 'just sentiments' will easily find the *first principles of Ethics*: but to the corrupt man they will never be visible at all and he can make no progress in science. Plato before him had said the same."[12] Lewis called the correct view of ethics the "doctrine of objective value," defining it as

> ... the belief that certain attitudes are really true, and others really false, to the kind of thing the universe is and the kind of things we are. ... And because our approvals and disapprovals are thus recognitions of objective value or responses to objective order, therefore emotional states can be in harmony with reason (when we feel liking for what ought to be approved) or out of harmony with reason (when we perceive that liking is due but cannot feel it). No emotion is a judgment: in that sense all emotions and sentiments are alogical. But they can be reasonable or unreasonable as they conform to Reason or fail to conform. The heart never takes the place of the head: but it can, and should, obey it.[13]

Lewis observed that Gaius and Titius scattered their view of ethics throughout *The Green Book*, and he concluded that it may have been their intention to get the students who used their text to make a clean sweep of traditional values and start with a new set. However, he was quick to point out that this new set of values was in another world—the world of pure subjectivity. This is the world of "facts, without one trace of value, and the world of feelings without one trace of truth or falsehood, justice or injustice."[14] In this kind of world there can be no reconciliation or harmony between reason and feeling, between the mind and the heart.

The end result of training young people to believe in this fact/value dichotomy is quite serious. When it is carried over to the personal dimension, it

[10]Ibid., 16–17.
[11]Ibid., 22.
[12]Ibid., 26 (emphasis added).
[13]Ibid., 29–30.
[14]Ibid., 30.

becomes a what/who dichotomy. In other words, what we do (our public image) does not have to be necessarily connected to who we are (our personal integrity). In practice it works out to something like this: as long as we are good at what we do (our profession), we need not worry about who we are (our character).

So according to this fact/value dichotomy, one could do whatever it takes to be good at a profession and become popular and powerful. This could be achieved without really caring about one's character and therefore placing the quest for power over the quest for character. We need not mention how high up, into the political arena especially, this "public image/personal integrity" dichotomy can go. It is certainly a sad commentary on our society when the highest office in the nation becomes the focus of this kind of duplicity. It is even more tragic when the American people care more about an elected official's job performance (what she does) than that official's integrity (who she really is).

This moral decay is not just confined to politics; it has reached epidemic proportions in every major profession. A survey conducted by *Time* showed that declining morality in the business world, political arena, law practice, and medical profession was the direct result of personal pride. In the final analysis *Time* said that these professionals all tended to "sweep ethics complaints under the rug" and that this inclination to avoid moral integrity was a direct result of a *"protective obsession with self and image."*[15]

Our society is not only accustomed to having this public image/personal integrity dichotomy—hypocrisy—as part of our culture, but we are even seeking out ways to be good at it! A book recently published by two authors is titled *The 48 Laws of Power*. Written on the dust cover of this work is a brief paragraph describing it as "amoral, cunning, ruthless, and instructive. . . . A synthesis of in-depth research into the philosophies of such great thinkers as Machiavelli, Sun-tzu, and Carl von Clausewitz and the legacies of statesmen, warriors, seducers, and con men throughout the ages, *The 48 Laws of Power* is the definitive study of power and the essential guide to modern manipulation. . . . All of the 48 laws provide an understanding of the strategies used by others, the tactics to avoid or live by."[16]

In all fairness to the authors, they have tried to write their book objectively by observing and documenting what it takes to gain power and keep it. A brief excerpt from the preface of this book will provide us with an idea of what many

[15]Ezra Bowen, "Looking to Its Roots," *Time*, May 25, 1987, 26 (emphasis added).
[16]Robert Greene and Joost Elffers, *The 48 Laws of Power* (New York: Penguin, 1998), dust cover.

individuals in our society are striving to attain and what it will take to get it. The authors say,

> No one wants less power; everyone wants more. In the world today, however, it is dangerous to seem too power hungry, to be overt with your power moves. We have to seem fair and decent. So we need to be subtle— congenial yet cunning, democratic yet devious. This game of constant duplicity most resembles the power dynamic that existed in the scheming world of the old aristocratic court. Throughout history, a court has always formed itself around the person in power—king, queen, emperor, leader. The courtiers who filled this court were in an especially delicate position: They had to serve their masters, but if they seemed to fawn, if they curried favor too obviously, the other courtiers around them would notice and would act against them. Attempts to win the master's favor, then, had to be subtle. And even skilled courtiers capable of such subtlety still had to protect themselves from their fellow courtiers, who at all moments were scheming to push them aside. . . .
>
> The successful courtier learned over time to make all of his moves indirect; if he stabbed an opponent in the back, it was with a velvet glove on his hand and the sweetest of smiles on his face. Instead of using coercion or outright treachery, the perfect courtier got his way through seduction, charm, deception, and subtle strategy, always planning several moves ahead. Life in the court was a never-ending game that required constant vigilance and tactical thinking. It was civilized war. . . . The court imagined itself the pinnacle of refinement, but underneath its glittering surface a cauldron of dark emotions—*greed, envy, lust, hatred*—boiled and simmered. Our world today similarly imagines itself the pinnacle of fairness, yet the same ugly emotions still stir within us as they have forever.[17]

The combination of power and pride are extremely corrosive to the internal character qualities of a person. This duplicity of public status and private morals—this lust for power coupled with the desire to protect one's image—can easily produce what C. S. Lewis referred to as "men without chests." He said that if the authors of *The Green Book* (and those who sanction and propagate subjective ethics) are successful, the very ideals that we hope to develop and nurture in our young people won't be possible. These are qualities that have long been considered hallmarks of integrity and virtue—courage, truthfulness, trustworthiness, honor, and the like. Lewis lamented,

---

[17]Ibid., *xvii-xviii* (emphasis added).

All the time—such is the tragi-comedy of our situation—we continue to clamor for those very qualities we are rendering impossible. You can hardly open a periodical without coming across the statement that what our civilization needs is more "drive," or dynamism, or self-sacrifice, or "creativity." In a sort of ghastly simplicity we remove the organ and demand the function. We make men without chests and expect of them virtue and enterprise. We laugh at honor and are shocked to find traitors in our midst. We castrate and bid the geldings be fruitful.[18]

Lewis then brings us to the pinnacle of his approach by asking the question, "Do not educators such as Gaius and Titius see their work as a means to an end?" He insists that they do and that their end is precisely the idea that makes *The Green Book* and the philosophy of subjective ethics self-defeating.

They write in order to produce certain states of mind in the rising generation, if not because they think those states of mind intrinsically just or good, yet certainly they think them to be the means to some state of society that they regard as desirable. . . . The important point is not the precise nature of their end, but the fact that they have an end at all. . . . And this end must have *real value* in their eyes. To abstain from calling it "good" and to use, instead, such predicates as "necessary" or "progressive" or "efficient" would be a subterfuge. They could be forced by argument to answer the questions "necessary for what?" "progressing towards what?" "effecting what?"; in the last resort they would have to admit that some state of affairs was in their opinion good for its own sake. And this time they could not maintain that "good" simply described *their own emotions* about it. For the whole purpose of their book is to condition the young reader that he will share their approval, and this would be either a fool's or a villain's undertaking unless they held that their approval was in some way valid or correct. . . .

A great many of those who "debunk" traditional or (as they would say) "sentimental" values have in the background values of their own which they believe to be immune from the debunking process. They claim to be cutting away the parasitic growth of emotion, religious sanction, and inherited taboos, in order that "real" or "basic" values may emerge.[19]

Lewis concluded his review by pointing out that from propositions about facts alone, no practical conclusions, with respect to values, can ever be drawn. In other words, if those who hold to the kind of philosophy upheld in *The Green Book* believed that their way of thinking will *preserve society* (offered as a

---

[18]C. S. Lewis, *The Abolition of Man* (New York: Macmillan, 1955), 35 (emphasis added).
[19]Ibid., 40 (emphasis added).

statement of fact), then that fact can never directly lead to the conclusion that *society ought to be preserved* (offered as a statement of value). It is impossible to derive prescriptive conclusions (what ought to be—values) out of a purely descriptive set of premises (what is—facts). In an effort to destroy all values, those who subscribe to subjective morality end up destroying the basis for their own view and that of objective values as well. Lewis suggested that if this is what subjective ethicists desire to do, then they need to be intellectually honest and forthright. He challenged them to take their philosophy seriously and "step outside" of the moral law altogether, into a world where there are no values:

> Very well: we shall probably find that we can get on quite comfortably without them [traditional values]. Let us regard all ideas of what we *ought* to do simply as an interesting psychological survival: let us step right out of all that and start doing what we like. Let us decide for ourselves what man is to be and make him into that: not on any ground of imagined value, but because we want him to be such. Having mastered our environment, let us now master ourselves and choose our own destiny. This is a very possible position: and those who hold it cannot be accused of self-contradiction like the half-hearted skeptics who still hope to find "real" values when they have debunked the traditional ones. This is the rejection of the concept of value altogether.[20]

Lewis forthrightly warned his readers of the looming danger resulting from the dismissal of ethics on purely subjective grounds. He said that when a society reaches the point of obliterating values altogether—by perfectly applying psychology and technology to humanity—that society is perilously close to the end. He explained what he meant by reminding his readers that we have conquered many things in nature, and that the things that were once our masters have now become our servants. Lewis argued that subjective ethicists are trying to conquer the final peak of nature—human nature itself—by using the instruments of eugenics, psychology, and education:

> I am only making clear what Man's conquest of nature really means and especially that final stage in the conquest, which, perhaps, is not far off. The final stage is come when Man by eugenics, by pre-natal conditioning, and by education and propaganda based on a perfect applied psychology, has obtained full control over himself. *Human* nature will be the last part of Nature to surrender to Man. The battle will be won. . . . But who precisely will have won it? For the power of Man to make himself what he

---

[20]Ibid., 62–63.

pleases means, as we have seen, *the power to make other men what they please.*[21]

Lewis referred to this final conquest of human nature as "the abolition of Man." Lewis is "spot-on" with respect to his prediction; consider the field of eugenics and the advent of human cloning. One thing seems certain: many people will not view human clones as having God-given or intrinsic value.

This is already true in human embryo research: in 1994, researchers Jerry Hall and Robert Stillman discarded numerous human embryos before successfully cloning one. Imagine the implications for researchers in two laboratories (the University of Texas and the University of Bath, England) who have created headless mice and tadpoles:

> Researchers found the gene that tells the embryo to produce the head. They deleted it. They did this in a thousand mice embryos, four of which were born. . . . Why should you be panicked? Because humans are next. "It would almost certainly be possible to produce human bodies without a forebrain," Princeton biologist Lee Silver told the London *Sunday Times.* "These human bodies without any semblance of consciousness would not be considered persons, and thus it would be perfectly legal to keep them 'alive' as a future source of organs."[22]

It's not hard to picture going to a company who specialized in "organ farming" and having them take a cell from your arm in order to clone you. They could then grow an unconscious body from the cell, which will become your own personal, perfectly matched, spare parts repository. As Aldous Huxley foretold in *Brave New World,* artificial wombs could be created to in-

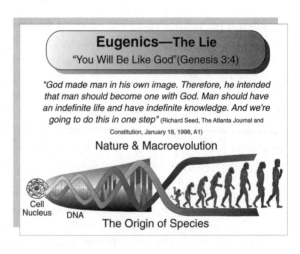

Eugenics—The Lie
"You Will Be Like God"(Genesis 3:4)

"God made man in his own image. Therefore, he intended that man should become one with God. Man should have an indefinite life and have indefinite knowledge. And we're going to do this in one step" (Richard Seed, The Atlanta Journal and Constitution, January 18, 1998, A1)

Nature & Macroevolution

Cell Nucleus   DNA   The Origin of Species

---

[21]Ibid., 72 (emphasis added).
[22]*Citizen,* "Of Headless Mice . . . and Men," (vol. 12, no. 3 *Focus on the Family,* March 1998), 9. Article by Charles Krauthammer, reprinted with permission from *Time,* January 19, 1998.

cubate tiny infants. This would help keep production costs and liability down, although it might not be easy to find sober-minded women who would carry headless babies to their birth. Organizations coming into existence for the purpose of producing human-organ spare parts? It leads us to exactly what Lewis said: "For the power of Man to make himself what he pleases means, as we have seen, the power to make other men what they please." It sounds like science fiction, but in theory an organization could *clone* a human and *own* that person as it would own any other asset—and, therefore, have "the power to make other men what they please."

The legal groundwork already exists. A journalist for the *Washington Post* reported the following:

> In a 5-to-4 decision in 1980, the U.S. Supreme Court [ruled] that . . . living things could be patented as long as they met the standard criteria for patentability. Seven years later, the office granted its first patent on an animal—a genetically engineered mouse—and it has since granted 79 other animal patents—including several on mice, rats and rabbits and one each for an engineered bird, fish, pig, guinea pig, sheep and abalone. More than 1,800 patents have also been granted for genes and lines of cultured cells, including human ones, that scientists believe have medical potential.
>
> "With cloning, Dolly [the sheep], with everything we've been hearing in the past couple of years, science is progressing and so these issues have come to the fore," said O'Connor, now executive director of the American Institute for Medical and Biological Engineering in Washington. "What does it take to be human? A cell line? A limb? A whole human? A chimera [beast of Greek mythology]? We don't have a definition of what a human being is for patent purposes."[23]

This is the logical and practical outworking of embracing the belief that all values are subjective. This belief rejects the concept that there is God-given value to every human life.

Now that we have pointed out the fallacious thinking involved with purely subjective ethics and the danger of rejecting the belief in objective values, we are ready to offer the reasons why it makes both theoretical and practical sense to believe in objective moral laws. We plan to show that the objective view of values is both logically consistent and existentially necessary for ethics to have personal meaning and social significance. Since we have presented the evidence for the historical reliability of the New Testament and the case for the deity of Jesus Christ, we turn to Him to see what He thinks.

---

[23]Rick Weiss, "Patent Sought on Making of Part-Human Creatures Scientist Seeks to Touch Off Ethics Debate," *Washington Post*, April 2, 1998, A12.

WHAT IS JESUS' FIRST PRINCIPLE OF ETHICS?

By now we hope to have made clear that *first principles are not conclusions found at the end of a set of premises but rather premises from which conclusions are drawn*. First principles are axioms, givens, or self-evident truths. They are as reasonable as other reasonable premises—in fact, so obviously reasonable that they neither demand nor admit proof. They are beyond direct proof because they are known to be true based upon their self-evident and inescapable nature. They also cannot be disproved because in making the effort to disprove a first principle (within any given field of study), one will only end up in self-defeating statements—as C. S. Lewis pointed out with respect to the subjective view of ethics. We have also shown this to be the case with logic, truth, science, law, justice, and evil (see chapters 1, 2, 4, 9, 10, and 11, respectively). As Aristotle said, each field of knowledge has a self-evident truth that forms the basis for deriving the other truths in that field. We now propose that the first principle of ethics is no different in nature than any of the other first principles previously examined in this work.

After Lewis finished his main critique of *The Green Book*, he justified and explained the necessity of first principles with respect to ethics and values. Consider again his argument:

> If nothing is self-evident, nothing can be proved. Similarly if nothing is obligatory for its own sake, nothing is obligatory at all. . . . Our duty to do good to all men is an axiom [first principle] of Practical Reason, and our duty to do good to our descendants is a clear deduction from it. . . . Natural Law or Traditional Morality or the First Principles of Practical Reason or the First Platitudes, *is not* one among a series of possible systems of value. *It is the sole source of all value judgments.* If it is rejected, all value is rejected. If any value is retained, it is retained. The effort to refute it and raise a new system of value in its place is self-contradictory. . . . You cannot go on "explaining away" forever: you will find that you have explained explanation itself away. You cannot go on "seeing through" things forever. The whole point of seeing through something is to see something through it. It is good that the window should be transparent, because the street or garden beyond it is opaque. How if you saw through the garden too? It is no use trying to "see through" first principles. If you see through everything, then everything is transparent. But a transparent world is an invisible world. To "see through" all things is the same as not to see.[24]

A prescriptive statement or judgment is one asserting that certain behaviors

[24]Lewis, *The Abolition of Man*, 53–54, 56, 91 (emphasis added).

"ought to" or "ought not to" be performed. This kind of statement imposes a prescription (ethical mandate) that may or may not be obeyed. Numerous ethical theories have been proposed concerning what causes individuals to behave in certain ways and what is meant by "moral goodness." These theories range from the self-love of Ayn Rand's egocentric ethics to the unselfish love of Erich Fromm's social ethics. We can study how human behavior is economically determined (Marx) or how it is socially determined (Skinner). We can embrace the belief that human ethics are self-determined (Sartre) or that they are genetically determined (Huxley). Ideas abound, but it is not within the scope of this work to examine all these ethical theories and critique each one.[25] *All* of these theories fall into the same general category of *The Green Book* (*humanity* is the basis for ethics) and are subject to the same essential criticism. Therefore, since we have already argued for the existence of the God of the Bible, for the historical reliability of the New Testament, and for the credibility of the claims of Jesus Christ, we can now focus on the Christian view of ethics. This view will be presented in light of the life and teachings of Jesus Christ and the New Testament authors.

We suggest that the first precept of Christian ethics was stated by Jesus in Matthew 7:12: "So in everything, do to others what you would have them do to you, for this sums up the Law and the Prophets." Jesus condensed the entire Old Testament ("the Law and the Prophets") into one concise ethical prescription or first principle. To see how this is applied in practice, think back to our earlier analogy about helping someone in danger. Imagine that we are passing by a burning house and an injured woman runs up to us pleading for help. She frantically tells us that her six-month-old infant boy is still inside, and she begs us to try to rescue him. Now, we would probably want to be safe (self-preservation) much more than we would want to help save the baby (herd instinct). Yet the moral law tells us to help the child all the same. This third thing that judges between the two instincts (self-preservation and herd instinct) and decides which should be encouraged is consistent with the first principle of Christian ethics—"In everything, do to others as you would have them do to you." If one of us were the parent of that child, would we not want someone to help save him? Of course we would—then do likewise.

WHAT DID JESUS SAY ABOUT MORAL GOODNESS?

When Jesus taught on the topic of moral goodness, He specifically explained how it was not to be found merely in the act itself but rather in the

---

[25]For a thorough analysis of ethical options, see Norman L. Geisler, *Christian Ethics: Options and Issues* (Grand Rapids, Mich.: Baker, 1989).

heart attitude behind the act. On the outside any action can appear to be morally good. However, according to Jesus the true state of morality is not measured by the outward behavior of people alone but by the internal condition of the heart. Unfortunately, the average person today believes that moral goodness is just a matter of keeping a set of rules and regulations—a list of do's and don'ts. For this reason, we see the teachings of Jesus as timeless and very applicable to the contemporary misconceptions of ethics. Therefore, let's take a closer look at the definition Jesus gave concerning moral goodness as He explained it in His Sermon on the Mount (Matthew 5–7).

According to Jesus, God is ultimately interested in developing our character and seeks for us to internalize moral principles so that the true measure of moral goodness is based upon who we are (personal integrity) and not just what we do (controlling our public actions). This view stands directly in the way of anyone who places image over integrity. In *The 48 Laws of Power* (cited above) the third, fifth, and sixth laws were formulated to help keep up the public image. That is, to help people develop conscienceless techniques of how to attain and keep power while maintaining an *outward appearance* of morality in order to protect their reputations (public image). The authors suggest,

> Keep people off-balance and in the dark by never revealing *the purpose behind your actions.* If they have no clue what you are up to, they cannot prepare a defense. Guide them far enough down the wrong path, envelop them in smoke, and by the time they realize your intentions, it will be too late. . . . Reputation [image] is the cornerstone of power. Through reputation alone you can intimidate and win; once it slips, however, you are vulnerable, and will be attacked on all sides. Make your reputation unassailable. Always be alert to potential attacks and thwart them before they happen. Meanwhile, learn to destroy your enemies by opening holes in their own reputations. Then stand aside and let public opinion hang them. . . . *Everything is judged by its appearance; what is unseen counts for nothing.*[26]

Contrast that last statement with what Jesus said concerning the hypocrisy of the religious leaders: "Everything they do is done for men to see. . . . Woe to you, teachers of the law and Pharisees, you hypocrites! You are like whitewashed tombs, which look beautiful on the outside but on the inside are full of dead men's bones and everything unclean. In the same way, on the outside you appear to people as righteous but on the inside you are full of hypocrisy and wickedness" (Matthew 23:5, 27–28). These are the two opposing views,

---

[26]Greene and Elffers, *The 48 Laws of Power*, ix (emphasis added).

one emphasizing the worthlessness of the internal moral state of humanity and the other, the view of Jesus, emphasizing that true worth and value are found on the inside—which is not seen by human eyes.

Jesus taught that moral goodness is not measured by behavior alone but rather by the internal state or attitude of the heart. The act itself does not make an individual morally good or virtuous. The primary indicator of a person's moral state is the heart attitude or mindset beneath the action; this is the true test of virtue that helps to build the internal character qualities of that person. If this were not the case, we might incorrectly conclude (as many people do) that God is only interested in our obedience to a set of mandates (what we do or don't do) and not interested in our inner being (who we are).

Jesus' definition of moral goodness is rooted in true love. Ultimately, God loves us and cares about our true happiness or ultimate fulfillment (which can only be found in Him). This contrasts the popular belief that God's laws were given to us to keep us from enjoying ourselves. We will explain why relational laws exist (the Ten Commandments) for our true happiness in more detail in chapter 15. For now, let's just say that true happiness and ultimate meaning depend upon an internal state of being (who we are) and not on external image or the possession of things (what we do or have).

This internal attitude of the heart was the fundamental issue Jesus addressed in Matthew 5–7. It was necessary for Him to lay down the foundational thoughts of what constituted true moral goodness so that the people could comprehend their need for God's help. Jesus was quick to point out to the people that they were being misled by the misinterpretations of their leaders, who believed that laws such as "Do not murder" and "Do not commit adultery" (Matthew 5:21, 27; Exodus 20:13–14) were external in nature and that true moral goodness was just a matter of obeying them—and thus *appearing* to have attained moral goodness. He had to correct these misapplications of God's laws by setting them in a relational context.

Jesus defined moral goodness more deeply when He said, "But I tell you that anyone who is angry with his brother will be subject to judgment. . . . Anyone who looks at a woman lustfully has already committed adultery with her in his heart" (Matthew 5:22, 28). Who has never harbored anger or bitterness? Who has never embraced lust? Who could keep that kind of standard without some kind of supernatural help? If Jesus was right, suddenly the idea of obeying a law for the sake of looking good lost its moral significance!

Jesus wanted us to understand that the Ten Commandments were given as a prescription for initiating and maintaining proper and healthy relationships. By this we mean the kind of relationships we were designed to have with God (the first table of the law) and with others (the second table of the law).[27] These commandments are given to remove the self-centered focus we naturally have and to raise up an ethical standard that is God-centered and other-centered. It is not that God is not interested in what we think about ourselves; on the contrary, true moral goodness requires a right view of self-esteem and value. However, this value can only be given by God, and it comes in the context of a healthy and loving relationship with Him.

With this kind of standard being raised back up by Jesus, one has to wonder—how hard does it get? In other words, if it's hard to keep hatred and lust under control, what else is expected from us? When a legal expert tested Jesus with the question, " 'Which is the greatest commandment in the law?' Jesus answered, 'Love the Lord your God with all your heart and with all your soul and with all your mind. And the second is like it: Love your neighbor as yourself. All the Law and the Prophets hang on these two commandments' " (Matthew 22:36–40; Mark 12:28–31).

These two commandments are concomitant principles. In order for us to love our neighbor, there must be a correct understanding of who we are and what it means to love ourselves; an appropriate view of self-love (valuing oneself) can only be understood in the context of a true and loving relationship with God. It is the Creator who endows us with intrinsic value and who seeks us out in order to love us. It is this intimate love relationship that must engulf our entire being, both inside and out—heart, soul, mind, and strength. According to Jesus, once we embrace God in a love relationship, love will manifest itself in the way we value and treat others.

If we are engaged in a pure, loving relationship with God, we will have no needs apart from Him. And if we are trusting God to meet every need we have, then we can love others by putting their needs first. This is how the whole of the law was condensed into the one first principle by Jesus: "In everything, do to others what you would have them do to you" (Matthew 7:12). This total abandonment—this all-consuming love of God—is a prerequisite for loving our neighbor. It is a perfect and selfless love. *It is the ultimate measure of moral goodness, and it is impossible to keep without God.* When the people heard Jesus explain the kind of standard God requires of them, they were most likely asking themselves, "What kind of a standard is this, and who could ever possibly keep it?" Jesus—knowing their hearts—left no room for misunderstandings: "Be perfect, therefore, as your heavenly Father is perfect" (Matthew 5:48).

---

[27]There were two tables of the law, and there are differing views with regard to how many laws were on each table. But there is general agreement that the first table reflected duty to God and that the second table reflected duty to other human beings.

God knows that human nature is corrupted and that it is impossible for us to be perfect. Jesus stressed this in the Sermon on the Mount! That's why toward the end of His sermon—and immediately following His first principle of ethics—Jesus said, "Enter through the narrow gate." The narrow gate He was referring to was His life and relationship with God, His Father. In John 10:9 He said, "I am the gate; whoever enters through me will be saved." Jesus understood that this first principle of ethics was humanly impossible to keep without entering into a loving relationship with Him and sharing in His life and His power. In order to understand why this is the case and what can be done about it, we need to turn to Jesus once again for His observations and guidance.

WHAT ARE JESUS' OBSERVATIONS ABOUT HUMAN NATURE?

Many things have changed in two thousand years, but one of the things that remains the same is the condition of human nature: fundamentally corrupted. Peter Kreeft observed that Western civilization is in need of an in-depth medical analysis. However, he is not referring to a physical analysis of the body.

> I mean by a medical analysis not an analysis of our material illnesses, such as poverty or starvation, but of our spiritual illnesses. It would be an analysis of the soul, not of the body; of the psyche, not of the soma [body]. It would be a cultural psychoanalysis; for civilizations, like individuals, have souls, and souls, like bodies, have diseases. Many individuals are hurting inside and going to soul doctors because our whole civilization is hurting inside. . . . It does not take a moralist to see that there is something not working in a civilization where, as C. S. Lewis says, "their rapid production of food leaves half of them starving, their aphrodisiacs make them impotent, and their labor-saving devices have banished leisure from their land."
>
> All practical philosophers, that is, all seekers of wisdom who think about what to do and how to live, say four basic things, simply because the structure of our existence is such that there are only four basic things to say, four basic questions to answer. These are the four steps of a medical analysis:
> 1. Observation of symptoms
> 2. Diagnosis of disease
> 3. Prognosis of cure
> 4. Prescription for treatment
> A four-step analysis of the human spiritual condition is in the tradition of all the great sages, the practical philosophers.[28]

---

[28]Peter Kreeft, *Back to Virtue* (San Francisco: Ignatius, 1992), 37–38, 44.

In keeping with this medical analogy, we plan to set forth Jesus' analysis of the moral condition of humanity in order to get to the root cause of human immorality. When Jesus walked this earth, He referred to Himself as a moral doctor, saying, "It is not the healthy who need a doctor, but the sick." He then went on to say, "I have not come to call the righteous, but sinners" (Matthew 9:12–13). In another passage He explained the difference between the two: "This is the verdict: Light has come into the world, but men loved darkness instead of light because their deeds were evil. Everyone who does evil hates the light, and will not come into the light for fear that his deeds will be exposed. But whoever lives by the truth comes into the light" (John 3:19–21). According to Jesus, there are only two kinds of patients: those who think that they are not patients at all and are not in need of a doctor, and those who face the truth about their moral disease and step into the physician's light (truth) in order to be cured. The former group live under the cloak of outer appearance (public image) to hide their immorality; the latter remove their cloaks by stepping into the light in order to dispel the darkness and see themselves for who they really are.

From these two passages we can note at least *six major observations that Jesus made concerning human nature.* First, Jesus declared that all people have a moral disease called sin, which He compared to darkness (evil). Second, He said He could only help people who acknowledged having this moral disease. Third, whether they acknowledge it or not, Jesus said that everyone recognizes that they are in darkness and that they love the darkness because their deeds are evil. Fourth, Jesus made clear that everyone hates the light because the light exposes their evil deeds. Jesus' fifth observation plainly states that all people have a choice to step out of the darkness and into the light. Finally, Jesus said some people choose to admit that they have a morally depraved (sinful) nature and make a decision to step out of the darkness (evil) and into the light (truth)—these are the people who know that they need a moral doctor.

We have already shown that God is the basis for absolute truth and that He is infinitely powerful, eternal, and good. It is essential to His nature to be these things, and He cannot change His nature—He is a perfect Being. It is this very fact of His perfection that raises a problem with respect to how imperfect beings like ourselves can enter into a loving relationship with a perfect God. How can people with dark (evil) natures enter into the relational presence of a Being who is perfect light (moral goodness)? The difficulty is that by the very essence of the basic differences between these two natures—one pure light, the other deep darkness—there is no way for them to coexist. In other words, without something being essentially changed in one of the natures, there is no hope of relational coexistence. People who embrace evil (darkness) cannot understand the true goodness and perfection (light) of God (John 1:5). Since God cannot change (Malachi 3:6; James 1:17) and since not even a hint of darkness can exist in pure light, there is a big issue that must be resolved in order for God and humanity to coexist in a loving relationship. This explanation may help us to comprehend the purpose for which Jesus stated He was born and how He came to offer the only solution to this fundamental chasm between God and humanity.

We cannot forget that God is also perfectly just, and since He cannot change, His justice requires that there be a punishment for violating His laws. Yet God is also loving and merciful, and realizing that it is impossible for us to change our own nature (the internal impurity of the human heart), there needs to be a solution that satisfies all of His attributes. He must find a way—through His love and mercy—to satisfy the just part of His nature as well. Since He is just, He *must* judge the evil deeds of humanity, and since He is loving and merciful, He *must* somehow offer forgiveness to us for the evil deeds we do. Jesus Christ offered Himself as the solution to this troublesome problem. In order for us to fully appreciate the answer Jesus offers to each one of us with respect to our relationship with God, we need to take a closer look at what He said about our condition.

WHAT IS JESUS' DIAGNOSIS OF THE CONDITION OF HUMANITY?

Since we will be using the terms *conscience, sin,* and *guilt,* we must ensure a basic understanding of what these words mean. *Conscience* has been defined as the "process of thought, which distinguishes between morally good or bad, commending the good, condemning the bad, and so prompting to do the former and avoid the latter."[29] We are using this word in the same manner the apostle Paul did when he said of all humanity that "the requirements of the [moral] law are written on their hearts, their consciences also bearing witness, and their thoughts now accusing, now even defending them" (Romans 2:15). So God's moral laws are written on every human heart, and to willfully violate His laws is what we mean by the term *sin. Guilt* is the mental awareness that we have broken one or more of those laws and therefore stand condemned by God.

If treated properly, this internal shame or guilt will bring us to the point

---

[29]W. E. Vine, *An Expository Dictionary of New Testament Words* (New York: Thomas Nelson, 1985), 122.

where we acknowledge the need for God's help. But this dimension of morality is often rationalized away or misunderstood. This internal dimension is sometimes referred to as *self-esteem* or *self-respect*. It has to do with having the right sense of valuing ourselves and being secure with who we are—our identity. The proper understanding of self and having a sense that we are truly valued can bring inner peace and harmony deep within the very core of our being. On the other hand, an improper understanding of self, or having the wrong kind of self-love, along with embracing a sense of not being valued, can cause deep psychological damage and breed inner confusion. So if we are to love our neighbors as ourselves, we must not listen to the lies of the rational-emotive and other cognitive therapies that say *"our feelings of guilt and shame are basically our own doing,* the results of our distorted thoughts and irrationality; we should learn how to get rid of them."[30] One of the most dangerous things we can do is to jettison legitimate feelings of guilt and shame. By "legitimate" we mean those feelings that are the direct result of breaking one or more of the commandments of God.

According to Jesus, a correct view of self and relational harmony with God will lead to a life of integrity through the internal development of the virtues. It is this inner strength of character that will foster right relationships with others. However, an improper view of self and relational disharmony with God will lead to a life of corruption through indulging in the vices. It is this internal corruption of self that will foster improper relationships with others. Every time we choose virtue over vice or vice over virtue, we are turning our hearts into something a little different than what it was before. When we take this truth and string it out over a lifetime, what Peter Kreeft noted makes sense. He cites the poet Samuel Smiles:

> Sow a thought, reap an act.
> Sow an act, reap a habit.
> Sow a habit, reap a character,
> Sow a character, reap a destiny.[31]

In order to keep ourselves from a destiny that leads us away from God and into darkness, it is necessary to deal with the root cause of our immorality. To find the root cause of our moral depravity, we must look beyond our actions or behavior and within ourselves—the thoughts of our minds and the attitudes of our hearts. Jesus said that the violation of God's moral law does not begin

---

[30]Schimmel, *The Seven Deadly Sins: Jewish, Christian, and Classical Reflections on Human Psychology*, 7–8 (emphasis added).
[31]Kreeft, *Back to Virtue*, 169.

with an immoral action but rather with an immoral heart attitude. For example, we may never murder anyone or commit adultery, but if we hate someone or have a lustful heart, then the law of God has already been broken, even though the act has not yet been consummated. In other words, if we consistently hate our neighbor, we have already murdered the relationship with him or her in our heart. In the same manner, if we continually lust after someone, the person is seen by us as an object or thing to be possessed and used rather than as a person with whom to build a healthy relationship. In both cases the end result is the devaluation of the other person, which constitutes a violation of God's relational moral laws.

It may be difficult for us to imagine how Jesus can call hatred and lust sins and put them on the same level as murder and adultery. If His statements baffle you, you are not alone. C. S. Lewis admitted that he had always been puzzled when he read Christian writers who seemed to be very strict at one moment and very free at another. He said,

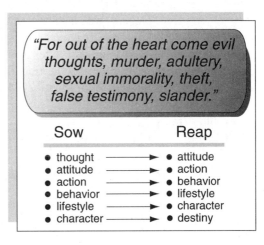

"For out of the heart come evil thoughts, murder, adultery, sexual immorality, theft, false testimony, slander."

Sow		Reap
thought	→	attitude
attitude	→	action
action	→	behavior
behavior	→	lifestyle
lifestyle	→	character
character	→	destiny

They talk about mere sins of thought as if they were immensely important: and then they talk about the most frightful murders and treacheries as if you had only to repent and all would be forgiven. But I have come to see that they are right. *What they are always thinking of is the mark which the action leaves on that tiny central self which no ones sees in this life but which each of us will have to endure—or enjoy—forever.* One man may be so placed that his anger sheds the blood of thousands, and another so placed that however angry he gets he will only be laughed at. *But the little mark on the soul may be much the same in both.* Each has done something to himself which, unless he repents, will make it harder for him to keep out of the rage the next time he is tempted, and will make the rage worse when he does fall into it. Each of them, if he seriously turns to God, can have that twist in the central man straightened out again: each is, in the long run, doomed if he will not. The bigness or smallness of the thing, seen from the outside, is not what really matters.[32]

---

[32]Lewis, *Mere Christianity*, 87 (emphasis added).

The people to whom Jesus was speaking had lowered the relational standard of God's moral law to a level that made them appear moral on the outside. But as Lewis pointed out, it is the mark on the soul that really counts. Jesus applied the standard to the root of where immorality begins—on the inside. The religious leaders of His day refused to acknowledge their hardened internal condition and applied God's standard to the outside in an effort to appear morally good to others. These leaders were teaching people that righteousness was all about keeping a list of do's and don'ts—external rules and regulations. They had their outer appearance nicely polished, and to the human eye they looked like the epitome of moral goodness. In reality, however, they actually *lowered* God's true standard, which called for an internal and relationally pure attitude of the heart. You can imagine how shocked they were, along with the crowd, when they heard Jesus say, "I tell you that unless your righteousness surpasses that of the Pharisees and the teachers of the law, you will certainly not enter the kingdom of heaven" (Matthew 5:20). In case they were too dull to catch the import of that statement, Jesus later called them sons of hell, blind guides, blind fools, greedy, self-indulgent, snakes, a brood of vipers, white-washed tombs, clean on the outside but rotting and dirty on the inside, and full of wickedness (Matthew 23).

Jesus' diagnosis of the root cause of sin (as manifested by guilt) was summarized by Him in one statement: "For *out of the heart* come evil thoughts, murder, adultery, sexual immorality, theft, false testimony, slander" (Matthew 15:19, emphasis added). He went directly to the locus of the problem of immorality and knew that everyone understood what He was talking about—all people stand guilty before God. C. S. Lewis said it quite appropriately: "All men alike stand condemned, not by alien codes of ethics, but by their own, and all men therefore are conscious of guilt."[33]

Jesus' verdict was even worse than we can imagine, because He said that we also love the darkness (our sin) and that we are afraid of being exposed by the light (truth). Some people refuse to listen to the inner testimony of the moral law and harden their hearts toward what they know to be the truth. However, some people are willing to confess that Jesus is right and step into the light to live by the truth. There is a clear choice that each of us must make—darkness or light.

WHAT IS JESUS' PROGNOSIS OF AND PRESCRIPTION FOR HUMANITY?

A prognosis involves two things: a prediction of the probable course of a disease in a patient and the prescription or sequence of action needed to

---

[33]Lewis, *The Problem of Pain*, 21.

achieve recovery. Jesus was quite forthright about the results of treating or not treating this moral disease called sin. He issued a warning about the nature of the disease in that it is terminal—if left untreated the result would be death. However He was not referring to mere physical death but rather to permanent relational death with God—a death that will last forever. In fact, the relational death is a reality right now. All of us are living in a state of guilt and have a conscious knowledge that we are standing condemned by God for breaking His moral laws. Jesus said that He did not come to earth to condemn us; we already stand condemned before God (John 3:17–18). Rather, He said He came to save us from having to pay the penalty we incurred by having broken God's moral law. Jesus said that all humanity stands condemned and that this life on earth is like being on death row. We are just waiting for the execution of the sentence to take place and what we need is to be pardoned—saved from death—to be set free (John 8:32).

To better appreciate the prognosis and prescription of Jesus, it will be necessary for us to spend some time on developing a biblically accurate and experientially sound perspective concerning the condition of humanity. The Bible tells us that we are created in the image of God—i.e., we are rational, psychological, volitional, and spiritual. The Bible also informs us that the first created humans (Adam and Eve) disobeyed God and severed their intimate relationship with Him. As a result, every human being has inherited what the Bible refers to as a sinful nature (original sin). All of us are born relationally dead to God, and, therefore, our basic inclinations are selfish and evil by our very nature. In other words, it seems self-evident that all of us are engaged in a personal struggle with sin and vice starting at an extremely early age when we become aware of what is right and what is wrong. Just consider the fact that no one has to teach a young child how to disobey or how to be selfish; it is in that child's very nature.

We all understand this inner conflict and what it means to live under the pretense of appearing to be someone we're really not. Duplicity produces an intense inner struggle as noted by one author:

> All of us are engaged to one degree or another in a personal, ongoing battle with sin and vice, although we may not think of our conflicts with our natures in those terms. Although our anger doesn't make most of us murderers, our lust doesn't make most of us rapists, and our greed and envy don't make most of us outright criminals, they, together with gluttony, arrogance, and sloth, *often make us and those who have to live with us miserable.* Moreover, when we give in to our low passions we debase our humanity. Our failure to live up to the best we can morally be is as tragic

as the unhappiness our evil causes. . . . Every deadly sin fuels harmful social phenomena: lust—pornography; gluttony—substance abuse; envy—terrorism; anger—violence; sloth—indifference to the pain and sufferings of others; greed—abuse of public trust; and pride—discrimination.[34]

If this is correct—and we believe there is sufficient evidence to show that it is—then sins against oneself cannot be divorced from sins against one's neighbor. Seemingly innocent and apparently "victimless" sins have tragic consequences. This is true not only for the individual who commits the sin but for those who are affected by that sin as well. With respect to the seven deadly sins mentioned above it has often been said that the sin of pride stands above the rest. Solomon Schimmel explains that through the centuries Christian theologians and devotional writers classified pride as the "deadliest" of the seven deadly sins. He refers to the medieval writer Gregory the Great, saying,

> Gregory did not include pride as one of the seven cardinal sins, but rather considered that it breeds the seven, which in turn breed a multitude of other vices. It is not difficult to see how *pride* leads to the other sins. The arrogant person who thinks so highly of himself believes himself entitled to what his heart desires, whether in the social or in the material sphere. Since he expects deference he is easily *angered* when he doesn't receive it. Assuming himself superior to others, he is especially prone to *envy*, which is a response to threats to one's self-esteem. Being self-satisfied the proud person does not feel compelled to activate himself in the pursuit of spiritual goals, and so commits the sin of *sloth*. Believing his "eminence" to be an entitlement, he will easily trample over the rights of others, as is so frequently done by the *greedy*, the *gluttonous*, and the *lustful*. It is not that pride inevitably leads to these vices, or that all manifestations of these vices are effects of pride. However, since these are frequently the case, Gregory accorded pride a separate status, designating it the mother and Queen of all vices.[35]

Pride is an inherent part of human nature and it is constantly at work trying to put us first, not only before other people but also before God. When this happens, we remove God from the picture and place ourselves at center-stage. When C. S. Lewis wrote about the uniqueness of Christian morality, he addressed the most repulsive of all the vices: pride.

---

[34]Schimmel, *The Seven Deadly Sins: Jewish, Christian, and Classical Reflections on Human Psychology*, 3–4 (emphasis added).
[35]Ibid., 33–34.

Today I come to that part of Christian morals where they differ most sharply from all other morals. There is one vice of which no man in the world is free; which every one in the world loathes when he sees it in someone else; and of which hardly any people, except Christians, ever imagine that they are guilty themselves. I have heard people admit that they are bad-tempered, or that they cannot keep their heads about girls or drink, or even that they are cowards. I do not think I have ever heard anyone who was not a Christian accuse himself of this vice. And at the same time I have very seldom met anyone, who was not a Christian, who showed the slightest mercy to it in others. There is no fault which makes a man more unpopular, and no fault which we are more unconscious of in ourselves. And the more we have it ourselves, the more we dislike it in others.

The vice I am talking about is Pride or Self-Conceit: and the virtue opposite to it, in Christian morals, is called Humility. . . . According to Christian teachers, the essential vice, the utmost evil, is Pride. . . . Pride leads to every other vice: it is the complete anti-God state of mind. . . . The Christians are right: it is Pride which has been the chief cause of misery in every nation and every family since the world began. . . . As long as you are proud you cannot know God. A proud man is always looking down on things and people: and, of course, as long as you are looking down, you cannot see something that is above you [God].[36]

From the creation of humanity and throughout all of recorded history, humans have somehow thought that putting oneself first and living a life apart from God would bring ultimate peace and happiness. Lewis commented on this hopeless and superficial endeavor:

Out of that hopeless attempt has come nearly all that we call history—money, poverty, ambition, war, prostitution, classes, empires, slavery—the long terrible story of man trying to find something other than God which will make him happy. The reason why it can never succeed is this. God made us: invented us as a man invents an engine. A car is made to run on gasoline, and it would not run properly on anything else. Now God designed the human machine to run on Himself. . . . God cannot give us happiness and peace apart from Himself, because it is not there. There is no such thing.

That is the key to history. Terrific energy is expended—civilizations are built up—excellent institutions devised; but each time something goes wrong. Some fatal flaw always brings the selfish and cruel people to the

---

[36]Lewis, *Mere Christianity*, 108–11.

top and it all slides back into misery and ruin. In fact, the machine conks. It seems to start up all right and runs a few yards, and then it breaks down. They are trying to run it on the wrong juice.[37]

God designed us to operate on Him and gave each one of us a moral nature—the sense of right and wrong—to help us stay on the right path. Throughout history there have been people trying to obey that moral sense in varying degrees. Yet, as Lewis said, "None of them ever quite make it." God also selected a group of people with whom He spent centuries "hammering into their heads the sort of God He was—that there was only one of Him and that He cared about right conduct. The people were the Jews and the Old Testament gives an account of the hammering process."[38] Even God's chosen people just could not seem to get it right. Then along comes Jesus who says, "God so loved the world that he gave his one and only Son, that whoever believes in him shall not perish but have eternal life" (John 3:16). When Jesus described the darkness of the human heart and the need to step into and live in the light (truth), He was referring to Himself: "I am the light of the world. Whoever follows me will never walk in darkness, but will have the light of life" (John 8:12).

To follow Jesus clearly calls for the death of pride or self-centeredness: "If anyone would come after me, he must deny himself and take up his cross daily and follow me" (Luke 9:23). Facing the truth about our own selfish nature will bring true liberation; Jesus promised, "You will know the truth, and the truth will set you free" (John 8:32).

Jesus said that He was born for two specific reasons. First, He came into this world to "give his life as a ransom for many" (Matthew 20:28). In other words, He came to pay the penalty for our sins, of which pride or self-centeredness is primary, and if we accept His payment for our sins, we can be pardoned by God and released from death row. Second, in a strong statement to Pilate, Jesus said, "For this reason I was born, and for this I came into the world, to testify to the truth. Everyone on the side of truth listens to me" (John 18:37). When Jesus speaks, He speaks the truth, and those who listen to Him are the ones who stand on the side of truth and step into the light. The Moral Doctor has spoken and offers the only cure—*Himself.*

Jesus' prescription to remedy eternal death (relational separation from God forever) is eternal life. Since we were born relationally or spiritually dead to God because of our corrupted human nature, we are utterly powerless to do any-

---

[37]Ibid., 53–54.
[38]Ibid., 54.

thing about it. There is only one cure that can help a dead person, and that cure is life! That life is the life that only Jesus can give. It is the truth that Jesus proclaimed over and over again—the truth that He is the only cure for the moral disease called sin. The only way to begin a new life in a loving relationship with God is His way. This is why Jesus said, "I am the way and the truth and the life. No one comes to the Father except through me" (John 14:6).

Sometimes there is only one path that leads to the top of the mountain; sometimes there is only one answer to a problem; sometimes a disease only has one cure. This is one of those times. Jesus presented Himself as the only cure for a morally sick and dying world; Jesus prescribed Himself as the medication to take in order to be cured and have eternal life. The medication for life eternal costs us nothing; it is a gift from God to us, freely dispensed by the grace of God. "For it is by grace you have been saved, through faith—and this not from yourselves, it is the gift of God—not by works, so that no one can boast" (Ephesians 2:8–9).

The nature of God is immutable: He is holy and just, yet He is also loving and merciful. Since He cannot change His nature, His justice requires that a penalty be paid for the sins of humanity. Jesus provided that payment at Calvary (1 Peter 2:24; 3:18) in a perfect and selfless act of love. Jesus, in grace and mercy, offered Himself as ransom for anyone willing to follow Him. When anyone decides to truly follow Him, they are put under the "protective umbrella" of Jesus Christ[39] and are shielded from the holiness and justice of God. The permanent cure that Jesus prescribed for His patients must be accepted by an act of faith on their part.

Once Jesus' payment is accepted by faith, the positive prognosis is assured, and the healing will begin. This process is described by God: "I will give you a new heart and put a new spirit in you; I will remove from you your heart of stone and give you a heart of flesh. And I will put my Spirit in you and move you to follow my decrees and be careful to keep my laws. . . . I will put my laws in their minds and write them on their hearts. I will be their God, and they will be my people" (Ezekiel 36:26–27; Hebrews 8:10).

True moral goodness begins on the inside with a new heart empowered by the Spirit of God to follow His laws, which are the ethical prescriptions necessary to engage in right and meaningful relationships (see Romans 8:2–4). If, however, the permanent cure of Jesus is rejected, then true moral goodness cannot be achieved, and those who reject Jesus must face God's holiness and justice on their own.

---

[39]See chapter 13 to understand the significance of the deity of Jesus Christ.

We have now completed the application of the test methodology to the three worldviews under examination in this work, with respect to the topics of truth, the cosmos, God (*Logos*), law, evil, and ethics.[40] The conclusions of our investigation show that atheism and pantheism fail to pass the test for truth. Consequently, as we look to answer the question of meaning, we turn to the worldview of theism, specifically Christian theism, which possesses the true view of reality. In the two chapters that follow, we will discuss how accepting or rejecting Jesus as the permanent cure for sin will have consequences in both this life and the next.

	Atheism	Pantheism	Theism
Truth	Relative, No Absolutes	Relative to This World	Absolute Truth Exists
Cosmos	Always Existed	Not Real– Illusion	Created Reality
God (Logos)	Does Not Exist	Exists, Unknowable	Exists, Knowable
Law	Relative, Determined by Humanity	Relative to This World	Absolute, Objective, Discovered
Evil	Human Ignorance	Not Real– Illusion	Selfish Heart
Ethics	Created by Humanity, Situational	Relative, Transcends Good/Evil	Absolute, Objective, Prescriptive

---

[40]See chapter 2 for reviewing the method of testing the truth claims of worldviews.

—15—
QUESTIONS ABOUT TRUE MEANING AND HEAVEN

The unexamined life is not worth living.

—SOCRATES

WHAT GIVES ULTIMATE MEANING TO LIFE?[1]

God loves us and cares about our contentment with respect to finding ultimate meaning, beginning in this life and culminating in the next. However, ultimate meaning cannot be found apart from God Himself. As we have established, ultimate fulfillment does not depend upon external things—what we do or what we possess; rather, it depends upon the internal state of our being— who we are. In chapter 14 we referred to C. S. Lewis's analogy of a car engine needing to run on gasoline because it was designed that way. In the same manner, God designed us to run on Himself, and apart from Him there can be no ultimate meaning—only temporary states of superficial fulfillment. To accept the permanent cure for sin that Jesus offers and to begin to have God work on

---

[1]In responding to the questions raised in chapters 15 and 16, we have incorporated many profound thoughts from the writings of C. S. Lewis. The majority of citations were taken from *Mere Christianity*, *The Problem of Pain*, and *The Great Divorce*. If you have never read these works, we highly recommend them.

the internal part of our being is to take the first step on the journey to finding life.

The journey with God begins by replacing the old corrupted value system of our former ways with a new set of values—God's. This first step is analogous to entering a gate, and we have already examined how and why Jesus claimed to be that gate. Once we come inside by accepting Jesus as the permanent cure for our moral depravity, we can begin to have true peace with God and enter into a loving relationship with Him. God designed and created us and knows both the general and specific purposes for our lives, and He will reveal those purposes through the process of permanently transforming our character.

No matter what we have done or what has been done to us, God's prescription for us is perfect because it has a fundamental ingredient known as *redemption*. Redemption is the promise that "in all things God works for the good of those who love him, who have been called according to his purpose" (Romans 8:28). The purpose of those who are loved by God and who love Him is also clearly articulated by God. He has called those He loves to be "conformed to the likeness of his Son" (Romans 8:29). Everyone who is loved by Him and who loves Him back is to become like His Son, Jesus Christ. How God accomplishes this purpose is up to Him, but true believers can be sure of one thing: what God sets out to accomplish, neither any person on this planet nor any power in the spirit realm can stop!

God always has the final say in everything, which is good news for the true believer. He is able to take even the most destitute lives and redeem their sufferings in order to accomplish greater good. We need only to look at Jesus— His life, death, and resurrection—to see this in action. An honest examination of the teachings, life, and passion of Jesus reveals that no one can thwart the purposes of God; He is in sovereign control of all that exists—both the living and the dead.

Technically speaking, since Jesus is the only person to live a sinless life (John 8:46), He is also the only one who has experienced truly "innocent suffering" at the hands of evil men. When the arrest party came to apprehend Jesus, Peter (His disciple) tried to take control of Jesus' destiny by the use of violence. Peter picked up his sword and used it in an effort to exert his own will over God's will and purposes for Jesus. Yet Jesus knew the plan His Father had for His life and said to Peter, "Do you think I cannot call on my Father, and he will at once put at my disposal more than twelve legions of angels?" (Matthew 26:53). Twelve legions of angels is somewhere between thirty-six thousand and seventy-two thousand angels—more than enough fighting power! However, Jesus chose not to call upon his Father to rescue Him, but to trust His Father's purposes for His life in every situation, even in death.

Jesus knew His Father loved Him and was sovereign over all things. Even when Pilate tried to get Jesus to stand down and submit to the power and authority of Rome by answering his questions, Jesus refused to be swayed. When Pilate said, "Don't you realize I have the power either to free you or to crucify you?" Jesus answered, "You would have no power over me if it were not given to you from above" (John 19:10–11).

Jesus teaches us that God has ultimate control even when evil people commit cruel and unjust acts. People who exercise their free will to act in wicked ways will never be able to interfere with God's plan. Hence, all who truly believe in God and submit to being a part of His purposes can never have the meaning of life stripped away—no matter what evil people do to them. In chapter 11 we quoted the following passage from C. S. Lewis, who concisely stated what we are attempting to say. Commenting on how God even uses the free will of the wicked to accomplish His purposes, Lewis said,

> The crucifixion itself is the best, as well as the worst, of all historical events, but the role of Judas remains simply evil. We may apply this first to the problem of other people's suffering. A merciful man aims at his neighbor's good and so does "God's will," consciously co-operating with "the simple good." A cruel man oppresses his neighbor, and so does simple evil. But in doing such evil, he is used by God, without his own knowledge or consent, to produce the complex good—so that the first man serves God as a son, and the second as a tool. For you will certainly carry out God's purpose, however you act, but it makes a difference to you whether you serve like Judas or like John.[2]

The choice is up to us. We can voluntarily be intimately involved in the purposes of God—like John. Or we can choose to act out our own purposes in this life, which God will ultimately use for His own ends anyway—like Judas. Either way, God's purposes *will* be accomplished; the difference it makes will matter only to us, will be experienced by us, and will be decided by us. The time to decide is now, while God gives us the freedom to choose, for when all is said and done and we come to the end of our lives, He will have the final word.

For unbelievers, if any purpose has been found in this life, it will end at death. For believers, however, death is merely the doorway to what God has planned for them. It is the resurrection of Christ that teaches us that God's ultimate purposes do not end with death, for it was in the death and resurrec-

---

[2]Lewis, *The Problem of Pain*, 111.

tion of His Son that God demonstrated His sovereignty and power over death by working all things for the greater good—and now all may have the opportunity of eternal life. This kind of hope can only be experienced by "the obedience that comes from faith" in Jesus Christ (Romans 1:5). If we believe in Jesus and reverently submit ourselves in obedience to God, He will not only redeem our lives from past failures and sufferings but also give us a future purpose and hope—true meaning. This is what He did, just as the Word of God says:

> During the days of Jesus' life on earth, he offered up prayers and petitions with loud cries and tears to the one who could save him from death, and he was heard because of his reverent submission. Although he was a son, *he learned obedience from what he suffered and, once made perfect, he became the source of eternal salvation for all who obey him.* (Hebrews 5:7–9, emphasis added)

God's plan was not to rescue Jesus from the hands of evil men, but instead to rescue Him from the hands of death itself! In defeating death, Jesus made it possible for us to do the same—to submit to God's plan and abandon ourselves into His loving arms. Jesus experienced fulfillment during the days of His life on earth as He obeyed the will of His Father. Yet the culmination of that meaning was not achieved until after His death. The Bible says that Jesus "for the joy set before him endured the cross, scorning its shame, and sat down at the right hand of the throne of God" (Hebrews 12:2).

Ultimate meaning is all about entering into the ultimate relationship with the Ultimate, a love relationship with the God who *is* love (1 John 4:16). Jesus said, "This is eternal life: that they may know you [God the Father], the only true God, and Jesus Christ, whom you have sent" (John 17:3). The knowledge Jesus was speaking of is not just head knowledge but rather a sound relational knowledge of God through Jesus Christ. This knowledge signifies an intimate union with God that brings about eternal life. Eternal life is not a quantity or length of time; it is a quality of life, shared with—and lived for—God. *Since God is the ultimate reality, being loved by Him and loving Him in response will bring ultimate meaning into our lives now and forevermore.*

WHY CAN'T TRUE MEANING BE FOUND APART FROM GOD?

Being conformed to the image of Jesus Christ (character development in this life) is certainly one of God's foremost purposes for every believer. With respect to finding ultimate meaning, we must consider what Thomas Aquinas called *the principle of finality*, which states that "every agent acts for an end."[3] In other words, God created us with a specific end in mind, and that end has to do with His glory and our true happiness. Without God we will merely achieve temporary states of superficial fulfillment in this life. In his book *Desiring God*, John Piper declares,

> The longing to be happy is a universal human experience, and it is good, not sinful. We should never try to deny or resist our longing to be happy, as though it were a bad impulse. Instead we should seek to intensify this longing and nourish it with whatever will provide the deepest and most enduring satisfaction. The deepest and most enduring happiness is found only in God. *The happiness we find in God reaches its consummation when it is shared with others in the manifold ways of love.* To the extent we try to abandon the pursuit of our own pleasure, we fail to honor God and love people. Or, to put it positively: *the pursuit of pleasure is a necessary part of all worship and virtue.* [As elaborated by the *Westminster Shorter Catechism of Faith*,]

> *The chief end of man is to glorify God and to enjoy Him forever.*[4]

How can the chief end of humanity be wrapped up in giving glory to God? Furthermore, how can glorifying God bring enjoyment or happiness?[5] It seems as though it's hard enough to find true meaning and achieve true happiness in a free society like ours; one that offers virtually unlimited things and ways to get those things. If it's hard to be happy in our own free society, how about people who have had their freedom denied? What would happen if our freedom were taken away along with our dignity? No freedom, no family, no possessions, and no honor or identity? Without these things, why bother with meaning? How can God be factored into lives that have been robbed of every important and meaningful thing this world has to offer? Well, as odd as it may seem, the more "things" we have in this world, the harder it is to find true meaning and happiness.

Viktor Frankl, a survivor of the Holocaust, wrote about his experiences in the context of trying to find true meaning in life. He told of his own sufferings at the hands of the Nazis and shared with his readers what it was like to have

---

[3]Norman L. Geisler, *Thomas Aquinas: An Evangelical Appraisal* (Grand Rapids, Mich.: Baker, 1991), 74.

[4]John Piper, *Desiring God* (Portland: Multnomah, 1986), 23 (emphasis added).

[5]It would be beyond the scope of this work to delineate what it means to take pleasure in knowing and glorifying God. If you are interested in following up on this concept, we suggest *Knowing God* by J. I. Packer (Downers Grove, Ill.: InterVarsity, 1973), or *Desiring God* by John Piper.

his freedom, family, and self-respect instantaneously stripped away. Frankl re-called how the Nazis treated their prisoners and took away from them every last thing of value this world had to offer, including their human dignity. One day—in the pre-dawn darkness and bitter cold temperature—Frankl was or-dered to join the ranks of a certain work detail. As he and the other prisoners were marching out to the work site, Frankl remembers thinking about his wife and their love for one another. Please follow this citation closely in order to grasp the depth of Frankl's insights. While marching out to the work site that day Frankl said,

> A thought transfixed me: for the first time in my life I saw the truth as it is set into song by so many poets, proclaimed as the final wisdom by so many thinkers. The truth—that love is the ultimate and the highest goal to which man can aspire. Then I grasped the meaning of the greatest secret that human poetry and human thought and belief have to impart: *The salvation of man is through love and in love.* I understood how a man who has nothing left in this world still may know bliss, be it only in a brief moment, in the contemplation of his beloved. In a position of utter deso-lation, when man cannot express himself in positive action, when his only achievement may consist of enduring his sufferings in the right way—an honorable way—in such a position man can, through loving contempla-tion of the image he carries of his beloved, achieve fulfillment. For the first time in my life I was able to understand the meaning of the words, *"The angels are lost in the perpetual contemplation of an infinite glory."* ... My mind still clung to the image of my wife. A thought crossed my mind: I didn't even know if she were still alive. I knew only one thing—which I have learned well by now: *Love goes very far beyond the physical person of the beloved. It finds its deepest meaning in his spiritual being, his inner self.*
>
> Another time we were at work in a trench. The dawn was gray around us; gray was the sky above; gray the snow in the pale light of dawn; gray the rags in which my fellow prisoners were clad, and gray their faces. I was again conversing silently with my wife, or perhaps I was struggling to find the *reason* for my sufferings, my slow dying. In a last violent protest against the hopelessness of imminent death, I sensed my spirit piercing through the enveloping gloom. *I felt it transcend that hopeless, meaningless world, and from somewhere I heard a victorious "Yes" in answer to my question of the existence of an ultimate purpose.* At that moment a light was lit in a distant farmhouse, which stood on the horizon as if painted there, in the midst of the misery and gray of a dawning morning in Bavaria. *"Et lux in tenebris lucet"*—and the light shineth in the darkness. ... *It is this spiritual freedom— that cannot be taken away—that makes life meaningful and purposeful.* ... A few days after the liberation [of Auschwitz], I walked through the country

past flowering meadows, for miles and miles, towards a market town near the camp. Larks rose to the sky and I could hear their joyous song. There was no one to be seen for miles around; there was nothing but the wide earth and sky—and then I went down on my knees. . . . I had but one sentence in mind—always the same: *"I called to the Lord from my narrow prison and He answered me."*

We all said to each other in camp that *there could be no earthly happiness which could compensate us for all we had suffered. We were not hoping for happiness—it was not that which gave us courage and gave meaning to our suffering, our sacrifices and our dying. . . .* But for every one of the liberated prisoners, the day comes when, looking back on his camp experiences, he can no longer understand how he endured it all. As the day of his liberation eventually came, when everything seemed to him like a beautiful dream, so also the day comes when all his camp experiences seem to him like a nightmare. *The crowning experience of all, for the homecoming man, is the wonderful feeling that, after all he has suffered, there is nothing he need fear any more—except his God.*[6]

What an amazing analysis of how meaning cannot be found apart from putting God into the equation! Indirectly, the Nazis helped Frankl to see that God has a better set of values that cannot be embraced by us until we see why they are more meaningful than anything this world has to offer. An eternal God offers eternal values that transcend the things of this world; therefore, in order to get our focus off this world and on Him and His purposes, He sometimes has to remove the worldly obstacles that so easily

> ### I Asked God
> *(Anonymous Letter to Ann Landers)*
>
> I asked God for strength, that I might achieve.
> I was made weak, that I might learn to obey.
> I asked for health, that I might do greater things.
> I was given infirmity, that I might do better things.
> I asked for riches, that I might be happy.
> I was given poverty, that I might be wise.
> I asked for power, that I might have the praise of men.
> I was given weakness, that I might feel the need for God.
> I asked for all things, that I might enjoy life.
> I was given life, that I might enjoy all things.
> I got nothing that I asked for, but everything I hoped for.
> Almost despite myself, my unspoken prayers were answered.
> I, among all men, am most richly blessed.

block our vision of Him and of what is truly valuable or meaningful.

With the right perspective, true believers can see their trials and sufferings as the tools God uses to carve out the image of His Son in their lives. Just as

[6]Viktor Frankl, *Man's Search for Meaning* (New York: Simon & Schuster, 1984), 56–58, 60, 87, 111, 114–15 (emphasis added).

the Italian Renaissance artist Michelangelo had to chip away at a raw block of stone to reveal the image of David inside, so too with God. When God looks at believers, He sees the embedded image of His Son and begins to chip away at vices and meaningless things of this world in order to reveal that image. Believers should not be focused on the chipping process but rather on the higher good and virtues that God has in mind. Remembering that we are ultimately made for heaven and not for this earth helps to ease the pains and sufferings of this life. C. S. Lewis said,

> The Christian view [of this world] is that men were created to be in a certain relationship with God (if we are in that relation to Him, the right relation to one another will follow inevitably). Christ said it was difficult for "the rich" to enter the Kingdom of Heaven,[7] referring, no doubt, to "riches" in the ordinary sense. But I think it really covers riches in every sense—good fortune, health, popularity, and all the things one wants to have. All these things tend—just as money tends—to make you feel independent of God, because if you have them you are happy already and contented in this life. You don't want to turn away to anything more, and so you try to rest in the shadow of happiness as if it could last forever. But God wants to give you a real and eternal happiness. Consequently He may have to take all these "riches" away from you: if He doesn't you will go on relying on them. It sounds cruel, doesn't it? But I am beginning to find out that what people call the cruel doctrines are really the kindest ones in the long run. . . . If you think of this world as a place intended simply for our happiness, you find it quite intolerable: think of it as a place of training and correction and it's not so bad. So what seems the ugly doctrine is one that comforts and strengthens you in the end.[8]

There are two ultimate ends: pleasing God or pleasing ourselves. When believers choose God over their own interests, a strange thing begins to happen. They begin to value the things that God values and desire the things that He

---

[7]Matthew 19:23; Mark 10:23; Luke 18:24.
[8]Lewis, *God in the Dock*, 51–52.

desires. For this reason, as they continue to take delight in God, He begins to fulfill their deepest longings. This is what the Bible means when it says, "Delight yourself in the LORD and he will give you the desires of your heart" (Psalm 37:4). As God changes the hearts of true believers—and with it their values—they truly begin to desire that for which they were made: God Himself. In doing so, they also begin to be conformed to the image of God's Son and display His glory in their lives; in this way they actually get the best of both this world and heaven. As so aptly put by C. S. Lewis: "Aim at Heaven and you will get 'earth thrown in': aim at earth and you will get neither."[9]

WHY CAN'T TRUE HAPPINESS BE FOUND IN THIS WORLD ALONE?

Before answering this question, we need to probe deeper into what is meant by the concept of happiness. In his book *Written on the Heart*, J. Budziszewski examines the various definitions of happiness and notes that there are basically four competing opinions. He uses Aristotle's knowledge as a filter to separate truth from error, revealing that Aristotle looked for the grain of truth mixed with the chaff (error) in each definition of happiness. Citing Aristotle's evaluation, he says,

> Is there some *highest* human good? If there is no highest human good—if we seek literally every good for the sake of some other—we might as well give up trying to give rational order to our lives, for we are like hamsters that run and run in their little wheels but never get anywhere. If there is a highest human good, however, we would do well to discover it. . . . The highest human good would have two qualities. First, other goods would be sought for its sake; second, it would be sought for its own sake. What do we know that's like that? Aristotle points out that almost everyone, in all times and places, gives the same answer to that question: happiness. . . .
>
> Aristotle accepts the idea that the greatest human good is happiness. But he immediately points out that it needs refinement. The reason is that the common opinion of mankind is not in agreement about what happiness is. However, the number of competing views is small:
> Definition 1: Happiness is *pleasure*.
> Definition 2: Happiness is *honor*.
> Definition 3: Happiness is *virtue*, or excellence.
> Definition 4: Happiness is *bodily and external goods*, such as health and wealth. . . .

---

[9]Lewis, *Mere Christianity*, 118.

Aristotle . . . considers whether in each one of the four opinions there might be a grain of truth mixed with chaff. If he can sift out the chaff, he can grind the grain into flour and bake bread.

Definition 1: Happiness is pleasure. *Grain:* No one would call a man happy who never experienced any pleasure at all. *Chaff:* Still, can we really say pleasure is the *same* as happiness? Unhappiness in the midst of pleasure is a common experience; it seems that, ultimately, mere satisfaction is unsatisfying. Not only that, pleasure comes and goes. By contrast we think of true happiness as something abiding, something that characterizes a whole life. Apparently pleasure is not the essence of happiness but merely its accompaniment or by-product.

Definition 2: Happiness is honor. *Grain:* No one would call a man happy who never received any honor for his excellences. *Chaff:* But even a seeker of honor admits that to be honored by other people for excellences that he knew he did not possess would be a hollow experience. So he does not want honor for its own sake after all; what he really wants is to *merit* honor. Besides, honor depends on those who confer it, and what is conferred can be taken away. But, as we said above, we think of true happiness as something abiding, something difficult to take away.

Definition 3: Happiness is virtue, or excellence. *Grain:* Unlike pleasure, virtue is abiding, and, unlike honor, it cannot be taken away by others. Not only that, we saw on closer examination that what the honor-seeker really wants is to merit honor. But one *merits* honor by possessing the virtues. *Chaff:* Imagine a man who is perfectly virtuous but who, by some dreadful mistake, is condemned to torture for crimes he did not commit. In the midst of his agony, is he happy? Socrates thought so, but Aristotle thought that view is absurd.

Definition 4: Happiness is bodily and external goods, such as health and wealth. *Grain:* Did we not just admit, in the example of the virtuous man undergoing torture, that happiness depends on outward conditions? *Chaff:* The example of the virtuous man undergoing torture did not prove that virtue is unnecessary for happiness; it only proved that virtue is insufficient for happiness.[10]

Even when we combine Aristotle's grains of truth, we still end up with some missing element to attaining true happiness because all of the definitions offered above depend on temporal things. In fact, these definitions of happiness were given with respect to the *greatest human good*. We have already explained how true happiness and ultimate meaning transcend humanity and are anchored in a *higher good—God*. Without God, we are left with extracting mean-

---

[10]J. Budziszewski, *Written on the Heart* (Downers Grove, Ill.: InterVarsity, 1997), 19–21.

ing and happiness from seeking and achieving the highest human good in this world; without God, ultimate happiness and meaning will always be—in the final analysis—elusive concepts. Yet if people looked in the right place, inside their own hearts, they would know that this world does not offer what they truly desire. C. S. Lewis describes this desire as

> . . . tantalizing glimpses, promises never quite fulfilled, echoes that died away just as they caught your ear. . . . It is the secret signature of each soul, the incommunicable and unappeasable want, the thing that we desired before we met our wives or made our friends or chose our work, and which we shall still desire on our deathbeds, when the mind no longer knows wife or friend or work. While we are, this is. If we lose this, we lose all.[11]

The Bible says that God has placed eternity in the hearts of all people (Ecclesiastes 3:11). There is a desire within the human heart to be of eternal import, to have value that transcends the temporal world. There is a longing deep within each of us to live the kind of life that, when all is said and done, will somehow have eternal consequences. However, the craving for eternal significance can never be satisfied within the limitations of a temporal world; only that which is eternal (God) can bestow eternal significance upon that which is temporal (humanity). This is why David said, "You have made known to me the path of life; you will fill me with joy in your presence, with eternal pleasures at your right hand" (Psalm 16:11). As Lewis said, "Earthly pleasures were never meant to satisfy . . . but only to arouse . . . to suggest the real thing," and that "real thing" is a relationship with God Himself. It is God who desires to bestow happiness upon us, and it is up to us to accept His gracious offer, delivered personally by His Son.

WHAT DOES THE FUTURE HOLD FOR SOMEONE WHO ACCEPTS JESUS?

When someone accepts Jesus Christ as her Lord and Savior, God goes to work in her life with the overall goal of molding her to be conformed to the image of His Son. In other words, God enrolls her into His character-development program, uses everything in her life, including people and circumstances, to turn her world into "a place of equipping and correction." The rest of her life on this earth will become the training ground to help prepare her for an eternity that will be spent in heaven. In time, she will come to

---

[11]Lewis, *The Problem of Pain*, 146–47.

understand that the vices once thought to bring fulfillment must now be shed and that the virtues once thought to be boring must now be embraced. The good news is that, for the first time in her life, God supplies the power and desire to choose the virtues over the vices. These choices will produce the kind of character that Jesus spoke of in His Sermon on the Mount.

In Matthew 5:3–10, Jesus began with the prescription for counteracting each of the seven deadly sins; the ingredients are known as the *Beatitudes.* For each of the seven deadly sins there is a specific beatitude that acts as an antidote to counteract the poison of the vice. Jesus called out each of the remedies by name, and we have placed alongside of each antidote the sin it was designed to cure. Peter Kreeft asserts that we understand things best by contrast and explained that there is a close parallel between the vices and the virtues. He lists the vices (seven deadly sins) and virtues (beatitudes) side by side, saying,

Pride is self-assertion, selfishness; poverty of spirit is *humility,* selflessness.

Vices (Seven Deadly Sins)	Virtues (Beatitudes)
• Pride	• Poverty of spirit (humility)
• Avarice (greed)	• Mercy
• Envy	• Mourning
• Wrath	• Meekness and peacemaking
• Sloth	• Hunger and thirst for righteousness
• Lust	• Purity of heart
• Gluttony	• Bearing persecution

Avarice is *greed,* the centrifugal reach to grab and keep the world's goods for oneself; *mercy* is the centripetal reach to give, to share the world's goods with others, even the undeserving. *Envy* resents another's happiness; *mourning* shares another's unhappiness. *Wrath* wills harm and destruction; *meekness* refuses to harm and peacemaking prevents destruction. *Sloth* refuses to exert the will toward the good, toward the ideal; *hunger and thirst for righteousness* does just that. *Lust* dissipates and divides the soul, desiring every attractive body; *purity of heart* centers and unifies the soul, desiring God alone. *Gluttony* needs to consume an inordinate amount of worldly goods; *being persecuted* is being deprived of even ordinate necessities.[12]

Taken together, the Beatitudes map out the curriculum that believers will be taken through by the Spirit of God. However, the seven virtues identified above are *not* an end in themselves. God is after integrity, and not just right actions or virtues. This is an important distinction, and it must be acknowl-

---

[12]Peter Kreeft, *Back to Virtue* (San Francisco: Ignatius, 1992), 92–93.

edged, for if it is not we might incorrectly conclude that God is only concerned in right actions, or in obeying a set of rules (what we do), rather than being primarily concerned about our character (who we are). If such were the case, right things could be done for the wrong reasons, and we could do them unwillingly or out of selfish motives. *God wants our actions to flow out of a pure heart.* C. S. Lewis confirms this:

> A man who perseveres in doing just actions gets in the end a certain quality of character. Now it is that quality rather than the particular actions which we mean when we talk of "virtue." . . . The point is not that God will refuse you admission to his eternal world if you have not got certain qualities of character: the point is that if people have not got at least the beginnings of those qualities inside them, then no possible external conditions could make a "Heaven" for them—that is, could make them happy with the *deep, strong, unshakable happiness* God intends for us.[13]

Heaven is the final destiny for those who accept or receive Jesus Christ into their lives. They will live forever in relational harmony with God and with all people who truly love Him. The Word of God tells us that living in this world is like seeing a "poor reflection as in a mirror," but heaven is a place where all things will be made clear. We only know in part now, but in heaven we shall "know fully" (1 Corinthians 13:12).

If you can imagine a world where all of the inhabitants are truly humble, selfless, meek, righteous, merciful, compassionate, pure in heart, and at peace with God and each other, then you have a glimpse of what heaven will be like. Heaven can be likened to a place of perfect harmony—like listening to a superb orchestra. The musicians (believers) have a singular focus on their conductor (Jesus Christ), and their performance consists of unending love songs to their God (Revelation 5:11–13). Heaven is a place of pure joy and rejoicing in all that God is and all that He has done for those He loves, who love Him and who have trusted in His Son, Jesus Christ (Revelation 7:9–12). Heaven is a place where there will be no more pain or suffering and where every tear will be wiped away by God Himself (Revelation 21:3–5). It is a place where there will be no more night or darkness because God will be the light that guides His people (Revelation 21:23–24). In heaven there will be no more lies, deception, broken promises, disappointments, betrayals, or vices because there will be no evil in heaven; evil will have been defeated and eternally quarantined (Revelation 21:27).

---

[13]Lewis, *Mere Christianity*, 77–78 (emphasis added).

Everyone in heaven will have custom-fit bodies, specially engineered for a heavenly environment. Their bodies will be the same physical bodies they had on earth but resurrected and glorified (1 Corinthians 15:39–49). One form of the word *glorified* means "manifested perfection" or "completion." In other words, those who enter heaven will know what it means to be fully or completely human—more human than could ever be imagined here on earth. There will be complete compatibility in heaven with respect to the natural and the spiritual.

Just as Nature and Spirit will be fully harmonized in heaven, so too will the glorified bodies, souls, and spirits of all believers. Once in heaven, the vices will no longer hinder the flourishing of the virtues, and believers will be able to reach full spiritual maturity. However, God does not want His people to wait until heaven to experience spiritual growth. The growing process begins the moment anyone personally accepts Jesus Christ as Lord and Savior. It is this process of becoming whole or complete that is a significant part of bringing meaning to life both now and forever. Conversely, those who decide to reject Jesus as Lord and Savior will cultivate the depravity that already exists in their lives. With this in mind, we turn our attention to examining the effects of human depravity when people choose not to call upon God to save them from it.

WHAT ARE THE TEMPORAL CONSEQUENCES OF REFUSING GOD?

When people refuse to acknowledge their need for God and to follow His prescriptions for how to live their lives, they can, and often do, end up living a self-destructive lifestyle. To show how this can happen, we will take a look at a man who chooses to ignore God's prescriptions for how to be sexually fulfilled and decides to seek out other ways to achieve that fulfillment. We will use the example of lust and pornography, since it is commonly thought to be a "private" and "victimless" matter.

God's directive clearly states that sexual fulfillment is to take place within the context and boundaries of a marriage covenant. Moreover, in keeping with Jesus' analysis of the root cause of sexual immorality, we want to show how and why a person's thought life can and often does lead to sexually immoral behavior. To illustrate our inquiry, we will use C. S. Lewis's analogy of the "human machine" and how God designed it to run within certain design specifications. When a man decides to reject God's design criteria and run on any fuel he chooses, it will only be a matter of time before his human machine begins to break down.

Let's say that a man chooses to operate his human machine on a counterfeit fuel such as softcore pornography (nudity) to fulfill his sexual appetite. As he continues to consume this false fuel, he seemingly gets fulfilled and continues the habit. For a relatively brief period of time the pornographic material appears to be working for him, but eventually he discovers that the fuel has lost its ability to truly satisfy. What this person fails to understand is that his human machine has actually started to become less efficient (it has morally deteriorated) as a result of being forced to run on fake fuel. He is under the impression that the fuel he is using (softcore pornography) no longer has the energy necessary to keep him running. In reality, however, the fuel he is using has not changed: *he has*. His efficiency—his moral condition—has decreased, with a proportional increase in lust, and the result is a need for a more potent fuel. So he looks elsewhere to find something that will satisfy his increasing desire for sexual pleasure.

His search for a more potent fuel brings him in touch with the world of hardcore pornography. He does not know it yet, but as his habitual choices increase, his human machine will begin to "cycle down." In other words, as his lust/pornography cycle continues in an unrestrained manner, he will eventually get deeper and deeper into this habit as he searches for more powerful fuels to meet his ever-increasing, aberrant sexual desires. This man may begin to act in ways he never thought he could or would in order to find the kind of fuel mixture he needs (even illegal forms of hardcore pornography) to fulfill his seemingly insatiable cravings.

He may not realize it, but he has taken a journey into a lifestyle that can have devastating results. He has become addicted and is leading a sexually deviant and morally bankrupt lifestyle. In many respects, he is no better off than a drug addict. Furthermore, if he does not acknowledge his addiction and get help, he can easily be in as much danger as a drug addict is of overdosing. Allow us to explain why this is so.

There exists a body of scientific evidence to support the conclusion that behavioral activities do, in fact, lead to a change in human brain chemistry. The result of something like a prolonged habit of a certain kind can have the same effect on a person as that of chemical addiction. Research continues to confirm that memories of experiences that occurred at times of behavioral arousal (including sexual arousal) are difficult to erase and produce a sort of "bonding" or "addictive behavior" to that which caused the stimulation. In an article on addiction research, an analyst from *Time* said,

The degree to which learning and memory sustain the addictive process is only now being appreciated. Each time a neurotransmitter like dopamine floods a synapse, scientists believe, circuits that trigger thoughts and motivate actions are etched onto the brain. . . . At a purely chemical level, every experience humans find enjoyable—whether listening to music, embracing a lover or savoring chocolate—amounts to little more than an explosion of dopamine in the nucleus accumbens.[14]

Habitual actions with respect to virtuous behavior help to reinforce good habits. Likewise, the more a bad habit is reinforced, the deeper it gets etched onto the brain's circuitry, which results in addiction. Addiction research and the criminal justice system use three basic terms to describe an addiction: habit, tolerance, and dependence. A *habit* is an overpowering compulsion to do or have something and to go to almost any extremes to do or get it. For example, with respect to pornography, first there is an addictive stage where the individual is hooked on obscene materials and develops a desire to keep coming back for more until a tolerance level is reached. *Tolerance* is the term used to describe an individual's progressive decreased response to the habit or drug. As a result, that person needs to do or get more of the same thing in order to be fulfilled, which forces that individual to delve deeper into the habit. For the user of pornography, this is the escalation stage where there is a need for more sordid materials in order to get the same kind of stimulation as before. Finally, there is a psychological and/or physical *dependence* on the habit that becomes necessary in order to function normally. The person must continually fuel himself with pornographic materials in order to act "normally."

Yet over a period of time, there is also a diminishing effect that the materials have on the user of pornography. This is the inevitable downward cycle we referred to above. What was once shocking and exciting becomes commonplace and acceptable at this stage, which prompts the user to find more stimulating and morally depraved materials. When an individual has gone this far with pornography, there exists the probability that he will try to get the needed fulfillment by "acting out" his fantasies—what was once purely imaginary now becomes a desired reality. What was once nudity has now fully blossomed into all kinds of sexual perversions and possibly criminal offenses for those addicted to pornography, such as rape, child molestation, child pornography, and other manufactured horrors of the dark and depraved human imagination—including the murder of their victims in an effort not to be identified by them.

Ted Bundy is a sad and sobering example of how pornography can be both

---

[14]Madeleine J. Nash, "Addicted: Why Do People Get Hooked?" *Time*, May 5, 1997, 72.

addictive and deadly. Bundy was a promising young law student who began abducting women from college campuses. After using them to satisfy his own perverted desires, he would kill them. He killed twenty-eight women before he was caught, his last victim a little girl who was only twelve years old. Following his arrest, he was convicted and ultimately ended up on death row where he spent ten long years. Just two days before his execution, he requested an exclusive interview with Dr. James Dobson. In that interview Dobson probed Bundy for the root cause of his moral disease and asked, "How did it happen? Where did it start?" Bundy went back to his childhood and explained how he became addicted to softcore and then hardcore pornography. Bundy explained, "But pornography will only go so far. I reached the jumping off point." He then explained what he meant by the "jumping off point." He said he needed "more" than books and pictures and a "normal" sexual relationship. Pornography was the path that led him to kill twenty-eight women, imprisoned him, and ended his life.[15]

Bundy is not an isolated case. The authors of the book *Journey Into Darkness* document various cases of sexual crimes. In describing the utter futility in rehabilitating sexual predators, the authors use the analogy of baking a cake with dirty hands that had been covered in axle grease. As the baker mixed the ingredients together, the grease became part of the cake mix along with the other ingredients. The cake would be fine if there was some way to get the blended axle grease out of the cake mix. Speaking about serial killers, the authors say,

> The fact of the matter is that in the vast majority of cases, the urges, the desires, the character disorders that make them hurt and kill innocent men, women, and children are so deeply ingrained in the recipe of their makeup that there is no way to get out the axle grease. The case of author Jack Henry Abbot is just one example of many. I recall one particular heartrending story which also makes the point. Back in the early 1990s, a child molester-killer who had escaped from prison was featured on the television program "America's Most Wanted." This individual happened to see the program himself, and realized that others who knew him in his assumed identity would undoubtedly see it as well, that they would finger him, he'd be rearrrested, and the jig would be up. Knowing this, and knowing his remaining time in freedom would be short, he left home, set out in his car, and kidnapped, molested, and killed another child before the police got to him. He knew that he would be going back to the slam-

---

[15]Dr. James Dobson, *Life on the Edge*, Focus on the Family & Word Inc., 1993, 1994, videocassette.

mer permanently, where he wouldn't have access to any little children, so he'd better do something while he had the chance.[16]

THE BASIC CONSEQUENCES OF REFUSING GOD AND IGNORING HIS MORAL LAW

As we see it, the root cause of the character disorders (moral corruption) mentioned above is directly associated with a person's refusal to acknowledge and act upon what is morally right and reject what is morally wrong. It becomes harder and harder for the individual to get help with his character disorder because of the increased moral depravity. This increase is associated with greater levels of insensitivity in that person's conscience. For example, during the progressive moral deterioration in the life of the person who uses pornography, his sequence of feeling-to-thought-to-deed proceeds with less and less intervention of the inhibitory mechanism of conscience and guilt. The Bible depicts this condition as a "seared conscience" (1 Timothy 4:2).

When people seriously burn themselves, the body forms scar tissue in that location. As a result, there is a deadening of the sensitivity level. In a similar manner, the habitual violation (burning) of one's conscience (ignoring or disobeying the moral law) and the suppression of associated guilt will eventually result in a declining sensitivity toward evil. Apply this concept to any form of evil and in due time people will lose

"The requirements of the law are written on their hearts, their consciences also bearing witness, and their thoughts now accusing them." Romans 2:15

Pornography

"seared conscience" (1 Timothy 4:2)

their ability to think clearly about right and wrong. The Bible describes people who reach this condition as having become "futile" in their thinking and represents their hearts as becoming "darkened" (Romans 1:21). In describing this progressive immoral condition, C. S. Lewis said,

> When a man is getting better, he understands more and more clearly the evil that is still left in him. When a man is getting worse, he understands his own badness less and less. A moderately bad man knows he is not very good: a thoroughly bad man thinks he is all right. This is com-

---

[16]John Douglas and Mark Olshaker, *Journey Into Darkness* (New York: Simon & Schuster, 1997), 362–63.

mon sense, really. You understand sleep when you are awake, not while you are sleeping. You can see a mistake in arithmetic when your mind is working properly: while you are making them you cannot see them. You can understand the nature of drunkenness when you are sober, not when you are drunk. Good people know about both good and evil: bad people do not know about either.[17]

Lewis just summarized one of the basic consequences of refusing God and ignoring His moral law. Another consequence is the impact on other people: whenever we turn away from God and focus on fulfilling our own selfish desires in any way we choose, we not only harm ourselves but also those around us. There is no such thing as private or isolated sin. The individual decisions people make and the attitudes they choose to have will eventually affect their family members and/or friends—and ultimately society. In fact, the problems we face as a nation can and have been traced right back down to an individual level and people's decisions to be self-centered. This selfish state of existence is not only the root cause of individual corruption but is also responsible for the destruction of families and has now led to a national moral crisis.

In chapter 14 we noted how "private vices" have public consequences, and we cited one author who says, "Every deadly sin fuels harmful social phenomena: lust—pornography; gluttony—substance abuse; envy—terrorism; anger—violence; sloth—indifference to the pain and sufferings of others; greed—abuse of public trust; and pride—discrimination."[18] We also suggested that pride, the attitude of putting oneself first, i.e., selfishness, is the root cause of all the other vices. Now we want to show how a nation can be, and has been, affected by a self-styled individualism or selfishness that is the driving force behind the vice we call pride.

There is an unbelievable amount of unbridled egotism in our contemporary culture that encompasses the entire spectrum of society—from young students to professionals in business and politics, and all the way up to the office of the president of the United States. A *Newsweek* cover story once surveyed the American people to find out what they thought was the cause of America's moral decline. They cited a poll indicating that 76 percent of adults agree that the United States is in moral decay.[19] This story was just one among many documenting the eroding moral fiber of our country. In an effort to isolate the root cause of this decline, a few years earlier, *Time* did some investigative re-

---

[17]Lewis, *Mere Christianity*, 87.
[18]Schimmel, *The Seven Deadly Sins: Jewish, Christian, and Classical Reflections on Human Psychology*, 3–4 (emphasis added).
[19]*Newsweek*, June 13, 1994.

search. Their findings appeared in an issue titled "What Ever Happened to Ethics? Assaulted by Sleaze, Scandals and Hypocrisy, America Searches for Its Moral Bearings." In this issue *Time* interviewed some of the top ethicists in the country. Their study led them to identifying the root cause as a "protective obsession with self and image." The author of the article said,

> In a recent poll for *Time* conducted by Yankelovich Clancy Shulman, more than 90% of the respondents agreed that morals have fallen because parents fail to take responsibility for their children or imbue them with decent moral standards; 76% saw lack of ethics in businessmen as contributing to tumbling moral standards; and 74% decried failure by political leaders to set a good example. Lawyers are often seen not as the guardians of the law but as sophisticated manipulators who profit from rule beating. Even the ethics counsel for the 313,000-member American Bar Association, Lisa Milord, concedes that all too many lawyers "are looking out for their own interests rather than the integrity of the legal system." . . .
>
> Doctors, wandering through ethical thickets freshly grown from a technology that gives them daunting new powers over life and death, are held in low esteem by many who see them as self-serving money chasers. Dr. Richard Kusserow, inspector general for the U.S. Department of Health and Human Services, claims that physicians' peer-review boards, out of concern for the profession's good name, tend to sweep ethics complaints under the rug. "They protect each other's incompetency from the public," he says.
>
> This protective obsession with self and image, say behaviorists, also permeates family living. Carlfred Broderick, a sociology professor at the University of Southern California, says increased emphasis on what he calls "personhood"—as opposed to duty—has helped to unravel traditional family obligations. . . . "Individual rights play a significant role," he says, "and that's where the tension arises" in today's families. Irene Goldenberg, a psychology professor at the University of California, Los Angeles, concludes that the cult of personhood has brought about a more selfish view of the "responsibilities in marriage," including the responsibility for divorce. Goldenberg adds that the diminished sense of commitment has seeped down to children, leaching out old feelings of loyalty to the family. In consequence, she says, today's children are "taking care of themselves first."[20]

According to some of the top ethicists in America, the moral decay of our culture can be traced right back to the family and tracked down to the individ-

---

[20]Ezra Bowen, "Looking to Its Roots," *Time*, May 25, 1987, 26.

ual moral corruption of each member. In analyzing the root cause of the moral decline at a national level, *Time* returned to the individual problem of selfishness.

In conclusion, a person's temporal consequences for rejecting God and living a self-centered life are many; we will list three. First, there will be a price to pay individually as her life slowly slips into darkness and away from the true light of God's moral law. Second, she will bring harm to those who are related to or closely associated with her—family and friends. Third, society as a whole will reap the bitter harvest of selfishness and pride, which manifests itself in many ways and will ultimately be the essential factor underlying the moral collapse of an entire nation. These temporal consequences, in many respects, serve as a preview or warning of what the eternal state of living without God (hell) will be like, which is the subject matter of our next chapter.

—16—
QUESTIONS ABOUT TRUE MISERY AND HELL

I willingly believe that the damned are, in one sense, successful, rebels to the end; that the doors of hell are locked on the inside.

—C. S. LEWIS

WHAT ARE THE PERMANENT CONSEQUENCES OF REFUSING GOD?

The simple and direct answer to this question was given by Jesus: "I told you that you would die in your sins; if you do not believe that I am the one I claim to be, you will indeed die in your sins" (John 8:24). To die in sin is to die forever separated from being in a love relationship with God. Jesus asked of the hypocritical religious leaders who rejected Him, "How will you escape being condemned to hell?" (Matthew 23:33). According to Jesus, if we do not believe in Him, we will not only die a physical death but a spiritual one as well. The Bible refers to this spiritual death as the second death (Revelation 20:6, 14), resulting in eternal separation from God. The name for this eternal separation or quarantine of evil for people who reject God is called *hell*. Hell was not created for human occupation but rather for the fallen angels—angels who chose to go their own way instead of obeying their Creator (Matthew 25:41). All who reject God will ultimately be cast out of His presence and live forever in a conscious state of eternal separation from God in hell.

But does it seem fair that just because a person sins in this lifetime he should spend an eternity in hell? How does the punishment (eternal condemnation in hell) fit the crime (sinning in this temporal life)? In order to fully appreciate Jesus' proclamation, we must consider the kind of Being God is (His divine nature) and the kind of beings we are (our human nature). If God is fair and loving and just, then hell must be a fair and loving and just place.

First, hell is fair because throughout our entire lives we have the choice not to go there. God has given us enough evidence (such as presented in this book) to choose Him and live with Him forever in heaven, or to reject Him and live without Him forever in hell. The people who reject Him freely choose to live without Him forever.

Second, God's love demands that hell be a reality. God respects the choice people make to reject His love, and since forced love is a contradiction in terms, God cannot force His love on unwilling people. God's love is always persuasive and never coercive. To coerce someone into a relationship would itself be an unfair, unloving, and evil act of which God is incapable. Jesus expressed this truth when He stood over Jerusalem and cried out, "O Jerusalem, Jerusalem, you who kill the prophets and stone those sent to you, how often I have longed to gather your children together, as a hen gathers her chicks under her wings, *but you were not willing*" (Matthew 23:37, emphasis added).

Third, hell is just because it punishes evil. Since God is just, He must judge everyone who has sinned and broken His moral law. The Stalins and Hitlers of the world, as well as all of humanity, must be brought to justice, and God ultimately sees that justice is carried out. Thus, the existence of a place of punishment for unrepentant people (those who are unwilling to admit their guilt and ask for forgiveness) after this life is necessary to maintain the justice of God.

WHY DO "DECENT" PEOPLE GO TO HELL?

Some think that hell seems like an appropriate place for a Stalin or a Hitler, but what about the average person who appears to have led a somewhat decent life? First, what *we* may call decent and what is decent in the eyes of *God* can be worlds apart. When Jesus denounced the cities that ignored the miracles He performed, He indicated that their judgment would be more severe than other cities. For example, He said that the people of Capernaum would suffer a more strict judgment than the people of Sodom (Matthew 11:24). Think about it: Capernaum was just guilty of ignoring Jesus, while the sins of Sodom are associated with sexual immorality. God sees indifference to Himself as a "greater" sin than sexual immorality. This is not to make light of sexual sins; they are repulsive in the eyes of God. This example merely helps us to illustrate how far off we can be when we try to judge levels of sin.

God judges rightly, and the weight of the sins committed will be met with the proper level of punishment. Furthermore, there are other places in the Bible that support the idea of varying degrees of sin and corresponding levels of punishment. In fact, Jesus told Pilate that Judas was guilty of a "greater sin" (John 19:11). The Bible also tells us that each person will be judged according to his or her deeds (Romans 2:6; Revelation 20:12) and that God is right and just when He judges (Psalm 51:4b).

Second, since the moral law is based upon the nature of God, any violation of that law is in reality a violation against God alone (Psalm 51:4a). This includes all sins—even sins against ourselves—because we are created in God's image, and all that is good in us is a reflection of the image of God. When we devalue ourselves or devalue others, it is equivalent to devaluing the true image of God in us and in them. So whether we deface (sin against) the image of God in us or in someone else, we ultimately sin against God.

Third, since God exists outside of time (He is an eternal Being) and we exist in time (we are temporal beings), our sins have eternal consequences even though they are committed in time. From God's perspective, He has had our sins before Him throughout eternity; therefore, the consequences of the punishment must also have eternal ramifications. God has all of temporal time in view in one "eternal present state"; He acts in time from eternity. Our actions, however, are performed in time, are eternally before Him—to think otherwise is to think incorrectly about the nature and consequences of sin. One particular line of faulty thinking is based on the idea that mere time cancels sin. Thinking that a past sin needs no accounting for because time has passed is an error. In his clear, candid, and simply profound way, C. S. Lewis argued,

> I have heard others, and I have heard myself, recounting cruelties and falsehoods committed in boyhood as if they were no concern of the present speaker's and even with laughter. But mere time does nothing either to the fact or to the guilt of a sin. The guilt is washed out not by time but by repentance and the blood of Christ. . . . All times are eternally present to God. Is it not at least possible that along some one line of His multi-dimensional eternity He sees you forever in the nursery pulling the wings off a fly, forever toadying [being insincere], lying, and lusting as a school-

boy, forever in that moment of cowardice or insolence as a subaltern [navy officer]? It may be that salvation exists not in the canceling of these eternal moments but in the perfected humility that bears the shame forever [Christ].[1]

This eternal component of the consequences of sin raises yet another truth about the need to have an eternal covering over our sins. Since from God's perspective our sins have always existed, there needs to be an atonement (payment) that also extends into eternity. If Jesus was truly who He claimed to be—God in the flesh—then His atoning work on the cross also exists in the eternal realm. In other words, since Jesus has two natures, His divine nature exists in eternity and acts as a shield protecting us against the consequences of our sins before God from all eternity—past, present, and future. For that reason, the Bible says Jesus was "slain from the creation of the world" (Revelation 13:8). This means that from God's perspective evil and all injustices have been dealt with—from eternity. For us, however, since we are creatures of time, we have yet to see the end and how God sets things right. Every evil that exists *will* be forever cast into hell, and those who find themselves there will willingly choose to be there. Consider the following illustration.

Let's suppose that one day NASA develops a special kind of protective capsule that permits astronauts to take an expedition to within a very close proximity of the sun. This allows them to study the sun's nature while shielding them from its deadly heat and lethal radiation. Let's also suppose that space travel has reached a point where someone from the public domain is afforded the opportunity to accompany these astronauts on their expedition as an observer. One day a certain man receives a call from NASA explaining how he has been chosen for a journey to the sun. He is also told about the specially designed capsule that was made to shield him from the sun. Yet for some stubborn reason this man refuses to agree to step inside the protective capsule—NASA cannot convince him otherwise—and he still insists upon going anyway. However, NASA cannot allow him to go because his nature and the nature of the sun cannot coexist at such a close proximity. Therefore, since NASA is responsible for him, values his life, and respects his choice, they cannot permit him to go.

Likewise, in order for sinful people to relationally coexist with God, we need to be protected from that part of His nature known as *wrath*. Simply stated, wrath refers to the characteristic of God's righteous anger toward our willful violations of His laws. Just as the nature of the sun cannot be changed

---

[1]C. S. Lewis, *The Problem of Pain* (New York: Macmillan, 1962), 61.

to accommodate us to coexist in nearness to it, so too the nature of God—it cannot change. Since He cannot alter His nature, and since He desires to have an intimate and loving relationship with us, His solution to the problem of our sin nature is Jesus Christ. The covering of our sins by the imputed (credited) righteousness of God, achieved through the blood shed on the cross by His Son, acts as an eternal shield to protect the true believer from the wrath of a holy and awesome God. God's attributes shine down upon each one of us. However, just as the sun hardens clay and softens wax, so some will melt and soften

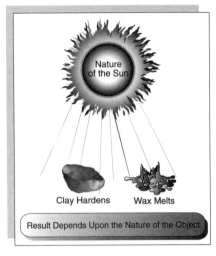

under the truths and the attributes of God, while others will only become hardened to Him. These are the ones who refuse to accept God's gracious offer of an eternal covering of their sins.

For those who reject this divine covering, there is no way that God can allow them to relationally coexist with Him. He cannot force His love upon them, and He respects their choice. When God's love is rejected, the result leaves the rejecters in a state of eternal indebtedness toward God. They must pay their own penalty for the sins they have committed. Since they refuse to be pardoned, they will remain in a state of relational separation from God forever. We must remember that it cannot be otherwise.

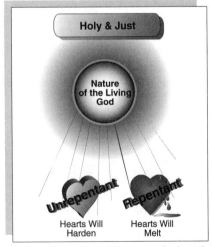

God is both a just judge and a loving Father, and, as such He must deal with the final state of unrepentant rebellion.

WHY DOES ANYONE GO TO HELL?

To bring this question of hell to closure and down to a practical level, consider what C. S. Lewis said:

Picture to yourself a man who has risen to wealth and power by a continued course of treachery and cruelty, by exploiting for purely selfish ends the noble motions of his victims, laughing the while at their simplicity; who, having thus attained success, used it for the gratification of lust and hatred and finally parts with the last rag of honor among thieves by betraying his own accomplices and jeering at their last moments of bewildered disillusionment. Suppose further, that he does all this, not (as we would like to imagine) tormented by remorse or even misgiving, but eating like a schoolboy and sleeping like a healthy infant—jolly, ruddy-cheeked man, without a care in the world, unshakably confident to the very end that he alone has found the answer to the riddle of life, that God and man are fools whom he has got the better of, that his way of life is utterly successful, satisfactory, unassailable. . . .

Supposing he will not be converted, what destiny in the eternal world can you regard for him? Can you really desire that such a man, *remaining what he is* (and he must be able to do that if he has free will) should be confirmed forever in his present happiness—should continue for all eternity, to be perfectly convinced that the laugh is on his side? . . . Soon or late, the right should be asserted, the flag [of truth] planted in this horribly rebellious soul, even if no fuller and better conquest is to follow. In a sense it is better for the creature itself, even if it never becomes good, that it should know itself a failure, a mistake. . . . The demand that God should forgive such a man while he remains what he is, is based on a confusion between condoning and forgiving. To condone an evil is simply to ignore it, to treat it as if it were good. But forgiveness needs to be accepted as well as offered if it is to be complete: and a man who admits no guilt can accept no forgiveness.

I willingly believe that the damned are, in one sense, successful, rebels to the end; that the doors of hell are locked on the *inside*. . . . In the long run the answer to all those who object to the doctrine of hell is itself a question: "What are you asking God to do?" To wipe out their past sins and, at all costs, to give them a fresh start, smoothing over every difficulty and offering every miraculous help? But He has done so, on Calvary. To forgive them? They will not be forgiven. To leave them alone? Alas, I am afraid that is what He does.[2]

Again, we must realize that *everyone who goes to hell has chosen to be there.* They would rather spend an eternity filled with misery in hell than an eternity filled with meaning by glorifying God forever. Heaven is the place where ultimate meaning is found through worshiping forever the One who is worthy of

---

[2]Ibid., 120–22, 127–28 (emphasis added).

adoration. A foretaste of that ultimate meaning can be had here and now, in this life, by accepting Jesus Christ as Lord and Savior. Conversely, rejecting God and His truth in this life and choosing to live a life apart from Him may bring temporary meaning in this life, but with it comes a foretaste of hell. The final choice boils down to this:

> There are only two kinds of people in the end: those who say to God, "Thy will be done," and those to whom God says, in the end, "Thy will be done." All that are in Hell, choose it. Without that self-choice there could be no Hell. No soul that seriously and constantly desires joy will ever miss it. Those who seek find. To those who knock it is opened.[3]

---

[3]C. S. Lewis, *The Great Divorce* (New York: Macmillan, 1946), 72–73.

APPENDIX: FIRST PRINCIPLE RESPONSES TO ETHICAL QUESTIONS

God, who gave us life, gave us liberty. Can the liberties of a nation remain secure when we have removed a conviction that these liberties are the gift of God? Indeed, I tremble for my country when I reflect that God is just, that his justice cannot sleep forever.

—Thomas Jefferson

Before we attempt to answer the following ethical questions, we need to set the context in which our answers ought to be understood. We have already argued for the credibility of biblical theism based upon the academic first principles presented throughout this work. We came to the overall conclusion that an uncaused, infinitely powerful, eternal, and intelligent Being (God) exists. Moreover, we have shown that this God is personal, loving, just, and merciful, and that all of these attributes of God are found only in the Bible. We also presented arguments for the God-given value of human life, which serves as the basis for human rights. This logically follows from the belief in a Creator, and we reminded our readers that the belief in a Creator and creation are considered to be the self-evident truths stated in the founding documents of the United States of America, namely, the Declaration of Independence.

Once the credibility of God as the Creator and basis for the human rights and value of human life has been argued for, all other ethical questions must yield to this truth. By this we mean, if there is a God who gave us life and bestowed value upon us, then no human being has the right to devalue human life or take away human rights, especially the right to life.[1]

WHAT ABOUT ABORTION?

Here are arguments in favor of abortion:

1. A woman has a right to privacy over her own body.
2. There are therapeutic situations where abortions are necessary for the "well-being" of the mother, including the need to alleviate the inseparable indignity that pregnancy by rape forces upon a woman.
3. An unwanted pregnancy results in making a child vulnerable to neglect and abuse.
4. Compassion is needed for women whose lives may be theoretically threatened from illegal abortions by "rusty coat hangers in back alleys."
5. All abortions are inherently and primarily medical decisions.

These reasons appear to have merit and even seem rather compelling. However, the *one major assumption* built in to all of these reasons—an assumption that the Supreme Court based its decision upon in *Roe v. Wade*—is that the unborn child is not truly a human person but only a potential human life or person. If the unborn is not a person or individual human being, but merely a tissue or unnecessary appendage, then the arguments for abortion are convincing. If, however, the unborn child is truly a person, then all these arguments (and other similar ones) turn out to be nothing more than an emotional appeal without moral justification.

For example, who would argue—on grounds similar to those used by proabortionists—that Hitler had the right to kill Jews because they were deformed or undesirable? Or what abortionist would insist that since Jews were being killed anyway by rusty knives in back alleys, passing laws to ensure them a sanitary death by sterile instruments was justified? Surely no reasonable abortionist would insist that the mother of the famous singer Ethel Waters has the

---

[1]For a thorough biblical and philosophical analysis of these ethical issues, see Norman L. Geisler, *Christian Ethics: Options and Issues* (Grand Rapids, Mich.: Baker, 1989). Also see Norman L. Geisler and Frank S. Turek III, *Legislating Morality: Is It Wise? Is It Legal? Is It Possible?* (Minneapolis: Bethany House, 1998).

moral right to kill her daughter years after she was born because the mother was yet haunted with memories about the rape by which Ethel was conceived. But why should abortionists admit that these types of killings are obviously wrong and yet insist at the same time that abortion, *for the same reasons,* is not wrong? The overall rationale is that they do not grant the unborn a personal status; they believe that prohibition against murder does not apply.

On the other hand, even the *Roe v. Wade* decision admits that if the suggestion of personhood is established, the appellant case collapses because the fetus's right to life is then guaranteed by the Fourteenth Amendment. In the final analysis only one basic issue needs to be resolved, and this issue is neither legal nor medical—it is moral. The essential question is, "Is the unborn child a person?" If so, then *Roe v. Wade* is allowing murder. In this case, to argue that abortion is essentially a medical decision is as ludicrous as claiming that capital punishment by the electric chair is primarily a problem of electrical engineering. If we are dealing with a human being, whether in capital punishment or abortion, then intentionally taking that life is a moral issue.

If the unborn child is a person, then the American slaughter of nearly 1.5 million unborn babies annually, over 4,000 a day (about one every twenty seconds), is a significant moral issue—an American holocaust. Stalin killed at least eighteen million people, and Hitler at least twelve million. *As a nation, we have killed over forty million unborn children in abortion chambers (1973–present). This is more than the combined mass genocide of both Hitler and Stalin.* There are so many elements surrounding the issue of abortion that it can become a rather complex and confusing debate. In order to clear up some of this, we intend to answer two essential questions with respect to abortion and human rights.

IS THE FETUS HUMAN OR NONHUMAN?

Genetically, science has demonstrated that human life begins at conception. All genetic characteristics of a fully developed and distinct individual human being are *actually,* not *potentially,* present from the moment of conception. Gynecologists are thus urged to consider the unborn their "second patient." In fact, the cover story of the February 1991 issue of *Discover* (the "news magazine of science") reads, "Surgery Before Birth: The Challenge of Medicine's Tiniest *Patients.*"[2] Unless *Discover* journalists are in the habit of misusing simple terms, the word *patient* indicates not only human life but also the commitment on

---

[2]Pat Ohlendor-Moffat, "Surgery Before Birth," *Discover,* vol. 12, no. 2, February 1991, 58–65 (emphasis added).

behalf of the doctor to take responsibility for the well-being of that life. *Webster* defines the word *patient* as "a *person* receiving care or treatment, especially from a doctor."[3]

A few years ago, the National Institutes of Health (NIH) appointed a panel to procure federal funding for conceiving human embryos in the laboratory. The *Wall Street Journal* reported on their task.

> A panel of 19 experts appointed by the National Institutes of Health has recommended federal funding for conceiving human embryos in the laboratory for the purpose of subjecting them to experiments that will destroy them. . . . Creating, using and destroying human embryos cannot be entirely separated from the question of abortion. . . . The NIH readily acknowledges that we can answer the question of when human life begins. *Science leaves us no choice: It begins at conception.* The embryo from the very beginning, we are told, deserves *"serious moral consideration."* . . . Scientists agree that from the earliest moments the embryo has the capacity to articulate itself into what everyone acknowledges is a human being.[4]

Biologically, life is a continuous human flow—at no point does it stop and then later abruptly begin. Human life is passed on through conception from parent to offspring without interruption. When human sperm unites with a human ovum, the result is a separate human zygote: *a distinct human being.*

So the question of when human life begins is not really a question at all. When there are forty-six chromosomes present,[5] there is human life; a new life with a new genetic code. It is not the code of the mother, nor is it the code of the father. Based upon the genetic evidence alone, the fetus ought to be recognized as an individual *human* life, and it is.

IS THE FETUS A PERSON OR A NONPERSON?

Are all human beings persons? This was also the overriding question being debated with the NIH. The panel agreed that embryos are human life; the debate was over whether or not that human life was a person. The *Wall Street Journal* reported,

---

[3]David B. Guralink, ed., *Webster's New World Dictionary: Second College Edition* (New York: Simon and Schuster, 1980), 1041 (emphasis added).
[4]Richard John Neuhaus, "Don't Cross This Threshold," *The Wall Street Journal*, October 27, 1994, A–20 (emphasis added).
[5]This is not to say that those with forty-five or forty-seven chromosomes are not human. They certainly are, just as persons who have four or six fingers on a hand are humans who have a unique defect.

Having acknowledged that human life is at stake and that some respect must be paid, the NIH panel has the difficult task of explaining why it is *morally right* to produce lives in order to use them for lethal experiments. . . . *The critical questions posed by this proposal are not narrowly scientific. They are ethical and philosophical.* The conceptual framework at the center of the panel's reasoning is that of "personhood." It switches the question from "When does human life begin?" to "When does a human being become a person?" Persons, under this construct, are "protectable." Nonpersons or those who are something less than persons are "not protectable." . . . And *how do we decide which human beings are persons and which are not?*[6]

Who has the right to decide who is a person and who is not, and on what basis? If we define personhood in terms of genetic purity, then we must be logically consistent and declare that anyone in our society with genetic deformities, such as Down's syndrome, sickle cell anemia, and the like, should also be declared a nonperson. If we define personhood by age (number of months), why not exclude others from human society because of age, such as the elderly? Likewise, if personhood is defined in terms of its size, why not exclude dwarfs or pro-basketball centers? If a person is defined in terms of location (outside the womb), why can't one also discriminate against sections of our society because of their location ("from the other side of the tracks" or "from the ghetto")?

If personhood is not a gift that is bestowed upon us from our Creator and considered to be concomitant with human life, then it is up to us to determine who is a person and who is not. In fact, this is exactly what is being recommended by institutions such as the NIH. They said,

In the panel's view, *personhood is a social status that we, who are certified persons, bestow.* We decide who will and who will not be admitted to the circle of those who are recognized as persons and are therefore entitled to respect and protection. . . . On behalf of its view, the panel cites an article by Prof. Robert Green of Dartmouth. . . . The article asserts that there are no "qualities existing out there" in any human being that require us to respect him or her as a person. . . . Personhood is entirely a "social construct." *Whether someone is too young or too old, too retarded or too sick, too useless or too troublesome to be entitled to personhood is determined by a "decision on our part."*[7]

---

[6]Op. cit. (emphasis added).
[7]Ibid. (emphasis added).

Nevertheless, there are only two options concerning the issue of personhood. Human beings are either persons at the moment of conception—the moment they become a human life or being—or human beings become persons at some later point in time and for some other reason apart from the fact that he or she possesses a human nature. Let's take the time to explore the validity of each option and the consequences of bestowing personhood on someone apart from that individual having a human nature. The following summary endeavors to analyze both of these options and draw the consequences associated with each position.[8]

First, the debate over the distinction between persons and humans may be legally irrelevant. For example, baby eagles and corporations are both protected by the government. In fact, the United States Supreme Court unanimously declared corporations to be persons under the Fourteenth Amendment (*Santa Clara v. Sanford* case of 1886). So, even if the unborn were only potential persons, there is no reason why they should not be protected. There are good reasons why they ought to be protected, since only by their birth are they able to become adult persons.

Second, making a distinction between humans and persons is arbitrary. There is no essential grounds for declaring humans as nonpersons, only functional ones. If functional distinctions are made, that is pure discrimination on the basis of ability, rather than to discern on the basis of their true nature.

Third, making a distinction between humans and persons on functional grounds would justify killing children and adults who have lost these same functions. Anyone who suffers brain damage or loses consciousness are still persons while they are temporarily comatose. The sleeping and the unconscious are all persons even when not functioning as such.

Fourth, basing personhood on function confuses function with essence. Function is a result of essence, not the reverse. There is no essential difference between a human being and a human person, only a functional one. For example, no one doubts that day-old humans have fewer current abilities than day-old cows. But this does not convince us that they have less inherent worth.

Fifth, since there is no agreement on when personhood begins, [and] the Roe decision placed it at birth, all types of brutality can be justified. For example, some say that personhood begins at the point of self-consciousness, which is not until the second year after birth. If it is decided that this is true, it would justify the killing of any child up to that age.

---

[8]For the most part this summary was excerpted from *Matters of Life and Death* by Francis J. Beckwith and Norman L. Geisler (Grand Rapids, Mich.: Baker, 1991), 84–86.

These are some of the reasons why there should be no discrimination made, based upon functional differences, between being human and being a person. Since there is no essential difference between humanness and personhood, it only stands to reason that all humans are persons and ought to be protected by the Fourteenth Amendment. Furthermore, since one of the fundamental reasons we appoint Supreme Court justices and elect legislators to make the laws is based upon the belief that they are among some of the wisest people in our land, we then ask, "What is the wisest thing to do?" If we cannot reach agreement on whether or not human life and personhood are essentially one and the same thing, then would it not be wiser to make laws that favor the protection of human life? Especially human life that is supposed to be in one of the most sacred, protected, and loving places it can be—in the womb of its mother? When is it ever wise to take human life based upon ignorance? Peter Kreeft illustrates our point in an imaginary dialogue, set in modern-day Athens, between an abortionist named Herrod and Socrates.

> Herrod: They [the pro-life supporters] claim to know what they really do not know: that the fetus is a human person from the moment of conception.
> Socrates: And you—you do not claim to know that it isn't?
> Herrod: No. There is my advantage and my wisdom. I do not claim to know what I do not know. They do. They are the dogmatists. Theologians, philosophers and scientists have argued about this for many years without agreeing. It is clear dogmatism for anyone to claim certainty about such a moot point. . . . We simply do not know when the fetus becomes a human person. Anyone who claims to know is a fool because he claims to know what he does not know.
> Socrates: You do not know whether the fetus is a person, correct?
> Herrod: Correct.
> Socrates: And your work here is to kill fetuses, correct?
> Herrod: Socrates, I am continually shocked by the language you choose to use. I abort unwanted pregnancies.
> Socrates: By killing fetuses or by something else?
> Herrod: (Sigh.) By killing fetuses.
> Socrates: Not knowing whether they are persons or not?
> Herrod: Oh. Well . . .
> Socrates: You said a moment ago that you did not know when the fetus became a person. Do you know now?
> Herrod: No.
> Socrates: Then you kill fetuses, not knowing whether they are persons or not?

Herrod: If you must put it that way.

Socrates: Now, what would you say of a hunter who shot at a sudden movement in a bush, not knowing whether it was a deer or a fellow hunter? Would you call him wise or foolish?

Herrod: Are you saying I am a murderer?

Socrates: I am only saying one question at a time. Shall I repeat the question?

Herrod: No.

Socrates: Then will you answer it?

Herrod: (Sigh.) All right. Such a hunter is foolish, Socrates.

Socrates: And why is he foolish?

Herrod: You never stop, do you?

Socrates: No. Wouldn't you say he is foolish because he claims to know what he does not know, namely, that it is only a deer and not his fellow hunter in the bush?

Herrod: I suppose so.

Socrates: Or suppose a company were to fumigate a building with a highly toxic chemical to kill some insect pests, and you were responsible for evacuating the building first. If you were unsure whether there were any people in the building and you nevertheless gave the order to fumigate the building, would that act be wise or foolish?

Herrod: Foolish, of course.

Socrates: Why? Is it not because you would be acting as if you knew something you really did not know, namely, that there were no people in the building?

Herrod: Yes.

Socrates: And now you, Doctor. You kill fetuses—by whatever means, it does not matter; it may as well be by a gun or a poison. And you say that you do not know whether they are human persons. Is this not to act as if you knew what you admit you do not know? And is that not folly—in fact, the height of folly, rather than wisdom?

Herrod: I suppose you want me to meekly say, "Yes indeed Socrates. Anything you say, Socrates."

Socrates: Can you defend yourself against the argument?

Herrod: No.

Socrates: It has indeed devoured you like a shark, as surely as you devour fetuses.[9]

We believe what Socrates, through the pen of Kreeft, articulated, namely, that wisdom implores us to treat unborn babies as persons. We have already

---

[9]Peter Kreeft, *The Unaborted Socrates* (Downers Grove, Ill.: InterVarsity, 1983), 69–72.

presented our rationale for why we believe God endowed each human person with value and why human rights do not depend upon the arbitrary dictates of any human form of government or unfounded assumptions of any panel, such as the NIH (see chapters 9 and 10). We believe the rationale presented is sound and consistent with three basic truths contained in the following statement:

> We hold these Truths to be self-evident, that [1] *all men are created equal,* that they are [2] *endowed by their Creator with certain unalienable Rights,* that among these are Life, Liberty and the Pursuit of Happiness. That [3] *to secure these rights, Governments are instituted* among men.

These three fundamental truths are the cornerstone of our great national heritage and provide the foundation for our government. According to these "self-evident truths," governments are instituted to secure the rights that have already been bestowed upon human persons by their Creator. Among those rights are the right to life, liberty, and the pursuit of happiness. Abortion denies human persons the most fundamental rights they have. We enjoy the freedoms offered in this country, but let's not forget the cost of that freedom and the foundation upon which it was built. As we saw earlier, one journalist noted,

> Interestingly, and perhaps reassuringly, some of the most thoughtful ethicists feel that *the elements for an enduring moral consensus are right at hand—in the Constitution and the Declaration of Independence,* with their combination of Locke's natural rights and Calvin's ultimate right. "It's all there, it's all written down," says Colgate Philosopher Huntington Terrell. *"We don't have to be converted. It's what we have in common."* Terrell calls for a move "forward to the fundamentals," in which people put their lives where their mouths have been: in line with the country's founding principles.[10]

We live in a world full of countries that do not believe in our form of government and in contrast have atheistic and/or naturalistic constitutions to prove it. Moreover, they have set up their own criteria to determine human rights based upon their constitutions. So people who disagree with "self-evident truths," as stated by our Founding Fathers, are free to leave this country and find other countries that have constitutions consistent with their respective worldviews. Countries where "Personhood is entirely a 'social construct.' *Whether someone is too young or too old, too retarded or too sick, too useless or too*

---

[10]Ezra Bowen, "Looking to Its Roots," *Time,* May 25, 1987, 29 (emphasis added).

troublesome to be entitled to personhood is determined by a 'decision on . . . [their] part.' "[11]

As for us, we echo the words of Abraham Lincoln: "The Declaration [gave] liberty, not alone to the people of this country, but hope to all the world. It was that which gave promise that in due time the weights would be lifted from the shoulders of all men, and that all should have an equal chance."[12]

Have we learned anything as a nation from our own history with respect to what happens when governments or those in leadership positions determine who is a person and who is not? Have we not learned our lesson from tragedies such as slavery, when the courts decided blacks were not persons? Was not the belief that Jews and other minorities were not considered persons (the Holocaust in Nazi Germany) enough to teach us the dangerous grounds upon which panels of institutions like the NIH and others are treading upon? History shows us that there is a high price to pay when we refuse to learn from it. "The disadvantage of men not knowing the past is that they do not know the present. History is a hill or high point of vantage, from which alone men see the town in which they live or the age in which they are living."[13] As wisely said, "Those who cannot remember the past are condemned to repeat it."[14]

WHAT ABOUT EUTHANASIA?

Logically, abortion, infanticide, and euthanasia are inseparable issues. Every argument for abortion is also an argument for infanticide and euthanasia. For example, some babies are born with genetically deficient diseases, such as Turner's syndrome (forty-five chromosomes) or Down's syndrome (forty-seven chromosomes). The case of Infant Doe in Indiana (April 1982) is an example of how genetically inferior newborns are legally allowed to starve to death, even when other couples have a desire to adopt. Nobelist Dr. James Watson argued that no newborn infant should be declared human until it has passed certain tests regarding its genetic endowment. He said, "If a child were not declared alive until three days after birth, then all parents could be allowed the choice . . . [to] allow the baby to die . . . and save a lot of misery and suffering."[15]

[11]Neuhaus, "Don't Cross This Threshold," A–20 (emphasis added).
[12]Adler, *Haves Without Have-Nots*, 219–20.
[13]G. K. Chesterton (1874–1936), British author. *All I Survey*, "On St. George Revivified" (1933) *The Columbia Dictionary of Quotations*© is licensed from Columbia University Press. © 1993 by Columbia University Press.
[14]George Santayana (1863–1952), U.S. philosopher, poet. *Life of Reason*, "Reason in Common Sense," chap. 12 (1905–6). William L. Shirer used this quote as an epigraph in his *The Rise and Fall of the Third Reich* (1959). *The Columbia Dictionary of Quotations*® is licensed from Columbia University Press. © 1993 by Columbia University Press.
[15]J. C. Wilke and Barbara Wilke, *Abortion: Questions and Answers* (Cincinnati: Hayes, 1985), 204.

At the other end of the spectrum is euthanasia. Euthanasia does not refer to allowing someone to die with dignity, and it does not mean removing a mechanical means of prolonging the experience of dying. Euthanasia speaks to the readiness of some people to either directly or indirectly kill someone who if treated properly could go on living. Frankly speaking, it is the killing of a human being on the grounds that he or she is better off dead. It usually hides behind euphemisms like "mercy killing."

The word *euthanasia* comes from the Greek language: *eu* means "good" and *thanatos* means "death." The meaning of the word has evolved from the concept of "good death." It now refers to the act of ending another person's life, at their request, in order to minimize suffering. It comes in two main forms: (1) *active euthanasia,* causing the death of a person through a direct action, and (2) *passive euthanasia,* hastening the death of a person by removing life support equipment (e.g., a respirator), stopping medical procedures, medications, etc., or stopping food and water and allowing the person to dehydrate or starve to death.

The term *assisted suicide* is vaguely related to euthanasia. It usually refers to a situation in which information and/or the means of committing suicide (e.g., drugs, carbon monoxide gas) are given to a person to help terminate her own life without further assistance. The term *voluntary passive euthanasia* (VPE) is becoming commonly used. One writer actually suggested the use of the infinitive *to kevork*,[16] derived from the name of Dr. Jack Kevorkian, a Michigan doctor who has promoted VPE and has assisted at the deaths of dozens of patients.

We are adamantly against euthanasia for the following reasons:

1. It is unethical.
2. It is unconstitutional.
3. It is easily corruptible.
4. It is detrimental to the health care system.
5. It fatally ignores the limits of medical prognosis.

It is unethical. The Hippocratic Oath, which doctors have pledged since ancient times, says, "That into whatsoever house you shall enter, it shall be for the good of the sick to the utmost of your power, your holding yourselves far aloof from wrong, from corruption, from the tempting of others to vice. That you will exercise your art solely for the cure of your patients, and will give no drug, perform no operation, for a criminal purpose, even if solicited, far less

---

[16]Martin Levin, "Verdicts on Verdicts About Easeful Death," *The Globe and Mail,* Toronto, August 10, 1996, D–5.

suggest it." It is a sad commentary on the medical profession when those who pledge to preserve life turn out to be the ones who destroy it.

Tragically, the practice of giving lethal injections, even though it is illegal, is a "well-established underground practice." In 1997 the U.S. Supreme Court heard pleas from lawyers representing physicians and terminally ill patients urging the justices to declare that the Constitution grants individuals a right to have their physicians help them commit suicide. The *Wall Street Journal* reported,

> "We have a well-established underground practice of physicians hastening death of the terminally ill," declared one lawyer arguing for the new constitutional right. Justice Ruth Bader Ginsburg then asked Solicitor General Walter Dellinger, who opposed the proposition, whether that didn't mean the whole court battle is "a great sham, because physician-assisted suicide goes on for anybody sophisticated enough to want it." "We looked, and we don't know," responded Mr. Dellinger. "There is no evidence," he said. The Justice Department did not look very hard. There has always been such an "underground" practice. In 1988 the *Journal of the American Medical Association* stirred a furor with an anonymous article called "It's Over, Debbie." A doctor-in-training told how he gave a lethal injection to a young woman dying of ovarian cancer. He had never met the patient before he entered her hospital room that day.[17]

We must not forget that "the massive eugenics and euthanasia programs carried out in Nazi Germany required the collusion of an entire generation of German doctors, enlisting them in a mass violation of the simple principle that underlies the Hippocratic oath: " 'First, do no harm.' "[18]

It is unconstitutional. Both the Fifth and Fourteenth Amendments, along with the Declaration of Independence, guarantee the right to life. But there is clearly no constitutional guarantee of the right to take a life, even if it is one's own life that is being taken.

It is easily corruptible. As noted in the article above, the practice of euthanasia is already being abused, and legalization of euthanasia has a very high risk for overexpansion and corruption, which would result in even more personal and social harm. Providing euthanasia for competent, terminally ill adults will expand to incompetent adults. Voluntary euthanasia will eventually give way to involuntary euthanasia.

[17]Eugene H. Methvin, "A Compassionate Killing," *The Wall Street Journal*, January 20, 1997, A–14.
[18]Lois Wingerson, *Unnatural Selection: The Promise and the Power of Human Gene Research* (New York: Bantam, 1998), 170.

It is detrimental to the health care system. Legalized euthanasia will erode patient trust that the health care system will do everything possible to relieve their suffering rather than relieve them of their life. Knowing the state has legalized their death "by lethal injection," how can patients be sure of doctors' intentions? This is especially true if the patient becomes a financial burden to the state.

It fatally ignores the limits of medical prognosis. More than one patient has been wrongly diagnosed as terminally ill. Innumerable patients who thought they would never live, have. Many patients have recovered from prolonged comas, supposedly incurable diseases, or even "brain death." Given the irreversibility of euthanasia, the benefit of the doubt should be given to helping people live, not helping them to die.

On June 26, 1997, the Supreme Court ruled that the average American has no constitutional right to a physician-assisted suicide. The vote was 9 to 0, an unusual unanimous decision. On the other hand, the Court implied that there is no constitutional bar that would prevent a state from passing a law that permits physician-assisted suicide. Oregon has done exactly this. The battle, then, must be fought on a state-by-state basis.

Some justices discussed the dual effect theory. This is a situation in which a physician prescribes an adequate level of morphine or other drugs to control pain, even while knowing that it will shorten the patient's life. They found that this was acceptable behavior. Some of them expressed concern about any laws that permitted assisted suicide; they were worried that such laws might be abused, and that they might be the first of a series of laws that might generate a slippery slope toward a society that has wide-open assisted suicide without effective controls.

We believe the justices who showed concern for the slippery slope are right: consider the horrific parallels between Nazi Germany and the United States with respect to the progression of medical atrocities and the disregard for human life. This devaluation raises one of the most important questions that must be answered: "Who has the right to determine whether or not a human being (person) has the right to live?" Once again, we are brought back to the same answer: human rights are not bestowed upon us by any government or individual, but rather are given to us by the Creator Himself.

It is the belief in the *God-given value of human life* that answers the questions surrounding abortion, infanticide, and euthanasia. Yet for all practical purposes, as a nation, we have removed God from government and from the classroom. By our example we have taught our children that God is not necessary, and by the practices of abortion and euthanasia we have taught our children that we do not value human life. In fact, surveys tell us that one of the greatest fears American children have is that they will be a victim of violence at school. We must realize that it matters little *what we say* to our young people in lecture halls and classrooms; it is *what we do* that is passed on as a legacy to them. It is our collective behavior, not our superficial words, that teaches young Americans the value of human life. As Guy Doud, the 1986 National Teacher of the Year, said,

> *I'd rather see a sermon than hear one any day;*
> *I'd rather you walk with me than merely point the way.*
> *The eye's a more ready pupil than ever was the ear,*
> *Fine counsel is confusing, but example's always clear.*[19]

WHAT ABOUT BIOMEDICAL ISSUES?

Among the biomedical ethical issues that ought to be addressed are organ harvesting, organ transplants, fetal tissue research, reproductive technologies, cryonics, and genetic research. Since the scope of this work is limited, we have chosen to address the hotly debated issue of eugenics (genetic engineering). Of course, this topic is directly linked to human cloning, which will be critiqued under that heading. For now, we are merely giving you some of the historical background and stating the realities of how the science of eugenics served as one of the essential objectives (if not *the* objective) of Nazi Germany. Furthermore, we want to make you aware of the dangerous grounds upon which our nation is treading and to show how the science of eugenics is directly based upon a false belief in macroevolution[20] and the erroneous proposition that we have a duty to engineer a genetically pure or superior race.

Eugenics (from the Greek *eugenes* or "well-born") has been defined as an "outgrowth of the study of human heredity, aimed at 'improving' the genetic quality of the human stock."[21] One author correctly links the origin of eugenics to the theory of macroevolution and shows how other organizations sprang up to carry the eugenics torch further onto American soil. She says,

> The term eugenics was coined in 1883 by the English mathematician Francis Galton, a cousin of Charles Darwin. He defined it as the science of improving humanity by enhancing the chances that the "fittest" would produce more offspring than the "less fit." The eugenicists felt a mandate

---

[19]Guy R. Doud, *Molder of Dreams* (Colorado Springs: Focus on the Family, 1990), 83.
[20]See chapter 7.
[21]Microsoft® Encarta © 97 Encyclopedia. © 1993–1996 Microsoft Corporation. All rights reserved.

to help human evolution along. . . . The bible of the popular eugenics movement was *The Passing of the Great Race*, published in 1916. "The laws of nature require the obliteration of the unfit," wrote its author, Madison Grant, "and *human life is valuable only when it is of use to the community or race.*" . . .

The mission statement of the American Birth Control League . . . lamented that "*those least fit to carry on the race are increasing more rapidly*" and that "funds that should be used to raise the standard of our civilization are diverted to the maintenance of those who should never have been born."[22]

Margaret Sanger, the founder of Planned Parenthood, went so far as to say, "The merciful thing a large family can do for one of its infant members is to *kill it.*" [23]

Phrases such as "survival of the fittest" and "struggle for existence" came into use at the end of the nineteenth century when eugenics societies were created throughout the world to popularize genetic science. The U.S. Immigration Restriction Act of 1924 favored immigration from northern Europe and greatly restricted the entry of persons from other areas referred to as "biologically inferior." Between 1907 and 1937 thirty-two states required sterilization of various citizens viewed as undesirable: the mentally ill or handicapped, those convicted of sexual, drug, or alcohol crimes, and others viewed as "degenerate."

By the 1920s various German textbooks incorporated ideas of heredity and racial hygiene, and German professors were participating in the international eugenics movement. The Kaiser Wilhelm Institute of Anthropology, Human Heredity, and Eugenics was founded in 1927; by 1933 a sterilization law that had been titled "Eugenics in the service of public welfare" indicated compulsory sterilization "for the prevention of progeny with hereditary defects" in cases of congenital mental defects, schizophrenia, manic-depressive psychosis, hereditary epilepsy, and severe alcoholism.[24]

---

[22]Lois Wingerson, *Unnatural Selection: The Promise and the Power of Human Gene Research* (New York: Bantam, 1998), 136, 138–39 (emphasis added).

[23]Cited in Francis J. Beckwith, *Politically Correct Death: Answering the Arguments for Abortion Rights* (Grand Rapids: Baker, 1993), 174 (author's emphasis). Originally quoted in *Woman and the New Race* (New York: Brentano's, 1920), 63.

[24]For more information on historical background and current status of eugenics and The Human Genome Project, visit http://guweb.georgetown.edu/nrcbl/scopenotes, which is a web site known as "The Eugenics Watch." The Human Genome project is a thirteen-year effort coordinated by the U.S. Department of Energy and the National Institutes of Health. The project originally was slated to last fifteen years, but rapid technological advances have accelerated the expected completion date to 2003. Project goals are to *identify* all of the approximate 100,000 genes in human DNA, *determine* the sequences of the 3,000,000,000 chemical bases that make up human DNA, *store* this information in databases, and *develop* tools for data analysis.

Eventually, this led to the darkest period for eugenics—when Nazi Germany embarked on the "final solution" to the "Jewish question," or the Holocaust. The Nazi racial hygiene program began with involuntary sterilizations and ended with mass genocide. "Survival of the fittest" was incorporated into the mindset of the Nazis along with the rise of Adolf Hitler and the "struggle" to save a languishing Germany. The "struggle for life" became the theme of Hitler's book—*Mein Kampf* (My Struggle)—and in 1924, a mere sixty-five years after the publication of *On the Origin of Species*, Hitler wrote,

> The stronger must dominate and not mate with the weaker, which would signify the sacrifice of its own higher nature. Only the born weakling can look upon this principle as cruel, and if he does so it is merely because he is of a feebler nature and narrower mind; for if such a law did not direct the process of evolution then the higher development of organic life would not be conceivable at all. . . . If Nature does not wish that weaker individuals should mate with the stronger, *she wishes even less that a superior race should intermingle with an inferior one;* because in such a case *all her efforts, throughout hundreds of thousands of years, to establish an evolutionary higher stage of being, may thus be rendered futile.*[25]

Nazi Germany, influenced by social Darwinism, enacted laws that were based on the assumptions that (1) they needed to eliminate the "unfit" and that (2) eugenics would improve the general level of industrial and personal efficiency in the working class and eventually give rise to a "superior Aryan race." Since World War II, interest in the type of eugenics popular in the early half of the century has changed. Utilizing gene therapy, genetic testing and screening, and genetic counseling, scientists and clinicians use knowledge of inherited disease or other genetic problems to change (for the better) those persons who can be assisted. Still, questions are raised about the morality of changing human genes, the limits of those changes, and the wisdom of acting when no cure is available.

Ultimately, eugenics is dedicated to the proposition that all are created *unequal* and that the "more highly evolved" must take the destiny of humanity and the "less evolved" into their own hands. World War II saw the advent of Hitler and his attempts at controlling the gene pool through eugenics. Now we have the technological know-how to transform our own society into a genetically superior race. We also now share the same goal as the Nazis, which makes this a perilous time for our nation. In addition, consider the fact that panels like the one cited above (NIH) are pushing to arbitrarily redefine personhood

---

[25]Adolf Hitler, *Mein Kampf* (London: Hurst and Blackett, 1939), 239–40 (emphasis added).

and, eventually, with that redefinition the right to life will also be subject to human opinion. Who will say *enough*? And even if the line is attempted to be drawn, where will it be drawn and who will draw it?

In the *American Journal of Law and Medicine,* an article was written presenting a model for government protection to allow parents to select certain traits in their offspring while proposing limits in the event the traits were damaging to the future child.[26] The truth is that eugenics spread steadily in Western culture throughout the twentieth century. Even after the German embarrassment, the eugenicists kept right on pursuing the same goals they had always pursued—*the same goals that Hitler pursued.* Yet the spread of eugenics after World War II in the United States is not well studied or documented.

Consider the fact that *the philosophy of eugenics was then, and is now, perfectly meshed with the principles of macroevolutionary science*—most notably natural selection and the survival of the fittest. "National Socialism," said Nazi party leader Rudolf Franz Ferdinand Hoess at a mass meeting in 1934, "is nothing but applied biology."[27] Nazi scientists saw themselves as "cultivators of the genes and caretakers of the race."[28] In principle, are we not guilty of the same thinking? Are we not looking to "breed out" the unfit through the science of eugenics?

Consider also prenatal testing. What is its ultimate purpose, and what kind of message are eugenicists sending out to individuals who have some of the same genetic "deficiencies" that genetic testers and eugenicists are hoping to eliminate? Ruth Ricker confronted this issue one Saturday in March 1995. She is a very articulate and candid woman who happens to be as tall as a third grader. Ricker has achondroplasia, an inherited form of dwarfism. In a public statement she said,

> What are the chances that a couple of generations from now there's going to be a lot fewer healthy dwarfs? . . . *It concerns me what the rest of society considers as normal and healthy.* A few years from now when average people are going to be able to screen for this, you know there's going to be a shopping list. We're going to see a whole lot less [dwarfs]—and I'm not necessarily comfortable with that.[29]

---

[26]Owen D. Jones, "Reproductive Autonomy and Evolutionary Biology: A Regulatory Framework for Trait-Selection Technologies," *American Journal of Law and Medicine,* 1993, 19 (3), 187–231.
[27]Lois Wingerson, *Unnatural Selection: The Promise and the Power of Human Gene Research* (New York: Bantam, 1998), 171.
[28]Ibid.
[29]Ibid., 46 (emphasis added).

Another example of the same kind of message being sent out to individuals who have genetic defects was documented by the same author when she cited a boy's school project.

> In the spring of 1995 . . . [fifteen-year-old] Blaine Deatherage-Newsom conducted a survey on the Internet. . . . Blaine posed five questions: "If we had the technology to eliminate disabilities from the population, would that be good public policy to do so? What are the Pros? What are the Cons? What is your answer? Why do you feel the way you do?"
>
> Blaine added that he has spina bifida and hydrocephalus (the accumulation of fluid on the brain), "so I have my own feelings and answers to these questions." . . . The results of Blaine's survey were mixed. . . . That uncertainty generated interesting comments. Some people wanted to know what Blaine meant by "eliminate" (he had been thinking of genetic engineering). . . . What could Blaine make of all this?
>
> "*I wonder if people are saying that they think the world would be a better place without me,*" he wrote. "I wonder if people just think the lives of people with disabilities are so full of misery and suffering that they think we would be better off dead. . . . Most of the time I am very happy and I like my life very much." (Blaine spends most of his day in a wheelchair, cannot make most people understand what he says aloud, and had undergone surgery eleven times by the time he conducted the survey.)[30]

The message is loud and clear, even for a fifteen-year-old boy to understand: "The world will be a·better place without you." The science of eugenics teaches us that the value of human life is directly proportional to the genetic purity of that life. We will address the ethical principles that supporters of eugenics and human cloning use to advance their views in our response to human cloning. For now, we merely want to respond to the fallacious thinking involved with the idea that somehow science must take on the responsibility to produce a superior race. *Those who advocate the science of eugenics are in principle no different than the Nazis.* In a book titled *Biomedical Ethics: Opposing Viewpoints,* one of the contributing authors, Rebecca Ryskind, quoted from an article written by Nazi researcher Joseph Sobran. She said,

> The fact remains that, as Joseph Sobran noted (in a column titled "The Angel of Choice"), the Nazi researchers shared the same premises of some of those who think they are the opposite of Nazis. Writing of Dr. Joseph Mengele, the Nazi "angel of death" who spent the latter years of his life working as an abortionist in Argentina, Sobran says:

---

[30]Ibid., 54–56 (emphasis added).

He saw himself as a progressive, and he was right. He had liberated himself from the stifling moral traditions, and he was in the vanguard of change, seeking new scientific answers through experimentation. He shared the Darwinian materialism of his time, which is still our time, even if the Nazi wing has gone a little out of fashion. Abortion, fetal experimentation, surrogate motherhood, genetic engineering—*he would have been right at home with these new developments. In fact, he could fairly consider himself a pioneer, a casualty of progress who was ahead of his time.*

The "murderous science" of the Nazis didn't begin with Hitler and it didn't begin overnight. Eugenics programs—always begun in the name of high humanitarian principles—were well established during the Weimar Republic. *Germany didn't accidentally wake up evil one morning; the German people simply got slowly accustomed to breaking down the safeguards separating science from atrocity.*[31]

As noted above, the Darwinian mindset cannot be divorced from what happened in Nazi Germany, nor should it be overlooked in our present situation here in the United States. The famous evolutionist Julian S. Huxley contended, "In light of evolutionary biology man can now see himself as the sole agent of further evolutionary advance on this planet, and one of the few possible instruments of progress in the universe at large."[32]

Responses to the exaggerated expectations of producing a superior race based upon the Darwinian mindset have already been addressed in a previous work from which the following excerpt is taken.

First of all, there is no real evidence that the present race was produced by any naturalistic evolutionary process. Both Scripture and the scientific evidence point to God as the cause of the human species.[33] Second, science, with all its technology and touted brilliance, has not been able to permanently improve even a fruit fly. We have a long way to go to "improve" man. Third, even if we could make permanent changes in the human species there is no ethical reason why we should. "Can" does not imply "ought" any more than "is" implies "ought." *Just because we can do something does not mean that we should do it.* Ability does not imply morality. Fourth, even if we were able to actually produce changes in the human species, how would we know they were better, not merely different? *By*

---

[31]Rebecca Ryskind, "The Use of Fetal Tissue Would Encourage Abortion," quoted in *Biomedical Ethics: Opposing Viewpoints*, Terry O'Neill, ed. (San Diego: Greenhaven, 1994), 140–41 (emphasis added).
[32]Julian S. Huxley, *Essays of a Biologist* (Harmondsworth: Penguin, 1939), 132.
[33]See chapters 6 and 7.

what standard would we judge them better? It would beg the question to answer, "by the desired human standard."[34]

Of course, the question being begged is "whose standard?" *Who* determines what a "better" human being is? Scientists, panels like the NIH, government, or society in general? The closer we get to actually cloning a human being, the more we advocate the same basic moral principles of Nazi Germany. *There is no escaping this truth.* Getting rid of society's undesirables, the weaker or less "fit" individuals, is what the Nazis set as their goal. Remember fifteen-year-old Blaine's words: *"I wonder if people are saying that they think the world would be a better place without me."* Those who advocate eugenics with the goal of "improving" the human race have answered his question with a resounding yes!

WHAT ABOUT HUMAN CLONING?

For years scientists have used cloning techniques to help produce better crops and gardens, and genetic engineers have worked with livestock. The medical breakthroughs that led up to Dolly (a sheep cloned from an adult cell) began around midcentury. Using cloning-type methodology and gene alterations, scientists are attempting to create new organs such as livers, kidneys, and even the possibility of human hearts. This kind of research is technically not cloning, but to the public it is considered to be the same.

The Human Genome Project, an ongoing effort to identify the location of all the genes in the human genome, continues to identify genetic diseases. Where and when the line is crossed is the question. The place where the line is drawn is related to the question on where medical purposes end and where genetic "improvement" begins; drawing that line leads us into our question concerning ethics. Even skeptical scientists believe that no matter what, the technique concerning human cloning will continue somewhere in the world. They claim that it will only be a matter of time before it happens. Yet few people realize that the success of Dolly followed 277 failed attempts. What happens to the unsuccessful attempts at human cloning?

We have argued for the belief that God created humanity and that human life begins at conception. On that basis, we believe in God-given human rights and the value of human life that is protected by our constitution. One thing is for certain right now: if human cloning research is allowed to continue in an unmitigated manner, *the life created by scientists will not be viewed as having*

---

[34]Norman L. Geisler, *Christian Ethics: Options and Issues* (Grand Rapids, Mich.: Baker, 1989), 178 (emphasis added).

God-given human value or human rights—in fact, this is already occurring in human embryo research (as noted earlier).

The NIH panel's recommendation concerning embryos and personhood, and the current practice in embryo research, leads us to another ethical question: "If human embryos are not considered to be persons, then what are they?" They are certainly living organisms. But what if living organisms, in particular human embryos, are not considered to be persons and have no human rights? This is no longer a speculative question; it has been addressed and continues to get dangerously close to viewing human life as a "thing" and not a "person." Consider the following excerpts from a *Washington Post* article, some of which we have already noted:

> A New York scientist has quietly applied for a patent on a method for making creatures that are part human and part animal in a calculated move designed to reignite debate about the morality of patenting life forms and engineering human beings. The scientist, Stuart A. Newman, a cellular biologist at New York Medical College in Valhalla, said he has not created such creatures and never intends to. Indeed, he said, although the hybrids could be extremely useful in medical research, his goal is to stop the technology from being used by anyone—and to force the U.S. Patent and Trademark Office and the courts to reexamine this country's 18-year history of allowing patents on living creatures, which he considers unethical and immoral.
>
> Patents are not allowed on human beings, but patent law experts said there is nothing in U.S. patent code that would preclude someone from winning a patent on a partially human creature. Already, the patent office has awarded several patents on animals with minor human components—including laboratory mice engineered with human cancer genes or human immune system cells. Even if the patent is not awarded to Newman, several experts agreed, the ploy could achieve its primary goal of forcing a national debate about the commercialization of life in an era when genes, cells, tissues and organs are being shuttled increasingly across species barriers and blurring the distinctions between humans and nonhuman animals.
>
> "It is a classic slippery slope," said Thomas Murray, director of the Center for Biomedical Ethics at Case Western Reserve University. "If we put one human gene in an animal, or two or three, some people may get nervous but you're clearly not making a person yet. But when you talk about a hefty percentage of the cells being human . . . this really is problematic. Then you have to ask these very hard questions about what it means to be human." . . . The patent office's policy of not granting patents on human beings is based on the 13th Amendment to the Constitution,

which blocks slavery. But the office has never been faced with the question of "how human" an animal would have to be before it was deemed worthy of that protection. . . . For years, the patent office assumed that living things could not be patented and agreed to grant patents on some plants and seeds only after Congress passed specific laws commanding it to do so. The office rejected the first request for a patent on a bacterium—one engineered to digest oil spills—in 1978. But in a 5-to-4 decision in 1980, the U.S. Supreme Court overruled that decision, saying living things could be patented as long as they met the standard criteria for patentability. Seven years later, the office granted its first patent on an animal—a genetically engineered mouse—and it has since granted 79 other animal patents—including several on mice, rats and rabbits and one each for an engineered bird, fish, pig, guinea pig, sheep and abalone. More than 1,800 patents have also been granted for genes and lines of cultured cells, including human ones, that scientists believe have medical potential.

"With cloning, with Dolly, with everything we've been hearing in the past couple of years, science is progressing and so these issues have come to the fore," said O'Connor, now executive director of the American Institute for Medical and Biological Engineering in Washington. "What does it take to be human? A cell line? A limb? A whole human? A chimera [beast of Greek mythology]? We don't have a definition of what a human being is for patent purposes."[35]

Seems as though we're back to the same argument as with abortion and euthanasia, but with a different application. In principle, there is no difference: we stand firm on the same argued grounds. Human rights are based upon the classical understanding of natural law and the God-given value of human life.[36] As science moves forward with the human cloning project, the idea is fostered that some individuals can have total dominion over the existence of others (human sovereignty over life) to the point of programming their biological identity—selected according to arbitrary or purely utilitarian criteria (that the end somehow justifies the means). This selective concept of human life will have, among other things, a heavy cultural fallout beyond the (numerically limited) practice of cloning, since there will be a growing conviction that human value does not depend on human personal identity but only on those biological qualities that can be appraised and therefore selected (the so-called quality-of-life principle). Moreover, there is this belief that since we have become so advanced in our technology, there exists some obligation to guide the

[35]Rick Weiss, "Patent Sought on Making of Part-Human Creatures: Scientist Seeks to Touch Off Ethics Debate," *Washington Post*, Thursday, April 2, 1998, A12.
[36]See chapters 9 and 10.

future of macroevolution in order to create a superior race.

It is not a stretch of the imagination to posit a country that would one day finance a national program, based upon social Darwinism, similar to that of Nazi Germany (genetically engineering humans to maximize certain traits and achieve genetic superiority). Once the "perfect human" was developed, embryo cloning could be used to replicate that individual and conceivably produce un-limited numbers of clones. The same approach could be used to create a ge-netic underclass for exploitation: e.g., individuals with subnormal intelligence and above-normal strength. Beyond that, one can imagine all kind of evil and hideous scenarios, especially if the technological know-how gets into the hands of immoral leaders.

This is the state of affairs regarding the science of eugenics and human cloning; with it come the ethical questions that are tragically lagging behind. The primary ethical principles and views that favor human cloning are:

1. The quality-of-life principle
2. Human sovereignty over life
3. The duty to create a superior race
4. The end-justifies-the-means ethic (utilitarianism).

We now offer our response to each of these ethical principles in an effort to show why they fail to be valid rational justifications for eugenics and human cloning.[37]

THE QUALITY-OF-LIFE PRINCIPLE

The quality-of-life principle is simply another form of utilitarianism (the greatest good for the greatest number). Yet one must ask, "What does 'quality of life' mean?" Often, it is an ill-defined and ambiguous catch-all term used to justify actions that lack ethical quality. Furthermore, who decides what "qual-ity" means? The patient? The doctor? Special panels? Society? How do we know for sure what procedures would bring about this elusive "quality of life"? One would have to be God in order to know all the factors necessary to predict that our genetic tinkering would really improve the race. It might cure some problems—and cause others. Genetic superiority may make a person arrogant, prideful, greedy, and violent. Genetic superiority could lead to creating a race determined to conquer the world.

---

[37]These responses are a summarized version of a more in-depth analysis given in the book by Norman L. Geisler, *Christian Ethics: Options and Issues* (Grand Rapids, Mich.: Baker, 1989), 173–92.

HUMAN SOVEREIGNTY OVER LIFE

To think that humanity exercises sovereignty over life is erroneous. We did not create the DNA code; we merely discovered it. Efforts to duplicate the creation of life from scratch have failed. In spite of all our medical advances, *death continues to prove to us that we are not sovereign over life.*

THE DUTY TO CREATE A SUPERIOR RACE

To believe that we have such a duty is fallacious. Horrendous past attempts should have put this to rest. Once again, this idea assumes that genetic superiority is somehow related to making humanity better. Yet there is no ethical reason why we should do this. As we said earlier, "can" does not imply "ought" any more than "is" implies "ought." That we *can* do something does not mean that we *should* do it. As C. S. Lewis said, "There is no sense in talking about *becoming better* if better means simply *what we are becoming*—it is like congratulating yourself on reaching your destination and *defining destination as the place you have reached*."[38]

THE END-JUSTIFIES-THE-MEANS ETHIC

The only way to know that the ends justify the means is to know what the end will be. However, we do not know what will happen. Hence, means must have their own justification; the same with ends. Not every goal is good, even if the majority of society believes that it is. It must be shown to be the case— and *that* implies a standard. Many Germans believed that their goal, to make a better world, justified their means. *They were wrong!* Also, if good or better ends justified any means, then logically one would have to agree with the Nazis. One could imagine all kinds of parallel scenarios to get rid of medical, psychological, social, and political problems with such an ethic.

In conclusion, apart from the God-given value of human life and human rights, we see no hope for stopping the science of eugenics and the desired goal of cloning "genetically superior" human beings. Halting the human cloning project is a moral duty that must also be translated into cultural, social, and legislative terms. We need to be able to distinguish between the progress of scientific research and the rise of *scientific Nazism*. Those who advocate the "progress" of eugenics ultimately foster the necessary condition for any society to collapse: treating humans as means to other ends.

Finally, we want to say that we should never forget that denial of the belief in God-given human rights and the value of human life creates new forms of

---

[38]C. S. Lewis, *God in the Dock* (Grand Rapids, Mich.: Eerdmans, 1970), 21.

slavery, discrimination, and profound suffering. God has entrusted the created world to the human race, giving us freedom and intelligence. *We must set the limits to our actions by learning where God has set the boundaries between good and evil.* The place to learn where the essential boundaries have been set by God is in His Word, the Bible. The chief difference should again be pointed out between life as a gift from God and the belief that life should be viewed as a commercial product. Scientific research loses its dignity, and a country will ultimately fail, when science turns on human life and devalues it.

As a nation, we have forgotten that human life and liberty are God-given gifts. Do not forget the warning of the author of the Declaration of Independence, Thomas Jefferson, which is etched in marble on the northeast wall of the Jefferson Memorial in Washington, D.C.

> *God, who gave us life, gave us liberty. Can the liberties of a nation remain secure when we have removed a conviction that these liberties are the gift of God? Indeed, I tremble for my country when I reflect that God is just, that his justice cannot sleep forever.*

BIBLIOGRAPHY

Adler, Jerry. "The Last Days of Auschwitz," *Newsweek*, January 16, 1995, 47.

Adler, Mortimer J. *The Great Ideas: A Lexicon of Western Thought* (New York: Macmillan, 1992).

———. *Haves Without Have-Nots* (New York: Macmillan, 1991).

———. *How to Think about God* (New York: Macmillan, 1980).

———. *A Second Look in the Rearview Mirror* (New York: Macmillan, 1992).

———. *Truth in Religion: The Plurality of Religions and the Unity of Truth* (New York: Macmillan, 1990).

Annas, George J., and Michael A. Grodin, *The Nazi Doctors and the Nuremberg Code: Human Rights in Human Experimentation* (New York: Oxford University Press, 1992).

Archer, Gleason L. *Encyclopedia of Biblical Difficulties* (Grand Rapids, Mich.: Zondervan, 1982).

Asimov, Isaac. *Asimov's Guide to Science* (New York: Basic Books, 1972).

Audi, Robert, ed. *The Cambridge Dictionary of Philosophy* (Cambridge: Cambridge University Press, 1995).

Beckwith, Francis J., and Norman L. Geisler, *Matters of Life and Death* (Grand Rapids: Baker, 1991).

Behe, Michael J. *Darwin's Black Box: The Biochemical Challenge to Evolution* (New York: Free Press, 1996).

Bennett, William R., Jr. *Scientific and Engineering Problem Solving With the Computer* (Englewood Cliffs, N.J.: Prentice Hall, 1976).

Bloom, Allan. *The Closing of the American Mind* (New York: Simon & Schuster, 1987).

Bowen, Ezra. "Looking to Its Roots," *Time*, May 25, 1987, 26–29.

Bruce, F. F. *The New Testament Documents: Are They Reliable?* (Grand Rapids, Mich.: Eerdmans, 1985).

Budziszewski, J. *Written on the Heart: The Case for Natural Law* (Downers Grove, Ill.: InterVarsity, 1997).

Buswell, James Oliver Jr. *A Systematic Theology of the Christian Religion* (Grand Rapids, Mich.: Zondervan, 1962).

Chesterton, G. K. *Orthodoxy* (New York: Doubleday, 1959).

Clark, Ronald W. *Einstein: The Life and Times* (New York: Avon Books, 1972).

Cowen, R. "Repaired Hubble Finds Giant Black Hole," *Science News*, vol. 145, no. 23, June 4, 1994, 356–58.

———. "New Evidence of Galactic Black Hole," *Science News*, vol. 147, no. 3, January 21, 1995, 36.

Darwin, Charles. *On the Origin of Species* (New York: NAL Penguin Inc., 1958).

Davies, Paul. *God and the New Physics* (New York: Simon & Schuster, 1983).

———. *Superforce* (New York: Simon & Schuster, 1984).

———. *The Cosmic Blueprint* (New York: Simon & Schuster, 1988).

Dawkins, Richard. *The Blind Watchmaker* (New York: W. W. Norton & Company, 1987).

———. *The Selfish Gene* (Oxford University Press, 1976).

Denton, Michael. *Evolution: A Theory in Crisis* (Bethesda: Adler & Adler, 1986).

Dobson, James. *Life on the Edge*, Focus on the Family & Word Inc., 1993, 1994, videocassette.

Doud, Guy R. *Molder of Dreams* (Colorado Springs: Focus on the Family, 1990).

Douglas, John, and Mark Olshaker, *Journey Into Darkness* (New York: Simon & Schuster, 1997).

Federer, William J. *America's God and Country Encyclopedia of Quotations* (Coppel: FAME Publishing, 1994).

Felsenthal, Edward. "Man's Genes Made Him Kill, His Lawyers Claim," *The Wall Street Journal*, November 15, 1994, B1.

Fleming, Gerald. "Engineers of Death," *The New York Times*, July 18, 1993, E19.

Fletcher, Joseph. *Situation Ethics: The New Morality* (Philadelphia: Westminister, 1966).

Foster, David. *The Philosophical Scientists* (New York: Dorset, 1985).

Frankl, Victor. *The Doctor and the Soul: Introduction to Logotherapy* (New York: Knopf, 1982).

———. *Man's Search for Meaning* (New York: Simon & Schuster, 1984).

Gallup, George H. *Scared: Growing Up in America* (Harrisburg, Pa.: Morehouse Publishing, 1996).

Geisler, Norman L. *Baker Encyclopedia of Christian Apologetics* (Grand Rapids, Mich.: Baker, 1999).

———. *Christian Ethics: Options and Issues* (Grand Rapids, Mich.: Baker, 1989).

———. *Christian Apologetics* (Grand Rapids, Mich.: Baker, 1976).

Geisler, Norman L., and J. Kerby Anderson, *Origin Science: A Proposal for the Creation-Evolution Controversy* (Grand Rapids, Mich.: Baker, 1987).

———. *Is Man the Measure?* (Grand Rapids, Mich.: Baker, 1983).

Geisler, Norman L. *Miracles and Modern Thought* (Grand Rapids, Mich.: Zondervan, 1982).

———. *Philosophy of Religion* (Grand Rapids, Mich.: Zondervan, 1974).

————. *Thomas Aquinas: An Evangelical Appraisal* (Grand Rapids, Mich.: Baker, 1991).

Geisler, N. L., and R. M. Brooks, *When Skeptics Ask: A Handbook on Christian Evidences* (Grand Rapids, Mich.: Baker, 1990).

Geisler, Norman L., and Thomas Howe, *When Critics Ask: A Popular Handbook on Bible Difficulties*, 1992).

Geisler, Norman, and William Nix, *A General Introduction to the Bible* (Chicago: Moody Press, 1982).

Geisler Norman L., and Frank S. Turek III, *Legislating Morality: Is It Wise? Is It Legal? Is It Possible?* (Minneapolis: Bethany House, 1998).

Geisler, Norman L., and William D. Watkins, *Worlds Apart: A Handbook on World Views* (Grand Rapids, Mich.: Baker, 1989).

Gibbons, Ann. "Mitochondrial Eve: Wounded, but Not Dead Yet," *Science*, vol. 257, August 14, 1992, 873.

Gish, Duane. *Evolution: Challenge of the Fossil Record* (El Cajon, Calif.: Creation-Life, 1985).

Gould, Stephen J. *Eight Little Piggies: Reflections in Natural History* (New York: W. W. Norton & Co., 1993).

————. "Impeaching a Self-Appointed Judge," *Scientific American*, July 1992, 120.

————. *The Mismeasure of Man* (New York: W. W. Norton & Co., 1981).

————. *The Panda's Thumb* (New York: W. W. Norton & Co., 1982).

————. "The Verdict on Creationism," *The New York Times Magazine*, July 19, 1987, 32–34.

Greene, Robert, and Joost Elffers, *The 48 Laws of Power* (New York: Penguin, 1998).

Guralink, David B., General Editor. *Webster's New World Dictionary: Second College Edition* (New York: Simon & Schuster, 1980).

Hawking, Stephen W. *A Brief History of Time* (New York: Bantam, 1988).

Heidegger, Martin. *An Introduction to Metaphysics* (New York: Anchor Books, 1961).

Heisenberg, Werner. *Physics and Philosophy: The Revolution in Modern Science* (New York, 1958).

Henry, William A. III. "The Price of Obedience," *Time*, February 3, 1992, 23.

Hick, John. *The Existence of God* (New York: Macmillan, 1964).

Hitler, Adolf. *Mein Kampf* (New York: Hurst and Blackett, 1942, trans. and annot. James Murphy).

Hume, David. *An Enquiry Concerning Human Understanding: Great Books in Philosophy* (Buffalo, N.Y.: Prometheus, 1988).

Hunter, George. *A Civic Biology: Presented in Problems* (New York: American Book Company, 1914).

Huxley, Julian S. *Essays of a Biologist* (Harmondsworth: Penguin, 1939), 132.

Jackson, Robert H. *The Case Against the Nazi War Criminals* (New York: Knopf, 1946).

Jackson, Robert H. *The Nuremberg Case* (New York: Cooper Square, 1971).

Jastrow, Robert. *God and the Astronomers* (New York: W. W. Norton & Co., 1992).

Johnson, Phillip E. *Reason in the Balance* (Downers Grove, Ill.: InterVarsity Press, 1995).

Jones, Owen D. "Reproductive Autonomy and Evolutionary Biology: A Regulatory Framework for Trait-Selection Technologies," *American Journal of Law & Medicine*, 1993, 19 (3) 187–231.

Kaku, Michio. "What Happened Before the Big Bang?" *Astronomy*, vol. 24, no. 5, May 1996, 36.

Kelman, Mark. *A Guide to Critical Legal Studies* (Cambridge, Mass.: Harvard University Press, 1987).

Koppel, Ted. Commencement speech, Duke University, May 10, 1987.

Krauthammer, Charles. "Of Headless Mice . . . and Men," *Time*, vol. 151, no. 2, January 1998, 68.

Kreeft, Peter. *Back to Virtue* (San Francisco: Ignatius Press, 1992).

———. *Making Sense Out of Suffering* (Ann Arbor, Mich.: Servant, 1986).

———. *The Unaborted Socrates* (Downers Grove, Ill.: InterVarsity Press, 1983).

———. *Three Philosophies of Life* (San Francisco: Ignatius, 1989).

Kurtz, Paul. *Forbidden Fruit: The Ethics of Humanism* (Buffalo, N.Y.: Prometheus, 1988).

Kushner, Harold S. *When Bad Things Happen to Good People* (New York: Avon Books, 1981).

Lasota, Jean-Pierre. "Unmasking Black Holes," *Scientific American*, May 1999, 42.

Leff, Arthur Allen. "Unspeakable Ethics, Unnatural Law," *Duke Law Journal*, December 1979, Number 6.

Lemonick, M. D. "Echoes of The Big Bang," *Time*, vol. 139, no. 18, May 4, 1992, 62.

———. and J. M. Nash, "Unraveling Universe," *Time*, March 6, 1995, 77–84.

Lester, Lane P., and Raymond G. Bohlin, *The Natural Limits to Biological Change* (Grand Rapids, Mich.: Zondervan, 1984).

Levin, Martin. "Verdicts on Verdicts About Easeful Death," *The Globe and Mail* (Toronto), August 10, 1996, D–5.

Lewis, C. S. *God in the Dock* (Grand Rapids, Mich.: Eerdmans, 1970).

———. *Mere Christianity* (New York: Macmillan, 1952).

———. *Miracles* (New York: Macmillan, 1960).

———. *Screwtape Letters* (Springdale: Whitaker House, 1984).

———. *Surprised by Joy* (New York: Harcourt Brace & Company, 1955).

———. *The Abolition of Man* (New York: Macmillan, 1955).

———. *The Great Divorce* (New York: Macmillan, 1946).

———. *The Problem of Pain* (New York: Macmillan, 1962).

Liles, G. "The Faith of an Atheist," *MD*, March 1994, 59–64.

MacArthur, John. *How to Study the Bible* (Chicago: Moody Press, 1982).

Martin, E., M. Ruse and E. Holmes, eds. *Oxford Dictionary of Biology* (New York: Oxford University Press, 1996).

McDowell, Josh, and Bart Larson, *Jesus, A Biblical Defense of His Deity* (San Bernardino, Calif.: Here's Life, 1983).

McDowell, Josh. *More Than a Carpenter* (Wheaton, Ill.: Tyndale House, 1973).

McKeon, Richard., ed. *The Basic Works of Aristotle* (New York: Random House, 1941).

Metzger, Bruce. *The Text of the New Testament* (New York: Oxford University Press, 1964).

Methvin, Eugene H. "A Compassionate Killing," *The Wall Street Journal,* January 20, 1997, A14.

Montgomery, John Warwick. *History and Christianity* (Minneapolis: Bethany House, 1964).

——. *The Law Above the Law* (Minneapolis: Bethany House, 1975).

Moreland, J. P. *Christianity and the Nature of Science* (Grand Rapids, Mich.: Baker, 1989).

Moreland, J. P., and Kai Nielsen, *Does God Exist?* (Nashville: Thomas Nelson, 1990).

Nash, J. Madeleine. "When Life Exploded," *Time,* December 4, 1995, 49–56.

Nash, J. Madeleine. "Addicted: Why Do People Get Hooked?" *Time,* May 5, 1997, 69–76.

Newman, Robert C., and Hermand J. Eckelmann, *Genesis One & the Origin of the Earth* (Downers Grove, Ill.: InterVarsity Press, 1977).

Niebuhr, Reinhold, ed. *Marx and Engels on Religion* (New York: Schocken, 1964).

Nietzsche, Friedrich. *The Gay Science,* in the portable Nietzsche, trans. Walter Kaufmann (New York: Viking, 1968).

Ohlendor-Moffat, Pat. "Surgery Before Birth," *Discover,* vol. 12, no. 2, February 1991, 58–65.

Orgel, Leslie. *The Origins of Life* (New York: Wiley, 1973).

Packer, J. I. *Knowing God* (Downers Grove, Ill.: InterVarsity Press, 1973).

Patterson, Colin. "Evolutionism and Creationism," speech given at the American Museum of Natural History, New York, November 5, 1981. Transcript by Wayne Frair.

Peacock, Roy E. *A Brief History of Eternity* (Wheaton, Ill.: Crossway, 1990).

Polkinghorne, John. *One World* (London: SPCK, 1986).

Robertson, Archibald T. *An Introduction to the Textual Criticism of the New Testament* (Nashville: Broadman, 1925).

Ross, Hugh. *The Fingerprint of God* (Orange, Calif.: Promise Publishing, 1991).

——. "Searching for Adam," *Facts & Faith,* vol. 10, no. 1 (1996), 4.

Russell, Bertrand. *"Why I Am Not a Christian" and Other Essays on Religion and Related Subjects,* ed. Paul Edwards (New York: Simon & Schuster, 1957).

Ryskind, Rebecca. "The Use of Fetal Tissue Would Encourage Abortion," quoted in *Biomedical Ethics: Opposing Viewpoints,* Terry O'Neill, ed. (San Diego: Greenhaven Press, 1994), 140–141.

Sagan, Carl. *Cosmos* (New York: Random House, 1980).

Sanders, C. *Introduction to Research in English Literary History* (New York: Macmillan, 1952).

Sheler, Jeffery. "Is the Bible True? Extraordinary Insights From Archaeology and History." *U.S. News & World Report,* October 25, 1999, 50, 52, 58–59.

Schimmel, Solomon. *The Seven Deadly Sins: Jewish, Christian, and Classical Reflections on Human Psychology* (New York: Oxford University Press, 1997).

Schroeder, Gerald. *The Science of God* (New York: The Free Press, 1997).

Shreeve, James. "Argument Over a Woman," *Discover,* August 1990, 52–59.

Smoot, George, and Keay Davidson, *Wrinkles in Time* (New York: Avon Books, 1993).

Stoner, Don. *A New Look at an Old Earth* (Eugene, Ore.: Harvest House, 1997).

Tierney, John, Linda Wright, and Karen Springen, "The Search for Adam and Eve," *Newsweek,* January 11, 1998, 46–51.

Vine, W. E. *An Expository Dictionary of New Testament Words* (Nashville: Thomas Nelson, 1985).

Warfield, Benjamin B. *An Introduction to the Textual Criticism of the New Testament* (London: n.p., 1886).

Watchtower. *Reasoning From the Scriptures* (New York: Watchtower Bible and Tract Society, 1985).

––––––. *You Can Live Forever in Paradise on Earth* (New York: Watchtower Bible and Tract Society, 1984).

Weaver, Richard M. *Ideas Have Consequences* (Chicago: University of Chicago Press, 1948).

Weiss, Rick. "Patent Sought on Making of Part-Human Creatures Scientist Seeks to Touch Off Ethics Debate," *Washington Post,* Thursday, April 2, 1998, A12.

Westcott B. F., and F. J. A. Hort, eds. *The New Testament in the Original Greek.* 2nd ed. (New York: Macmillan, 1928).

Wingerson, Lois. *Unnatural Selection: The Promise and the Power of Human Gene Research* (New York: Bantam Books, 1998).

Whitfield, L. Simon, John E. Sulston, and Peter N. Goodfellow, "Sequence Variation of the Human Y Chromosome," *Nature,* vol. 378, no. 6558, December 14, 1995, 378–80.

Wilder-Smith, A. E. *The Natural Sciences Know Nothing of Evolution* (Costa Mesa, Calif.: T.W.F.T., 1981).

Wright, Robert. "Infidelity: It May Be in Our Genes." *Time,* August 15, 1994, 46–56.

Yockey, Hubert P. *Information Theory and Molecular Biology* (Cambridge: Cambridge University Press, 1992).

––––––. "Self Organization, Origin-of-Life Scenarios and Information Theory," *Journal of Theoretical Biology,* vol. 91, 1981, 13–31.

SCRIPTURE INDEX

INDEX

Biden, Joseph, 197–198, 216
Big Bang, 95, 101
Big Crunch, 104
Bigotry, 205
Biology, class in, 61–65
Biomedical Ethics: Opposing Viewpoints, 388
Biomedical issues, 384–390
Black box, 115
Black holes, 99–100
"Blind men and the elephant," 36–37, 51–52
Bloom, Allan, 33–34
Bodily goods, happiness as, 349–350
Bohlin, Raymond G., 125
Boundary conditions, 134
Brave New World, 322
A Brief History of Eternity, 94–95
A Brief History of Time, 81, 94
Bruce, F. F., 271
Budziszewski, J., 191, 225, 349
Bundy, Ted, 356–357
Burrows, Millar, 271

Cancer, reason for, 242–245
Category mistake, 77, 109
Causality principle, 73–74
  applying to God, 78
  quantum physics and, 76–77
  reliability of, 74–75
Causes. *See also* Intelligent cause; Past causes
  of the cosmos, establishing, 87–89
  kinds producing highly specified complexity, 127–131
  for the rise of positive law theory, 192–195
Cells
  complex nature of, 117–119
  Darwin's understanding of, 115–117
  kinds of coded information utilized by, 119–121
Center for Biomedical Ethics, 391
Challenger space shuttle, 13
Chesterton, G. K., 72
Christian theism, 232, 234, 340
Chromosomes, defining, 186n
Civil War, 212–213
Claims of Jesus Christ, 284–287
Claudius, 270
Cloning. *See* Human cloning
COBE satellite, 96
Coded information, utilized by a cell, 119–121, 394
Coincidence of testimony with collateral facts, and telling the truth, 279
Completeness of the fossil record, supposed, 159–163

Complexity
  of the cell, 115–119
  highly specified, 127–131
Computer models, use of, 150–155
Conceit, 336–337, 352
Conclusions. *See* Personal conclusions about Jesus Christ
Condition of humanity, Jesus' diagnosis of, 331–334
Conflict, apparent, of the Biblical age of humanity with modern science, 185–188
Conformity of testimony with experience, and telling the truth, 279
Confusion, among worldviews, 60–61
Consequences, of refusing God, 354–361, 363–364
Consistency, and telling the truth, 279
Constitution, U.S., 199–201, 212–214, 382, 391
Correspondence to reality, defining truth as, 139–140, 227–228
Cosmological evidence, origin model fitting best, 101–103
Cosmology
  differing from cosmogony, 89–90
  quantum, 107–110
Cosmos
  as an eternal steady state, 105–106
  establishing cause of, 87–89
  as oscillating (or pulsating), 104–105
  questions about, 15, 87–110
  and sufficiency of usable energy, 92–93
  the Superforce bringing into existence, 103–104
Creator, appealing to, 84–85
Credibility, of absolute truth, 47–48
Crick, Francis H., 122
Crimes against humanity, 222
Criminal justice, jeopardizing, 195–196
Critical legal studies, 195
Cuozzo, Jack, 183n

Darwin, Charles, 141, 159, 161–162, 193, 205, 384
  understanding of the complex nature of the cell, 115–117
Davies, Paul, 94
Dawkins, Richard, 142, 151–153, 155, 162
Death, Jesus' resurrection from substantiating His claim to be God, 305–308
"Decent" people, going to hell, 364–367
Declaration of Independence, 199–201, 212–214, 372, 395
Deissmann, Adolf, 255
Deity of Jesus Christ, questions about, 16, 283–308
Denial of basic human rights, 209–211

Laws of science, 90–92
Leff, Arthur Allen, 198
Legal theory, relationship to concepts of personal morality, 214–227
LEM. *See* Law of excluded middle
Lester, Lane P., 125
Lewis, C. S., 16, 26, 32, 46, 64, 68, 72–73, 83, 89, 113, 191, 220–221, 226, 231, 235–241, 252, 282, 286, 307, 310–325, 333–338, 341–343, 349–353, 358–359, 363–367, 394
Liberalism, 39–40
LID. *See* Law of identity
Life
    forces of nature unable to account for, 131–133
    human sovereignty over, 394
    what gives ultimate meaning to, 341–344
Lincoln, Abraham, 189, 207, 212–214, 380
Links. *See* Missing links
Living organisms, from nonliving matter, 126–127
LNC. *See* Law of noncontradiction
Local knowledge, specific, in the New Testament, 274–276
Locke, John, 225–226
Logic
    applying to reality, 26
    beginning with, 21–22
    first principle of, 22–23
    questions about, 14, 19–29
    using as a test for truth, 28–29
    using Eastern, 26–28
Logos, 139–140, 340

Macroevolution
    defining, 141–142
    questions about, 15, 141–168
    support for, 147–149
    variations of, 142–143
Macroevolutionary model of origins, theistic, 114, 169–172
A man (with only a finite human nature), view of Jesus Christ as, 290
Manuscript, defining, 254n
Marx, Karl, 58, 193, 325
Matching up
    design models with the scientific evidence, 172–175
    the progressive view with the evidence, 175–177
Matter. *See* Mind or matter
McAuliffe, Christa, 13
McDowell, Josh, 289, 305–306
Meaning of life
    true, 344–349

ultimate, 341–344
Mein Kampf, 57, 207, 216, 219, 386
Mengele, Josef, 209–210, 388
Mere Christianity, 307, 313
Metaphysics, defining, 72n
Michelangelo, 348
Microevolution, 115n, 169
Mill, John Stuart, 193, 195, 208
Milord, Lisa, 360
Mind or matter, precedence of, 111–113
Miracles
    defining, 63–64
    possibility of, 252–253
    substantiating Jesus' claim to be God, 303–305
Miracles, 252
Missing links, fossil record except for, 159–163
Models. *See* Computer models; Design model; Hawking's model; Origin-of-life models; "Punctuated equilibria" model; Theistic macroevolutionary model
Modern science, apparent conflict of the Biblical age of humanity with, 185–188
Molecule. *See* DNA molecule
Montgomery, John Warwick, 255, 259, 277
Moral goodness, Jesus' statements about, 325–329
Moral laws, existence of absolute, 311–313
Morals. *See also* Personal morality
    defining, 309–311
    questions about, 16, 309–340
Morris, Desmond, 194
Murray, Thomas, 391

National Socialism, 206–207, 387
Natural selection
    defining, 141n
    and support for macroevolution, 147–149
Nature. *See* Human nature
Nazareth Decree, 270
Nazi Germany, 15, 56–57, 204–223, 345–347, 380, 382, 388–390, 393–394
Necessary conditions, 153
New Age movement, 59
New Testament
    bibliographical test of, 254–258
    external test of, 255, 264–277
    internal tests of, 255, 259–264
New Testament authors
    as contemporaries, 279–280
    reliability as eyewitnesses, 277–281
    Simon Greenleaf's rules for credibility, 277–279

UNSHAKABLE FOUNDATIONS COMPANION CD FOR TEACHERS

Southern Evangelical Seminary and Legacy of Truth Ministries
offer their resources to help teachers be better prepared to teach apologetics.

Southern Evangelical Seminary

"The Scripture cannot be broken."—John 10:35

Teachers may want to consider taking classes on apologetics through the Veritas Graduate School external studies program at Southern Evangelical Seminary (SES). For information on the courses offered, call SES at 1-800-77-TRUTH or visit their Web site at www.ses.edu.

"Tell it to the next generation." —Joel 1:3

Legacy of Truth Ministries is offering a CD that contains the color version of many of the visual illustrations found in this book (formatted for Microsoft PowerPoint). The *Unshakable Foundations* CD for teachers contains 508 slides in two layouts:

The Classroom Layout Includes:
• A set of color overheads for each of the chapters in *Unshakable Foundations*. These overheads are designed to illustrate and stress the main points of each chapter. Moreover, many of them were created as animated slides for teachers who may want to use Microsoft PowerPoint for a computer-generated presentation.

• A set of teacher's notes explaining the main points of each chapter and how they relate to the entire theme of the book. These notes also include some of the more noteworthy quotes from significant authors.

• A set of student handouts for each chapter that follows the overheads or slide presentation.

• In addition to the above, suggested exercises are included to help teachers motivate their students to learn how to apply these principles in a hands-on manner and to help them get involved in principle-oriented discussions.

The Seminar Layout Includes:
A basic overview of *Unshakable Foundations* consisting of a series of overheads, notes, and quotes that taken together constitutes a five-to- six-hour seminar.

To order this CD Visit our Web site at www.legacyoftruth.org, or write to:
> Legacy of Truth
> *Unshakable Foundations* CD
> PO Box 920063
> Norcross, GA 30010-0063

Unshakable Foundations—A CD for Teachers
Color Overheads, Exercises, Student Handouts, & More
Committed to training reliable and qualified leaders (2 Timothy 2:2)